ANTIQUES ROADSHOW

A Z
OF

ANTIQUES HUNTING

ANTIQUES ROADSHOW

A-Z OF ANTIQUES HUNTING

with an introduction by
HUGH SCULLY

Editor:
HUON MALLALIEU

Consultant Editor:
DAVID BATTIE

Colour Library Direct

This book was created by Headwater Communications, a trading name of
Wallington, Irving, Jackson Ltd. It is a substantially revised version of the Antiques Roadshow
A–Z of Antiques Hunting published by Headwater Communications in parts
over the first 20 weeks of 1995.

First published in volume form in Great Britain in 1996 by Boxtree Limited.

This edition published in 1997 for Colour Library Direct,
Godalming Business Centre, Woolsack Way, Godalming, Surrey GU7 1XW

Editor: Huon Mallalieu
Consulting Editor: David Battie
Consultants:
Paul Atterbury
Hilary Kay
Christopher Payne
Ian Pickford
Art Director: Norma Martin
Designer: Peter Charles
Chief Sub-Editor: Graeme Ewens
Illustrators: Ruth Rowland; Tim Slade
Editorial Director: Peter Jackson
Publishing Director: Jeremy Wallington

For photographic credits please see final page

Colour Reproduction by Wace Publication Imaging, London
Printed by Toppan Printing Co., (China) Limited

A CIP catalogue entry for this book is available from the British Library

ISBN 1 85833 741 0
CLD 20424

Introduction

BY HUGH SCULLY

From the north of Scotland to the coast of Wales and south west tip of Cornwall we have spent nearly twenty years assessing Britain's hidden treasures. They have come in plastic bags, brown paper parcels, wooden boxes and wrapped in yesterday's newspapers.

Each year, the 'Antiques Roadshow' sets out on another journey of discovery and we know that among the countless scores of items brought to the experts tables there will be some real surprises - perhaps it will be a priceless piece of porcelain, or a long lost picture by an old master, or a 19th-century bronze by a famous French maker - whatever they are and wherever they come from, one thing is sure: some important discoveries will be made.

This annual journey is not only professionally satisfying, it also produces some great personal finds too. Most of us on the 'Roadshow' are collectors of something. Henry Sandon will be scouring the antiques shops of the towns and cities we visit on the look out for interesting pots. David Battie will be wanting to add to his fine collection of porcelain. Clive Farahar will have his nose in the second-hand bookshops and Philip Hook will certainly be calling-in to some of Britain's great art galleries, or looking at private collections in our country houses. I always find it comforting to know that our experts do exactly the same off screen as they do in front of the cameras - always in search of unusual, rare and interesting things to add to their collections. Perhaps Bunny Campione will find another bunny.

Having all this wonderful expertise on hand gives me the unique opportunity of being able to do my own buying with the best of advice readily available. A year or two ago, for instance, I was at an antiques fair in London presenting some prizes to *Radio Times* competition winners.

There, on one of the stands, was a beautiful 19th century mahogany dining table, just the thing needed for our house in Cornwall. I called John Bly over and asked him to have a good look at it. He confirmed my view about its quality , thought the price being asked was very reasonable, and, as a result, the table was soon on its way to our Cornish dining room.

Not long afterwards there was some Derby porcelain that came up in a local auction and I was able to get an idea from John Sandon about how much I should pay. His estimate of what it would fetch was absolutely right and I made the right bid. Later, on a trip to Dublin, I bought some glass, again with the advice of a 'Roadshow' expert to hand.

Now, within the pages of this book, you have access to exactly the same expertise that I have been able to enjoy privately for so many years. You too can learn from the experience of my friends and colleagues who have spent their lives assessing the quality and the value of antiques and other works of art. You can happily browse through Britain's antique shops, auctions, fairs and car boot sales, in the company of your favourire expert from one of our most popular and enduring television programmes.

I know it will be an enjoyable experience.

With this guide to help you there is every chance it might also be very rewarding.

Introducing our team of experts

HUON MALLALIEU

Huon Mallalieu, editor of the *Antiques Roadshow A-Z of Antiques Hunting* worked for Cristie's for four years from 1969 before becoming a full-time writer on art and antiques and appearing on the BBC's early 'Antiques Roadshows'. He is the author of the standard and reference works on English watercolours and other books, and has been a regular contributor to *The Times* since 1976. His work has featured in many other newspapers and magazines. In 1990 he was appointed saleroom writer of *Country Life*, which is one of the most prestigious positions in British antiques journalism.

DAVID BATTIE

David Battie is a specialist in ceramics and Oriental works of art. He trained as a graphic designer and worked for three years for *Reader's Digest* before joining Sotheby's in 1965 as a book porter. He is now a director of the company and married to Sotheby's former glass expert. He has written articles on various art subjects as well as the price guides to 19th-century pottery and porcelain. His appearances on the 'Antiques Roadshow' go right back to the first series in 1978.

PAUL ATTERBURY

The curator of the Pugin Exhibition at the Victoria and Albert Museum, Paul Atterbury is a freelance writer and lecturer specialising in 19th- and 20th-century art and design, particularly ceramics. He was formerly historical adviser to Royal Doulton and Minton and was editor of *The Connoisseur*. His recent books include *The Parian Phenomenon*, *Moorcroft Pottery*, *Dictionary of Minton*, *See Britain by Train*, *The North of France* and *Exploring Britain's Canals*. His other interests include printed ephemera, fountain pens, kitchenalia and railway relics.

HILARY KAY

Hilary Kay started her career with Spink & Son, fine art dealers of St James's, London, and left to join Sotheby's in 1977. In 1978 she became head of their Collectors' department and an auctioneer specialising in mechanical musical instruments, scientific instruments, toys, automata, dolls, models and rock'n'roll ephemera. Now a senior director, she regularly broadcasts, lectures and contributes articles to specialist magazines. She has edited a general guidebook to British antiques, and is the author of a history of rock memorabilia, *Rock'n'Roll Collectables*.

What's it worth

Valuation is an imprecise art and pieces can vary for many reasons, including the condition of a piece, fashion and regional interest. Throughout the Antiques Roadshow A-Z of Antiques Hunting, the valuations given are estimated auction prices. Since auctions take place in the public arena, this is considered the most accurate pricing guide. Experts sometimes suggest an insurance value considerably higher than the auction value. This is because in surance values are based on replacing the item from the open market . Prices in antique shops may also be higher because a dealer , having bought goods at auction, marks prices higher to make a profit.

In addition to prices for individual pieces illustrated in the A to Z section, the listing columns carry symbols giving a more general guide to the scale of prices likely to be asked for examples in fine condition:

£ = £1-£9

££ = £10 - £99

£££ = £100 - £999

££££ = £1000 - £9999

£££££ = £10,000 - £99,000

R indicates that this category is especially rare.

Where to go

The A- Z section carrys symbols giving a basic indication of the places where antiques are most likely to be up for sale:

BOOKSHOP

PAWNBROOKERS

COUNTRY HOUSE SALE

ANTIQUE SHOP

AUCTION

CAR BOOT SALE

SECOND-HAND SHOP

MARKETS

CHRISTOPHER PAYNE

Son of a Midlands antiques dealer, Christopher Payne worked at Sotheby's where he was a director of the Furniture Department for nearly 25 years. He is now fine art consultant at Phoenix Film Hire and adviser to private collectors . His books include *19th Century European Furniture* (1981) and *Animals in Bronze* (1985). He is also general editor of Sotheby's *Encyclopaedia of Furniture*.

IAN PICKFORD

Ian Pickford entered the antique silver trade on leaving Westminster City School. Six years later, he began lecturing at the University of London and the University of Surrey, and for NADFAS (the National of Decorative and Fine Art Societies) and the National Trust. His writings include the now standard reference book on silver flatware, and he is the editor of *Jackson's Silver and Gold Marks*. In 1981 he was made a Freeman of the Worshipful company of Goldsmiths.

My 10 Golden Rules of Antiques Hunting

BY DAVID BATTIE

There is a terrible trap into which all of us on the Antiques Roadshow and others in the world of works of art are likely to fall: that of assuming that the terms we use are generally known and understood. Many articles and reference books also liberally spice their texts with words and phrases which are all too often met with a blank stare or a shake of the head. What is needed is a helpful guide which lists the terms that the collector will at sometime run into, and will expand on the subject that interests him. This book aims to do that. Apart from being armed with an *aide memoire* to collecting terminology, the collector could do worse than bear in mind the following golden rules:

1. Concentrate your collection; do not buy at random; have a distinct theme.

2. Try to buy objects which are well made.

3. Buy objects which are in as good a condition as possible - they will give you the most satisfaction - but do not reject damaged pieces out of hand. Better to have something damaged than not at all.

4. Buy objects which encapsulate the time in which they were made.

5. Do not buy with investment in mind; those who do, invariably come unstuck.

6. Spend the most you can afford on the best possible example - and sell three good examples to buy one exceptional.

7. Try to avoid following a trend - very often prices are higher than they merit and may take a tumble. In other words: follow your own instinct.

8. Dedicate time to your collecting; time spent is of more value than money.

9. Spend not only on your chosen objects, but also on books, magazines, visits to collections and lectures. They will all enhance the pleasure you get from your collection.

And finally:

10. Buy only what you really, truly love.

GOOD HUNTING!

lishments used the same decorators—after all the owners were cousins. However, Abbotsford does not seem to have produced the large pigs which are the best-known Wemyss products. The pottery had no connection at all with Walter Scott—except to prove how bankable his name still was 70 years after his death.

 **££-£££**

ACAJOU MOUCHETÉ
French term for spotted or 'fiddleback' mahogany. It has a ripple pattern, similar to the veneers used for the backs of the best violins.

ACANTHUS
The most prolific foliage to flourish as a decorative motif on architecture, furniture and works of art of all kinds (see illustration below). Derived from the Mediterranean *acanthus spinosus*, in the hands of artists it can also resemble thistle, poppy or parsley leaves. It is the basis of the Corinthian and Composite ORDERS, and easily turned into a scroll. Even Gothic and Romanesque architects and craftsmen employed it, and from the Renaissance to the mid-19th century it was consistently in favour. Eventually, however, one critic was complaining of 'the inevitable acanthus leaf as if in the whole range of vegetable life this was the only kind of foliage worth imitating', and another that 'it requires so little thought'.

ABBOTSFORD FURNITURE

Extravagant neo-Gothic furniture made during the 1820s and '30s and named after Sir Walter Scott's Scottish baronial house. It is heavy and spiky, and sometimes crudely made up from genuinely old fragments. The architect A. W. N. PUGIN, while admitting that he had designed such stuff for Windsor Castle, said of it: 'All the ordinary articles of furniture, which require to be simple and convenient, are made not only very expensive, but very uneasy... A man who remains any length of time in a modern Gothic room, and escapes without being wounded by some of its minutiae, may consider himself extremely fortunate.'

 R ££££-£££££

ABBOTSFORD WARE
Brilliantly decorated pottery in the WEMYSS style produced by the Fife Pottery's neighbour and rival, the Kirkcaldy Pottery of David Methven and Sons, in the late 19th and early 20th centuries. It is most likely that the two estab-

ABACUS
The precursor of the pocket calculator is still sometimes found built in to playpens. It is a frame with wires across it, each threaded with 10 beads. It is at least as old as the ancient Greeks (the word is Greek for 'cyphering table', since it can also be used to teach writing), and it was modified by the Chinese. Rather crude examples from British schools and nurseries are common enough, but the elaborate one shown above was made by the 17th-century mathematical instrument maker Robert Jole.

££-£££

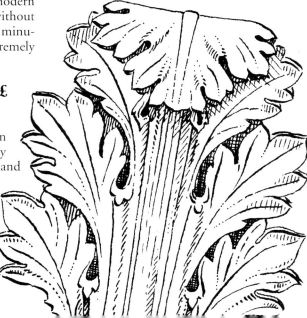

ACKERMANN, RUDOLPH (1764-1834)

An immensely influential London designer, publisher and bookseller, whose monthly *Repository of Arts, Literature, Commerce, Manufacture, Fashions and Politics* (1809-28) set the style of the REGENCY period. He is credited with the introduction of lithographic illustrations to Britain, and he designed Nelson's elaborate funeral catafalque. His premises in the Strand, also named The Repository of Arts, were a publishing house, print and artists' materials shop, drawing school and lending library, and catered for fashionable amateurs as well as professional artists and craftsmen. One of the best known of his other publications is *The Microcosm of London*, with prints after Augustus Charles Pugin (the father of the architect) and the caricaturist Thomas Rowlandson.

ACORN CUPS

Cups made from silver or gold in the form of giant acorns, they were popular in the late 16th- and early 17th-century England. They are usually on twiggy stems, and the cover—the acorn itself—may well be engraved with a coat of arms. In the 18th and 19th centuries, the acorn appears in wood as a TREEN novelty, and sometimes in pottery for pepper and salt pots.

    R ££££

ACT OF PARLIAMENT CLOCK

A popular but misleading name for a Coaching Inn or Tavern Clock, which arose from the extraordinary idea that philanthropic landlords might wish to save their clientele the expense of Pitt's Act of 1797, taxing clocks and watches. They are hanging, weight-driven wall clocks, with short trunks, large, wooden, white dials and bold, black Roman numerals or japanned black faces with gilt numerals. They were used in coffee houses as well as coaching inns, and were later enlarged and adapted for station waiting rooms.

    ££££

ADLERHUMPEN

Tall, cylindrical German drinking glasses, sometimes with covers, which are enamelled with the double eagle of the Holy Roman Empire. Its wings carry the armorial bearings of the 56 *Adel* (noble) families that combined to make the Hapsburg inheritance. They were particularly popular from the middle of the 16th century.

    R £££££

AEGRICANES

A technical term from the Greek for the goat's or ram's head motif used in antiquity to decorate altars. It was revived as a decorative device during the Renaissance (shown below as a skull rather than a head), and was particularly used by late 18th-century furniture designers. Since the ram was closely associated with Bacchus, it is common to find ram's mask handles and hoof feet on such items as wine coolers.

AESTHETIC MOVEMENT

This might be called the 'arty' end of the Arts and Crafts Movement. It

▼ **Paste medallion portrait** of Robert Adam (1728-92) by James Tassie

▲ **The Eating Room** at Osterley Park designed by Robert Adam

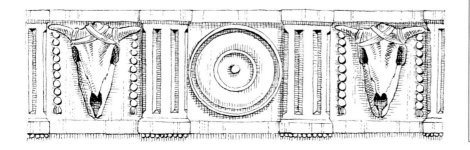

▼ **Watercolour design** for the Painted Breakfast Room, Kedleston Hall, Derbyshire

▶ **Design for the North Lodge** at Kedleston Hall, 1759

▶ **Adam's tapestry** at Osterley Park, London (below right)

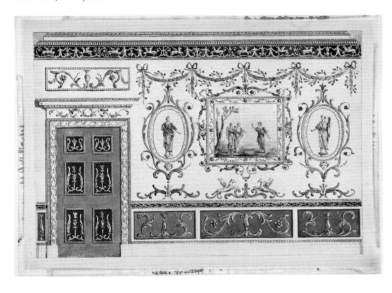

Master of classical motifs worked on a grand scale

ADAM, ROBERT (1728–92)

The NEO-CLASSICAL architect and designer Robert Adam created a distinct style which will always be associated with his name. In partnership with his brothers John, James and William (with whom he developed the Adelphi in London's Strand district), he produced complete schemes for decorating and furnishing houses, employing many eminent cabinet- and chairmakers. He often employed painters such as Angelica Kauffmann to provide decorative roundels for both ceilings and furniture.

His Grand Tour (1754–58) took him to Rome, Venice and the ruins of Diocletian's Palace at Split in Dalmatia, which he later turned into influential engravings. He returned with a large and sophisticated repertory of classical motifs, which he used with a light touch. He intended to 'transfuse the beautiful spirit of antiquity with novelty and variety', but the results occasionally justify Horace Walpole's disparaging comment: 'filigrane and fan painting, gingerbread and snippets of embroidery'.

The significant characteristics of his style are the use of classical figures, mainly maidens, in togas and carrying stiff leaves or other devices. Borders are commonly swags of laurel leaves tied with ribbons and the ANTHEMION is a frequent motif. His influence on ceramics was considerable.

As a designer, Adam had most success with mirrors, wall furniture and decorative pieces, and he appears to have invented the sideboard. He also designed some Gothic revival furniture, carpets and occasional pieces of silver. But some of the best Adam-style furniture, made by CHIPPENDALE, was not actually designed by him. His influence is also seen in the metalwork of Matthew BOULTON. On Wedgwood and Adams (no relation) basaltes and jasper, white relief maidens stand out against the blue or black grounds between small leaf borders and in stoneware, large numbers of jugs have moulded neo-Classical style reliefs. The general feel of the Adam style is of airiness and with much of the background left blank. In the hands of the unskilled it can be lifeless and boring.

There was a reaction against Adam during the Regency and William IV periods but from the 1860s the Adamesque became acceptable to the Victorians and was ultimately a major component in what became known as Edwardian Reproduction or Chippendale Revival furniture.

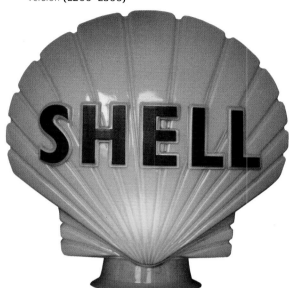

▼ **Shell illuminated sign** designed by Raymond Loewy to be fitted to the top of petrol pumps, 1950s version (**£200-£300**)

◀ **Double Diamond** display figure from the 1950s in Beswickware (**£150**)

Packaging and 'puffs' keep the sales message alive

ADVERTISING

Advertising is as old as barter and the market place, and almost anything can and has been used as an advertisement. When it survives, the mass-produced and supposedly ephemeral object can become rare and much prized. Because there is so much choice of material, there are specialist collectors for all sorts of advertisements, from engraved 18th-century trade cards to pottery Guinness toucans, labels, posters, large enamelled metal street 'puffs' (as they became known in the 19th century), and shop signs such as barbers' poles, and opticians' spectacles.

There are calendars, bookmarks and paperweights; clothes hangers and shoe trees; thermometers and ashtrays; biscuit tins, bar furnishings and beer mats. Amongst the first deliberate attempts to sell through attractive packaging, was the POT LID.

Packaging is a vast subject and in the 1980s a museum devoted to advertising and packaging was set up in Gloucester.

One of the most ephemeral of all advertising media is the cereal packet. From the 1930s there were cut-outs to collect from their backs, and the few that were not destroyed or discarded are now sought after, as are some of the tin and plastic toys which came inside the packets.

In recent years there has been a proliferation of painted and carved wooden signs, which shout 'fake!' even in theme pubs. Genuine pub signs, on the other hand, are likely to be quite modern. When examined they are often more crudely executed than one might expect— after all they are not supposed to be seen close to. Enamelled metal signs are expensive, but are probably too complicated and time-consuming for reproductions of them to be made .

Advertising has even reached the hallowed halls of fine art with Andy Warhol's Campbell's soup can paintings. Such icons are now priced in hundreds of thousands of pounds, whereas the collectors of the real thing can spend as little as £1. Even the most expensive will set them back only a few thousands.

Collectors have a wide choice and the smart ones can build a collection for nothing. House clearance skips can be raided for the chuck-outs from the kitchen cupboards and there are not a few with an eye to the future who save the give-aways that come with cereal packets – complete with wrapping, of course. Collectors have a wide choice of items to suit their tastes and their pockets.

▶ **Huntley and Palmer 's** high-rise winter biscuit tin (£40–£50)

▼ **McVitie's biscuit tin** based on a Martinware bird. Its bright colours have been lost, perhaps through over-zealous cleaning and its value diminished (£80–£100)

was a reaction to the flamboyant ornamentation loved by Victorians. From the 1840s a new purity of design was championed by Pugin and Owen Jones, and in the 1860s the ideal of Art for Art's Sake was taken up by the culturally aware. The Movement drew on diverse sources, from Japanese and Chinese to Queen Anne and traditional metalwork. Walter Crane summarised it well in 1889: 'plain materials and surfaces are infinitely preferable to inorganic or inappropriate ornament.' The simple lines, and fan-shaped motifs on the nursing chair brought into the Huddersfield Roadshow (right) are entirely Aesthetic. Alas, the original fabric covering was in poor order.

AFFENKAPELLE

Porcelain monkey orchestras, comprising about 20 figures, were probably first produced by J. J. Kändler at Meissen in around 1755. The theme came from Dutch and Flemish painters, such as David Teniers II. Paintings of 'monkeyana' subjects became popular again in the early 19th century. A late but pretty set turned up at the Newcastle Emlyn Roadshow.

   £££

AGATE GLASS

A Renaissance technique of blending molten glass of two or more colours to imitate semi-precious stones. The mixture was then turned into decorative objects. Depending on the mix,

▶ **Aesthetic Movement** low chair in ebonised wood with original upholstery c1880 (£200)

agate chalcedony, onyx or jasper might be aimed at.

   R ££££–£££££

AGATE WARE

An agate-like pottery made with blended clays by the Romans, and latterly by WEDGWOOD and other Staffordshire potters.

££££

AIRTWIST

An 18th-century English method for stretching bubbles into single or double spirals in the stems of glasses (right). Sometimes the spirals were coloured.

£££

TALKING ANTIQUES

'AGAINST YOU'

This phrase is usually used by the auctioneer to make it plain to a bidder who is unsure where the bidding has got to and whether the bid is with him or not. He may repeat it several times for emphasis and if there is no forthcoming bid will sell to the last bidder.

ALABASTER

A fine-grained white, yellow or reddish limestone, or gypsum, which can be cut so thinly as to be translucent. It was even used for glazing small church windows in the Middle Ages. From the middle of the 14th century, Nottingham was known as a centre for small-scale religious carvings in alabaster, but the English industry was killed in the 16th century by the Reformation.

ALABASTRON

Originally a small, ancient, Egyptian or Greek cosmetic bottle carved from alabaster. Later examples were made of glass, pottery and other materials. Cylindrical, with a round base and spreading rim, they are often iridescent after being buried for years.

£££

ALBARELLO

A cylindrical apothecary's drug jar of a type that came to Europe from Persia in the 15th century. It has a flanged neck, flared foot and slightly waisted body. The flange enabled a parchment cover to be tied on. The form was adopted by the Italian MAIOLICA potteries in particular, but was also popular in England, France, the Netherlands, Portugal and Germany. Its popularity lasted well into the 18th century, and there was a revival in the 19th. Reproductions tend to be over decorated and the outlines can look mechanical. Dates and inscriptions are too flowery. Turning rings should be visible on the inside.

£££-£££££

◀ Albarelli later became objects for display rather than for use (£300-£400)

ALBERT

The Prince Consort (1819-61), Queen Victoria's husband, is commemorated in the name for a gold watch chain, and also for a FLATWARE pattern.

££-£££

ALCORA POTTERY

A Spanish FAIENCE factory founded around 1727 with craftsmen enticed from Moustiers in France. The high rococo wares include plates, plaques, pyramidical table-centres and statuettes. In the French Revolutionary period neo-Classicism took over, while from 1810 to 1858 the factory imitated Staffordshire figures. The mark is a capital A with something like large, flat, clown's feet.

££-£££

ALDINE BINDINGS

Aldus Manutius (1449-1515) founded the Aldine Press at Venice in 1494. His style of bookbinding was widely imitated in northern Italy, so not all gold-tooled 'Aldine' bindings are from his press. They tend to be decorated with strapwork patterns or rectangular panels with the title or author's name stamped in the middle. The 'Aldine fleuron', a small trefoil leaf, may be used at the corners.

R ££££

ALE FLUTE

A tall, trumpet-shaped glass with a long or short stem and spreading foot, used in 18th-century Britain for beer and ale drinking. If engraved, the most common motif is the hop vine.

££-£££

ALENÇON LACE

The lace industry was founded at Alençon in France in 1675, by a group of Venetians brought in by the French minister Colbert and subsequently encouraged by the government. By the time of Napoleon Bonaparte, the complex designs were becoming simpler and most Alençon lace dates from around that time. The town gave its name to *point d'Alençon* needlepoint, which was also made elsewhere.

££-£££

AMATI FAMILY

The first of the great violin-making family born at Cremona in northern Italy was Andrea (1511-80). He was succeeded by Antonio (born *c*1540), Hieronymus Girolamo (1561-1630) and Nicolo (1596-1684). Nicolo was the master of STRADAVARI

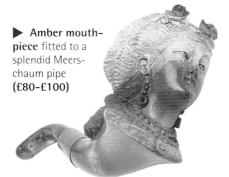

▶ Amber mouthpiece fitted to a splendid Meerschaum pipe (£80-£100)

AMBER

A fossil resin chiefly found on the southern shore of the Baltic. Translucent, it has a rich, nicotine yellow-brown colour. It has been popular since the Middle Ages for decorative items and embellishments to furniture, as well as for beads and jewellery.

AMBOYNA WOOD

Pterocarpus indicus. A hard, light brown wood from the Moluccas islands. It is used in MARQUETRY.

AMEN GLASSES

A rare type of JACOBITE wine glass engraved with the Stuart anthem ending 'Amen' and a crowned 'JR 8' for James III (and VIII of Scotland). These are almost certainly post-1740, and probably post-1746. As with many Jacobite glass patterns, some convincing fakes were made in the 1930s, using genuine old glasses. These tend to have tiny chips or 'frits' along the engraved lines and the copied writing does not look natural.

R £££££

Sawbones' tools of trade

AMPUTATION TOOLS

It is extraordinary to discover that stone-age man was conducting trepanning (making holes in the skull) operations with a flint. In ancient times, surgeons became skilled at amputations after battles. These early instruments must have been crude and, without anaesthetics, the operations extremely painful.

Even so, the later knives, small and large bone saws, scalpels, catheters, trepanning drills, lithotomy instruments, obstetric specula, forceps and so on can be unexpectedly beautiful. The basic forms of surgical instruments hardly changed from the mid 16th century to the late 18th. Indeed, some show virtually no evolution before the coming of the laser. A guide for dating them, however, can be found in the handles. Before about 1875 sets of instruments often had handles of carved ebony but after that they were made to be sterilised

by boiling and were replaced by metal.

A set which does not contain gynaecological instruments suggests that it was for use by a naval or military surgeon and, from the 18th century, service surgeons would usually carry their instruments in fitted, brass-bound wooden cases. These are often superb examples of cabinet making in their own right. Country doctors might still prefer a simple leather wallet. Bleeding knives or cups were included until about 1940. Most collectors seek out complete sets, but there are those are specialise in one type of instrument. Single saws, for example, from the 16th or 17th century can be valuable as the handles were often intricately carved ivory or bone — a perfect breeding ground for potentially fatal bacteria!

▼ Two sets of field surgeon's instruments by J. Weiss of London c1835 (£1,500–£2,000 each)

AMERICAN CLOCKS

The most commonly found American clock in Britain is the mass-produced, late 19th-century, wooden wall or mantel clock by the Ansonia Clock Co. They may have pediments or flat tops and painted or transfer-decorated panels below the dials. They are worth between £50 and £100. However, during the same period American makers were capable of better quality, and more impressive items (right) were also exported.

 ££-£££

AMPULLA

A small, usually glass vessel for oil or perfume, used by the Romans to beau-

Mantel clock made by Young of Boston (c1860); has a mercury-compensated pendulum and mahogany case **(£300–£400)**

tify the living and anoint the dead. It is usually round with a narrow neck and will probably show a pleasing iridescence. The name and shape passed into ceremonial Christian use for coronations.

 ££-£££

ANAMORPHOSCOPE

From the Greek for 'to form anew'. A small-scale cylindrical mirror which, when placed near a distorted drawing, would make it recognisable. It was a popular parlour entertainment from the 16th century onwards.

 £££

ANDIRONS OR FIREDOGS

Wrought- or cast-iron supports for logs, which were made in pairs from

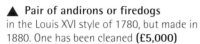

▲ **Pair of andirons or firedogs**
in the Louis XVI style of 1780, but made in
1880. One has been cleaned **(£5,000)**

the 15th to the 18th century, when coal replaced wood for heating most houses. They are vaguely dog-shaped, with upright stems, usually on two feet, and horizontal 'backs' running to a hind foot. Most are simple and rustic, but great houses had grander versions in bronze, brass or even silver. Many of these were purely decorative, and were replaced by smaller, humbler versions for actual use.

 ££-££££

ANEROID BAROMETER

'Aneroid' means 'containing no liquid', and this form of barometer is so called because it uses atmospheric pressure on a partial vacuum rather than on mercury. The invention goes back to Leibniz (1646-1716), but its first commercial use was by Lucien Vidie and his competitor Eugène Bourdon in the mid 19th century. Desk or mantelpiece versions with visible workings were popular, and pocket types were also made in many sizes with gold, silver or brass cases. They should not be confused with anemometers or wind-gauges.

 £££

ANHUA

Secret decorations incised or painted in white slip on Chinese porcelain in such a way that they are only visible when the piece is held up to the light, rather like a watermark in paper.

ANIMALIERS

Nineteenth-century sculptures of animals in bronze—principally French.

Dramatic groups of lions, tigers and the like, in combat, were popular with the Romantics, and from the 1830s sculptors such as A. L. Barye (1796-1875) and P. J. Mêne (1810-79) supplied the market with table or mantelpiece groups. Hunting dogs and birds sold well.

 **£££-££££**

ANTHEMION

A classical flower motif (from the Greek *anthos*, a flower), resembling honeysuckle. It was much used in the 18th century for architectual adornment and on furniture. Virtually indistinguishable from the palmette, it was often used in conjunction with it by the Adams and other neo-Classical designers.

ANTIQUE

A term used in the past to describe Greek and Roman artefacts, but since Victorian times it has widened to include anything over 100 years old. This is the legal definition for export and other purposes.

ANTLER FURNITURE

Antler and horn tables and chairs became popular in Germany and Scotland during the middle of the 19th century. Chairs, in particular, look dangerous as well as uncomfortable. In the United States buffalo horns were used in a similar manner.

 £££-££££

APPLIED AND APPLIQUÉ

Decoration that is 'applied', or stuck on, to a surface, such as crests applied to the backs of chairs. A popular idea in the early GEORGIAN period was for faceted, carved, turned or moulded ornaments to be applied to panels of doors or the flat surfaces of cabinets. Appliqué is fabric decorated in the same way, with shaped pieces forming a pattern on the material to which it is stitched.

▼ **Animalier bronze**
A bitch and pups by P.J. Mêne **(£800-£1,200)**

APPRENTICE PIECES

Technically known as 'prentices' pieces, these models of furniture, usually 8in to 10in long, are supposed to have been made by cabinetmakers as 'masterpieces' to show their skills on completion of their apprenticeships. This may be true of some miniature pieces, but other examples served as travellers' samples and shop window advertisements. Almost all small furniture is likely to have been intended for children and their dolls. In recent years at least one London firm of dealers in antique and reproduction furniture has encouraged its craftsmen to make similar items.

▶ **Miniature walnut** 'prentice-type dining chair, *c*1680 **(£5,000-£6,000)**

Saintly attributes cast in silver

◀ **Apostle spoon**
Dating from 1490, with a figure of St James the Great, this is one of the very earliest examples and has traces of gilt on the finial (**£15,000–£20,000**)

▶ **London leopard's head** hallmark

▼ **Spoon by Samuel Cawley** of Exeter (below and top right) with pseudo marks put on because, as a Royalist, c1650, he needed to keep his head down (**£1,500-£2,000**)

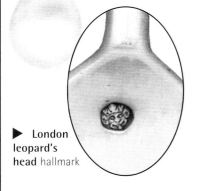

APOSTLE SPOONS

Silver spoons with fig-shaped bowls and handles topped by figures of apostles or—in the case of the master spoon of a set of 13—by the figure of Christ. A number of full-length figures of the Virgin Mary are also known. Popular in England, Germany and elsewhere from about 1490 to 1675, they became collectable in Victorian times and have been faked, forged and reproduced ever since. No complete sets of 13 are known to remain from before the 16th century.

The earliest finials on English spoons were the acorn knop from the 13th century and the diamond point from the 14th. The seal top, with a flat disc above a rather architectural baluster, is the most common from about 1500, but from the mid-15th century there were also heraldic finials, such as the lion sejant, or the head (poll) of the de la Pole Earls of Suffolk. The type known as the maidenhead, a bust-length Virgin figure, was associated with the Mercers' Company, who used it in their crest. From around the Charles II period until the early 18th century, the trefid (or trifid) terminal is common, (see spoon bottom left). As here, initials and occasionally a date are found pricked into the flat end. These will be on what would now be considered the underside as spoons were then laid on the table as in the photograph.

The maker's mark is generally punched on the back of the stem near the bowl, but the London leopard's head and some provincial town marks appear in the bowl itself close to the stem. In the 17th century bowls became more oval and stems a little flatter and less tapering.

The Victorians revived the design, in miniature, for coffee spoons, and modern fakers have often produced 'apostles' by reshaping stems and bowls of 18th-century spoons and soldering on cast figures. Usually only one mould was used for the figure although he may have had a different attribute—Peter's keys, Andrew's cross—soldered on. Pairs of large apostle spoons in fitted boxes occur quite commonly from the turn of the 19th and 20th centuries, usually given to commemorate some event of religious significance such as the laying of a foundation stone. The proportions and casting of modern examples are often too perfect.

▶ **Early finials** (top to bottom) Acorn knop, diamond point, seal top and plain knop

AQUAMANILE

A medieval bronze ewer for washing guests' hands at table. The Mosan enamellers and metalworkers produced lovely examples in the 13th century, often in the shapes of lions, mythical beasts or mounted knights.

 R £££££+

ARABESQUE

Decoration of intricate, interweaving, scrolling foliage, calligraphy or flowing lines—also known as Saracenic or Moresque decoration. If it contains human figures it becomes Grotesque.

ARCHITECT'S TABLE

Otherwise known as an artist's or draughtsman's table. There were many variants in the 18th century, but the common link is an adjustable, rising, drawing-board top. Usually there are slides, candle slides, drawers and compartments for pens and ink pots. Some have central pillars and tripods, but usually they had four legs and storage space for sheets of Double Elephant paper (26.5in by 40in).

 ££££

ARGYLE OR ARGYLL

An 18th-century English gravy-warmer, drum-shaped like a tea pot. The gravy was in a central cylinder connected to the spout, and surrounded by hot water. It was generally made of silver or other metals, but there are also pottery versions, notably in Wedgwood creamware. Argyles are recorded from about 1760, and are said to be named after the 4th Duke of Argyll.

 R £££-££££

ARITA PORCELAIN

The earliest Japanese porcelain factories were founded near Arita by a Korean who discovered a source of kaolin in 1616. White wares were produced, decorated with underglaze blue like late Ming, and exported to Europe by the Dutch. Later in the 17th century enamelled Kakiemon and Imari wares were made, and in the 18th century much of the best Japanese porcelain was made there.

ART DECO

Taking its name from the Paris Exposition Internationale des Arts Decoratifs of 1925, Art Deco is associated with the late 1920s and early 1930s, with emphasis on richly-coloured and semi- abstract pattern, exotic materials and styles and a decorative approach to modernism. Although that is the historically correct but rather narrow definition, Art Deco is now widely used to describe anything made between 1920 and 1940. Amongst the rich materials used for furniture were ebony, particularly the yellow-striped form, palmwood and zebrawood, shagreen (sharkskin) and black and cream lacquer. The French ebonistes Emile-Jacques Ruhlmann, Pierre Legrain and Jean Dunand (lacquer) are the best known as well as the Briton Eileen Gray

Its roots lie in some facets of ART NOUVEAU, particularly the formal geometry exemplified by Charles Rennie MACKINTOSH. The influence of Christopher DRESSER is also obvious, indeed some of the pieces he designed in the 1880s could pass for Art Deco.

Also important in its formation were elements of Cubism and abstract art, primitivism, Russian revolutionary art, modernist architecture and jazz. Another major influence was the American film, particularly the musical, to such an extent that the style is also known as Odeon, after the cinema chain, and even modern methods of transport.

There are two distinct phases of Art Deco. The first is colourful, dramatic, abstract and angular, with a traditional use of materials, and is seen at its best in textiles, (see AXMINSTER) ceramics and graphics. Often garish and abrasive in its extreme approach to modernist decoration, this phase is epitomised by the pottery of Clarice Cliff, by the fashions of the period, and by an extreme use of geometry and symbols such as the ziggurat and the lightning flash.

The second, later phase, associated with the 1930s, reflects a cooler, more elegant approach to design, with pastel and ice-cream colours, rounded forms and an understanding of modernism that is more than purely decorative. Powerfully inspirational were Hollywood styles: streamlined shapes of ships, trains and planes were applied to objects as diverse as cinemas, teapots and radios. This second phase, with its international appeal, paved the way for the novel styles of the 1950s. Amongst the most distinctive and collected works of art of the period are the bronze and ivory figures of maidens, youths and children, often in dramatic dancing poses. Names to look for include Ferdinand PREISS and Demetre Chiparus

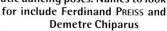

▶ **Car mascot by Lalique**
Called 'Spirit of the wind', this one blew into the Guernsey Roadshow (**£5,000**)

Streamlined design for the jazz age

▲**A typical angular** Art Deco dressing table from a bedroom suite **(£300–£400)**

▶ **'Ada May'**, a Cochrane girl chryselephantine figure by Ferdinand Preiss (1882-1943) marked 'PK' for Preiss Kässler **(£8,000)**

◀**Chrome-plated** Zeppelin-shaped cocktail shaker containing all the necessary equipment. German, 1920-25 **(£200)**

◀ **Silver and enamelled necklace** A fine piece representative of the Art Nouveau style (£250–£350)

▶ **Liberty-style cabinet** c1900 in the style of the designer J.S. Henry (£1,000)

Setting the style for a new century

ART NOUVEAU

Associated particularly with the Paris Exhibition of 1900, this is a complex style whose apparent modernism, designed to reflect the new century, was actually drawn from historical sources. ROCOCO, GOTHIC and naturalism all played their part in the creation of a style whose distinctive feature was a sinuous, flowing linearity.

Highly significant also was the influence of Celtic motifs, particularly strong in the Glasgow School. The leading light here was Charles Rennie MACKINTOSH whose furniture particularly could be rectilinear and apparently hard to fit into the organic lines of art nouveau. His wife, Margaret Macdonald, her sister Frances and Herbert MacNair made up the

'Glasgow Four'. Also important was the book illustrator Jessie M.King.

Essentially decorative and often excessive, Art Nouveau emerged almost simultaneously during the 1890s in Europe, North America, Japan and Australia. The illustrator Aubrey Beardsley, famous for the cover of *The Yellow Book*, was one of first to promote the style, but its progenitor is arguably Arthur Heygate Mackmurdo.

At the time the style had many names, including *Jugendstil* in Germany and *Stil Liberty* in Italy, which reflected a sense of youthful modernism and the desire for revolution and change. The main centres were France, Austria, Belgium and Holland, but it was a powerful force in the USA, notably in the work of Tiffany; in Spain in the

extraordinary architecture of Gaudí and in central Europe, each country adding a twist of its own. It was the first style which was truly international and one in which the numerous art magazines enabled influences to be felt rapidly from one centre to another. In England, the *Studio* magazine and the London store, Liberty's, were the major driving forces.

The flowing curves of Art Nouveau were applied to buildings, furniture, metalwork, jewellery, ceramics, tiles, textiles, wallpapers, stained glass, books and posters.

There were a number of popular decorative themes, notably stylised plants and flowers; insects and birds, especially the peacock; elements from JAPANESE ART and various aspects of the female form.

▼ **Shell and tendril** desk lamp in the style of Gustav Gurschner incorporating a real sea shell (£2,000)

ARMORIAL PORCELAIN

Primarily, this refers to Chinese export porcelain decorated with the coats of arms of European, American or Brazilian families. From around 1700, drawings and instructions were sent to the Jingdezhen factories, but the majority of the arms enamelled in the centre or rims of plates or on tureens and so on, were executed in Canton. As the decorators had no idea of what heraldry (or the written instructions) meant, hilarious mistakes were frequently made. Complete services are uncommon but single pieces appear on the market not infrequently.

£££-££££

▲ **Armorial bowl,** mid to late 18th-century. Although crudely painted it has a recognisable coat of arms **(£300)**

ASH

A tough, light brown wood, used for making country furniture and decorative veneers. When polished up, it can resemble olive.

ASTBURY, JOHN (1686-1743)

A leading Staffordshire potter, who is said to have learned to make red stoneware from the Elers brothers but who is most famous for his brown, lead-glazed earthenware vessels decorated with applied white clay vines, hops and so on. He also produced figures of mounted ladies and gentlemen, musicians and others, modelled in two types and colours of clay. In all this his work is similar to that of Thomas WHIELDON, and their pieces are often catalogued Astbury-Whieldon when it is impossible to say which potter produced what. Astbury's most typical wares are always unmarked, and the impressed mark 'Astbury' dates from about 1760-80, by which time he was already dead.

££££

ASTLEY COOPER CHAIR

A high chair with an oval, caned seat, sabre legs and turned spindle splats, it was designed around 1800 by the orthopaedic surgeon Sir Astley Cooper to encourage children to sit upright. Then as now, however, doctors disagreed. As Loudon's *Encyclopaedia* (1833) notes: 'It is proper to observe that some medical men do not approve of these chairs.'

£££

ASTRAGAL

In classical architecture this is a small, semi-circular moulding, generally used with the Ionic ORDER. To cabinetmakers, however, an astragal is a glazing bar on the glass-fronted doors of case furniture such as bookcases and escritoires.

▲ **Tudric clock** *c*1900-1920. Supplied by Liberty, great commercial popularisers of the style **(£500)**

TALKING ANTIQUES

'AS FOUND OR ALL FAULTS'

A/F on a sale ticket is a warning: the piece is in some way defective, usually chipped, cracked or restored. 'As is' or 'As bought' are less common but may indicate that no claim is made as to date or origin.

ASTROLABE

(Often miswritten as astrolobe.) An instrument used to determine the altitude of stars, and thus latitude and distance travelled. Small versions were used at sea from the 11th century. Originally they consisted of a flat brass plate 3in-12in across, engraved with a map of the heavens, the names written in Arabic, Persian, Indian or Latin. On the front is a 'rete', (star pointer). Only 66 authenticated examples prior to 1650 are known to survive, many dated between 1600 and 1640. Almost everything else will be later or a fake.

 £££-£££££

ATHÉNIENNE

A lidded urn on a classical tripod, invented in 1773 as an imagined Roman sacrificial altar. It was adapted to many uses, such as a perfume burner, a candelabra, a plant stand or even a wash-hand basin.

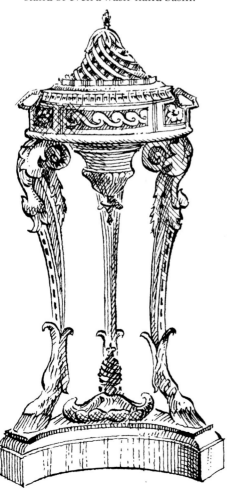

AUBUSSON

Tapestries were made at Aubusson, between Clermont-Ferrand and Limoges in France, from the early 16th century, and unlike the practice at other centres the weavers worked at home rather than in factories. Many were Huguenots who left after the Revocation of the Edict of Nantes (1685), but the industry was revived from 1732 and still continues, often using designs by leading modern artists. From 1742, carpets were also made there. Most famous are the smooth, tapestry-woven carpets, which were produced prolifically in the late 18th and 19th centuries when actual tapestries were out of fashion. The designs tend to be delicate and feminine.

 ££££-£££££

AUGUSTE, ROBERT JOSEPH (*c*1723-1805) and HENRI (1759-1816)

Among the leading Parisian silversmiths of their day. Robert Joseph made the coronation regalia for Louis XVI, but this was destroyed during the Revolution and he has to be judged by his table silver in other royal collections—sophisticated, severe and strictly classical. The work of son Henri is heartier and less smooth; and he supplied a ewer and basin for Napoleon Bonaparte's coronation. Despite this, he went bankrupt. He died in Haiti.

£££££

AUGUSTUS THE STRONG (1670-1733)

More properly Frederick Augustus I, Elector of Saxony (1694) and King of Poland (1697). He founded the MEISSEN porcelain factory in 1710 to exploit the introduction of the first European hard-paste porcelain by Count von Tschirnhausen and the alchemist Johann Friedrich BÖTTGER. Pieces

▼ **Doll automaton** with musical movement in the base. She raises her lorgnette to her bisque head. *c*1885 (£6,000-£8,000)

14

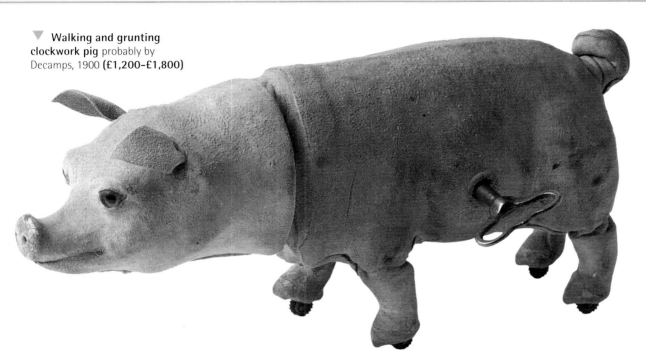

▼ Walking and grunting clockwork pig probably by Decamps, 1900 (**£1,200–£1,800**)

Clockwork curiosities

Animated figures, have been made since well before the time of Christ. In the Middle Ages moving figures were often associated with clocks and bells in public places, as they still are today, and the Germans, who were fine clockmakers, led the field in making smaller automata as table ornaments. Some of the 16th-century automata, with cannons firing from silver gilt galleons as musicians played on deck, were exceptionally elaborate and ingenious as well as extravagantly opulent.

In the 18th century the fashion for rich musical moving toys continued to grip Europe, and Swiss, French and British makers competed to produce such novelties as gem-studded mice and caterpillars, or

cages of singing birds. The leading English automaton maker was James Cox, who was working from before 1757 until 1791. He produced automata for the East India Company to present to potentates such as the Emperor of China. French competitors included Henri Maillardet and Henri Jaquet-Droz.

In the 19th century, along with much else, mass production made them more widely available and makers such as Vichy and his competitor Leopold Lambert aimed at a less sophisticated audience with pierrot, clown and bisque-headed doll figures. Some, such as a doll pulling another in a cart, made by

▶ French clockwork acrobatic bear c1900 (**£400**)

Roullet & Decamps, c1890, no longer even had a musical component — movement was all. However, since Regency times, domestic organs, and later other musical boxes, had included moving figures, while automata of ships in storms and moonlit water-mills often had musical accompaniment. These last are frequently

protected by glass cloches.

Most commonly found automata date from the second half of the 19th century or the beginning of the 20th. But modern fakes can deceive even experts.

marked with an underglaze blue AR monogram (left), for Augustus Rex, were intended either for his own palaces or as royal gifts. However, this mark, which may refer also to Augustus II is extremely rare and the majority of pieces with it were made in the last quarter of the 19th century by Helena Wolfsohn in Dresden. He built up a vast collection of oriental ceramics and furniture

    £££-£££££

AUCTION

Victorious Roman armies used to divide their loot—and slaves—by auction. In England the first record of auctioneering comes only at the end of the 15th century, with an official of Henry VII's court known as the King's Over-Roper. To 'rope' was to shout out for sale (which might give one a 'ropey' throat) and the word survives in Scotland and northern England where sales may be called 'roups'. After the Restoration of Charles II in 1660, auctions became common in London, with Covent Garden as the centre of the trade. Among the oldest British firms to survive are Sotheby's, which stems from Baker's book sales beginning in 1744, and Christie's, founded in 1766. Dreweatt Neate of Newbury also has its origins in the 1760s. Bonhams, which is still in part a family-run firm, and Phillips, founded by James Christie's sales clerk, followed at the end of the century. Other countries may have longer traditions, but today British auctioneers effectively sell up the world.

Pedalling back into motoring history

AUSTIN

The J40 Joy Car, made by Austin, was one of the most coveted of pedal cars, which have been made for children for almost as long as petrol-powered automobiles have been available for their parents. When lovingly restored, such pre-war treasures as a French carriage-shaped car driven by rat-trap pedals and made around 1905, or a 1939 coach-built two-door drophead Mulliner MG, in maroon and beige, can sell for £5,000, £6,000 or more. However, these were always luxury toys, and such price levels are normally only reached by electrically-driven children's vehicles of lesser vintage.

The company which stands out among post-war British pedal car manufacturers is Austin, which from the 1940s produced small cars as well as large. The J40 Joy Cars were beautifully constructed and finished, and in unworn condition they are now comparatively scarce, and worth £2,000 plus. They were based on the design of the full-sized Austin Somerset and Devon, which also has fanatical followers. Still more desirable in the covetous eyes of adults nowadays are pedal racing cars such as the Pathfinder Special of about 1949. Alas for those with fond memories of them, the tinnier and less robust products of Tri-ang and other competitors have fewer fans these days and fetch much lower prices.

AVENTURINE

A glass made by mixing copper crystals with molten glass. The process was discovered by chance at Murano in the 16th century. The result is gold-like flecks in the, usually, coloured glass. A similar type was produced in antiquity, and the effect was also used in both Japanese and European lacquer-making.

 ◀ Axminster rug
by Edward McKnight
Kauffer, 1925

AXMINSTER

The first carpet factory at Axminster, Devon, was established in 1755. It supplied a Chinoiserie carpet for the Brighton Pavilion and a Turkish one for Sir John Soane's House. In 1835 it closed and its equipment was taken over by the WILTON factory. Since then the term Axminster has applied to carpets produced mechanically by Wilton and those from the Kidderminster carpet factory.

££££

BACCARAT GLASS

This comes from a glasshouse founded at Baccarat near Luneville in 1765, which is still making high-quality glass today. It specialised in coloured and opaline glass as well as lead crystal and is most famous for its paperweights manufactured from 1846. These fetch high prices and were extremely complicated to make. Thin sections of coloured cane and clear glass were arranged in a pattern, placed in an iron mould and fused together and the whole enclosed by a blob of clear glass. MILLEFIORI (bunches of coloured glass rods) and coloured patterns are the most common designs; insects and animals are rarer. Some examples are signed 'B', followed by the date.

££££-££££

◀ Baccarat blue and white buttercup paperweight, mid-19th century (£2,200)

▼ Baccarat faceted bouquet paperweight (£2,800)

BACCHUS

The Roman god of wine and fertility. He is generally depicted as a fat, bearded drunk or sometimes as a youth. His many attributes include the grapevine, laurel, dolphin, serpent, ivy, panther, tiger, ass and ram. Bacchic ornament was used especially in dining rooms and on dining-room furniture and tableware, and was popular throughout the 18th and 19th centuries.

BACCHUS GLASS

A Birmingham glasshouse which produced the first English pressed glass in the 1830s. This was formed into cast-iron moulds by a plunger. From the 1850s the factory produced cased glass as well, where one colour is covered by a thin layer of another, which can be cut away to make cameo glass. Bacchus also imitated cut glass and produced paper-weights and tableware.

£££

◀ Burr walnut bachelor's chest with opening top, c1730 (£8,000–£10,000)

BACHELOR'S CHEST

A small, low chest of drawers which was made from the 18th century. Either the top is hinged and opens up, supported by slides to be used as a dressing table, or a brushing slide can be pulled out for the same purpose.

££££

BACK SCREEN

A small screen, often made of wickerwork, which could be attached to the back of a dining-room chair to shield the sitter from the full heat of the fire. They are found from the mid-19th century

R £££

▼ Bacchus snake paperweight, c1850 (£3,800)

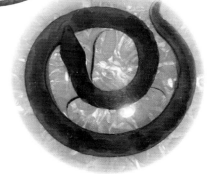

17

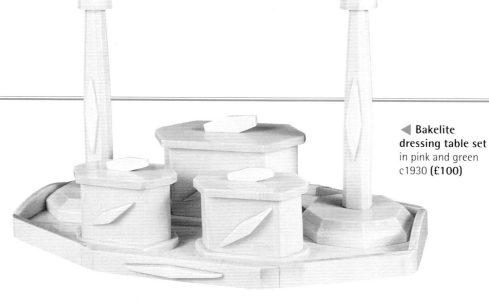

◄ **Bakelite dressing table set** in pink and green c1930 (£100)

Origins of the age of plastic

BAKELITE

An unmeltable, transparent but easily coloured resin, created by the reaction of phenol and formaldehyde with alkaline and acid catalysts. It was first discovered in 1872, and then rediscovered in 1907 by L H Baekeland (1863-1944), who gave it his name. It is the most universal and long-lasting of early plastics and could be used for anything from jewellery to light switches,

Thermos jugs, tea sets (which can be worth up to £100) and even furniture. The most popular colours were mottled blue and green, but plain brown, and cream — used to imitate ivory — are common.

Although the first commercially successful plastic, Bakelite was not the first. Earlier claims to the name (although there is argument about the exact definition) would be BOIS DURCI, made from ground ebony and blood,

Parkesine (cellulose nitrate), shellac from insect secretions and gutta-percha based on bark. There was also Vulcanite or ebonite from rubber, Celluloid from camphor and casein from milk.

These early plastics are now widely collected and the range of articles is seemingly endless: jewellery, book bindings, pseudo-bronze plaques, combs, fountain pens, photograph frames, shoe horns, and salad servers.

For identification, wet Bakelite smells of carbolic and celluloid smells of camphor when rubbed with a cloth.

The best-known and most expensive items are the circular Ekco AD 75 radios of the 1930s, which can make £400-£500, as could a Senora 'Cadillac' of 1946. Standard radios of the Forties and Fifties range from £40 to £200, with well-designed examples, such as the Bush DAC 90 or the Murphy SAD 94 at the upper end.

▶ **Art Deco vanity set** 1930s (£30)

◄ **Radio Rentals** wireless from the 1950s (£40)

BACK STOOL

A stool which had a separate back fitted to it for increased comfort. They are most common in the mid 17th century.

 R ££££

BACON CUPBOARD

A useful item of farmhouse furniture which provides both seating and storage. A tall cupboard forms the back of a settle and there may also be drawers beneath the seat. Such pieces are likely to be made of elm, or, perhaps, oak. They were made from the Middle Ages to at least the second half of the 18th century.

 ££££

BAGUETTE

A semi-circular moulding with a bead and reel ornament, also known as an ASTRAGAL, and often used for the glazing bars of furniture.

BALDWIN, CHARLES HENRY (1859-1943)

One of the most important painters at the WORCESTER factory, where he worked from 1874 to 1909. He specialised in birds —especially swans — and moonlight scenes and landscapes. On leaving the factory he became a water-colourist, mainly in the north of England. Most of the porcelain he decorated (left) is signed in full.

££££

BALL FOOT AND BALL TURNING

A ball foot is exactly what it sounds like - a turned spherical foot for a heavy piece of furniture which was popular in the late 17th century and early 18th centuries. Ball turning is one of the oldest styles of furniture ornament, consisting of strings of equally sized balls on the legs and stretchers of tables and chairs. It was used by the Macedonians and was popular in the 17th and early 18th centuries and again in Victorian times.

BALL, WILLIAM

A Liverpool porcelain-maker, active c1755-69. All the pieces once thought to be by him have now been re-attributed by scholars to the VAUXHALL factory.

BALTIC CHEST

A type of 16-th century chest made on the Baltic coast, possibly at Danzig, and imported into England. The earlier ones are carved with religious scenes. The later ones are also known as NONESUCH CHESTS (meaning unequalled) and are richly decorated with marquetry designs of fantastic architecture.

££££

BALUSTER

A columnar form which swells at the base and narrows at the top. It was first developed during the Renaissance and was quickly adapted for use in furniture legs, glass stems, candle sticks and lamps. Rows of balusters of wood or wrought iron are known as balustrades.

BANDING

A decorative effect used to finish off the edges and rims of furniture. Coloured veneers are cut at varying angles to the grain: straight banding is cut along the length of the grain, cross-branding across it; and feather or herringbone banding is cut diagonally across it.

BANJO CLOCK

An American pendulum wall-clock in the shape of a lyre. They were introduced by the Willard family of

BALLOON BACK

The archetypal Victorian chair, it has a back which is formed like a balloon-shaped oval held in an inverted U, which narrows towards the seat.

They can either be very simple or highly decorated and elaborate. Some have heart-shaped balloons, rather than ovals, and many are bowed for comfort.

The seats may have been upholstered if the chairs were intended for dining or sitting room use, or made of simple cane in beechwood frames if they were intended for bedrooms.

After the 1860s deep upper rails became a more popular feature. Also, after this time, the balloons themselves were sometimes elaborated, as in the example illustrated.

▲ **French, 19th-century** rosewood balloon back chair, 1860 **(£150)**

Sitting around

Boston and made from c1802 to 1860. They have round faces and the pendulum case and rectangular base were decorated with painted glass panels. In later ones glass was replaced by painted wooden panels.

 £££

BARBEAUX

The French word for cornflowers which became a common decorative motif on 18th- and 19th-century porcelain. Believed to have been introduced at SÈVRES in 1782 to please Marie-Antoinette. English porcelain decorators quickly adopted the same motif.

BARBEDIENNE, FERDINAND (1810-92)

He established a famous bronze foundry in Paris in 1838 in partnership with Achille Collas who had invented a machine for the reduction of sculpture. They cast bronzes for Barye and other leading sculptors and also produced silverwares and reproduction furniture with bronze mounts in a wide range of styles.

BARBER'S BOWL

A shallow oval basin with a semi-circular notch to fit the neck of a person being shaved or having his beard washed by a barber. They are most commonly made of porcelain or pewter, and occasionally silver.

▲ Arita porcelain's barber's bowl
Japanese, late 17th-century (£800-£1,200)

Taking a measure of the pressure

BAROMETER

Galileo's notes on measuring atmospheric pressure were discovered after his death by an apprentice called Evangelistia Torricelli (1608-47) who improved on the master by using mercury instead of tubes of water. A scale was added to his first barometer only after his death, by the French philosopher Descartes.

Barometers were introduced to England in the 1680s, in both the basic stick and the wheel types. The stick, which stands on three little legs, was popularised by the Irish scientist Robert Boyle (1627-91). It had a visible vacuum at the top of the mercury column. The wheel type, invented by Boyle's former assistant, Robert Hooke (1635-1703), has a U-bend at the bottom of the tube.

In the19th century, Clerkenwell was full of Italian barometer-makers as well as clockmakers. One of the most common mid- to late 19th-century types is the FITZROY, invented by the commander of the Beagle on Charles Darwin's South American voyage. Most Fitzroy barometers have Victorian Gothic oak frames.

◀ Fitzroy type barometer in Victorian Gothic style wood case, late 19th century (£350-£500)

▶ Torricelli type, French, early 19th century. The mercury column is concealed at the back (£1,500-£2,500)

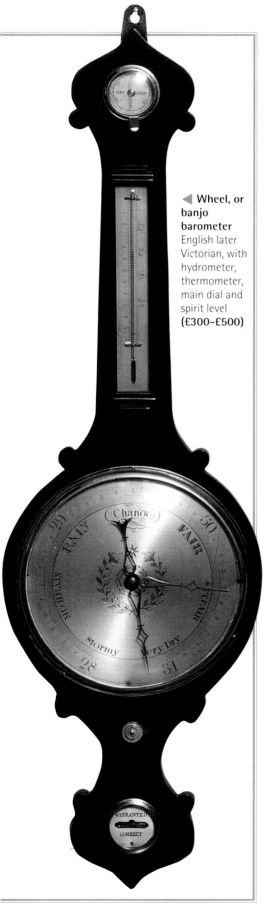

◀ **Wheel, or banjo barometer**
English later Victorian, with hydrometer, thermometer, main dial and spirit level **(£300–£500)**

BARGELLO WORK

A type of embroidery used mainly for upholstery in which each element of the flame-shaped pattern is worked in a single graduated colour. It is also known as flame, or Hungarian, stitch. English examples tend to be in wool and Italian ones in silk.

◀ **Doulton biscuit barrel** by H. Barlow, 1878 **(£700)**

BARLOW, HANNAH (1851–1916)

From the 1870s onwards she worked for the DOULTON factory in Lambeth together with her sister Florence (d1909). They used *sgraffito* (see BOLOGNA), to decorate stoneware, usually with animals and birds. Their work is widely collected.

£££–££££

BAROQUE

The style originated in Italy and was fully developed in 1620. It uses exuberant decoration, both figurative and architectural, and extravagant curvaceous forms. Its influence spread across Europe, but reached England quite late. Baroque furniture uses

elaborate inlays, gilded wood, japaning and lacquer. Silver, ceramics and glass tend towards bulbous shapes.

BARR, FLIGHT AND BARR

Thomas Flight bought the Worcester porcelain works in 1783 and Martin Barr joined him in 1792. In 1840 their company merged with the rival factory of Robert CHAMBERLAIN.

BARREL CHAIR

Round-backed easy chair, either cut from a barrel or made to look like that.

££

BASALTES WARE

A hard, unglazed, black stoneware also known as black balsate, developed by WEDGWOOD in the 1760s. It was made from Staffordshire clay, iron - stone, ochre and manganese and was used for vases, busts and tablewares. Vases are sometime bronzed with lightly fired metallic gold or painted to resemble Attic red figure wares.

£££

▶ **Black basaltes teapot** c1800. A damaged item **(£150)**

BASKET CHAIR

A woven cane or wicker chair extremely popular in the 19th century. They can be round-seated single chairs or lounge chairs with foot rests.

£££

BASKET STAND

A work table with two circular tiers on a columnar stand, it may have developed from the DUMB WAITER.

R ££££

Family who set the standard for silver

BATEMAN, HESTER (1708-94)

The most famous of female London silversmiths was also a brilliant businesswoman. The interest in Bateman is odd, in that Hester's work in particular is not of any great quality, certainly not compared to many of her contemporaries. Americans are the greatest supporters of her work and much of what appears for sale goes to the States. Often the silver sheet is thin and pieces light and one should be wary of re-engraving as the gauge can be so thin that the piece may have worn through. Hester Bateman was not the only silversmith to register the mark HB, although the others are earlier and less likely to be encountered.

Much of her work was done on commission from other retailers rather than directly for her own clients, so it is not uncommon to find her mark overstruck by theirs. She started in the 1760s, making mainly flatware, particularly spoons, but expanded into a wide range of domestic silverware. Especially sought after were her crescent-shaped wine labels and seals. She used simple forms, ornamented with beaded, bright-cut, pierced and engraved decoration.

She retired in 1790 but her sons Peter and Jonathan continued the business. Jonathan was succeeded by his widow Ann and in 1800 they were joined by Hester's grandson William. Ann retired in 1805 and Peter died 10 years later. William's son, William II, registered his first mark in 1827 and was still making silver until

his death in the 1870s. Thus the family worked from the heyday of neo-Classicism to the High Victorian era.

Today Hester's HB mark is much more highly valued than any of the others, although William II was far the best of the family. It must be re-emphasised that the initials HB were those of several other makers. The date of the piece and the shape of the enclosing punch must also be considered.

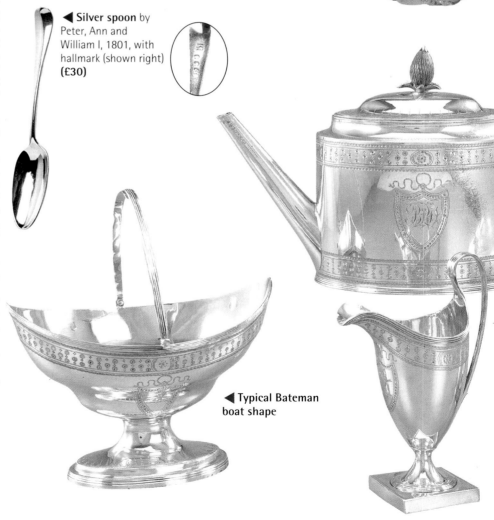

◀ Silver spoon by Peter, Ann and William I, 1801, with hallmark (shown right) (£30)

◀ Typical Bateman boat shape

▶ Four piece tea set and caddy in silver by Peter and Ann Bateman, 1791 (£8,500)

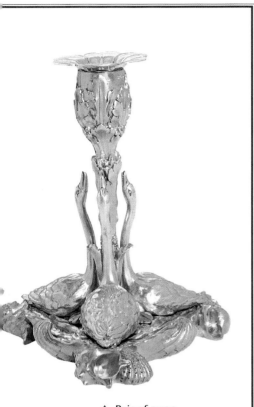

▲ **Pair of swan candlesticks** by William II, after Marot (**£25,000**)

BATH CHAIR
A chair on three wheels which was invented by James Heath of Bath in about 1750 for use by invalids. A long steering handle attached to the front wheel swivelled to allow the chair to be pulled from the front or, with the passenger steering, to be pushed from the back.

£££

BATHING COSTUMES
Recreational sea bathing was indulged in during the early 18th century, but it was only when it was advocated by George III's doctors that it became in any way popular. Bathing machines, and their ferocious, usually female attendants appeared at south coast resorts such as Weymouth, Sidmouth, Lyme and Brighton, and elaborate all-encasing dresses were worn by bathers. On less fashionable coasts no form of dress was thought necessary until well into the Victorian era. In 1853 a visitor to Barmouth noted that the machines were not used, and that the young preferred 'a state of nature to putting on those ugly blue sacks politely termed Bathing Gowns'. However, this would have been 'called exceedingly improper for our English ladies at Scarboro'. In the 1870s and '80s—as recorded by so many Punch artists—ladies' costumes had several layers of skirt over culottes, while gentlemen wore combinations.

These became less elaborate until the one-piece arrived in something like its modern form in the 1930s. The bikini owed its name to the exotic South Sea atoll on which atom bomb tests were carried out in the 1950s. Since then one-piece, two, or none has been dictated by fashion and audacity rather than aesthetics or moral sensibilities.

£

BAXTER PRINTS
George Baxter patented a new process for producing coloured prints in 1835. Colour was applied through a succession of engraved wood blocks tied by a black engraved steel plate. Prior to Baxter, coloured prints were rare and expensive, employing much hand work. Baxter produced more than 300 images and, under increasing pressure from his competitors, he offered six licences for the use of his process in 1849. Among those who took them up were Kronheim and le Blond, whose work is of lesser quality. They used fewer colours and Baxter's prints, which were nearly always signed, are considered to be of finer quality.

BAXTER, THOMAS
Probably the finest English ceramic painter of the early 19th century. He had studios in London, then Worcester, Swansea and again at Worcester (CHAMBERLAIN).

◀ A costume from the 1950s (**£10**)

▲ Black velvet handbag with gold beads and sequins, French, c1930, **(£150)**

BEADWORK

Coloured glass beads used to decorate textiles, often in elaborate designs. Beadwork became popular in England in the late 16th and 17th centuries for the decoration of objects such as caskets and frames. Far more common are 19th-century examples from chair covers to small purses.

BEAR JUGS

English pottery jug shaped like a bear, often hugging a dog to represent bear-baiting. The detachable head can be used as a cup. They were made during the 18th century in brown stoneware at Nottingham and Derby and in white salt-glazed stoneware in Staffordshire.

££££

◀ Brown stonewear bear jug and cover, late 18th century **(£800-£1200)**

A time to sleep and a time to lie

BEDS

Beds raised above the ground became widespread only in the 17th century. However, in grand households the bed had a ceremonial significance and was always one of the most important items of furniture.

Early beds are on raised platforms with carved head and foot boards. From the Renaissance the super-structure becomes more elaborate with a canopy, or tester, and side curtains to protect the sleeper from dirt and draughts. Early beds sometimes had a wheeled truckle bed beneath, which pulled out for a maid or valet to use. The canopies could be hung from the walls and ceiling, supported on the headboard and foot posts or on four posts. Decoration was lavished on the textile hangings.

In the 19th century beds became less elaborate, with the drapery gradually disappearing. More humble beds include: a press bed which fits into a cupboard, a sideboard or even a piano; a narrow day bed, with a head and arms, and a camp or field bed of light framework and folding legs.

One of the most elegant early 19th-century types is the 'lit à bateau', or boat-bed with S-shaped head and foot. These, usually Continental, are often inexpensive, but sizes rarely match modern mattresses which may have to be specially made.

Victorian and Edwardian bedheads, the sizes of which usually match today's, are inexpensive considering the craftsmanship. They may be carved in mahogany or in inlaid satinwood and are a practical alternative to a modern veneered chipboard. Popular too, are elaborate brass examples. The most elegant are Adam revival designs in square or ribbed section. Once polished they should be lacquered to prevent endless cleaning. Beware brass on cast iron, it may disintegrate.

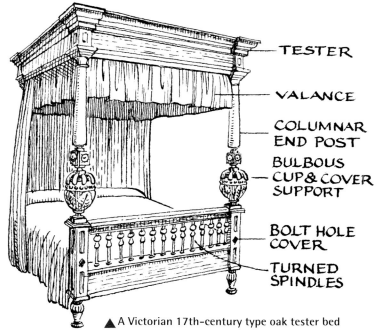

TESTER

VALANCE

COLUMNAR END POST

BULBOUS CUP & COVER SUPPORT

BOLT HOLE COVER

TURNED SPINDLES

▲ A Victorian 17th-century type oak tester bed

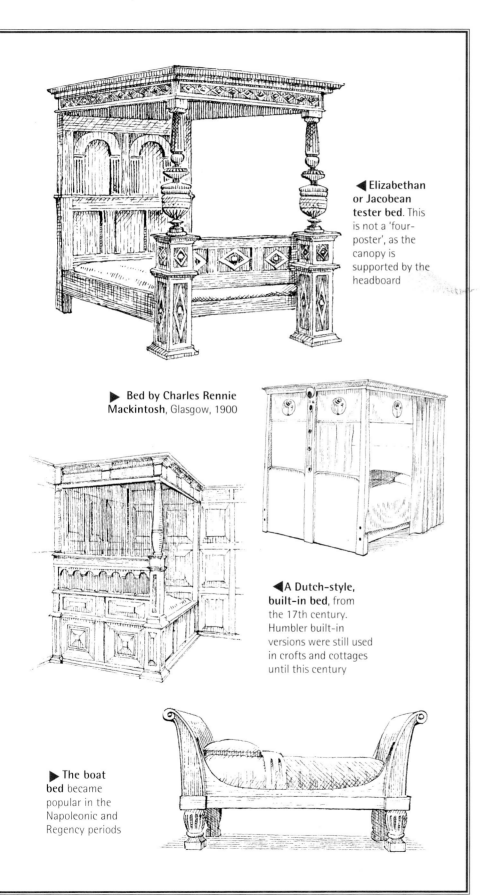

◀ **Elizabethan or Jacobean tester bed**. This is not a 'four-poster', as the canopy is supported by the headboard

▶ **Bed by Charles Rennie Mackintosh**, Glasgow, 1900

◀ **A Dutch-style, built-in bed**, from the 17th century. Humbler built-in versions were still used in crofts and cottages until this century

▶ **The boat bed** became popular in the Napoleonic and Regency periods

BED STEPS
A set of steps for climbing into high 18th-century beds. Some incorporate a small cupboard for storing a chamber pot.

£££

BED TABLE
A tray with folding legs to fit across the bed and provide a firm surface. In the 19th century a type was made which swivelled on a pillared base and could be adjusted in height.

££

BED WAGON
An open wooden frame with a canopy over it and a platform for a charcoal-burning pan. Used for airing rather than warming beds.

R £££

BEDROOM CHAIR
Light chairs of japanned beech or painted pine were made for bedrooms from the late 18th century, often with rush seats. A light BALLOON BACK has a cane seat.

££-£££

BEILBY, WILLIAM (1740-1819)
The most famous enameller on English glass, he and his sister Mary (1749-97) were working at Newcastle upon Tyne from about 1762 to 1778, when William went to London to teach drawing. Later they settled in Fife. Their brother Ralph was a silversmith and engraver and Thomas Bewick, the wood engraver, was his apprentice. The Beilbys decorated glasses and mallet-shaped decanters in full colour or a bluish-white enamel, which complemented white-twist stems on wine glasses. Coats of arms, masonic devices and decorations of fruit, flowers and birds, landscapes and skating scenes all appear. Occasionally pieces are signed with the surname, and there is a long-held assumption that a butterfly also serves as a signature. (This may or may not be true.) Glass-

The heavy hand of time

BELGIAN 'MARBLE' CLOCKS

Clocks made from Ardennes (Belgium) or Welsh slate, polished to look like black marble, were mass-produced with French movements from about the 1870s, and they became very popular in Britain and across the Continent. They are solid and heavy, and have incised decoration, and sometimes granite bases for decorative columns. The favourite shapes are rectangles with pedestals, or a flowing curve. Despite being mass-produced they were dependable and of some quality.

Although American makers quickly copied the form, they first used painted cast iron, even imitating flecks of gold as in the slate, and then painted wooden versions. This killed the Belgian and British industries within a matter of 20 years. At both the country house Roadshows in 1995 — Luton Hoo and Blenheim Palace — clocks made of all three materials turned up.

◀ **Rusty patches** give away this cast-iron clock by the American Ansonia Co., c1890 (**£100**)

▶ **French marbled** wooden version, c1865 (**£100**)

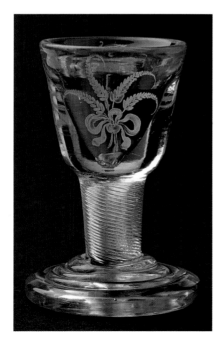

▲ **Beilby enamelled** toastmaker's glass with butterfly, c1760 (**£7,000-£8,000**)

making was big business on Tyneside and many pieces with enamel decoration that are attributed to the Beilbys are just not good enough. Genuine Beilby glasses often have gilt rims, but these were not 'fired on' and tend to have worn badly. Beilbys should not be confused with 'Mary Gregory' glasses which have figures in white enamels, usually on a coloured metal, and were made in Austria or Bohemia at the turn of the 19th/20th century

R £££££

BELLANGÉ, PIERRE-ANTOINE (1758-1837)

French cabinetmaker patronised by Napoleon, but most of his recorded furniture dates from the *Restauration* period when he became official *ébéniste* (originally a veneer specialist) to Louis XVIII. He worked mainly in mahogany and other dark woods in a wide range of styles. His brother Louis-François used lighter woods often decorated with porcelain plaques. Pierre-Antoine's nephew, Alexandre-Louis, inherited both their businesses. He became *ébéniste du roi* to Louis-Philippe and supplied furniture to George IV for Carlton House.

BELLARMINE

Sturdy, round-bellied stoneware jug made in 16th-century Cologne. The neck is decorated with a grotesque bearded face associated with Cardinal Roberto Bellarmino, governor of the Spanish Netherlands, who was hated in the Protestant countries for his counter-Reformation zeal. They were made as late as the 19th century and were copied, possibly by J. DWIGHT, in England where they went under the name Greybeards.

£££-££££

BENTWOOD

Wood which has been bent by heat, steam or pressure. The bowed back of a WINDSOR chair is one of the earliest forms. More common are the mass-produced, 19th-century bentwood chairs with cane or plywood seats.

££

BÉRAIN, JEAN (1637-1711)

A French architect and ornamental designer who helped to create the Louis XIV style. In 1674 he became *dessinateur de la chambre et du cabinet du roi* and provided designs for the royal festivals and ballets. His work is light and whimsical with grotesque masks and fanciful figures. In 1711 a collection of his designs extended his influence throughout Europe.

BERGÈRE

A rectangular, or slightly rounded, armchair with canework or padded back and sides. A variety of 18th-century types gradually fused into one of the most typical shapes of the Regency. Full caned versions usually had loose leather cushions, but some were fully upholstered. Edwardian reproduction bergères often have Sheraton shell motifs in the centre of caned backs.

£££-££££

▶ Bergère chair, mahogany, George III, *c*1805, with caned back and bowed cane sided arms (£1,380 the pair)

Sea-shell shiny

BELLEEK

The factory, which was founded at Belleek in Co Fermanagh by David McBirney in 1857, became famous for its pearly, highly-translucent porcelain. The basic PARIAN-like body was covered with a clear and particularly lustrous glaze of a type influenced by Royal Worcester. The most notable products were vases and dishes decorated with shells, particularly sea-urchins, and other marine life, or grasses and flowers. The shell lines were designed by a Dublin architect, W.R. Armstrong, and first shown at the Dublin Exhibition in 1865. The factory also produced plain white and coloured, utilitarian jugs, basins and spirit barrels in earthenware.

An ex-employee took Belleek's secrets to Ott and Brewer of New Jersey, who produced nacreous ware marked 'Belleek' from 1872. One of their employees in his turn set up the Lenox Co. in Trenton in 1889. Other American Belleek imitators were Knowles Taylor and Knowles of East Liverpool, Ohio, producing 'Lotusware'.

American 'Belleek' is usually more colourful and still more ornate than Irish. True Belleek wares, when coloured, are in pastel tones, usually the flowers in woven baskets and vegetation on tea sets. On some the leaves, which were modelled by young women and children with particularly supple fingers, can cut the clumsier fingers of admirers. Belleek is now widely collected in Ireland and by Americans claiming Irish descent.

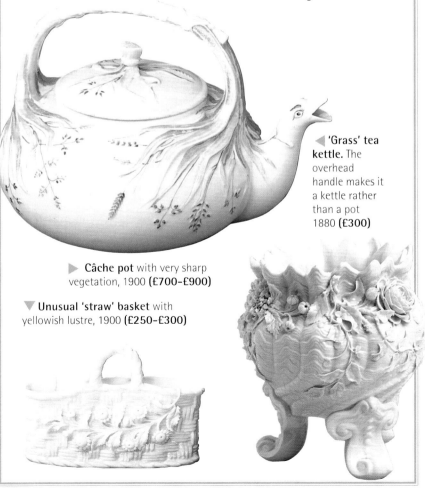

◀ 'Grass' tea kettle. The overhead handle makes it a kettle rather than a pot 1880 (£300)

▶ Câche pot with very sharp vegetation, 1900 (£700-£900)

▼ Unusual 'straw' basket with yellowish lustre, 1900 (£250-£300)

▼ Betjemann miniature tantalus
with Bramah lock, c1890 **(£150)**

BERLIN IRONWORK

Fine cast-iron jewellery which became especially fashionable in 1813-15 during the Prussian war of independence. Women were asked to give up their jewels to finance the war and received cast-iron jewellery instead. It was cast by the Prussian Royal Iron Foundry, initially in Silesia and from about 1804 in Berlin. The earliest pieces are neo-Classical in style, later examples becoming influenced by the Gothic revival. It remained popular until well into the mid-19th century.

££££

▲ Berlin ironwork belt, made in the 1840s-50s, towards the end of the style's popularity **(£300)**

BETJEMANN

The late Poet Laureate Sir John Betjeman's great-great-grandfather set up George Betjeman & Sons in 1820 to make household items for the rich. In the 1860s the second 'n' was added to the name, reflecting the fashion for all things German. During the First World War the family dropped it again. The firm had many fine lines, but its prosperity was based on the tantalus, patented in 1821, designed to keep spirit

decanters safe from servants. There were four grades; the one shown here is a B, with brass bar and Bramah lock. The factory was in the Pentonville Road, London.

Making plates for the Great

▼ Mid-19th-century bowl which demonstrates the factory's high standard even though it is marked 'reject' underneath **(£70)**

▶ Plaque of Princess Louise, perhaps by Richter, 1870-80 **(£4,000-£6,000)**

BERLIN PORCELAIN & PLAQUES

The first Berlin factory, founded by Wilhelm Kaspar Wegely in 1752, lasted for five years, producing hard-paste porcelain tableware influenced by MEISSEN and VINCENNES. Some of the craftsmen then joined the Berlin Porcelain factory established in 1761 by the financier J.E. Gotzkowsky. This was bought by Frederick the Great in 1763.

The products of the first decade are finely modelled with great delicacy in the Rococo style. Superb tableware was produced for the king, and figures after models by F.E. and W.C.Meyer. The factory's painters included K.W. Bohme, J.B. Bormann and K.J. Klipfel.

Around 1770 there was a marked change of style: the introduction of a different type of kaolin produced porcelain of a much colder, whiter tone and the factory developed a more severe type of decoration.

It used to be assumed that after Frederick's death in 1786 standards declined. But it is now recognised that the factory produced many fine pieces in a variety of styles until well into the 19th century, including magnificent Directoire, Empire and Restauration dinner services and vases. Often they are decorated with impressive topographical subjects. Berlin decorators also imitated marble, micromosaic and lapis. Later there were lively Art Nouveau and other lines.

From 1827 the factory made transparent lithophanes — thin porcelain plaques to be held against the light — which were mounted in brass as lamp shades or could be hung over a window. As the light passed through an image in tones of light and dark appeared. Berlin made huge numbers of porcelain plaques, a few of which were then painted in the factory with subjects after the Old Masters and the more sentimental works of the Munich School. However, the vast majority of plaques were sold as blanks to

BETTY LAMP

A primitive lamp used in America in the 18th century. It is a flat, iron vessel with a floating wick usually suspended from a nail or adjustable stand.

 £££

BEVEL

The sloping, angled edge of a flat metal, wood or glass surface, or book covers.

BEZEL

The metal ring that encircles and frames the glass over a clock face (shown right). It is usually hinged.

BIBLE BOX

Portable oak box with a hinged lid, dating from the 17th century. There is often carved decoration on the front. The name dates from the Victorian period when they were mistakenly believed to have been designed to hold the family bible.

£££-££££

BIDET

A stool, originating in 18th-century France, with an inset metal or ceramic basin. Travelling bidets were made as chests with removable tops.

£££

BIEDERMEIER

A furniture style named after a philistine bourgeois character invented by the satirist Ludwig Eichrodt. It was applied to the furniture and furnishings of new rich Germans and Austrians of the period 1815-48, between the fall of Napoleon and the year of revolutions. It tends to be comfortable (*gemütlich*) and opulent, with embossed metal ornaments. Once dismissed as 'exuberantly vulgar', it is now increasingly appreciated, like its equivalents in France (*Restauration* and Charles X) and in Britain (William IV).

BILLER FAMILY

Prominent Augsburg silversmiths throughout the 18th century, they were a Protestant family who specialised in secular domestic plate. Five of them reached prominence, and Johann Jacob published two sets of engraved designs for goldsmiths' work.

BILLIES AND CHARLIES

These are mid-19th-century forgeries of medieval amulets, small figures and seals. They are made of poor-quality pewter with relief decoration and were forged by William Smith and Charles Eaton of Tower Hill, London. They claimed to have found them by digging in the Thames riverbed but the pieces were discovered to be forgeries because their dates were in Arabic rather than Roman numerals.

 ££-£££

▲ **Austrian Biedermeier** mantel clock, giltmetal-mounted giltwood, stained fruitwood and alabaster. On this example the bezel is clearly visible (£1,500-£2,000)

BILLINGSLEY, WILLIAM (1758-1828)

An important English porcelain maker and painter, who worked in numerous factories and specialised in delicate naturalistic flowers. Apprenticed at DERBY, he established, in 1795, a factory at Pinxton in Derbyshire. He left in 1799 and worked as an independent decorator at WORCESTER. In 1814 he started the NANTGARW factory, closing it about 1822. He left to work for COALPORT. Indeed, Coalport paste at this period can be mistaken for Nantgarw.

 £££

outside decorators, particularly in Dresden. These are now very collectable, particularly in Japan.

Marks include a blue W for Wegely; an underglaze G for Gotzkowsky; and a variety of sceptres from 1763 on. From the 1790s various dashes and numbers gave a precise date, and during the 19th century an orb might join the sceptre, the initials KPM (Konigliche Porzellan Manufactur) and an eagle.

Trinket boxes for the masses

▲ Novelty patch box, c1800 (£600–£800)

◀ Bilston bird snuffbox (£400–£600)

BILSTON AND BATTERSEA ENAMEL

Mid-18th-century enamel boxes, often called 'Battersea', are likely to come from Bilston or Birmingham. From the 1740s Bilston enamels were a cheaper, mass-produced alternative to hand-painted porcelain boxes. They were transfer printed on prepared surfaces. Despite the quality of its products, the Battersea factory, where the French engraver S.F. Ravenet was chief designer, lasted only from 1753 to 1755. Thereafter many of the craftsmen migrated to Bilston and Staffordshire. Their enamels are generally executed in monochrome red, purple or sepia. More common are brightly coloured boxes,

often in novelty shapes with complementary scenes on the lids, also made at the Bilston and Wednesbury factories. Others were made in Birmingham by BOULTON. Most easily recognised are Bilston souvenir boxes with homely mottoes. Other wares included caddies, candlesticks and scent bottles. In the second half of the 19th century SAMSON of Paris produced 'Battersea' enamels.

▶ Bilston tea caddy, c1770, of the sort copied by Samson (£3,000–£5,000)

BING TOY FACTORY

The Gebrüder Bing factory, founded in Nuremburg in 1865, did not begin manufacturing tin toys until

▲ Bing clockwork O-gauge train set, in original box, 1920s (£600–£700)

1895. Model ships were popular around 1900. Expansion was rapid and high production levels were achieved in the 1920s with train sets. The business was a hit by the economic slump of the 1930s and went into receivership in 1932. The toys are stamped GBN Bavaria.

BIRD CAGE

Cages for song birds were fashionable in Italy and France from the Renaissance and throughout Europe from the early 18th century. They could be made of wood, wickerwork, brass or copper wire, and varied enormously according to the fashionable style of the period. The most elaborate of them copied contemporary architecture and were an important decorative feature of a room. In the 19th century mechanical AUTOMATA of birds in cages were also made.

 £££–£££££

BISCUIT

Earthenware or porcelain which has been fired but not glazed. 'Bisque' is a corruption used for dolls' heads.

BLACK FOREST CLOCK

The Swiss did not invent the cuckoo clock - German peasant clockmakers in the Black Forest did so in about 1730. Theirs had wooden moving parts and the earliest examples used stones as weights. They did not keep good time. Striking versions also appeared about 1730 and pendulums 10 years later, although these were in front of the dials rather than behind. Dials were wooden, and then painted paper stuck to wood. Metal parts took over in the 19th century and from the 1840s picture clocks had movements set in scenes such as moonlight villages. They also made cheaper copies of mass-produced American clocks and those from other areas and countries, such as the elaborate hanging Vienna Regulator.

 ££-£££

BLACK JACK

A 17th-century British leather jug, shaped like a tankard, often with silver mounts. It can vary in size from a quart to a gallon or more.

R £££-££££

BLANC-DE-CHINE

Chinese porcelain which is pure white with a lustrous glaze, made at Dehua in south-east China. Large quantities were imported into Europe, especially in the 17th and 18th centuries, and they were an important influence on porcelain factories.

£££

BLANKET CHEST

A chest with two drawers under a box with a hinged lid. American examples look like a chest with four drawers but the top two drawers are false and conceal the chest section.

£££-££££

BLEU CÉLESTE

A brilliant turquoise enamel ground colour developed at VINCENNES in 1753 and later used at WORCESTER.

BLUE DE ROI

An intense royal blue enamel introduced at SÈVRES by 1760, and also known as *gros bleu*, *bleu nouveau* and *beau bleu*.

BLIND TOOLING

A decorative bookbinding technique. The design is stamped into the leather, but left 'blind', without any gold leaf or colouring. Subtle and restrained, it is a very old form of decoration, dating back to the Middle Ages when it was used on manuscript bindings.

Tons of 'toys' from Brum

BIRMINGHAM SILVER

Birmingham became a manufacturing centre for silver and jewellery in the early 18th century and it soon became known as the 'Toyshop of Europe'. Toys in this sense meant small metal objects such as buckles, buttons, boxes, 'seals, tweezers and toothpick boxes, smelling bottles and filigree work, watch chains, stay hooks, sugar nippers, etc' (*Sketchley's Birmingham Directory*, 1767). In 1762 Matthew BOULTON, the future partner of James Watt, set up his Soho factory. He produced SHEFFIELD plate as well as steel and pure silver items.

In 1773 Sheffield and Birmingham were granted their own assay offices, taking their crown and anchor marks from a London pub where their representatives met. Such was Birmingham's predominance in early 19th-century toy-making that it is almost a surprise to find anything but the anchor on a VINAIGRETTE or CADDY SPOON. From the 1830s, Boulton's position as doyen of the trade was taken by Elkington, the firm which held the ELECTROPLATE patent. Inevitably there was a snobbish reaction against 'Brummagem's' success, with A.W. PUGIN dismissing Birmingham and Sheffield as an inexhaustible mine of bad taste, which was unfair.

In the late 19th century, silver card cases with raised views of famous buildings or sporting subjects were popular, as were fancy pin-cushions in the form of animals such as pigs and elephants. Other notable Birmingham products included Jennens and Bettridge's PAPIER-MÂCHÉ furniture, steel pens, artificial eyes and pins — of which 500 tons were being produced each week by 1900.

▲ **Silver cheroot case,** with engraved scrolling decoration and initials, 1900 (**£150**)

▲ **Caddy spoon** by Joseph Williams, 1842 (**£120**)

◀ **Elephant pin-cushion** with shell cart, 1909 (**£200-£250**)

BLOOR, ROBERT

Bloor bought the DERBY porcelain factory in 1811 and, although he went mad in 1826, his name is still used as a label for the period up to 1848 when the factory closed down. The products of the time when he was involved are mostly undistinguished.

BLOWER

A wooden or brass box which encloses a fan for blowing a fire. They were made in the 18th century. A handle on the outside turns the fan and the air is directed through a metal tube to the fire.

£££

BLUE-DASH CHARGERS

Large tin-glazed earthenware dishes made at Lambeth, Brislington and Bristol from c1640 to the early 18th century. They were highly ornamental, decorated in MAIOLICA colours with borders of slanting dashes. Designs include stylised portraits of Charles I and II, James II, William III, equestrian portraits, Adam and Eve and flower designs recalling ISNIK pottery.

££££

BLUNDERBUSS

Developed from the short cavalry carbine, the blunderbuss was a favourite weapon for self-defence from the 1670s to the 1840s, when it was superseded by much more effective pistols and shotguns. Because of the typical trumpet barrel it is often assumed that it had a wide spread but in fact the opposite is true. The wide muzzle was designed for easy loading on a bucking coach or pitching ship. Thus, although it was generally inefficient, it was popular on stagecoaches and with the navy. It was good for physical intimidation, especially when fitted with a spring bayonet.

£££-££££

◀1820s blunderbuss (£900)

When the West looked East

Essentially, the Chinese tradition of blue and white porcelain began in the 14th century and continues today. Their wares were prized by Moslem rulers, and made their way to European courts in the 16th century. In the same way, the taste moved eastwards, first to Korea and then to Japan.

In the mid-16th century the Portuguese, followed by the Dutch from the early 1600s, began to import directly, and this stimulated European potters to compete. Blue and white became standard for Dutch delft, and much was produced elsewhere in Europe by makers of MAIOLICA and FAIENCE. No European imitations could compare with the quality of the imported Kangxi porcelain wares (1662-1722) which were avidly collected by connoisseurs. The Dutch sent to Japan delft-decorated wooden samples of the designs they wanted, which were then turned out en masse by the Japanese potters at Arita. Blue and white retained its popularity despite the discovery of true or hard-paste porcelain by Johann BÖTTGER.

Once the English factories such as Worcester, Lowestoft and Liverpool came into production in the mid-18th century, they each made blue and white, as did Staffordshire earthenware potters. Part of its popularity was due to its cheapness as against coloured wares. Shapes were largely derived from silver designs, and the decoration either imitated the Chinese directly or built up its own Rococo Chinoiserie world – of which the willow pattern later became the most famous example.

▶ Qianlong 'mark and period' piece (1736-95) (£20,000-£30,000)

▲ One of a pair of Chinese shell dishes, modelled after European silver (£700-£900 the pair)

▼ The Battle of Portobello (1739) an early English delftware plate, c1740, (£1,500-£2,500)

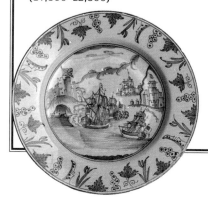

▶ **Bologna sgraffito jug**, late 15th century (£15,000–£20,000)

◀ **A Chelsea group** of rustic lovers-who might well be given hay-fever by their bocage! (£5,000–£8,000)

be filled with colour or a double layer of slip applied and then engraved. The piece was then glazed and fired. The earliest are fairly crude, but in the late 15th century the Bolognese tried to compete with the MAIOLICA factories and produced much finer wares decorated with PUTTI, youths and maidens within a border of stylised leaves. *Sgraffiti* like the trilobed jug (above) were made at Bologna until the 18th century with, from 1749, a factory making cream-coloured earthenware.

££££-£££££

BOCAGE

The three-dimensional vegetation that forms the background to porcelain and earthenware figures made in Germany from about 1740 and England from around 1760. The leaves, which often resemble those of the hawthorn, are arranged in groups usually with coloured flowers at the centre of each group.

BOIS DURÇI

A compound which imitates ebony carvings, and was popular in France and England, *c*1850-1900. Sawdust, water and blood are combined by heat treatment and then die-stamped into decorative features.

BOKHARA RUGS

A popular name given to a large group of carpets woven by the Turkman nomads of central Asia. Since the late 19th century Bokhara has been their trading centre although the rugs are not actually made there. They are woven by the Salor, Saryq, Yomut, Afghan and Tekke tribes, each of whose work has distinguishing characteristics. In general they have a warm but sombre colour scheme, with dull red and black predominating. Octagons are a dominant

motif. Those woven by the Tekkes are considered the finest, with the octagons filled with small stars, flowers and trefoils.

££££

BOLECTION MOULDING

A distinctively shaped convex moulding often used to disguise the join between two surfaces on different levels. Found on panelling, and on surrounding fireplaces, from the late 17th century, but it rarely appears after the year 1710. On furniture it is often used to cover the joints between panel and frame.

BOLOGNA POTTERIES

It was here that the best *sgraffito* (scratched) wares of the late 16th and early 17th centuries were made. The clay vessel was dipped into liquid clay (slip), dried, and the decoration scratched through to the underlying colour before firing. The lines could

▲ **Swedish bombé commode** In kingwood and parquetry. 18th century (£4,200)

BOMBÉ

A French term meaning 'blown out', which refers to the exaggerated convex swelling curve given to the fronts of commodes and chests-of-drawers, especially during the early 18th century.

▲ Chelsea bonbonnière
(£2,500–£3,500)

BONBONNIÈRE

Small 17th- or 18th-century box for sweets also known as a sweetmeat or comfit box. They resembled snuff-boxes, and could be made in all sorts of materials including PIQUÉ enamel and gold.

£££–££££

BONE CHINA

A porcelain made of KAOLIN with the addition of up to 50% bone ash/calcinated ox bones. It is softer than hard paste porcelain and more durable and less expensive than soft-paste. It was introduced in the late 18th century and is the standard English body, still in use today.

BONHEUR-DU-JOUR

A lady's small writing table with a cabinet of shelves, drawers or pigeonholes. They appeared first in mid-18th-century France and were found soon after in England. Made in a variety of styles, they are always delicate, essentially feminine and often richly decorated, either painted or inlaid. The origin of the name is unknown.

££££

◄ Boulle work bonheur-du-jour mid-19th century (£3,000–£4,000)

BOOKCASE

Free-standing bookshelves that are glazed, rather than being left open. Early libraries tended to have fitted cases. The free-standing version dates from the 17th century. In the 18th century they became large architectural pieces with two glazed doors, often with a BREAKFRONT where the central section projects in front of the sides. Smaller versions, frequently with display shelves for curios, appear towards the end of the century.

£££–£££££

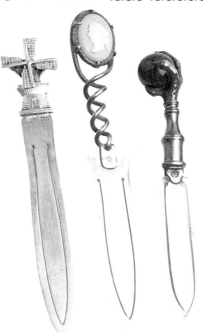

▲ Three from a vast collection of bookmarks brought into the Taunton Roadshow (£20–£50 each)

BOOKMARKS

These are made from a wide variety of materials and date from the 19th century onwards. They were often trowel-shaped with a slit cut in them to slip over the page. The most costly were made of delicately engraved silver, with ivory handles, but base metals, wood, bone and, from the 1930s, plastics were also used. They often had a souvenir or commemorative function. Later, many were produced in silks, card or leather as advertisements.

£–££

▼ A group of moulded medicine or sauce bottles
With proprietory names. Late 19th century (£5–£10 each)

Empties that are full of interest

BOTTLES

From about 1650 English bottles were made from dark green or brown bottle glass which contains no lead. They had a bulbous body and long neck with a deep kick in the base. During the 18th century they gradually become taller with slightly curved sides and rounded square shoulders. From around 1830 they approximate more closely to the shape we know today, following the custom of stacking wine bottles in bins. The early bottles were made in clay moulds and have a distinct bulge at the base. Later, metal moulds were used and the bulge disappears.

Machine-moulded bottles date from about 1840. Before that, they should have a PONTIL mark on the base. Bottles from the 17th and 18th centuries often carry seals with the names or crests of the owners, including Oxford pubs and colleges.

◀ **English wine bottle** with the seal of Trinity College Common Room, c1790 (**£70**)

▼ **English mallet-shaped wine bottle** c1740 (**£60-£90**)

◀ **Bohemian enamelled liquor flasks** with short, narrow necks and pewter mounts, c1760 (**£700-£1,000 the pair**)

BOTT, THOMAS and THOMAS JOHN

Royal Worcester painters specialising in 'Limoges Enamel' subjects. T. J. Bott later became art director at COALPORT.

BÖTTGER JOHANN FRIEDRICH (1682-1719)

Inventor of the first European hard-paste porcelain at MEISSEN in about 1708, after experiments in red stone-ware. An alchemist who worked for AUGUSTUS THE STRONG, in 1707 he abandoned the attempt to turn base metals to gold and, with Count von Tschirnhausen, made the almost as valuable discovery of the secret of porcelain. In 1708 they produced red porcellaneous stoneware, and translucent white porcelain followed a year later. He was appointed first director of MEISSEN in 1710.

◀ **Böttger coffee pot and cover** Made in red stone-ware for the Turkish market, c1712 (**£7,000-£8,000**)

BOTTLE LABEL

Small silver or enamel label suspended on a chain to identify the contents of a bottle or decanter, and made from about 1725 until around 1860. Many bear now unfamiliar names such as Rhenish, Negus and Hollands. In 1861 it was made legal to sell wine by the bottle, provided it

▶ **Bottle label** Simple silver design, c1820 (**£50-£100**)

bore a paper label, and it then became acceptable for bottles to appear on the table. The labels tended to follow fashions in silver design and decoration. A few were also made in SHEFFIELD plate, mother-of-pearl and porcelain.

 ££-£££

◀ Breakfront
display cabinet
boulle work, c1850
(£5,000-£6,000)

▲ Detail of
ormolu mount

The ins and the outs of it

BOULLE, ANDRÉ-CHARLES (1642-1732)

The most celebrated of Louis XIV's furniture-makers, he was appointed ébeniste du roi in 1672 and worked almost exclusively for the royal palaces, especially Versailles. His furniture is sumptuous and monumental, with brass mounts of outstanding quality. He perfected an old Italian technique of tortoiseshell and brass inlay, which then became known as 'boulle work'. A sheet of tortoiseshell is glued on top of a brass one, and the design is cut through both. When the two sheets are separated, the designs can be inlaid into their opposite backgrounds. A brass design laid into tortoiseshell is known as première partie, and its opposite is contre-partie.

In this way pairs of tables or commodes might be decorated as negative/positive images of one another. Similarly, first-part and counter-part panels might be used on either side of a door. Areas which had no inlay were usually veneered in ebony or mounted with ORMOLU.

Boulle's sons carried on the business, and the technique passed from them to many of the great late-18th-century ébenistes. Green tortoiseshell was fashionable in Germany, and boulle work remained popular there and in England throughout the 18th century. It was revived in the 19th. Imitators often tried to paint an already gaudy lily by colouring the backs of the tortoiseshell sheets, or adding inlays of pewter, mother-of-pearl or brightly stained horn.

In fact, in many cases, particularly in the 19th century, horn replaces the more expensive tortoiseshell, its back coloured in imitation. The complex construction of boulle work means that the brass often lifts. This is caught by passing dusters and is bent back. Restoration of boulle work is fiendishly expensive and buying damaged pieces may be a serious mistake. On less good quality 19th-century furniture the ebony veneer may be replaced by ebonising. This can usually be detected on edges where paler wood will show through worn patches. Considering the craftsmanship needed to produce boulle work, it is at present comparatively inexpensive due to the current disfavour in which black is held.

▼ French side cabinet
In boulle work, lacking
its marble top, c1855
(£1,000-£1,500)

BOURDALOUES

Oval, slipper-shaped chamber pots used by ladies when travelling and possibly carried concealed in muffs. They are supposedly named after the famous preacher Louis Bourdaloue (1632-1704) whose sermons at Versailles were so popular that his congregations had to assemble hours in advance. However, the earliest surviving examples date from 1710. They are generally made of porcelain, beautifully decorated and often mistaken for sauce-boats.

£££-££££

BOW

Soft-paste porcelain factory founded at Bow, London, *c*1747 and closed in 1776. It produced a wide range of figures and domestic ware which were often enamelled in KAKIEMON style or with botanical flowers in soft colours. After 1760 the quality deteriorated. When the factory closed, many of the models were taken by William Duesbury for use at DERBY . Marks include: incised planet symbols, blue and white marked with B, script G, or planet symbols in underglaze blue. Marks on later figures include anchor and dagger in red, underglaze blue letters, dots and crescents.

£££-££££

◀ **Bow figure** It represents the actress Kitty Clive, *c*1750 (£8,000–£9,000)

BOWIE KNIFE

A hunting knife named after the American frontiersman and soldier James Bowie (1795-1836). The exact design of the original knife is uncertain but the term came to mean any knife with a clipped-back blade-for fighting, hunting or clearing ground. The blades were from 9in to 15in long and curved at the end. They were made by smiths in Mississippi, Arkansas, Louisiana and Texas, and later exported by English cutlers to America and the colonies.

£££

◀ **Bowie knife by W. Sanson of Sheffield** Made for the American market, *c*1860. The horse's head version is the most sought after (£2,000)

BOX IRON

An early form of hollow iron which has a metal box, similar in shape to a flat iron, attached to a handle. A heated piece of iron, coal or a small hot brick was placed inside .

££

BOX WOOD

A hard, smooth, pale yellow wood generally used for decorative inlays.

Thanks to buttons

▶ **Ormolu-mounted blue john candelabrum.** From the Boulton workshop (£42,000)

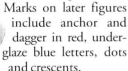

BOULTON, MATTHEW (1728–1809)

At his great Soho works near Birmingham, begun in 1762, Boulton made steel jewellery, silver, ORMOLU (gilt bronze) and SHEFFIELD PLATE items, using designers such as ADAM and William Chambers, as well as in-house workers. Manufacture of buttons, buckles, watch chains and the like had to help finance more ambitious products such as ormolu-mounted blue john chimneypiece decoration. Despite clients such as George III and the Empress of Russia, and a strong market in France, ormolu production was stopped in 1785. Boulton retired in 1800, but his son carried on the business until 1846.

TALKING ANTIQUES

'BOUGHT IN'
A term applied to an object that fails to reach its RESERVE at auction. Bought by the auctioneer on behalf of the vendor. It may be taken away or re-offered later.

BRACKET

A right-angled wall fitting to support a clock, lantern, inn or shop sign. From the Middle Ages they were made of wrought iron or brass, sometimes in elaborate and scrolling designs. From the 18th century they are more often made of wood, which can be decoratively carved, and gilt.

BRAMAH, JOSEPH (1748-1814)

The inventor of, among other things, the Bramah lock. This was held to be unpickable until the 1851 Great Exhibition when an American won £200 by opening one. However, a Bramah lock is usually a sign of quality on 19th- century furniture, and it was a feature of the BETJEMANN tantalus.

BRAS DE LUMIÈRE

The French name for a wall light or SCONCE. In the 17th century some were made in the shape of an arm with the hand clutching the candle, hence the name.

BREAKFAST TABLE

A small four-legged table with two hinged flaps which open up to double its size. Made from the mid-18th century.

£££-££££

BREAKFRONT

A piece of furniture with a central section standing proud of its flanks. It was a standard feature of 18th- and 19th-century cabinet-making, and breakfront bookcases, in particular, were often topped by broken pediments. The two sections of these could be either rigidly triangular or scrolling 'swan-necks'.

▲ **Breakfront bookcase** with swan-neck broken pediment, attributed to Thomas Chippendale, c1775 (£200,000-£300,000)

BRETBY ART POTTERY

A pottery set up near Melbourne, Derbyshire, by Christopher Dresser's potting assistant Henry Tooth in 1882. It produced some of Dresser's Linthorpe Pottery designs as well as its own wares. Some of the novelty lines are great fun, but the half life-sized figures of Italian peasant children can only be appreciated by those with a sweet tooth. The pottery closed in 1887 but many of the designs then passed to one of the partners, William Ault, who ran his own business at Swadlincote until the early 20th century.

££-£££

BRIGHT CUT

An engraving technique executed with a double-edged graving tool,

▶ One of a pair of Bretby figures c1885, one slightly damaged (£800-£1,000 the pair)

which removes a sliver of silver and burnishes the cut facets giving a glittering effect. Found mainly on 18th-century silver and SHEFFIELD plate, especially flatware.

BRISTOL GLASS

Bristol was established in the 1740s as an important centre for English glass, specialising in making decanters, goblets and vases. The most famous Bristol glasses are the opaque white resembling porcelain, decorated with flowers, birds or Chinamen by the porcelain painter Michael Edkins, and the very rich blue decorated with gilding by the Jacob brothers. Similar glassware was made at Newcastle and other English factories and often attribution can be extremely difficult.

£££

▲ Set of three Bristol decanters
in original toleware stand, 1790
(£1,200-£1,500)

◀ Blue and white
tankard from Benjamin
Lund's Bristol factory
c1750 (£10,000)

▶ Bristol
Temple Back
pearlware
plate c1790,
(£50-£80)

◀ Bristol blue-dash
charger of
Queen Anne, c1702,
(£4,000-£5,500)

From homely to stately

BRISTOL POTTERY AND PORCELAIN

Potteries at Bristol and neighbouring Brislington and Wincanton produced delftware in the 17th and 18th centuries. Their marks, if any, were not consistent, and it can be difficult to tell their products, including plates and tiles, from Lambeth or Liverpool delft. BLUE-DASH chargers were a feature in the late 17th century, and blue and white Chinoiserie patterns followed from the 1720s.

From 1755 'bianco sopra bianco', a technique of painting opaque white designs on a bluish white ground, was sometimes used. Creamware was produced at the Temple Back factory from the 1770s to 1884.

Soft-paste porcelain was first made in Bristol by Benjamin Lund in 1749. He was taken over by WORCESTER in 1752. In 1770, W. COOKWORTHY moved to Bristol and made hard-paste wares, including groups and figures. His patent was taken over by Richard Champion in 1774, but legal challenges from Wedgwood and the Staffordshire potters forced him to close in 1782. Bristol porcelain styles range from the homely to imitations of SÈVRES. Marks include BRISTOLL (first period); B with a 7 below and to the right of it; and a variety of xs and crossed swords (second period).

When armies marched to beat of Britain's drum

In 1893 William Britain (1826-1906) put a new spin on the toy soldier business. He moulded his lead figures as did other makers, but then forced the excess out of the holes in the tops of their heads by a quick spinning movement. This produced a perfect, light and hollow figure cheaply. Previously almost all the lead soldiers sold here were foreign-made—Britain's

themselves had made mechanical and other kinds of toy. These were gradually discontinued due to the success of the new soldiery.

Five sons and two daughters were with him in the business, and once Britain's first set, the Life Guards, was launched at Gamages' Holborn store their future was assured.

After a few years movable arms were introduced but, unlike French and German cavalrymen,

Britain's horses and riders were cast as a unit. Topicality was all-important and. alongside the ceremonial soldiers, sets of miniature warriors were inspired by events such as the Spanish-American war of 1898, the Russo-Japanese war of 1905, the Balkan struggles which preceded the First World War, and various colonial conflicts.

At first khaki proved unpopular with boy generals but, like their elders,

they fell into line. However, more exotic uniforms, such as those of Haile Selassie's Abyssinians and their Blackshirt and Carabinieri adversaries in 1935, still retained their appeal.

By 1910 Alfred Britain could boast of having driven German-made soldiers from the country. Models were re-used, being re-painted to serve in different armies, and some even took the pledge: the bandsmen of the King's army re-

▲ Brigade of Guards band 1930s (£250-£350)

mustered as Salvationists in 1910 (not always successfully, as recorded in Saki's *The Toys of Peace*).

The popularity of other subjects, such as the village idiot, suggested by George V, means they are now forged — as are the most sought after military figures.

Largely unjustified fears about lead poisoning led to the end of production in 1967. Already plastics had been infiltrating the ranks and extending to rural life. Early plastic sets of elaborate gardens now have their own devotees.

As so often with toys, sets of Britain's figures which have retained their boxes in good condition are considerably more valuable than those which have not.

Britain's are thought of

as producing only figures, but they also made other pieces. Amongst the rarest is the Barrage Balloon. This was made of rubber and very few have survived unperished. A complete set with its lorry and winch would make around £1,000, the latter alone only £200. There was an Auto gyro which makes around £500–£700; Campbell's Bluebird £200–£300 and the rarer Cobb's Railton Special £300–£500. These have detachable bodies so that the chassis and engine can be seen.

After the First World War, thoughts turned to more peacable pursuits and the farm, garden and hunting series appeared. Britain's was always in the forefront of new trends.

▲ Salvation army band and officers *c*1910 (£1,400–£1,600)

BRITANNIA METAL

A tin, antimony and copper alloy made as a popular cheap substitute for pewter. It is lighter in colour and weight and very easy to work. Large-scale manufacture began in about 1780, and around 1804 James Dixon in Sheffield established the factory that became the leading producer, exporting large quantities to America.

BRITANNIA STANDARD

A silver standard higher than sterling, introduced from 1697 to 1720. It consists of 928 parts per 1,000 (11oz 10dwt per lb Troy). It was introduced to prevent the coinage from being melted down to make domestic ware. The hallmark is Britannia seated together with a lion's head 'erased'. After 1720 both Britannia and STERLING were used.

BRUSHING SLIDE

A flat wooden surface which slides out of the top section of a chest-of-drawers for brushing clothes on. It is one of the features that make a bachelor chest.

BRUSTOLON, ANDREA (1622-1732)

An Italian sculptor who specialised in furniture which is quite unique in its fantastical, exuberant, sculptural design. Born in Belluno, he worked in Venice (1684-96) where his masterpiece is the furniture carved for the Palazzo Rezzonico. The

▼ German-made British Guards band with clockwork conductor, *c*1910 (£600–£800)

chairs incorporate negro boys with ebony heads and arms, and the GUÉRIDONS are of naked slaves in ebony with boxwood chains. Many of his designs, including his drawings for elaborate looking-glass frames, are in the Museo Civico, Belluno.

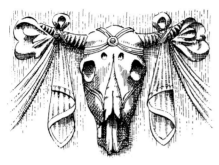

BUCRANE
A garlanded ox skull originally used to ornament classical architecture. It is often found as a motif on late 18th-century furniture and porcelain. Also known as a bucranium.

BUEN RETIRO PORCELAIN
Spanish factory established by Charles III in the Buen Retiro park, Madrid, in 1759; it closed in 1812. The equipment and modellers were all transported from CAPODIMONTE, so the early products are close to the Neapolitan factory. Italian materials were abandoned in the 1770s and a yellowish paste replaced the creamy tone. From 1748 a fine glassy white paste was produced. The factory's most famous product is the porcelain room modelled for the palace of Aranjuez. Figure groups, water stoups, mirror frames, chandeliers, ewers and basins were also made but there were very few useful wares until after 1804.

R £££££

BRONZES

Bronze is an alloy of copper and tin which was first cast into tools and figurines about 2500BC, and gave its name to the European Bronze Age from around 2000BC.

As early as the Shang Dynasty (c1700 BC) the Chinese discovered hollow, rather than solid, casting and the LOST WAX method, both of which saved metal. These techniques were known in Europe by the 4th century BC. Sand moulding was not developed until about the same time. Decoration applied after casting involves 'cold working' with hammers, chisels and gravers. Fire or mercury gilt bronze is known as ORMOLU or in France, *bronze doré*.

In the West the Greeks, Romans and Celts all used bronze with a high degree of

◀ **1930s Art Deco kneeling maiden**, which may originally have been one of a pair (£1,000)

▶ **French bronze** of man fighting lion, marble base, c1880 (£1,500–£2,000)

The alloy which broke the mould

artistry, and had a direct influence on the masters of the Romanesque period (from the late 10th century), when the medium came to the fore once again.

Many of the greatest works of Romanesque art are in bronze, including the wonderful MOSAN fonts, AQUAMANILES, crucifixes, reliquaries and candlesticks.

Since the Renaissance, bronze has chiefly been used for small-scale sculpture, and for *bronzes d'ameublement*, decorative mounts for furniture, clock cases and the like. During the 19th century there was a vogue

for small bronze groups, especially warriors, horsemen and ANIMALIER subjects. As this was an international taste there is a distinct kinship shown between the Cossacks, Arabs, British camel scouts and cowboys. The most famous maker of the last was Frederic Remington, whose bronzes have been forged .

So popular were bronzes in the 19th century that SPELTER versions were made for those who could not afford the real thing. Bronze casters in Vienna specialised in small figures, often animals, which were cold painted.

Throughout the MING dynasty in China, bronze figures were produced of Buddhistic significance, along with incense burners, usually bearing the reign mark of the Emperor Xuande (1426-35), a practice that has continued to the present day.

In Japan in the second half of the 19th century, the Tokyo school produced superb figural groups and animals to rival those of the Anamalier school. Amongst the best are those signed Miya-o. They also cast incense burners, vases and jardinières, some with inlaid

▲ Remington cowboys reproduction, *c*1980. An original might be ten times the price (£2,500-£3,500)

gold, silver and copper details which are amongst the highest quality works of art in bronze. Just as the art nouveau style was influenced by Japan, so were, in turn, Japanese bronzes influenced by art nouveau.

Huge bronzes in vaguely oriental and in animalier style are being made today and passed off as old, but the 'painted' look to the patination is usually a give-away.

▼ Japanese bronze koro by Unno Moritoshi (1834-1906) (£20,00-£25,000)

▶ 'The Cossack's Farewell' Russian bronze after Gratcheff, 1910 (£4,000-£5,500)

BUFFET

The medieval name given to tiers of shelves used to display silver, china and glass generally in the dining room. By the late 18th century the SIDEBOARD had replaced the buffet. The early buffet is also known as a court cupboard, and had no doors, but after it had gone out of fashion the name was revived for various enclosed stands. SHERATON took it for an ornamental cupboard with elaborate shelves above, intended as 'the repository of a tea equipage'.

◄ **Strasbourg bullet-shaped teapot** and cover, 1748-54 **(£1,800)**

▼ **George II bullet-shaped teapot**, 5in high, 1751 **(£2,000-£3,000)**

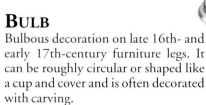

► **Bulle magnetic pendulum clock** Should be covered by a glass cloche, *c*1920 **(£250-£350)**

BULB

Bulbous decoration on late 16th- and early 17th-century furniture legs. It can be roughly circular or shaped like a cup and cover and is often decorated with carving.

BULLE CLOCK

A French, battery-operated clock with the pendulum mounted on a bar made of two joined magnets. The dial, with a central aperture to show the movement, is on a column which contains the battery. As soon as the battery is connected the pendulum starts itself due to the arrangement of the magnets. The original large versions were made from about 1920 and smaller ones

became popular in Britain after being seen at an early Ideal Home Exhibition. Bulle made them until the Second World War, and others produced similar clocks later.

 **£££**

BULLET TEAPOTS

An early 18th-century English silver teapot with a spherical, bullet-shaped body. The lid is not raised but cut out of the upper body. The shape was adopted by Continental potters.

 **££££**

BUN FOOT

A ball-shaped foot flattened at the top and bottom and dating from the mid-17th century.

He created Napoleon's home from home

BULLOCK, GEORGE (1777/8 – 1818)

One of the most vigorous and original furniture-makers of the Regency period, Bullock was in business in Liverpool as a cabinetmaker in 1804. He moved to London 10 years later, and built himself workshops on Oxford Street at the end of his garden. At this time he was prosperous, with a fashionable clientele, including Sir Walter Scott, and among his business concerns were marble quarries on Anglesey. His most famous commission was from the government, to provide the furnishings for Napoleon's exile on St Helena.

Unfortunately by the middle of 1816 he was facing serious financial problems, including a dishonoured bill from one client and late payments from another (BOULTON's son). While Bullock was primarily a neo-Classical designer, he also produced Gothic revival pieces. His passion was for native British woods, notably oak and holly, and he used marble slabs from his quarries as tops for cabinets.

Another characteristic was his plant-inspired brass inlay, which anticipates the work of such designers as PUGIN, OWEN JONES and DRESSER.

▲ Ormolu-mounted mahogany armchair, attributed to George Bullock, c1815 (£2,000–£3,000)

► Pen's-eye view of a tortoiseshell, brass and mother-of-pearl inkstand, (£26,000)

▲ Brown oak and ebony Regency dressing table, c1815 (£30,000)

► George IV window seats in the style of Bullock. Two of a set of three (£7,000 the set)

Why writing letters was once such a pleasure

▲ Continental walnut, marquetry and inlaid bureau, c1735 (£15,000–£20,000)

BUREAUX

Bureau is merely the French word for desk, derived from 'bure', a coarse cloth used to cover the tables at which medieval clerks worked. The 'bureau plat', a simple, flat-topped writing table, became popular in France in the 17th century, by which time leather had replaced linen.

The *bureau plat* in the 18th century often had a separate cabinet for filing papers at one end known as a *cartonnier* (made of board and leather covered), although this name was also given to a self-contained filing-cabinet.

In the course of the following centuries the basic bureau developed a wide variety of shapes and forms, of which the most common are the pedestal and kneehole desk, the '*bureau à gradin*', which has drawers or pigeonholes along one side (the CARLTON HOUSE desk is an example of this), the fall-front bureau and its derivative, the bureau-bookcase.

The fall-front bureau, which is now just referred to as a bureau in English, has a hinged flap which rests at 45° when closed, and provides a writing surface when open and supported by LOPERS. The interior is fitted and there are usually two short and two long drawers beneath.

These evolved from the writing slope and box on separate stand in the early 18th century and may be found in walnut, oak or mahogany.

English usage is not exact but the essential difference between a bureau and an ESCRITOIRE, or SECRETAIRE, is that the writing component of the latter is in a drawer with a folding front which slides out for use and closes flush with the lower drawers. The earliest form of this was the KNEEHOLE bureau table.

Early Georgian kneeholes did not generally go right through, but contained recessed cupboards A bureau cabinet has a cabinet above, with glazed doors and shelves

▲ Louis XIV 'bureau plat' attributed to Boulle c1720 (£310,000)

▲ **George II bureau bookcase** by Giles Grendey, c1740 (£250,000-£350,000)

for display purposes, while a bureau dressing table, made from the early 18th century onwards, is a bureau on cabriole legs, with two or three shallow drawers beneath the writing desk, and a looking glass mounted above.

A bureau bedstead, on the other hand, is unlikely to have any writing component, being merely a folding bed disguised as a bureau. '*Bureau Mazarin*' is a 19th-century term for a kneehole where the recess is mostly filled by a cupboard.

BURGES, WILLIAM (1827-81)

Architect and designer who worked in the highest Gothic Revival style. His most monumental buildings were Cardiff Castle and Castell Coch for the Marquess of Bute, where he designed furniture to match his grandiose re-ordering of the interiors. He thought his own home, The Tower House, Melbury Road, Kensington, looked 15th-century but, despite its medieval inspiration and colourfulness, it could not be more of its own time (1875-81). His furniture style is simplicity covered by fantastic and opulent decoration—painted birds, flowers and scenes (sometimes by leading artists such as Burne-Jones and Poynter), huge, out-of-scale, metal embellishments such as hinges and locks and inset trefoils and quatrefoils, sometimes with mirrors. The tops of his cabinets have pitched roofs or battlements and lower down there are columns and all sorts of architectural motifs. Tables may have *pietra dura* marble tops on supposedly Gothic frames. He also designed metalwork and jewellery and, while the inspiration is generally medieval, elements did creep in from Byzantium, China, Japan or ancient Assyria. He loved animals—both fantastic and real.

▲ **The library at Burges's Tower House,** painted by Axel Herman Haig (1835-1921) and exhibited in 1887

BURMANTOFTS

The Burmantofts art pottery—named after a district of Leeds—began by making sewage pipes in the 1840s. In the 1870s, decorative and coloured tiles were a successful line which led, in 1881, to the establishment of the art pottery.

 £££

▶ **Burmantofts art pottery vase,** 20in high, 1890s (£400-£500)

BURR

A bulbous growth on the trunk or root of a tree which produces a very decorative grain when cut. Especially used in oyster veneers with walnut, elm or yew.

BUSTELLI, FRANZ ANTON (1723-63)

One of the greatest modellers of porcelain, Bustelli was born in Switzerland. He was *Modellmeister* at the Nymphenburg Porcelain Factory in 1754-63. His celebrated figures are slim and delicate and capture intricate curving poses. Some of his favourite subjects include the figures of the Commedia dell'Arte, Chinese and Turkish characters and impassioned lovers. He either used restrained colours or left his figures unpainted.

£££££

◀ **Commedia dell'Arte figure** modelled by Bustelli *c*1760 **(£20,000–£25,000)**

BUTLER'S TRAY

A tray with carrying handles mounted on a folding stand. Used by butlers from the early 18th century for serving drinks and removing empty glasses.

£££

▶ **Butler's decanter tray,** late 18th century **(£1,000-£1,500)**

BUTTONING

A decorative upholstery technique. Padding is placed between the frame and the outer material, strong thread is stitched through both, drawing them into a quilted pattern, and the stitches hidden behind a covered button. Especially popular on Victorian and Edwardian furniture.

BUTTONS

Medieval buttons are known from paintings but none survive from before the 16th century. At that point they were small and either acorn or bead-shaped, but richly worked. In the second half of the 18th century button-making was a staple of BIRMINGHAM toy makers, and from the 1770s they were a definite feature of male and female dress. By the 1870s women's buttons were highly decorative.

▲ **Set of enamel buttons,** late 19th century **(£10-£15)**

CABARET

A porcelain tray with matching tea or coffee set, especially popular in the 18th century. If it has two cups it is called a *tête-à-tête*. With only one cup it is a *solitaire*.

££-£££££

CABRIOLE

A furniture leg based on an animal's hind leg. It has a broad convex knee curving outwards, which tapers to a narrow concave curve above a ball and claw, paw or mask foot. It was in use in the late 17th and 18th centuries.

CADUECEUS

The snake-enwrapped and winged rod which was an attribute of Mercury (Hermes), messenger of the gods. Without wings, such a rod represents Aesculapius and medicine. From 1722 to the early 1730s it was used as a MEISSEN porcelain mark: a vertical stroke inside a spiral, which looks like Mercury's rod, in underglaze blue.

CADDY SPOON

A small silver spoon with a short stem for taking tea leaves from a caddy. They were made from the late 18th century. The earliest have shell-shaped scoops. Later they came in shapes

▶ **Caddy spoon** by George Unite, Birmingham, 1835 (£55-£65)

such as acorns, jockey caps, leaves, thistles, shovels and horses' hooves. Tin spoons were produced for events such as the 1951 Festival of Britain (See TEA THINGS).

££-£££

CALLOT, JACQUES (*c*1592-1635)

A decorative engraver, painter and etcher, celebrated for crowd, peasant and battle scenes, especially grotesque and comic figures. Callot was born in France but worked in Rome and Florence. After 1621 he lived mainly in Nancy. Paintings after his designs appear on FAIENCE and MAIOLICA but his name is best known for the grotesque little porcelain figures of dwarfs made throughout Europe in the 17th and 18th centuries. These were mostly taken from a book of engravings published in his style in 1716.

CAMEO

A gem, hard stone or shell with two different coloured layers. The upper one is cut away and carved

▶ **Cameo** hardstone brooch/pendant in gold, enamel and gem set mount, *c*1865 (£1,500-£2,000)

▼ **Shell portrait**, 1858 (£550-£650)

in relief and the lower one left as a contrasting background. The technique was known from Greek and Roman times, when portraits or mythological scenes were popular. There were revivals in the Renaissance and neo-Classical periods when cameos were mounted in elaborate frames or worn as jewellery. James Tassie (1735-99) (see page 2) developed a technique for making imitations which even experts find hard to identify.

££-£££

CAMEO GLASS

A decorative glass made of different-coloured layers. A cup of the outer layer is blown and then a blob of a different colour is dropped into it and the two (or more) are blown together. The outer layer (or layers) is carved, producing the design in relief. The technique was known to Romans and was popular for snuff bottles in China, but the most common type is that made in 19th-century Bohemia and at Stourbridge in England. The two main factories were: Stevens and Williams under the direction of John Northwood, and Webb & Co under George and Thomas Woodall. The finest examples are signed.

£££-££££

▶ **Two-colour cameo** bottle-vase by George Woodall, *c*1880 (£30,000-£32,000)

CAMERAS

The first commercially produced cameras were designed by L. J. M. Daguerre and made by Alphonse Giroux of Paris from 1839. They featured a pivoted brass plate which swung out of the way when the exposure was made. In the 1840s and '50s cameras had the lens in a front box, while a smaller box slid into the first and was adjusted for focusing. The bellows camera, patented in 1851, increased the range of extension and revolutionised camera design. From the 1850s there were numerous designs for folding cameras, usually made by cabinet-makers from mahogany with brass accessories. In the 1880s the gelatin dry plate replaced the wet plate, enabling shorter exposure times and making hand-held cameras practical. By the 1890s cameras were capable of holding up to a dozen plates. The Eastman-Walker roller, patented in 1884, held a continuous band of film inside the camera. In 1888 Eastman invented the leather-covered box Kodak which was sold ready loaded with a 100-exposure film. In the 1890s the first cine cameras were made.

◀ **35mm cine camera** in boxwood c1909 (**£500–£600**)

CAMPAIGN FURNITURE

Campaign furniture was made for officers to take on military campaigns. It is usually made of a robust hard wood like teak with flat surfaces, recessed brass handles and protective brass corners. Feet, which are generally small, unscrew to fit inside. Small chests-of-drawers are common, as are portable wash stands that can be unscrewed and packed flat. Much of it was made for the Peninsular and the Crimean Wars in the 19th century.

▲ **Campaign chest** in the form of a trunk brought into the Basingstoke Roadshow, c1880 (**£300**)

CANDLE BOX

A plain wooden or metal box which has a high back for hanging on the wall, and a hinged lid. Used for storing candles. In the 18th century they were occasionally JAPANNED (coated in glossy black lacquer).

   £££

CANDLE SCREEN

A miniature screen which slides on a pole to shield the face from the glare of a candle. Slightly larger versions are known as face, or pole, screens.

£££–££££

CANING

Woven cane was used for chair seats and backs from the mid-17th century. Rattan palm is interwoven to form a tough, open-work surface. Canework was popular in the 19th century and much more from this period survives.

◀ **Silver, four-light candelabrum,** by Robinson, Edkins and Aston Birmingham, 1843 (**£3,000–£3,500**)

◀ **Gothic-style** bronze candlestick, one of a pair, c1845 (**£300–£350 the pair**)

Casting light on the subject

CANDLESTICK

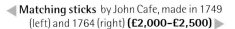

Few English silver candlesticks survived the Civil War, when all such things were melted down. By the Restoration the earlier pricket candlestick with the candle held on a spike and a separate grease-pan was superseded by a chunky baluster with a socket and large rim to catch the wax. These were cast in three sections — sconce, stem and base — and were heavy and solid.

During the late 18th century sheets of fine rolled and die-stamped silver were used around a core of metal rod, pitch and plaster. These were cheaper to manufacture.

Generally candlesticks can be dated by shape and size: 1660s, 9in high; 1700-1755, 7in; 1755-99, 10in; 1800 onwards 10-12 in high.

Certain smiths and families were specialist candlestick makers; the marks of the Gould and Cafe families appear again and again.

A standing candlestick with arms and nozzles for more than one candle is called a candelabrum. A low nozzle fixed in a saucer is a chamber stick, and may be made in anything from silver down to enamelled tin.

One or two bracket candlesticks fitted on a back plate (mirrored or polished to reflect the light) is called a wall sconce. Really elaborate rococo versions of these are known as GIRANDOLES. Miniature sticks, four to five inches high, are not for lighting but are taper sticks for melting sealing wax.

As well as silver and gold, less expensive candlesticks were made in wood, brass, pewter, glass and SHEFFIELD PLATE. Brass candlesticks were highly collectable in the late 19th and early 20th century, but are less sought after today. Regency period bronze sticks are still available in fair numbers and reflect the current styles: gothic, rococo revival and occasionally Eastern influences. Like brass, pewter is no longer popular and candlesticks are rare. The elaborate ormolu and marble candelabra of the Victorian period are back in fashion, as are porcelain candlesticks, particularly the decorative flower-encrusted sticks from Coalport and Meissen.

◀ **Matching sticks** by John Cafe, made in 1749 (left) and 1764 (right) **(£2,000-£2,500)** ▶

▼ **North European brass** stick, late 18th century **(£200)**

▶ **North European brass** stick, late 18th century **(£300-£400)**

▶ **Flemish brass** stick, late c1500 **(£900-£1,000)**

◀ **One of a pair** of gilt-bronze candelabra, French, 18th century **(£1,200-£1,800 the pair)**

◀ **German brass** stick, c1500 **(£800-£1,000)**

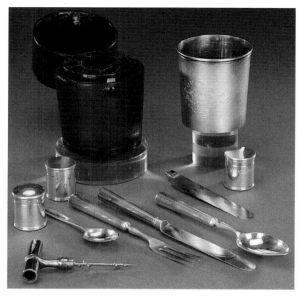

◀ **Canteen kit**
A particularly sumptuous example by Rawlings and Summers, London, 1851-54 **(£1,600)**

CANTEEN

Originally a small leather case containing personal eating utensils: spoon, knife, fork and beaker. When sets of matching cutlery came into use in the late 17th century, canteens were made to house them and stood on the sideboard. The earliest of these were probably of SHAGREEN or in the form of KNIFE BOXES with slots for spoons and forks as well. The standard, and much larger, wooden box type canteen to hold full dinner services that we know today was extremely rare in the Georgian period. Most surviving examples date from Victorian or Edwardian times.

£££-££££

CANTERBURY

In the late 18th century this was a table-side stand with three partitions to hold knives, forks and spoons and a curved end partition for plates. The name was also soon used for a low stand for sheet music or books. After the mid-19th century it was also employed, by extension of ideas, as a music stool with a hinged lid over a box for holding music.

£££-££££

CANTON ENAMELS

A generic term for Chinese painted enamel on copper. An object is first covered in a layer of white enamel and fired, and the design is then painted on in different colours fired at different temperatures. The technique was first developed in Europe at Limoges in the late 15th century and introduced into China by French missionaries in the 18th century. Just as European porcelain shapes were copied, enamel wares were made almost exclusively for the export market and decorated at Canton and

In the palace of paste

CAPODIMONTE

A porcelain factory founded by Charles III, King of Naples, in the grounds of his royal palace of Capodimonte in 1743. It made fine, white, delicately modelled translucent paste figures.

The decoration has a Neapolitan richness and exuberance even when it has been taken from prints after Watteau and other French artists.

The chief modeller was Giuseppe Gricci, who was best known for his energetic renditions of Commedia dell' Arte figures and realistic Neapolitan peasants.

He also made the large reliefs for the CHINOISERIE porcelain room at the royal palace of Portici.

In 1759 the factory moved to Spain with Charles, merging with BUEN RETIRO. The maker's mark is a fleur-de-lys in underglaze blue. Beware later pieces with crowned N mark offered for sale as genuine Capodimonte.

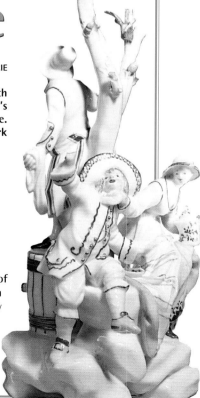

◀ **Gold-ground** pomade pot and cover c1750, one of a pair **(£44,000 the pair)**

▲ **Two-handled beaker** c1750 **(£900-£1,200)**

▶ **Group of Neopolitan revellers** by Giuseppe Gricci c1750 **(£80,000)**

other ports. In the 18th century FAMILLE ROSE decoration was especially popular and FAMILLE VERTE in the 20th century. The decoration is mainly floral but you also find figure scenes copied from European prints.

CARAT

A measure of fineness of gold based on 24 units. In its pure state, gold is too soft to work, so it is alloyed with other metals in various proportions. The finest in use is 22 carat, that is 22 parts of gold to two parts of base metal. A carat is also a measure of weight for precious stones. An average diamond in a ring weighs approximately one carat but where the gems are set the value is calculated by the size and depth of the stone.

CARD CASE

Elaborate 19th-century visiting rituals inspired silver calling-card cases. They were still being made until about the First World War.

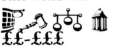

££-£££

▲ Silver card case 1878 (£200-£300)

CARLTON WARE

Pottery produced by Wiltshaw and Robinson at the Carlton Works, Stoke-on-Trent. The firm is best known for novelty earthenware produced from 1925—marmalade pots shaped like oranges, cruet sets in the form of chickens and embossed salad ware. Brilliant colours later gave way to more pastel shades. They also made advertising displays, and experimented with oven-to-table ware.

£-£££

◀ Carlton ware lamp with metal shade, 1960 (£200-£300)

◀ Mahogany and satinwood late Victorian Carlton House desk, c1900 (£2,500)

▲ Marbled wood Carlton House desk. This is a considerable rarity with its green and cream painted 'marble', c1800 (£78,500)

Fit for a Regent

CARLTON HOUSE

This was the magnificent palace which George IV built when Prince of Wales. Before being demolished in 1827, it occupied the site of what is now Waterloo Place in London. A leading connoisseur of the arts, George IV extensively altered Carlton House, building on a new façade and designing the interiors in the latest style.

In addition he made an outstanding collection of paintings, furniture, porcelain and silver, taking advantage of the political upheavals in France to acquire objects from the French royal and aristocratic collections.

Through the artists, designers and craftsmen he employed at Carlton House, George IV had an enormous influence on the decorative arts in Britain.

The palace even gave its name to the Carlton House desk or, more correctly, but less commonly, table which was designed for him as Prince of Wales. It has a superstructure behind the writing area containing drawers and pigeon-holes or a space for books. The top is D-shaped with the sitter on the straight side and the superstructure follows the curve to flank the writing space. The legs are often turned with reeded cappings. This table has been much copied and was especially popular in the late Victorian period when the shelving became taller at the centre than at the sides, which still retained their concave shape.

◀ **Striking carriage clock,** gilt brass and porcelain, by Moser c1850 (**£2,000–£2,500**)

▼ **Gilt brass** and pietra dura miniature clock c1840 (**£2,200–£2,700**)

▼ **Gilt brass and champlevé** enamel miniature c1830 (**£2,000–£2,500**)

◀ **French clock** with Limoges-style enamel face and sides (**£2,500–£3,000**)

CARRIAGE CLOCK

A small travelling clock, 3in to 12in high, with a brass frame and carrying handle. They were originally supplied with leather cases, which opened to show the face, and which may survive. The Swiss clockmaker Abraham-Louis Breguet (1747-1823) is credited with inventing them soon after 1800. Before this, travelling clocks looked like large watches and were known as COACH WATCHES.

They were made in France and England throughout the 19th century but, confusingly, French clocks may carry an English retailer's name. The movements often include alarms, striking mechanisms and calendars.

£££-££££

CARRIER-BELLEUSE, ALBERT ERNEST (1824-87)

A French sculptor, closely associated with the decorative arts, whose work typifies the hedonistic atmosphere of the Second EMPIRE period. In 1849 he came to England and worked as a modeller at the MINTON factory. He returned to Paris in 1855 and soon established himself as a fashionable sculptor. He specialised in small bronzes and elaborate *torchères,* while continuing to supply Minton with designs. From 1864 Auguste Rodin (1840-1917) worked as his assistant, producing reliefs and figures in unglazed

◀ **Terracotta bust** of a lady in Renaissance-style dress by Carrier-Belleuse, c1870 (**£8,000**)

earthenware. Carrier-Belleuse was artistic director of the SÈVRES factory from 1875 and also designed silver for Christofle, the largest firm of silver and plate manufacturers in France.

CARRON IRONWORKS

Following the improved techniques of coke smelting pioneered by the Derby family at COALBROOKDALE, John Roebuck set up the Carron foundry on the River Carron, near Falkirk, along similar lines. Roebuck was a man of science who formed a partnership with Samuel Garbett, a Birmingham businessman, and William Cadell, a skilled ironmaster. The engineers James Watt and John Smeaton were both closely associated with the Carron works and much of Watt's early experimental work on the steam engine was done here. As well as making ordnance, grates and stoves, the company was remarkable for the quality of the designers it employed. John ADAM was a partner in the company and his brothers James and Robert both produced elegant designs for railings, grates, verandahs, fireplaces and garden ornaments. William and Henry Haworth, who were skilled carvers and painters, also produced many of the elegant neo-Classical patterns found on Carron pieces. Along with the Coalbrookdale

◀ **Gilt brass and champlevé** striking carriage clock, Swiss (£2,000–£2,500)

◀ **Grande sonnerie clock** by Henri Jacot, with case, c1900 (£2,000–£2,500)

▶ **French repeating clock,** made for English mass market, with case, c1895 (£400–£600)

foundry and Macfarlane and Co of Glasgow, Carron were the main producers of decorative ironwork throughout the 19th century. Their catalogues continued up to the 1950s and included street furniture, tables, benches and chairs, a wide range of stoves, grates and garden furniture.

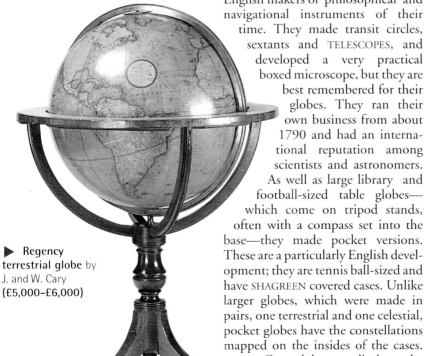

▶ **Regency terrestrial globe** by J. and W. Cary (£5,000–£6,000)

CARTOUCHE

A panel, often partly open and framed by a curving scroll shape. Usually elaborately decorated, they carry inscriptions or coats of arms.

CARY GLOBES

John and William Cary (1754-1835 and 1759-1825) were among the best English makers of 'philosophical' and navigational instruments of their time. They made transit circles, sextants and TELESCOPES, and developed a very practical boxed microscope, but they are best remembered for their globes. They ran their own business from about 1790 and had an international reputation among scientists and astronomers. As well as large library and football-sized table globes— which come on tripod stands, often with a compass set into the base—they made pocket versions. These are a particularly English development; they are tennis ball-sized and have SHAGREEN covered cases. Unlike larger globes, which were made in pairs, one terrestrial and one celestial, pocket globes have the constellations mapped on the insides of the cases.

Cary globes usually have the maker's details in CAR-TOUCHES, but all globes can be dated by the geographical features and discoveries that they show.

£££-£££££

CARYATID

A female figure serving as a supporting column. It was originally used in Greek and Roman architecture but was adapted as a motif to form the stems, handles and legs of small-scale decorative objects from the Renaissance onwards. The figures are invariably draped. If carrying a basket on her head she is a canephorus. Male or female bust-length figures, often armless, are called herms or terms.

CAST IRON

Iron which is melted in a furnace at high temperature, poured into a mould and left to cool. The technique became feasible from the 15th century when improved furnaces and water-powered bellows were developed. Early charcoal smelting produced a metal that was thick and impure and contracted on cooling, which caused any decoration to be ill-defined. It was used mainly for firebacks and stoves until the 18th century when foundries such as COALBROOKDALE and CARRON were set up using improved techniques of coke smelting which produced a purer and more molten metal. As well as being used for ordnance and architectural features, cast iron served for a range of decorative objects such as tables, benches, chairs, fenders and fire grates and in the 19th century was widely used in the construction of bridges and railway stations.

CASTEL DURANTE

One of the finest groups of 16th-century Umbrian MAIOLICA factories. The leading decorator was N. Pellipario, who specialised in *istoriato* decoration (high-quality wares decorated with mythological, historical or genre scenes). Castel Durante maiolica has an unusual palette of soft blues, greenish greys

▼ Castel Durante dish, c1530 (£10,000-£12,000)

and pale orange and purple and is covered in a clear, glossy outer glaze.

 £££££££

CASTLE HEDINGHAM

A pottery was first established here in 1837 by Edward Bingham, and made common earthenware. The founder's son, also Edward, produced more decorative glazed wares and in 1901 the firm was sold to the Essex Art Pottery Company. It closed in 1905. Many of the later works copy English forms of the 16th and 17th centuries: jugs, mugs, candlesticks, plaques with 17th-century dates incorporated into their decoration, and large rustic vases. They are not easily mistaken for the earlier objects.

££-£££

CASTOR

Small, pivoted wheel screwed onto the ends of legs of furniture. In the later 17th century they were wood or leather. Metal ones came into use in the 18th century.

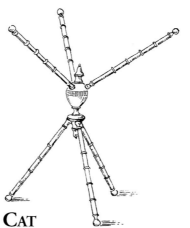

CAT

A plate-warmer made of three rods joined X-wise in the centre to stand before the fire. Generally made of turned wood or wrought iron.

££-£££

CAUGHLEY

A pottery factory was established at Caughley in Shropshire in about 1750. By 1772 this was making porcelain. In 1775 Robert Hancock, from the WORCESTER factory, was

employed and he introduced transfer printing in underglaze blue, similar to Worcester. Although the Caughley pigment is slightly brighter, the factory deliberately attempted to imitate Worcester and the two are hard to distinguish. Polychrome wares imitating Worcester and Lowestoft were also made, as well as BLUE AND WHITE painted wares, which were gilded by outside decorators. The factory closed in 1814. Marks: letters C, S, Sx and mock Chinese numerals.

£££-££££

CAXTON CHAIR

A cheap wooden chair invented in the mid-19th century, with a flat seat, slightly tapered legs and three straight bars in the back. They were made principally at High Wycombe, Buckinghamshire. The origin of the name is a mystery.

£-££

CAYENNE PEPPER SPOONS

A long-handled spoon with a shallow bowl and a cast devil's head finial to remind the diner of the pepper's extreme hotness. They would have accompanied a CRUET and mostly would have been made during the Victorian era.

££

CEDAR

An aromatic wood used for panelling, caskets and for the lining of drawers and wardrobes.

CELLARET

A free-standing chest or deep drawer in a sideboard, partitioned to hold bottles.

£££-££££

CELLULOID

The first wholly man-made plastic. Alexander Parkes discovered that celluloid nitrate could be moulded, and marketed it as celluloid from 1862. It continued to be used for table tennis balls and spectacle frames even after its competitors had taken over.

CELTIC REVIVAL

A 19th-century interpretation of the Celtic style which, in the British Isles, originally dated from about 650AD to 1150. It came about through an interest in archaeological discoveries and the publication of topographical accounts of Celtic artefacts, such as the standing crosses of Scotland, Northumberland and Ireland, metalwork, jewellery and the great illuminated manuscripts. Books such as Sullivan's *Facsimiles of National Manuscripts of Ireland* (1874-84) and Abbot's *Celtic Ornaments from the Book of Kells* (1892-95) made the interlocking designs, with their stylised bird and animal imagery, widely available. The Tara brooch, discovered in Ireland in

► **Celtic revival cloak clasps,** c1890-1910 in silver, using semi-precious stones **(£100-£400 each)**

1850, sparked off a revival of Celtic-style jewellery, in particular PEBBLE JEWELLERY made mainly in Scotland. ARTS AND CRAFTS designers such as William MORRIS, Walter Crane (1845-1915) and the members of the GLASGOW SCHOOL all adopted

Celtic motifs. In London, LIBERTY's Celtic-inspired Cymric silver and jewellery, and Tudric pewter, designed by Archibald KNOX, were immensely popular.

££-£££

The valley of the dolls

◄ **Snow White and the Seven Dwarfs** made in 1938. Wind-up doll of Snow White plays *Some Day My Prince Will Come* **(£2,000-£2,500)**

CHAD VALLEY TOYS

Chad Valley was established in Birmingham in 1823. In 1897 the firm moved to Harborne, making children's games and board games. In the 1930s it produced low-quality tinplate toys and in 1949 a small range of die-cast cars.

It is best known for board games and teddy bears, which have been made there since the 1920s. The bears come in a range of sizes and qualities. The early ones have a tin-plate button inscribed 'Chad Valley Hygienic Toys' and a woven label sewn to the foot. Bears produced after 1938 carry the Royal Warrant. In the 1950s the firm was given the sole rights to manufacture Sooty puppets.

Variations on an ancient theme

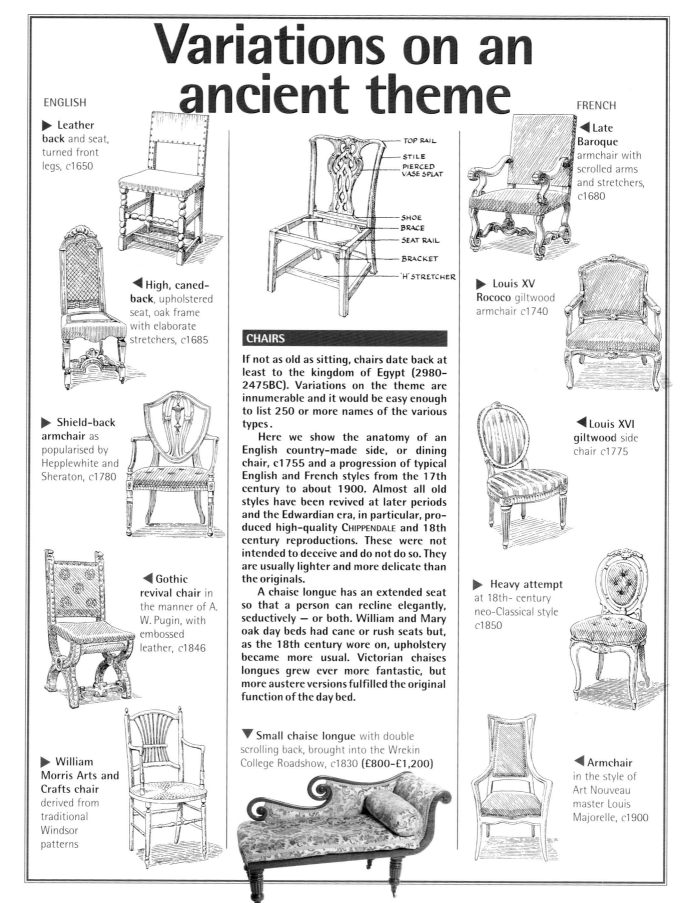

ENGLISH

▶ **Leather back** and seat, turned front legs, c1650

◀ **High, caned-back,** upholstered seat, oak frame with elaborate stretchers, c1685

▶ **Shield-back armchair** as popularised by Hepplewhite and Sheraton, c1780

◀ **Gothic revival chair** in the manner of A. W. Pugin, with embossed leather, c1846

▶ **William Morris Arts and Crafts chair** derived from traditional Windsor patterns

TOP RAIL
STILE
PIERCED VASE SPLAT
SHOE
BRACE
SEAT RAIL
BRACKET
'H' STRETCHER

CHAIRS

If not as old as sitting, chairs date back at least to the kingdom of Egypt (2980-2475BC). Variations on the theme are innumerable and it would be easy enough to list 250 or more names of the various types.

Here we show the anatomy of an English country-made side, or dining chair, c1755 and a progression of typical English and French styles from the 17th century to about 1900. Almost all old styles have been revived at later periods and the Edwardian era, in particular, produced high-quality CHIPPENDALE and 18th century reproductions. These were not intended to deceive and do not do so. They are usually lighter and more delicate than the originals.

A chaise longue has an extended seat so that a person can recline elegantly, seductively — or both. William and Mary oak day beds had cane or rush seats but, as the 18th century wore on, upholstery became more usual. Victorian chaises longues grew ever more fantastic, but more austere versions fulfilled the original function of the day bed.

▼ **Small chaise longue** with double scrolling back, brought into the Wrekin College Roadshow, c1830 (**£800-£1,200**)

FRENCH

◀ **Late Baroque** armchair with scrolled arms and stretchers, c1680

▶ **Louis XV Rococo** giltwood armchair c1740

◀ **Louis XVI** giltwood side chair c1775

▶ **Heavy attempt** at 18th- century neo-Classical style c1850

◀ **Armchair** in the style of Art Nouveau master Louis Majorelle, c1900

CHAFING DISH

A shaped metal container, often with a long, turned wooden handle, to hold charcoal for heating food in the dining room. Usually made in silver, copper, Sheffield or electroplate.

£££

CHAIR TABLE

An armchair with a hinged, circular back which swings forward and rests horizontally on the arms to form a small round table. They seem to have existed from the mid-17th century.

£££

CHAMBER POT

In the late 17th century pewter or earthenware pots were a feature of close or necessary stools. Before that fireplaces (when not otherwise in use) and closets behind tapestries did duty for lavatories. During the 18th century pots were secreted in different types of furniture, including bedroom pot cupboards, dressing tables and eventually commodes with close stools in the bottom drawer

£-£££

▲ **Staffordshire chamber pot** seen at the Newcastle Emlyn Roadshow, c1840 **(£150-£200)**

CHAMBERLAIN, ROBERT (b1735)

A porcelain decorator who worked for Dr Wall's WORCESTER factory before setting up his own business in 1783. At first he decorated the wares of others, including CAUGHLEY, COALPORT and NEW HALL, but from 1800 the factory went into large-scale production on its own account. It amalgamated with the older Worcester factory in 1840.

CHAMPLEVÉ AND CLOISONNÉ ENAMELS

An enamel is a vitreous substance, similar to glass, fused to a metal surface under heat. In the case of *champlevé* it is applied as a paste into a depression gouged from the the silver or bronze object. Once fired it is polished smooth. In the *cloisonné* technique the *cloisons* or compartments are formed by wires fixed to the surface. In both techniques the exposed metal divides one colour from another. Both forms have been used since Roman times in Europe ands *cloisonné* was perfected in China and Japan.

CHANEL, GABRIELLE (1883-1971)

The most famous *couturière* of the century, Chanel created a style that anticipated the changing role of women and their need for less formal and more comfortable clothes. She was abandoned by her father at an orphanage, leaving at 18 to work as an assistant in a tailor's shop. She designed and made her own hats and soon set up a millinery shop in Paris. In 1913 her wealthy boyfriend set her up in business and soon after she opened boutiques in Deauville and Biarritz. Her innovations remain classics. The untailored jersey or tweed suit, the little black dress and her simple evening dresses provide a simple but elegant wardrobe for the active and busy woman. Chanel also launched a range of merchandise which included costume jewellery and the famous Chanel No 5 perfume. Today there is a flourishing collector's market in classic Chanel couture and other products.

▲ **The famous Chanel No 5** bottle. A 1956 Chanel suit (below) photographed by Karl Lagerfield **(£400-£600)**. Innovative designs fetch highest prices

A-Z of Antiques Hunting

▲ **Chantilly green-ground** two-handled pot-pourri vase, c1750 **(£5,000)**

CHANTILLY

A porcelain factory founded by Louis-Henri de Bourbon, Prince de Condé, in about 1725. The prince was a major collector of Japanese ARITA porcelain. Only SOFT-PASTE porcelain was made, based on a recipe used at SAINT-CLOUD, early on covering it with an opaque tin glaze,

◀**Chantilly figure** of an oriental, c1740 **(£5,000)**

> **TALKING ANTIQUES**
>
> **'CHASING'**
> Technique for modelling the surface of metal using a hammer and punch. The background is hammered down over a leather-covered cushion, leaving the design in relief. When worked from the back it is known as embossing.

giving a chalk-white background for painted enamels. Early decoration was inspired by Chinese and Japanese porcelain, especially KAKIEMON. As well as useful wares, the factory specialised in grotesque figures of Chinamen. After 1750 the decoration was less inspired by the Orient. Floral decoration in the MEISSEN style was used and the factory succumbed to the dominant influence of VINCENNES-SÈVRES. This decoration gives way to more simple, delicate patterns such as the Chantilly sprig, a sketchy pattern of flower sprays, twigs, grasses or ears of corn often painted in underglaze blue and copied in other English and French factories. The factory closed in 1800 but many 19th-century forgeries exist. The mark is a hunting horn painted in enamel or incised or raised on white figures.

 **£££-£££££**

CHAPTER RING

The ring on a dial of a clock on which numerals or strokes indicating time divisions are marked.

CHATELAINES

These were elaborate ornaments hooked onto the waist and worn by both men and women in the 18th century. They had a useful function but they were primarily

◀**Well-equipped** silver chatelaine, late 19th century **(£300-£400)**

for show and were generally made of precious metal or enamel. Delicate panels were linked by chains from which were suspended a watch, crank key, fob SEAL, ÉTUI and other useful paraphernalia

£££

▲ **Earthenware cow's head** cheese dish cover, 1895 **(£350-£400)**

CHEESE CRADLE

A wooden trough with movable racks for supporting round cheeses on their edges, which was used on the table in the mid-18th century. It was superseded by pottery cheese dishes with covers. These came in all sorts of suitable and unsuitable shapes. They were made in great numbers during the 19th century in such Staffordshire potteries as Dudson.

 **£££**

Anchored in London's past

CHELSEA

The first successful English porcelain factory was founded in Chelsea, London, in 1745 by Nicholas Sprimont, a silversmith. All Chelsea was a SOFT-PASTE or 'artificial' porcelain. Production can be divided into four periods, with different marks — although not all pieces were marked.

Incised Triangle Period c1745-49. Produced in a beautiful glassy porcelain body with typical silver-like shapes, the mark being a roughly incised triangle under the base. The wares are rare and valuable.

Raised anchor period c1749-52. The body was more robust, slightly milky-white from the use of tin in the glaze. The mark was a raised anchor on a round pad. Popular decorations were copies of Japanese KAKIEMON, MEISSEN landscapes and *Aesop's Fables*. A few rare figure models and birds were produced.

▲ Chelsea figure of 'La Nourrice', c1756 **(£8,000)**

Red anchor period c1752-56. A great range of figure models was introduced, copied from Meissen or contemporary engravings and used as dessert table settings. As Horace Walpole wrote in 1753: 'Jellies, biscuits, sugar plums and creams have long given way to Harlequins, Gondoliers, Turks, Chinese and Shepherdesses.' Curious covered tureens in the forms of animals, birds and fish were somewhat eccentric, but table wares with coloured grounds in the style of SÈVRES pointed the way to the next period. Small 'toys'— tiny scent bottles and seals — were produced. The mark of a very small red-anchor appears on the back of figures and under the bases of plates and cups where the three 'spur marks' (remains of firing supports) are seen. When held up to a strong light the famous Chelsea 'moons' should be seen (scattered around lighter patches or bubbles trapped in the paste).

▲ Red anchor period basket, with handle missing, c1755. If complete it would fetch 15 times the price **(£100)**

Gold anchor period c1757-69. The figures become more elaborate, with masses of BOCAGE (modelled flowers). These were for display on mantelpieces or in cabinets, designed to be viewed only from the front. The glaze is clear, thickly applied, with a tendency to craze. The mark was a very small gold anchor. Wares of this period are less appreciated than they were years ago. Beware of 19th-century forgeries, usually in hard-paste with large gold anchor marks.

In 1769 the factory was sold and run in conjunction with the DERBY works until the closure in c1784. During the 'Chelsea-Derby' period, the mark changed to a conjoined anchor and D, while pad support marks are sometimes seen instead of spur marks.

▼ Teapot decorated by J. O'Neale, c1755 **(£25,000)**

▼ Group of goats painted in the workshop of William Duesbury, c1751 **(£9,000)**

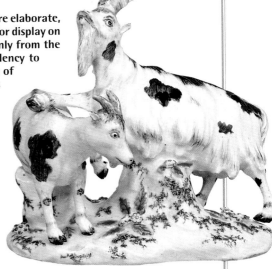

CHENILLE

A velvety trimming made from a cord with short threads of silk set at right-angles to it. It also describes types of imitation velvet in the 19th century.

CHERRY

A strong fruit wood often used for the turned members of chairs and tables, chair seats, table tops and chests.

CHEST-OF-DRAWERS

This was invented in England in the mid-17th century. Previously, clothes were stored in a chest, although later chests might contain small drawers fitted below the hinged chest compartment. At first the chest-of-drawers was mounted on a solid plinth or a stand with legs. The form we know today, with two or three long drawers below and two half-length drawers above and the carcass supported on feet, was developed in the mid-18th century.

£££-££££

CHEST-ON-CHEST

Also known as a tallboy, this is a high chest of seven or more drawers, in two sections resting one on top of the other. The lower part normally contains three drawers, while the upper part has three long drawers and two short ones below the cornice.

££££

George I burr walnut chest-on-chest, *c*1720 **(£10,000-£11,000)**

CHESTERFIELD

A late-Victorian name for a large, well-stuffed sofa.

£££-££££

CHESTNUT

The wood of the horse chestnut is not suitable for cabinetmaking, being soft and woolly in texture. White in colour, it can be used for carving and inlay in cabinet work.

Game, set ar

▲ **King piece** in stained ivory. Delhi, early 19th century (**£800-£1,100 the set**)

CHESS SETS

Games resembling chess have been found in Egyptian tombs and chess was certainly played in India from the 8th century and Persia from the 7th. The Moslem armies which conquered Spain introduced the game to Europe in the 8th century.

According to Islamic laws the pieces were entirely schematic and non-representational, but in medieval and Renaissance Europe the figures took on a highly representational and figurative form. During the 17th and 18th centuries interest in chess declined and it was largely replaced by card-playing.

The neo-Classical period saw a revival of interest in the game, but the pieces were once again designed as abstract shapes and it often became difficult to distinguish the different figures from each other.

There are some amusing sets made of bone during the French Revolution with the

▲ **Chess table**, 1840-50. This was brought into the Basingstoke Roadshow together with the silhouette (above) of players enjoying the use of the very same table in about 1850. (**£800-£1,000 the table**)

d checkmate

stylised heads terminating in spikes to enable them to be stuck in the ground on an improvised board. Many of these are PRISONER-OF-WAR WORK.

Another stimulus came from India, where British colonial officials and traders acquired wonderful sets with kings and queens riding in elephant howdahs, knights in chariots, Oriental castles and sepoy pawns. These were beautifully carved in ivory, with the bases or one side stained to denote black or white.

The most fantastic are from Madras, the men being asembled from numerous pieces so that elephants bristle with cannon and spears and the whole may be brilliantly coloured.

In 1849 Howard Staunton, an English chess master, lent his name to a set designed by Nathaniel Cooke in 1835. It was patented and the forms are are still used today. Chess sets are found in a variety of materials, including bone, ivory, wood, silver and bronze.

Ceramics sets are rare, but Wedgwood produced them and a Communist porcelain propaganda set was made in Moscow shortly after the Revolution.

▲ **Staunton ivory 'club' size set** in the now-familiar standard designs, made by Jaques of London — also famous for croquet sets, c1860 (**£4,000–£6,000**)

▲ **White knight** from ivory set, 'John Company' (East India Company), c1810 (**£10,000–£15,000 the set**)

▼ **Green-stained** and natural ivory set, Indian (**£800–£1,100**)

▲ **Cheval mirror** with adjustable candle brackets that are often missing, c1825 (£1,000–£1,200)

CHEVAL GLASS

Upright, full-length mirror which swings on a four-legged frame. The word *cheval* originated from a pulley or 'horse' which in some examples was part of the mechanism for moving it.

 £££

CHIFFONIER

A piece of 18th-century furniture, with open shelves and a drawer or cupboard below. Also an English 19th-century form of dining-room cupboard with a top forming a sideboard.

£££–££££

CHIMERA

A creature from classical mythology which breathes fire and has the head, mane and legs of a lion, the tail of a dragon, the body of a goat and the wings of an eagle. It was a popular motif in the neo-Classical, Empire and Regency periods.

CHINA

The country produced the supreme ceramic masters and the invention of translucent porcelain. This has given the names of china clay and china stone to the main ingredients of porcelain. The name is now used loosely for a great variety of ceramics.

Days of empire

Xuantong, or Pu-Yi, the hero of Bertolucci's film *The Last Emperor* (above) was heir to a largely unchanged tradition, in which court ceremonies were passed from reign to reign.

Chinese civilisation stretches back to the Neolithic period (c6500–c1500BC) when they were already producing impressive earthenware pots and bronzes. By the time of Christ, when the Roman Empire was still young, the Chinese Empire was already old.

Here we list the dynasties from that period and the individual emperors of the MING and QING dynasties down to Xuantong.

CHINESE DYNASTIES AND REIGNS

DYNASTIES		
c6500–c1500 BC		
	Neolithic cultures	
c1500–c1050BC		
	Shang dynasty	
c1050–771 BC	Western Zhou	
770–221 BC	Eastern Zhou	
221–207 BC	Qin dynasty	
206BC–220AD	Han dynasty	
221–280	Three Kingdoms	
265–420	Six dynasties	
420–589	Southern & Northern dynasties	
589–618	Sui dynasty	
618–906	Tang dynasty	
907–960	Five dynasties	
907–1125	Liao dynasty	
960–1279	Song dynasty	
1115–1234	Jin dynasty	
1279–1368	Yuan dynasty	
1368–1644	Ming dynasty	
1644–1911	Qing dynasty	

Ming Dynasty emperors	
Hongwu	1368–1398
Jianwen	1399–1402
Yongle	1403–1424
Hongxi	1425
Xuande	1426–1435
Zhengtong	1436–1449
Jingtai	1450–1457
Tianshun	1457–1464
Chenghua	1465–1487
Hongzhi	1488–1505
Zhengde	1506–1521
Jiajing	1522–1566
Longqing	1567–1572
Wanli	1573–1620
Taichang	1620
Tianqi	1621–1627
Chongzhen	1628–1644

Qing Dynasty emperors	
Shunzhi	1644–1661
Kangxi	1662–1722
Yongzheng	1723–1735
Qianlong	1736–1795
Jiaqing	1796–1820
Daoguang	1821–1850
Xianfeng	1851–1861
Tongzhi	1862–1874
Guangxu	1875–1908
Xuantong	1909–1912
1912–1949	Republic
1949–	People's Republic

▲ *The Empress of China in a Pavilion said to be in the Summer Palace*, attributed to Lamqua's studio, mid-19th century (£20,00–£30,000)

◄ **Chinese dressing table** made for the European market, late 18th century (**£1,800–£2,200**)

CHINESE FURNITURE

Little of this survives from before the 16th century, when it was made of lacquered softwood. Thereafter hardwoods such as Indian *dalbergia* rosewood and the similar *hua-li* were used, the most prized being *huang hua-li*. This was thought to have become extinct in the 18th century, but recently small supplies have become available again and it is used to imitate the styles and methods of Ming and Qing furniture-makers. Another highly valued wood was the hard, dark *tzu-tan* which carves well. Most traditional Chinese furniture was made to be dismantled for easy carriage by travelling bureaucrats and scholars, so it is pegged rather than glued. Another design feature was the 'floating panel', on large surfaces, allowing for contraction and expansion. Cupboards and chests were made of elm or camphor, and these were also used to line *huang hua-li* pieces to protect them from insects. Metal mounts might be brass or paktong , a silvery alloy. The classic period is held to be the century from the middle 1500s, when designs were bold, the carving fine and detailed, and lines flowing. After this, things became stiffer and heavier. As well as chests, chairs, beds and tables to their own designs, the Chinese made export furniture to suit Western tastes. These often failed to meet either Oriental or Occidental standards of craftsmanship.

CHINOISERIE

By the early 17th century, trade links with China were well established. As well as the Chinese producing wares for the European market, European designers began to imitate the Chinese style, taking their patterns from authentic porcelain or lacquer. Some of the earliest interiors to be designed in the Chinoiserie style were at Rosenborg Castle, Copenhagen, in 1655-68. By the end of the century European faience factories were producing wares decorated with Chinoiserie scenes, and travel books such as J. Nieuhof's *Atlas Chinesis or The Treatise on Japanning and Varnishing* made Chinese-style designs widely available.

Chinoiserie incorporates a whole range of Chinese motifs, dragons, pagodas, monkeys, Chinamen with moustaches and coolie hats, the hilly landscape and exotic birds and butterflies. It was a style ideally suited to the light, witty and frivolous ROCOCO movement, and by 1720 Chinoiserie had spread to every medium. Silver was engraved with Chinoiserie ornament, wallpaper hand-painted in the Chinoiserie style and furniture carved with elegant Chinoiserie motifs.

Thomas CHIPPENDALE, Batty Langley and J. Pillement were just a few of the designers who produced wide ranges of Chinese designs.

However, it was never accepted as a serious architectural style and was so whimsical that it was generally confined to only one room of a house. One of the last manifestations on a grand scale was probably the interior of the Prince Regent's Brighton Pavilion, 1802-20, although it has lingered on in designs for teahouses, fairgrounds and garden houses.

▲ **George II standing shelf**, lacquered in the Chinoiserie style (**£16,000**)

Block off the old Chipp

CHIPPENDALE, THOMAS (1718 – 79)

A Yorkshireman, he had established himself in London before 1745. He became one of the most influential furniture-makers of the time, in part because his business embraced both cabinet-making and upholstery. He supplied his clients with not only furniture, but also other household necessities such as wallpaper, curtains, bedding, carpets and other fittings.

On major commissions, such as that for Harewood House, near his birthplace, he was as happy to supply casing for lavatories as state beds and grand library furniture, and there are still houses in Covent Garden whose front doors may have come from his workshops at 60 St Martin's Lane.

The other principal source of his influence was the immense and immediate success of his comprehensive book of furniture designs, *The Gentleman and Cabinet Maker's Director*, 1754, and a second, enlarged edition in 1762. Influences are wide and GOTHICK and CHINOISERIE designs are there as well as NEO-CLASSICAL. In fact, the furniture often looks distinctly odd and unmakeable as one chair may combine two styles with the perspective a token gesture. It was by no means the first such pattern book, but it was far more ambitious than its predecessors in that it dealt with all branches of furniture and gave detailed designs with measurements along with instructions as to how each piece should be finished. It was both useful

to colleagues and flatteringly acceptable to customers. It has lasted as an invaluable guide to the designs and thinking of the period.

For these reasons Chippendale's name became synonymous with English furniture-making in the second half of the 18th century — so much so that only now are many of his competitors being brought back from obscurity.

John Channon (1711-c1783), William Vile (c1700 - 67) and John Cobb (c1715-78), Samuel Norman (active 1746- 67), and the LINNELLS may have been his equals, but they lacked his flair for advertisement.

The *Director* is essentially a ROCOCO manual. Even when it aspires to PALLADIAN sobriety, Rococo flair and frivolity intrude. Chippendale designs were intended

▲ Thomas Chippendale's label was attached to pieces made in his workshop

to be executed in mahogany, but country-made pieces in oak and elm exist. Some seat furniture was painted in the French style and Chippendale even imported French pieces unassembled (and was prosecuted for avoiding duty).

Chairs, which generally had upholstered seats, had lower backs than before with projecting 'ears' at the ends of the top rails, and carved cabriole front legs with scrolled feet, rather than claw and ball or

▲ A good provincial chair in Chippendale's style, c1770 (£600-£800)

▶ Fine rosewood and mahogany hexagonal tripod table, attributed to Chippendale, c1770 (£10,000– £15,000)

▲ George III mahogany secretaire-cabinet, attributed to Thomas Chippendale (£49,000)

▼ Mahogany bedside cupboard attributed to Chppendale (£30,000)

paw. Pierced back splats were sinuously carved with acanthus, ribbons, shells, shields, Gothic arches or Chinese trellis. Tables were designed for every different function that fashion might demand.

It is a testament to Chippendale's commercial acumen that the success of his designs and style did not prevent him from collaborating with Robert ADAM, the high priest of neo-Classicism. Equally, it is a testament to the power of his name that Victorian and Edwardian furniture-makers reproduced his work so reverently. These copies are often of great quality.

CHOCOLATE POT AND CUP

Chocolate was introduced into Britain in the mid 17th century and rapidly became fashionable. The pots resemble coffee pots but have a hole in the lid to stir the grounds. Cups are taller and larger than coffee cups, with two handles.

££-£££££

CHRYSANTHEMUM

The flower was a popular motif in Chinese and Japanese ceramics and symbolised autumn and friendship. From the MEISSEN period onwards it was used on European ceramics.

CIGAR AND CIGARETTE CASES

Cigars were introduced to Britain from America in the 1830s and rapidly overtook snuff in popularity. Cigar cases were made in silver and silver-mounted leather and crocodile skin, and were often engraved with BRIGHT-CUT or ENGINE-TURNED designs. Cigarettes appeared in the late 19th century, and scaled-down versions of the cigar case were made for them. The most popular today are the enamelled ones, especially those with erotic scenes or bright ART DECO patterns.

£-£££

CIGAR CUTTERS AND LIGHTERS

Cigar cutters and, later, lighters, which are often combined with them, come in all sorts of ingenious shapes and sizes, from the grandest table silver to witty pocket size.

£-££

▶ Silver cigar lighter, one of a pair which belonged to the Imjin Battery, 19th Regiment, The Highland Gunners, 1911, 26in long (£300 the pair)

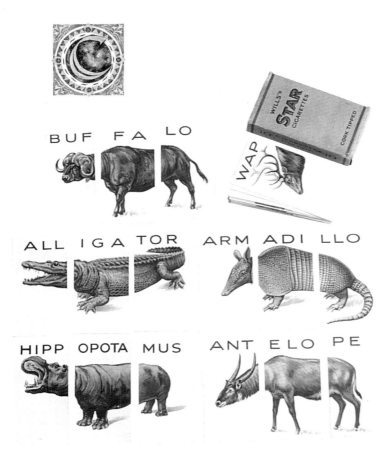

BUF FA LO

ALL IGA TOR   ARM ADI LLO

HIPP OPOTA MUS   ANT ELO PE

◀ **Cigarette cards** brought into the Taunton Antiques Roadshow. The 'Un-natural history' series comprised 16 animals, each in three sections which could be mixed in a variety of amusing ways (£25–£35)

CLICHY

This glasshouse was founded at Billancourt, Paris in 1837, and settled at Clichy-la-Garenne. It made cheap tableware for export and also specialised in fine CAMEO, FILIGREE, OPALINE and MILLEFIORI glass. It is specially well known for its brightly coloured, swirl-patterned paperweights incorporating a distinctive rose. Some are signed with a 'C'.

£££–££££

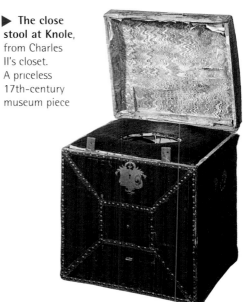

▶ **The close stool at Knole**, from Charles II's closet. A priceless 17th-century museum piece

CIGARETTE CARDS

These were introduced in America in the 1880s to stiffen paper cigarette packets. The first cards carried advertising but this was quickly replaced with colour pictures issued in series of up to 50 different images. They ranged from early nautical-inspired themes to Indian chiefs, flowers and film and stage beauties. Wills of Bristol was the first English firm to issue them in 1888, with the 'Soldiers of the World' series. In both quality and subject-matter the finest cards were made from 1900 to the 1930s, after which the quality deteriorates.

£–££

CLAW AND BALL

An eagle's talon clutching a ball appears in Chinese art and may derive from the legendary image of the Chinese DRAGON holding a flaming pearl of wisdom. Claw and ball feet appear in the late 15th century. The claw can be finely modelled while the ball provides a sturdy base for furniture or metalwork.

CLAY PIPES

Pipe smoking began in England around 1590. The first clay pipes had very small bowls—they were referred to as 'little ladels' with flat spurs beneath which might have had a maker's stamp. During the 17th century bowls grew larger, and the rims tilted forwards, with a milled ring around them. From about 1700 this ring disappeared, and the bowl edge was set parallel to the stem, which was a foot or more in length. From the mid-18th century bowls were moulded with subjects such as the fox and grapes and Turks' heads, royal and city guilds' arms, or patriotic incidents. Decoration became still more elaborate in the 19th century, with portraits, jokes, souvenirs, Masonic, sporting and even erotic subjects. Many pipes have the makers' initials or mark on the spur, and there are local variations of design. It is quite usual to find Dutch examples in Britain. Some WIG CURLERS could be mistaken for broken pipe stems.

£–££

▶ Selection of clay pipes, 1590–1750 (£1–£5)

CLOSE STOOL

An enclosed stool, often richly upholstered with silk and velvet, containing a pewter or earthenware pot. They were also called night stools, and from the Victorian period were known by the American euphemism of 'commode'.

££–£££

Bizarre success with the boldest patterns

CLARICE CLIFF (1899-1972)

Born at Tunstall, in Staffordshire, she was apprenticed at the age of 13 to learn freehand pottery painting. In 1916 she joined the firm of A.J. Wilkinson, where she stayed for the rest of her life.

Arthur Shorter had taken over the Wilkinson factory and later his sons Colley and John Guy also acquired the Newport factory. Clarice began experimenting with thickly applied, bold, bright, geometric decoration. Colley recognised her potential and marketed them under the title of Bizarre ware. They proved an enormous success and by late 1929 the entire factory was producing Bizarre ware. Clarice was made art director, employing 150 decorators. The peak period was 1929-34. Hundreds of ART DECO designs were made, including banding, geometric floral patterns, stylised landscapes and Cubist and line patterns. Patterns such as Crocus were applied to experimental shapes based on circles, squares and triangles. Applique was a range of wares produced by a specific process and Latona was associated with a milky glaze.

Matching dinner, tea and coffee services and centrepieces could be ordered in a huge range of patterns. Mass-produced, the wares were available in all the major retail outlets. Publicity stunts such as the Bizooka — a 5ft-high horse made entirely out of Bizarre wares — and painting demonstrations by the Bizarre girls boosted sales. By the late 1930s demand declined and Clarice returned to designing more conventional patterns. She married Colley Shorter in 1940 at the age of 41, after what had been widely rumoured to have been a long-standing love affair. The factory continued to produce conventional wares but Clarice did little designing. Colley died in 1963 and two years later the factory was taken over by Messrs Midwinter.

Interest in her work revived in the 1960s and a retrospective was staged at the Brighton Museum in 1972. Rare pieces can fetch thousands of pounds although it is debatable whether the wares are of serious merit. Examples will bear a facsimile signature as well as the pattern name and the maker, either Newport Pottery or Wilkinson Ltd.

▲ A Clarice Cliff conical bowl decorated with the Trees and Hope design in the pastel colourway and stamped Bizarre and Fantasque (£450-£550)

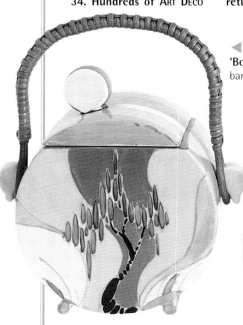

◄ A Bizarre 'Bonjour' biscuit barrel (£200-£300)

▶ A Bizarre baluster vase (£250-£300)

▼ Bizarre 'Bonjour' preserve pots (£100-£150 each)

Stone age success story

COADESTONE

Eleanor Coade (d.1796) was not the first artificial stonemaker in London, but she remains the most famous. She came from Lyme Regis, and around 1769 she set up her factory in Lambeth, to exploit a process discovered either by her father or her husband George Coade, who died in that year. The business, run by Eleanor and her nephew John Sealy (1749-1813), and then by her daughter and namesake, was an instant success, and they employed the best sculptors and designers. They produced terracotta pieces, including coats of arms, as well as Coadestone statues, seats and memorials.

Supposedly a revival of the lost Roman artificial cement, the secret was lost again with the closure of the business in about 1836. One of the best-known Coade figures is the lion which now stands at the Lambeth end of Westminster Bridge. The firm also supplied statues and friezes for Buckingham Palace. Coade's products were comparatively cheap. Eleanor claimed her stone had 'a property peculiar to itself of resisting the frost and consequently of retaining that sharpness in which it excels every kind of stone sculpture'. (See also GARDEN FURNITURE)

▲ Figure from a rare set of four seasons c1790 (£65,000–£75,000)

▲ English lion slaying a French eagle from a unique group (£30,000–£35,000)

▶ The Coadestone lion which stands on Westminister Bridge

CLOTHES PRESS
A large, enclosed piece of furniture with sliding shelves or trays on which the clothes were stored.

 £££-££££

CLUB CHAIR
A deep-sprung easy chair with a long seat for lounging in, which came into use in the mid-19th century. Sometimes fitted with a drawer below the seat, in which case it can also be called a smoker's chair.

 ££££

CLUB FENDER
A metal fender, with a padded upholstered leather seat, used from the mid-19th century. It is considerably higher than the Georgian fender stool.

£££-££££

COACH WATCH
A large, 18th-century pocket watch used for travelling, which was enclosed in a metal case. It was replaced in the 19th century by the CARRIAGE CLOCK.

 £££

◀ Coach watch with alarm and repeater by Cabrier of London, c1775 (examples £6,000 – £15,000, depending on elaboration)

Founders of tradition

COLEBROOKDALE IRON

Abraham Darby took on the lease of the Coalbrookdale works in Shropshire in 1708 and began the technique of smelting iron ore with coke rather than charcoal (see CAST IRON). Seven generations of Darbys continued to run the company until the early 20th century. The earliest products were pots, cooking utensils, and cylinders for the newly–invented steam engine.

Because the family were strict Quakers they did not get involved in the booming ordnance trade of the other British foundries. The year 1781 saw the building of the spectacular Iron Bridge at Telford, the first of its kind in the world, and thereafter the company specialised in bridge building and architectural components. By now it was one of the largest iron producing centres in England.

By 1800 they were making stoves and grates, progressing by the mid–century to more elaborate designs such as kitchen ranges.

Ornamental cast iron was introduced from the 1830s, and throughout the19th century it was a speciality of the company. They produced enormous catalogues which were distributed around the world and mounted spectacular displays at the International Exhibitions. Products included gates, fountains, inkstands, hat stands, garden benches and ornaments, cake plates, statuettes and relief plaques, some of which were made to designs from foundries in Berlin and Fuspang, Sweden. Marked Coalbrookdale they are easily identified.

By the 1920s the iron industry was in recession, and in 1929 the company became a subsidiary of Allied Iron Founders Ltd. In 1968 the Ironbridge Gorge Museum was set up and the foundry continues to make a limited range of decorative ironwork.

◀ **Mirror** stand with adapted Coalbrookdale cast-iron base, c1850s (£300)

▼ **Early Coalbrookdale** cooking pot, very rare dated 1714. In the Museum of Iron in Coalbrookdale

▼ **Inkstand** with Coalport china pots. Also in the Museum of Iron

COALPORT

Also known as the Coalbrookdale porcelain factory, it was founded in 1795 by William Reynolds, although John Rose was the driving force behind the factory. He was trained at CAUGHLEY and bought that factory in 1799 and NANTGARW in 1819, taking on WILLIAM BILLINGSLEY. The early wares are very similar to Caughley, decorated in underglaze blue. In 1820 a leadless feldspathic glaze was introduced and wares were sparingly decorated with flowers, moulded patterns and light-coloured gilding.

◀ **Two-handled vase** in typical Coalport style, c1835 (£400–£600)

Patterns were lightly transfer-printed and then hand-coloured, thus retaining the quality of hand-painted porcelain. From the mid-19th century products were inspired by the SÈVRES style with coloured grounds and finely painted fruit and flowers. The factory is still in production but has moved to Stoke-on-Trent. Marks include: CD, CDale, Coalport or Coalbrookdale, J or John Rose & Co, CBD monogram and CSN in an ampersand (&)

££-££££

◄**Silver wine coaster,** Mortimer and Hunt, London 1891 (£2,000 - £3,000)

COASTER

A tray or trolley for circulating food or bottles around the dining table. It was usually a low, round decanter stand with a silver or Sheffield plate gallery on a wooden base, the underside covered in baize. Boat or figure of eight shapes were made to take two bottles, and more fanciful forms also exist. They were used from the late 18th century when dining habits became more intimate, bottles were placed on the table and servants were not required to wait behind each chair.

£££-££££

COCK-FIGHTING CHAIR

An erroneous term for a reading chair which was first made in the early 18th century. It has broad, high arm rests and a reading desk fitted to the back so the reader could sit backwards, resting his elbows on the arms.

COCK-FIGHTING RELICS

Cockfights or 'mains' were introduced to Britain by the Romans, Illegal since 1836, the 'sport' was earlier banned by both Edward III and Oliver Cromwell. Relics include feather trophies and vicious steel spurs, which are sometimes framed and mounted as displays. The best cockfighting prints are mezzotints by Richard Earlom after Zoffany's *Colonel Mordaunt's Cock Fight* (1792) and by Charles Turner after Ben Marshall (1810 and 1812). There are also sets of aquatints after R. B. Davis (1810), C.H. Weigall (1839), and Newton Feilding (1853). In 1825 and 1842 cockfighting prints after Henry Alken were published.

These have been much reproduced and copied, and sometimes modern versions are coloured over to masquerade as oil paintings.

COFFIN STOOL

A rectangular stool with four turned legs held by rails above and stretchers below. They are correctly known as joint stools and were much used in the 16th and 17th centuries for sitting at the dining table. The term coffin stool was coined in Victorian times and may come from a reference in Pepys's diary to his uncle's coffin 'standing upon joynt-stooles'.

£££-££££

COIN GLASS

A drinking glass with a coin embedded in a knop in the stem. The first examples date from the early 18th century. Obviously the glass may not be as old as the date of the coin in it.

£££

▼ **Cockfighting memorabilia** including the rules of the 'sport", seen at the Guernsey Roadshow **(£500–£600)**

◄ **Coin goblet** commemorating the silver jubilee of George V and Queen Mary in 1935. The coin is visible in the bulb at the top of the stem **(£150)**

◀ **Commemorative coronation pencils** are worth a few pounds each

Transferring affections

COMMEMORATIVE ITEMS

Although commemorative pottery is known from the reign of Elizabeth I, and the slipware portrait chargers of Thomas TOFT are examples of the tradition, the industry got under way with the invention of TRANSFER PRINTING in the 1750s. Nelson's death at Trafalgar, George III's Jubilee in 1809, the death of Princess Charlotte in 1817 and George IV's attempt to divorce Queen Caroline are the earliest events to be commemorated on a large scale. Thereafter coronations, royal weddings, births, jubilees, elections and by-elections have all been memorialised on china, textiles and glass — and on almost everything else from pencils to biscuit tins.

It was during the Victorian period that the heroes (and not infrequently villains) of the period were commemorated. Staffordshire poured out a stream of portrait figures celebrating the Crimean War, murders, the theatre and religious and political leaders.

The now ubiquitous jug was moulded with the marriage of Albert Edward (later Edward VII), and Alexandra and was gaudily transfer-printed to glorify the jubilees of 1887 and 1897. Despite popular mythology, coronation mugs of Edward VIII, who was never crowned, are very common and worth about £15. As less time was available before his brother, George VI's coronation, these are rarer, but worth about the same.

◀**Commemorative bust** of King Edward VIII, 1936 **(£150)**

▶ **Royal Doulton** beaker presented to guests at one of the numerous 1902 coronation dinners **(£100)**

◀**George III** as patron of Lancastrian School Movement, c1805 **(£400-£500)**

▼ **Victorian** coronation mug,1838 **(£700-£1,000)**

▲**Limited edition** Coalport plate commemorating the Boer War **(£300-£400)**

sented a cross-section of contemporary society. The plays had no set text but were worked up from basic scenarios by the actors who sang, danced, played musical instruments and performed conjuring tricks and acrobatics. At the centre of the plot were two frustrated young lovers. The men were generally called Flavio, Lelio or Orazio and the women Aurelia, Isabella or Ginevra but the real heroes and heroines were the *zanni* or servants who provided the action. Brighella was a cunning rascal while Harlequin, who wore a patched costume, was carefree and funny.

CONSOLE TABLE

A table fixed to the wall, usually with a marble top and supported on curved, S-shaped legs which act as brackets. They were often placed below a wall mirror. See PIER TABLE.

££££

COOKWORTHY, WILLIAM

Credited with the discovery of china clay and china stone in Cornwall and the forming of these into the first English hard-paste porcelain at Plymouth, 1768-70, and later at Bristol.

All points north

COMPASSES

The use of the lodestone (magnetic iron oxide) to find north was discovered by the Chinese in the 1st century AD, and they made primitive compasses of magnetised iron slivers floating on straws in bowls of water. From the 11th century Arab sailors made refinements on these, and in the 16th French mariners developed the gimbal to keep a compass horizontal, whatever

the movement of sea and ship. Large steering compasses were mounted in teak and brass binnacles, which might be elaborately decorated according to the whim of the skipper or owner.

Efficient pocket compasses were developed during the 19th century, and those most frequently found today are military bearing compasses, in leather cases, which were made by the hundreds of thousand during the two World Wars.

◀ Gentleman's pocket compass late 18th century, (£1,800-£2,500)

▼ Silver pocket dial by Butterfield of Paris (£3,000-£4,000)

▶ Small ship's compass binnacle, 1920s, (£1,500-£2,000)

▶ Doccia commedia dell' arte figure of Columbine, as a pair with Harlequin (£8,000 the pair)

COMMEDIA DELL'ARTE

The popular theatre which originated in Italy in the 16th century was performed in various guises throughout Europe until the end of the 18th century. From the early 18th century the characters were frequent subjects for figures in porcelain and sets were made by most of the major European factories, including MEISSEN, CHELSEA, NYMPHENBURG and CAPODIMONTE. The theatre was based on stock characters who repre-

▶ Selection of wares designed by Susie Cooper. On the left and right are two slender ovoid vases in the 'Moon and Mountain' pattern, 9in (£1,300 each vase)

Self-made stylist

COOPER, SUSIE (1902-1995)

One of the most influential ceramic designers to emerge from Staffordshire this century. She was born in Burslem and worked from 1922 to 1929 as a painter for A. E. Gray & Co. Here she introduced her geometric and banded pattern designs. In 1930 she set up her own works, merging in 1932 with Wood and Sons, who supplied her with white ware for decoration. By the late Thirties her business was supplying Harrods, Peter Jones, Waring and Gillow, Selfridges and Heal's.

Her innovatory designs provided functional, modern, cost-conscious tableware. The hallmarks of her style were her use of free-hand painting, her experiments with crayon designs, banding and polka dots and innovative floral designs. She also pioneered an improved quality of lithographic transfers. In 1950 she purchased the Jason China Co and by the late Fifties china production had replaced earthenware. Her company became a member of the Wedgwood Group in 1966. In 1972 she resigned as director and the Susie Cooper pottery closed in 1980. Up to her death she was still designing on a freelance basis.

CONTENTS SALE

Auction held on the vendor's premises — usually at country houses, often in a marquee on the lawn. They can be a happy hunting ground for a 'sleeper', or un-catalogued lot, but generally they are social gatherings and prices are often driven up to ridiculous levels.

▲Rare Corgi 'pop art' Mini 1967 (£500, mint and boxed)

▲The Saint's Volvo (£40- £60 boxed)

▼ Milk jug from a Copeland and Garrett tea service, 1833-46 (£60-£90)

implements and relatively portable duplicating machines which came in neat, business-like wooden boxes fitted for writing.

£££

CORDIAL GLASS

An English drinking glass for a strong, sweet liquor, introduced *c*1700. About 6-8in high, it has a small, bell-shaped bowl or flute, tapering into the stem, and resting on a flared foot.

£££

▶ **English cordial glass** seen at Blenheim Palace Roadshow, *c*1780 (£150- £200)

enced the choice of the Welsh corgi dog as a trade mark. The cars were in direct competition with DINKY but slightly larger in scale, between 1:44 and 1:48. Before 1957 the metal base plate was pressed and after this die-cast. By the late 1950s the firm was releasing one new model a month.

Speciality ranges included a group of military models and the Corgi classic collection launched in 1964. In 1965 the popular television range was launched which went on to include the Saint's Volvo, James Bond's Aston Martin, Chitty Chitty Bang Bang and the Batmobile. In 1983 Mettoy went into receivership and a new Corgi Company was formed, concentrating on collectors' models. The Corgi range is of the highest quality and very undervalued compared with Dinky toys.

COPELAND

In 1833 W. T. Copeland and his partner Garrett took over the SPODE factory. From 1847 to 1867 the mark was Copeland Late Spode, then Copeland. The Spode name is now current.

COPIER

The 19th-century firm of Sampson MORDAN made all sorts of writing

CORDWAINING

High-quality leather which was used as wall hangings as an alternative to tapestries. It was embossed, gilded or painted and originally came from Córdova in Spain but from the 14th century the main centre of production was the Low Countries. The fashion for cordwaining declined in the 18th century with the rise in popularity of wallpaper.

CORGI TOYS

The range was launched by Playcraft Toys, a subsidiary company of Mettoy in 1956. The main manufacturing plant was at the Mettoy factory in Swansea, South Wales, and this, combined with the up-market association of corgis with the royal family, influ-

£-££

▲007's Aston Martin (£60-£80 boxed)
▼The Batmobile (£40-£60 unboxed)

▲Copying press by S. Mordan and Co, 1856 (£100- £200)

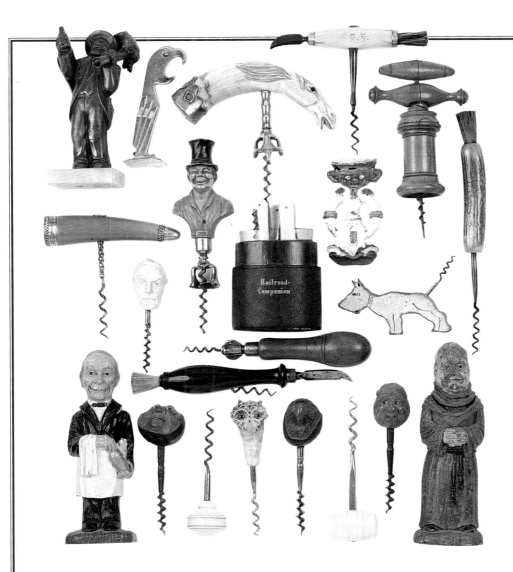

◀Collection of 19th- and 20th-century corkscrews. The various figurative and novelty screws can range from £5 to £50. More serious examples, such as the tusk-handled screws and the better earlier models can be valued at £100-£350

▼ Late 19th-century German novelty legs corkscrew (£80-£150)

They make you turn to drink

CORKSCREWS

The first patent for a mechanical corkscrew was taken out by the Rev Samuel Henshall in 1795 and this was manufactured by Matthew BOULTON as the Obstando Promoves Soho Patent. Over the next 100 years on average 10 patents per year were taken out in Europe and North America with about 350 in Britain.

Henshall's innovation was a fixed disc at the top of the worm which compressed the cork and limited penetration.

Boulton's former apprentice Sir Edward Thomason, patented a continuous action, brass-barrel screw in 1802. Among Henshall's and Thomason's British successors was H. N. S. Shrapnel — son of the bullet maker — with a steel, two-pillar screw with folding handles.

Also quite common are brass-barrel King's screws with ivory handles. Many early designs have a brush to remove dust and fragments of cork. The French introduced the concertina-action 'Zig Zag' and the Germans

late 19th-century novelties such as 'Lady's Legs'

Minature screws with plain bow handles were for opening medicine bottles while more elaborate versions with ivory or mother-of-pearl handles were made for scent bottles. Travelling corkscrews pack away inside their handles. In George III's reign these might be silver; in that of George V, steel.

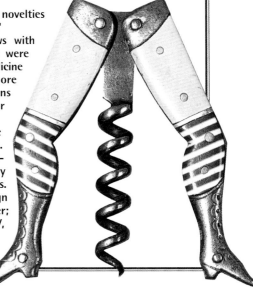

A-Z *of* Antiques Hunting

CORNER CUPBOARD

A free-standing or hanging cupboard made to fit into the corner of a room. It can be left open for the display of glass or china or closed with doors. Popular during the 18th century.

COROMANDEL WOOD

A type of EBONY with light-coloured stripes, also known as zebra wood. Used in 18th- and 19th-century cabinetmaking, especially for BANDING.

COTTAGE PIANO

The first upright pianos had an extremely high case but after 1826 Robert Wornum's crank action enabled the movement to be put into a smaller case. Throughout the 19th century this type was known as a cottage piano. It usually has a fretwork panel lined with silk above the keyboard.

  £££-££££

COT AND CRADLE

Originally a canvas bed suspended from the beams of a ship. This sea cot probably gave its name to swinging cribs or cradles used for babies, which are either suspended from a bar or mounted on rockers with a hood or canopy. Today, a child's cot is not designed to swing but has high, open, barred sides which can be dropped down, or left up to prevent the child from climbing out.

▼ **Mid-Victorian** mahogany cradle, c1850 (**£2,000-£2,750**)

▲ **Moonstone and sapphire** wisteria pendant by Fred Partridge, 1910. Seen at the Truro Roadshow (**£2,500-£3,500**)

▶ **Scottish-style Arts and Crafts** armchair c1910 (**£500**)

▼ **Stoneware jug** by Bernard Leach, 1953 (**£250-£350**)

◀ **Stoneware vase by** Leach, (far left) 1960 (**£5,000-£6,000**)

Pilkington's Royal Lancastrian double gourd vase, brought in to the Luton Hoo Roadshow (£50-£60)

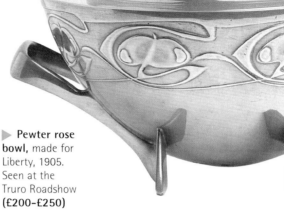

Pewter rose bowl, made for Liberty, 1905. Seen at the Truro Roadshow (£200-£250)

You have to hand it to them

ARTS AND CRAFTS MOVEMENT

Drawing its inspiration from designers and critics as diverse as A. W. N. PUGIN John RUSKIN, Dr Christopher DRESSER and William MORRIS, the Arts and Crafts Movement represented a switch of emphasis away from the highly finished and stylistically complex products of industry towards a more individual, hand-made and traditional type of object.

Truth to nature, the controlled and relevant use of ornament, vernacular styles and materials, and an exploration of the creative potential within the craftsmen or women were all part of a movement that affected Britain, many European countries and North America during the late 19th and early 20th centuries.

The revival of interest in local and predominantly pre-industrial styles, techniques and materials, the development of studios, guilds and other artistic associations and the avail-ability of new sales outlets and means of promotion, such as specialist shops, exhibitions and magazines, all helped the new generations of art students brought up on the teachings of Ruskin and Morris to make a major impact on art and design.

Along with its clear interest in handcraft skills, the movement also drew heavily on the continuing vogue for the decorative arts of Japan. The Arts and Crafts Movement affected most areas of the decorative arts, especially ceramics, wood and metalwork, silver and jewellery, textiles stained glass, typography and book design. At the same time, the characteristic simplicity of Arts and Crafts design radically changed the look of contempory architecture and interior decoration, establishing dateless and informal styles that are still popular today.

The social impact was also considerable, bound up as the movement was with the development of left-wing politics, trades unions, female emancipation and concerns about the quality of life in the workplace.

In Britain, key examples of the Arts and Crafts Movement include the pottery-decorating studios set up in the early 1870s by MINTON and DOULTON, the flourishing of small art potteries throughout the country during the 1880s and 1890s, the vogue for decorative tiling, the distinctively vernacular styles of furniture and woodwork associated with the Cotswold region, craft associations such as C.R. Ashbee's Guild of Handicrafts, department stores such as LIBERTY and HEAL'S and the architecture promoted by men including Ernest Gimson, C.F.A. Voysey, W.R. Lethaby, C. R. MACKINTOSH and, in the USA, Frank Lloyd Wright

There had been since the Middle Ages a tradition of ladies engaging in needle-work to while away the time. During the Arts and Crafts period, the loosening of the ties that held a woman at home meant that many now took up a more robust hobby. Hammering brass into picture frames, carving furniture, making pewter inkwells and jewellery, often inlaid with Ruskin cabouchons, hand-painting pottery, and for the more adventurous, enamelling and working in gold and silver. The worst of their efforts are appalling, but many attained acceptable — and collectable — results.

Inkwell by Birmingham Guild of Handicrafts, 1900 (£400-£500)

Queen of cream

CREAMWARE

A lead-glazed earthenware with a smooth cream body containing flint. It was first made by Enoch Booth of Tunstall, Staffordshire, but a better type, known as 'Queen's ware' in honour of Queen Charlotte, was developed by Wedgwood in 1765. It was much cheaper to produce than porcelain but was light, thin and durable. It was particularly suitable for open-work and could be hand painted or transfer-printed. It was soon copied by other factories, Leeds in particular.

▶ Creamware teapot, probably Leeds, c1770 (£800-£1,200)

CREWELWORK

A type of needlework done in brightly coloured wools on white, beige or linen grounds. Designs are bold and floral, derived from Indian cottons. It was widely used for bed hangings in the late 17th and early 18th centuries.

CRICKET TABLE

A small plain, circular table made in the 17th century. The term cricket is modern and may come from the three legs which resemble cricket stumps or from the use of the word cricket to describe a plain wooden stool.

 £££

◀ Christopher Payne admiring fine crewelwork at Florence Court, Enniskillen, given to the National Trust in 1953

CROSSED SWORDS
Classic mark of the MEISSEN factory, often imitated.

CROSSLEY CARPETS
Established by John Crossley at Dean Clough Mill, Halifax, in 1837, the factory originally made hand-loom carpets. In 1850 John's son Francis installed the first steam-powered loom for carpets and the business expanded rapidly. The factory specialised in wide, seamless jacquard carpets in a huge variety of patterns.

 £££-£££££

CRUET
A silver stand, often oval or boat-shaped, which supports a number of glass or silver vessels for spices and condiments.

CUCKOO CLOCK
A development of the wooden BLACK FOREST CLOCK first made c1730. A striking mechanism actuates a wooden cuckoo from behind a trap door, which pops out on the hour making a simulated bird sound produced on two small organ pipes.

££-£££

CUTCARD
Gold or silver APPLIED ornament cut from a thin sheet of metal and soldered on to the object. It was introduced to England on HUGUENOT silver, especially as a border around the body of a vessel.

CYLINDER TOP DESK
A desk where the writing area and upper storage space are closed by a pullover fall which slides back into the body of the desk when it is open. The fall is framed by a solid cylindrical section or a horizontally slotted tambour—a flexible sheet made of reed-like lengths of wood glued to fabric side by side. They date from the second half of the 18th century.

CYPRESS
An aromatic, close-grained hard wood introduced into England in the early 16th century.

which has been characterised as 'slightly less extravagant and much less refined' than that of GALLÉ.

£££-££££

DAVENPORT

The first little Davenport writing desk was made in the late 18th century by Gillow's of Lancaster for a Captain Davenport, perhaps a member of the Cheshire Bromley-Davenport family. Early examples were fairly plain, with the writing slope sliding forwards from a solid, squarish, pedestal of drawers. As the 19th century progressed, so variations on the Davenport theme became ever more elaborate, and it is rare to find two exactly alike. Constant elements are the pedestal case of four drawers, and the slope, which is usually fixed to project over knees in Victorian versions. There may be all sorts of galleries, slides, pen boxes and cabriole or column supports, and many exotic woods were used as well as walnut or mahogany.

▲ **Early walnut Davenport** with sliding top, seen at the Blenheim Palace Roadshow, 1810-20 (**£1,500-£2,000**)

▶ Walnut Davenport with rising stationery gallery, c1850 (**£3,000**)

DAMASK

A reversible figured textile on which the pattern is formed by two faces of the same weave, giving a damascened effect. As with the parent word, the term has expanded, and is now used to cover any silk fabric with a raised pattern.

DARLY, MATTHIAS (active 1741-1780)

A publisher, caricaturist, engraver and designer, who styled himself 'Professor of Ornament'. He was the first to publish GOTHIC REVIVAL furniture designs, and also popularised the CHINOISERIE and ADAM styles.

DAUM

From 1889 the glass factory set up at Nancy in Lorraine by Auguste (1853-1909) and Antonin (1864-1930). Daum produced decorative coloured glassware,

▶ **Daum vase** in yellow glass with applied crocuses, c1890 (**£2,400**)

▲ Stereoscopic daguerreotype of three Victorian graces, c1850 (**£2,500**)

DAGUERREOTYPE

Louis Daguerre (1787-1851) was quick to build on the work of Nicéphore Niepce, who had taken the first photograph in 1827. By 1839 Daguerre launched his daguerreotypes commercially, and thousands of studios opened in France and Britain, putting many portrait painters out of work. The process was complicated and slow, but essentially the image was fixed on a surface of silvered metal, which was then cased. The daguerreotype was soon displaced by the ambrotype, produced by a similar but much simpler process which meant that amateurs could make their own images. As a result daguerreotypes are rarer and more sought after.

£££

DAVENPORT POTTERY AND PORCELAIN

In about 1793 John Davenport set up at Longport, Staffordshire, producing cream-coloured, blue-printed earthenware. Around 1820 a porcelain works opened, making tea and dessert services in imitation of DERBY. The factory closed in 1887.

£-£££

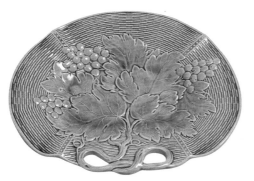

▲ **Davenport dish,** with moulded pattern of grapes and vine leaves (£40-£50)

DAYBED

A term used from the 16th to the mid-18th century for a long, upholstered or caned seat with one fixed or adjustable inclined end. If fixed, it was closer to a bed than a settee, but in any case it was the ancestor of the chaise longue.

 £££-££££

DEAN'S TOYS

Dean's Rag Book Company was a toy manufacturer which made not only printed rag books, but also dolls with moulded and painted faces. The 'Princess' range in the 1930s came with various accessories, including pet dogs.

▶ **Large cloth doll,** the 'Princess', made by Dean's, 1935. 3ft high (£300-£400)

DEAL

A general term for the woods of conifers such as pines or firs when cut into thin planks. Until the extraordinary craze for stripped pine in the 1980s, deals were intended to be used but not seen, and a distinction was made between valuable timbers and mere deals. Deals were used for flooring, the carcasses of pieces which were to be painted, drawer linings and the backs of furniture.

DEATHWATCH BEETLE

Xestobium rufovillosum, to be formal, particularly attacks oak and chestnut.

 Beetles appear in the months of April and May, when their tapping, which has a sexual rather than a morbid significance, is most likely to be heard.

DECANTER

A vessel, usually of glass, into which wine is 'canted' or poured for serving at table. The earliest, made by George Ravenscroft in the third quarter of the

▲ **Cut-crystal pillar wine** decanter, Anglo-Irish, c1830 (£260)

17th century, were still called 'bottles', but were more ornamented. Some had handles, but basically they followed the 'shaft and globe' design of wine bottles. During the 18th century other shapes, such as the mallet, the polygonal and the cruciform, were developed.

They were often engraved with bottle labels, trailing vines or hops, or cut into facets or flutes. Conical decanters, popular during the Napoleonic Wars, are known as ships' or RODNEY decanters. Jeroboam and magnum decanters exist, and miniatures of all styles were made, usually as 'toys'. Claret jugs, with handles and pouring lips, are also known as claret decanters. From the end of the 18th century

A man of

PAUL DE LAMERIE (1688-1751)

Paul de Lamerie was baptised on April 14, 1688, at s'Hertogen-bosch in the Netherlands. The family, as Huguenots, had fled France following the revocation of the Edict of Nantes in 1685. Paul's father served in the army of William III, and moved on to England in the train of the King.

At 15, Paul was apprenticed to Pierre Platel for a seven-year term, but it was not until 1713 that he became a Freeman of the Goldsmiths' Company and registered his first mark. This long apprenticeship suggests he was being groomed as Platel's successor.

De Lamerie had a cavalier attitude to authority. He was frequently in trouble, most often for not having work hallmarked and then not paying the resulting fine. On one occasion the authorities wished to inspect a large shipment of silver being sent to Russia of which about half was by de Lamerie. A little refreshment was suggested before boarding. When they eventually left the tavern, the ship had sailed!

He was also in trouble for sending pieces to be marked as if they were his own when they had been made by

◀ **Coffee pot** by de Lamerie, c1735 (£85,000)

sterling character

others who did not have registered marks. We do not know how many of 'de Lamerie's' early pieces are really from his own workshop. However, by 1716 he appears as a royal goldsmith and in 1717 he was made a Liveryman of the Goldsmiths' Company.

In 1723 he took out an insurance policy on his business for £1,000, and apart from this he had significant property holdings. This policy reveals that he was in partnership with the silver engraver Ellis Gamble, who is best known for having been the master of William Hogarth. There have been attempts to attribute the engravings on de Lamerie's pieces to Hogarth, and there were close links between them — de Lamerie even had his book plate engraved by Hogarth.

In 1732 de Lamerie registered his first sterling standard maker's mark. Interestingly, he was the last to do so of those who had been working in 1720 (when sterling was reintroduced as an alternative to BRITANNIA STANDARD).

Up to the early 1730s de Lamerie's work displayed a mastery of the formal BAROQUE, using the designs of Daniel MAROT as source material for some of his most important work. Then

there was a radical and rapid change as de Lamerie became the great leader of English Rococo. Whether this was the result of his own genius or of his employing a new designer/modeller is not clear.

When he died in 1751, his obituary in the London *General Evening Post* said: 'Last Thursday died Mr Paul de Lamerie of Gerrard Street much regretted by his Family and Acquaintance as a Tender Father, a Kind Master and an Upright Dealer.'

▲ Fine George II bread basket by de Lamerie (£66,000)

◀ Pair of George II tea caddies and matching sugar box, with later (c1770) ebony case. Value is reduced by removal and replacement of original arms (£15,000-£18,000)

▼ Two views of a de Lamerie marrowbone scoop, 1733, with detail of mark (right), seen at the Blenheim Palace Roadshow (£3,000-£5,000)

straight-sided decanters were made, which were more suitable for containing spirits. They were also used in sets in a frame such as the Victorian TANTALUS.

 £££-££££

DECEPTION TABLE

An 18th- and 19th-century table that looks like a PEMBROKE but, as Sheraton put it, serves for 'a pot cupboard, or any other private use which we would hide from the eye of a stranger'. One of the supposed gateleg flaps folds down to reveal compartments .

R ££££

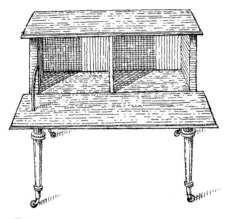

DECKCHAIR

First developed in the mid-19th century as the 'hammock chair'. The design of the adjustable deckchair has changed little since it was advertised in 1875 at 17s 6d in oak and canvas, or 25s in ebony with silk and wool.

££-£££

DELLA ROBBIA

Luca della Robbia (*c*1400-82) was the most prominent member of a family of Florentine ceramic sculptors. Typical products were reliefs of the Virgin and Child framed by fruit or flowers. Pale blue, yellow and orange are the most characteristic colours. Luca's nephew Andrea (1435-1528) and great-nephew Giovanni (1469-1529) extended the range. From the mid-19th century many forgeries were produced, and from 1894 to 1906 there was a pottery called the Della Robbia Company in Birkenhead.

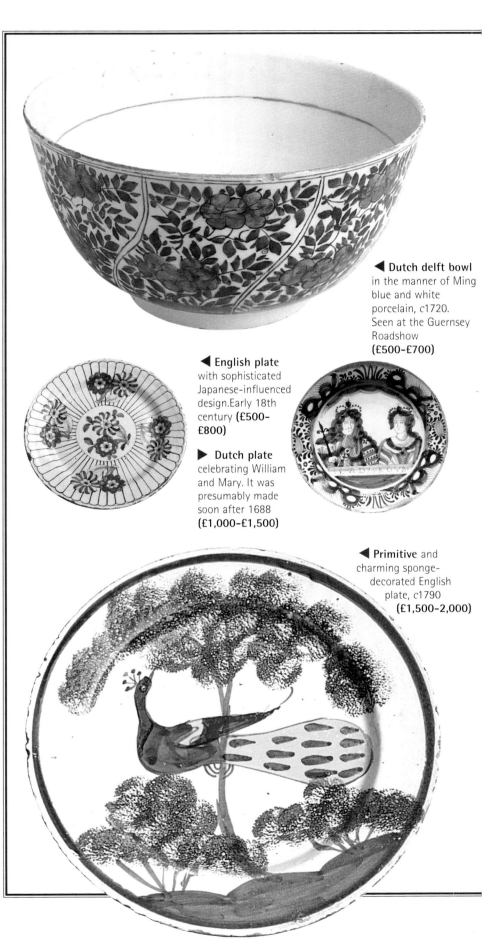

◀ **Dutch delft bowl** in the manner of Ming blue and white porcelain, c1720. Seen at the Guernsey Roadshow (£500-£700)

◀ **English plate** with sophisticated Japanese-influenced design.Early 18th century (£500-£800)

▶ **Dutch plate** celebrating William and Mary. It was presumably made soon after 1688 (£1,000-£1,500)

◀ **Primitive** and charming sponge-decorated English plate, c1790 (£1,500-2,000)

Delving deeply into blue and white

DELFT

The word has come to mean earthenware covered by a tin-oxide glaze made, not only in Holland, but in England. In France and Germany it is known as FAIENCE and in Italy and the Iberian peninsula, MAIOLICA.

The derivation is from 'delving' or digging the clay. Despite the name, delftwares were being produced in England and elsewhere in Holland before they were in Delft.

They were produced in Antwerp from 1508 and later at Amsterdam, Rotterdam and Haarlem. In Delft itself the most famed decorator is Frederik van Frijtom (active 1632-1702).

Most potteries there were located in disused breweries and they retained the former names such as The Metal Pot, The Double Bottle, The Old Moor's Head and The Peacock. During the 17th century they concentrated on BLUE AND WHITE, usually emulating Chinese porcelain and making tulip holders, dishes, vases and, in vast numbers, tiles. These often formed pictures spread over a number of tiles, whereas this is almost unheard of in England.

In the 18th century, competition from elsewhere in Europe as well as enormously increased quantities of Chinese porcelain, reduced standards and in the early 19th century, the industry died. It was revived in the late 19th century for the tourist trade, frequently copying old patterns.

The first English delftware was made at Aldgate, London, from 1571, and potteries at Southwark, Bristol, Lambeth and elsewhere soon followed. Records are poor and attribution to a particular site is haphazard. Much was of high quality and almost all have a naïve charm. Dated examples exist and sell at a premium.

▼ **English flower brick**
These were for plant propagation rather than use as a vase, c1730
(£300-£400)

► **English delft beer mug**, with rare pig-butchering scene, dated 1777 on base. Seen at the Newcastle Emlyn Roadshow
(£6,000-£8,000)

Modelled on past glories

DERBY

The story of porcelain manufacture in Derby has to be split into three parts — the original factory in Nottingham Road (c1748-1848), the Sampson Hancock factory in King Street (1848-1935) and the Derby Crown and later the Royal Crown Derby factory in Osmaston Road (from 1875 to the present). The first factory is thought to have been founded by Andrew Planché, a silversmith and son of a HUGUENOT immigrant, whose figures have great strength of modelling. These early figures, usually left 'in the white', are known as 'dry edge' for the way the glaze stops short at the foot, exposing the biscuity-looking body.

In 1756, the factory was taken over by William Duesbury the first, who also took over the CHELSEA factory, resulting in a period known as Chelsea/Derby when the Chelsea anchor was conjoined with the D of Derby.

His son William continued in 1786 and surrounded himself with a superb group of modellers, painters and gilders. At this point the major influence came from SÈVRES. In 1795 Duesbury took Michael Kean into partnership but died two years later. In 1811, the factory was rented by Robert Bloor but the business folded in 1848. This may have been due in part to the often poor quality of the paste which may turn brown and a glaze which cracks badly. The mark was a crowned D.

The King Street factory was formed by Sampson Hancock and some workers of Bloor's. The wares were very similar, as was the factory mark, with a crown above crossed batons and three dots with a D below and the initials S and H either side of the batons. The factory closed in 1935.

In 1875 Edward Phillips moved to Derby from WORCESTER, where he had been a director of Royal Worcester. He had a new factory built in Osmaston Road. Although many of the decorations and shapes were based on those of the past, new decorators revived the qualities of the 18th century. Perhaps the greatest was Desiré Leroy, whose painting, gilding and jewelling, developed at Sèvres, rank among the finest English porcelain work.

Their most frequently encountered products are the famous IMARI pattern in underglaze blue, red and gilding, still made today. The patterns were painted on miniature kettles, irons, cauldrons and so on, which are widely collected.

The title 'Royal' was granted by Queen Victoria in 1890 and the Royal Crown Derby Porcelain Company continues to this day. The current mark has the name in full as well as a crown over interlaced Ds.

▲ Royal Crown Derby dish, painted by W. Dean, 1921. Seen at the Derby Roadshow (£120-£150)

◀ Derby figure of a hind, c1770. Value diminished because it is chipped (£200)

DE MORGAN, WILLIAM (1839-1917)

One of the leading English pottery designers of the 19th century. He was working with William MORRIS from the 1860s, and was to pottery what Morris was to wallpaper. He set up his own factory in Fulham in 1888, and from 1892 he spent his winters working in Florence. He was particularly influenced by HISPANO-MORESQUE styles and techniques, as well as classical Greek and Persian and is best known for his revival of lustre decoration. He produced wonderfully bold plates and tiles, on which the figures manage to be both stylised and lively. He retired in 1905.

DENBY

A pottery founded in Denby, Derbyshire in 1809, which began by trying to emulate Staffordshire stoneware. Nowadays it specialises in simple, oven-proof kitchen pottery.

£-££

DENDROCHRONOLOGY

The science of dating wooden objects by the growth rings in their timber. It is obviously essential to know the area in which the tree flourished for a comparative study to be made. Annual growth rings in timber are to some extent dictated by weather conditions, which are often recorded.

DENTIL

A small, rectangular block, often used in a row, like teeth, below a cornice.

▲ Portable desk slope, 1874. Seen at the Huddersfield Roadshow (£1,500)

DESK SLOPES

Portable oak desks were known as writing boxes in the 17th century, and might be fitted with tills, drawers and pigeonholes for papers. In the 18th century and Regency periods they might be 2ft long and oblong when closed, and are generally in mahogany with military/style brass corners and handles, while the Victorians preferred shallower rectangular boxes, like the tops of DAVENPORT desks, and these are sometimes leather-covered. Fittings might include inkwells, tinder and sanding boxes, penholders and pen and paper knives. Similar boxes, but upright, were made to stand on *bureaux plats* and writing tables. These are fitted for stationery, and the fronts fold down to make a slope.

££-££££

DERUTA

A group of Umbrian potteries which began to make MAIOLICA in the late 15th century, reputedly under the patronage of Cesare Borgia. It is difficult to tell their wares from those produced at FAENZA or GUBBIO, and later the decorators imitated the styles of Urbino. Among the earliest wares are distinctive 'petal-backed' dishes, although products of the factory are still not firmly attributed and may be confused with those of from FAENZA or Sienna

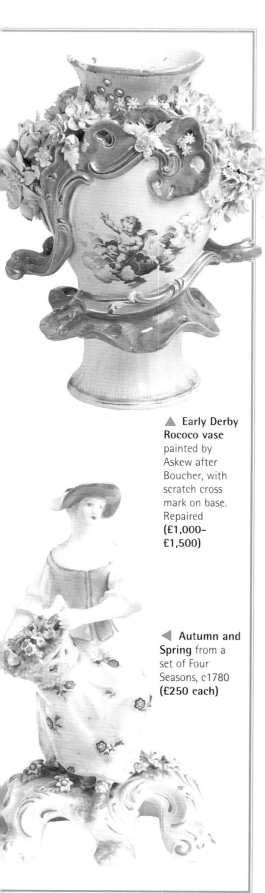

▲ Early Derby Rococo vase painted by Askew after Boucher, with scratch cross mark on base. Repaired (£1,000–£1,500)

◄ Autumn and Spring from a set of Four Seasons, c1780 (£250 each)

TALKING ANTIQUES

DISTRESSED

A term, mostly, of furniture, covering legitimate age or deliberate ageing. In the former any serious wear and tear gives rise to the condition which is one stage worse than 'country house condition'. Fakes and forgeries are often distressed by attacking with chains, hammer blows and spikes to simulate worm holes. A book which is in desperate need of rebinding may be described as 'distressed'.

DEUTSCHE BLUMEN

German flowers, also known as Strasbourg flowers, are naturalistically painted. Either used separately or tied into bouquets, they were employed as decoration on ceramics (illustrated below). Often they included insects buzzing around the plants. As a motif this originated at Vienna in about 1730, and the fashion was taken up by J.G. Horoldt at MEISSEN between 1750 and 1765, before spreading to many of the other European factories.

DIAPER ORNAMENT

A repetitive pattern of ornament such as lozenges, diamonds or rectangles, each of which encloses a motif. In textiles this is achieved by contrasting the warp and weft faces of the same weave. Similar effects are also used to decorate silverware and various other materials.

DIE-CAST TOYS

These are made by pouring molten metal (often lead) into moulds and pressing them. It is inexpensive and fast. The first die-cast toys were produced in America and France around 1914, but BRITAIN, and DINKY TOYS in particular, soon took over as the world's leaders.

£-££

DIE-STAMPING

Decoration on silver, using a die to create a pattern in relief.

DISHED SEAT

A flat wooden seat on a chair or stool, sunk below the seat rails so as to keep a cushion in place.

English

▲ FAB1, Lady Penelope's pink Rolls-Royce from Thunderbirds (£30-£40 unboxed)

Moving into

DINKY TOYS

Not everyone who played with their products may have realised that three of the greatest names of British 20th-century toy-making were divisions of the same corporation.

The first die-cast cars to be made by Meccano were announced by Frank HORNBY — famous for his 0- and 00-Gauge model trains — in 1933, but the first Dinky toys reached the market only in the following year. They were immediately successful and by the end of 1934 more than 150 models had been issued. It ensured that Meccano had a virtual monopoly of the British

market until the 1950s.

Pre-war models are avidly collected, especially such rarities as the mid-1930s Pickford's delivery van, or the model 36d Rover saloon with its tinplate driver.

Boxed aeroplane sets are also dear to the hearts of collectors — but the condition is always of prime importance to the value. Hairline cracks are the first sign of metal fatigue, and their discovery can strip hundreds of pounds from the price of even the most coveted rarity. There is a temptation that must be resisted to brighten up chipped paint with new colour. Repainting reduces the value considerably and

▼ Captain Scarlet's personal transport, and his maximum security vehicle (right), 1960s (£20-£30, each unboxed)

the money

▲ Junkers JU87B Stuka World War II plane in original box (£25-£35)

collectors need to be on their guard against 'freshening' the paintwork.

During the late 1930s Dinky Toys approached transport companies such as Pickford's with the proposal that they issue personalised toy vans in well-known liveries. All were loosely based on the contemporary Ford van, but they were individually decorated with transfers.

In a recent auction the only known example decorated in the colours of Bentalls department store in Kingston-upon-Thames sold for £12,650, more than double any previous price. Originally it had cost 6d – still well short of £1 in today's money. It must be emphasised that this

was exceptionally rare (if another were to turn up, it might not make as much), and in good order.

The Second World War saw aeroplanes issued in camouflage finish but after 1942 the factory was turned over to war work. In April 1946 post-war production re-started with a Jeep and a Lagonda.

In the 1950s Meccano suffered from increasing competition from other companies, such as Mettoy, with CORGI Toys, and LESNEY products with their Matchbox models.

As with all other toys, the original boxes are highly prized. Quite often a box in good condition will double the value of the toy which lacks it.

▼ No 12 postal set with Royal Mail van, pillar boxes and telephone box, in original box, 1930s (£300-£350)

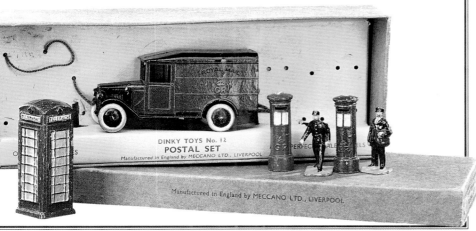

DISH RING AND CROSS
Supports for holding hot dishes, to protect polished surfaces. The crosses were hinged cruciform frames in silver or Sheffield plate. Because many of the pierced silver rings, usually about 3in high and 8in diameter, were made in Ireland during the 18th century, they are also, incorrectly, known as potato rings.

£££-££££

DISPENSARY
A small version of a MEDICINE CHEST, measuring from 9in to 12in high, 10in to 13in wide and perhaps 8in deep, with racks in the doors and other places for up to nine bottles as well as drawers, shelves and compartments for scales, measures, pestle and mortar and GALLIPOTS. There are a number of variations on the basic design.

££-£££

▲ Apothecary's dispensary chest by John Bell of London, complete with many original medicine bottles. Seen at the Inverness Roadshow, 1840 (£600-£900)

DIVAN EASY CHAIR
A late 19th-century, high-backed armchair with rollover arms and a long seat which projects beyond the arms in a bow shape. It is similar to a club chair, and if there is a little drawer in the front of the seat it is a smoker's chair.

£££-££££

◀ One of a pair of Doccia Commedia dell'Arte figures of Scaramouche and Ragonda (£17,000 the pair)

DOCCIA

A Florentine factory founded by Marchese Carlo Ginori in 1737, using Italian modellers and Viennese decorators. The earliest figures and tableware may look dull because of the greyish hard-paste and glazes used, but the large figures and groups are impressive. Armorial tableware can also be of high quality, and from the 1760s new bodies and glazes gave the porcelain a greater whiteness. After a flirtation with SÈVRES patterns the factory reverted to type in the 19th century. They made copies of CAPODIMONTE, marking them with the crowned N of Naples. The Ginoris remained in control until 1896, and their factory still flourishes. Unlike its backward-looking British counterparts, it produces fine modern designs and some of the best porcelain made in Italy today.

DOG

Apart from their own merits, and necessary use in hunting subjects, dogs in art may represent fidelity, watchfulness or the sense of smell. In the 18th century pug dogs may appear as a symbol of Freemasonry. William Hogarth's pug Trump not only appears in his self-portraits, but was popular as a model of fidelity, based on the sculpture by Roubilliac, which was used by both CHELSEA and WEDGWOOD.

DOG OF FO

A Chinese half-dog, half-lion which stood in pairs at the entrances to Buddhist temples, Fo being one of the many names of the Buddha. They also guard precious works of art. They may be shown playing with a silk ball and ribbon, and/or spitting flames. Western potters adopted them as finials from the late 17th century.

DOG TOOTH

A zig-zag, triangular decorative moulding, which was most popular from the Early English Gothic period to the 16th century. It appears on furniture and woodwork as well as in brick and stone.

◀ Chinese blanc-de-chine Dog of Fo, made for export to late Europe, late 17th century, 8in high (£300–£400)

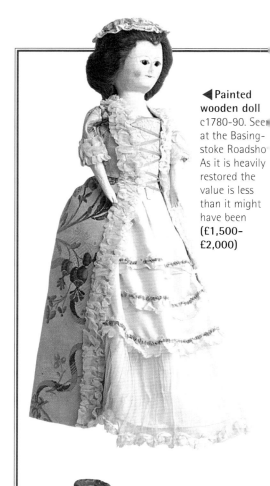

◀ Painted wooden doll c1780-90. Seen at the Basingstoke Roadsho As it is heavily restored the value is less than it might have been (£1,500–£2,000)

◀ South German peg-jointed wooden doll with papier mâché head and original clothes, c1820s (£1,000 £1,500)

It's a doll's life

DOLLS

Dolls have been made for thousands of years: fired clay examples date back to 3000BC. Wooden dolls from the 17th and early 18th centuries are rarely found today, and when one appears at auction it commands a high price. As early as 1974 two William and Mary wooden dolls sold at auction for a record £16,000 — they are now in the Victoria and Albert Museum. A similar doll, by the same craftsman, made a new world record of £67,100 in a London sale in March 1987.

During the first half of the 19th century dolls with PAPIER-MÂCHÉ heads and peg-jointed wooden bodies were produced in France and Germany. Today, one of these, with an elaborate moulded hairstyle, in good condition and wearing original clothes, can fetch up to £1,000 at auction. While these and the early wooden dolls have risen steadily in price, they do not have such a wide buying market as the later bisque ones.

English wax dolls of the 18th century are still found, though rarely in good condition, light and heat being their enemies. Poured wax, waxed papier-mâché and waxed-composition dolls were produced in large quantities in 19th century England and Germany. They are still undervalued and should be a good investment for first-time buyers. Some people, though, find them macabre, the wax lending rather too human a resemblance for their liking. Prices usually range between £500 and £1,000-plus for those in good condition with original clothes. The most famous makers were two Italian families working in London, Montanari and Pierotti.

Bisque (unglazed porcelain) dolls first appeared in France towards the middle of the 19th century. The early heads were pressed rather than poured into a mould, and then fired before being fitted snugly to bisque shoulder plates and secured to well-formed, stitched and waisted kid bodies. Clothed in coloured silks and satins, they were known as fashion dolls and portrayed the modish clothes of the day.

Famous early manufacturers were Casimir Bru, François Gaultier, Huret, Emile Jumeau, Radiquet et Cordonnier, Rohmer, Schmitt et Fils and Jules Steiner. Rabery et Delphieu and Thuillier came later. From 1899 many of these firms amalgamated to form the Societé Français de Fabrication des Bébés et Jouets (SBFJ). From this time only the rare mould numbers of SFBJ command four-figure prices.

Early German manufacturers in demand are Alt, Beck and Gottschalke, Bähr and Proschild, Kämmer and Reinhardt, J.D. Kestner, Kley and Hahn, and Simon and Halbig. The world auction record is held by mould number 108 by Kämmer and Reinhardt, manufactured in 1909, which sold in 1994 for £188,000.

Despite high prices for bisque dolls there is scope for the collector from a few pounds for 1950s stuffed dolls and there are devotees of composition (sawdust and glue, papier-mâché and even CELLULOID.)

As with most toys, condition is all important, cracks to the head decimating the value. Wear to painted papier-mâché limbs is less important, and detached or floppy parts can be re-strung, increasing the value. Old clothes in poor condition are better than any new clothes. Moving eyes often detach and can be reset and, if lost, replaced — although modern eyes are far less good than early ones.

▲ French bisque-headed doll by Gaultier, c1860s (£500-£700)

◀ Doll by Lenci of Turin, seen at the Luton Hoo Roadshow (£200)

Tiny Towers

DOLLS' HOUSES

It is hard to find early dolls' houses complete with their original contents. The earliest to be put up for auction was dated 1675. Although empty, it commanded a bid of £25,300 at Sotheby's in 1988.

One of the earliest fully furnished English houses, c1735, is at Nostell Priory in West Yorkshire. Queen Mary's doll's house at Windsor Castle, complete with wine cellar and miniature copy of *Country Life*, is one of the most famous today.

Titania's Palace, the most expensive dolls' house sold at auction, was lovingly built over 15 years by Sir Nevile Wilkinson for his daughter. On completion in 1922, it was officially 'opened' by Queen Mary. Titania's Palace contains an art gallery of miniature pictures by famous artists. Micro-mosaics are painted on walls and floors, and real gemstones adorn a jewel-encrusted throne. In 1978 it was bought at Christie's for the record price of £135,000 by Legoland in Denmark, where it is now exhibited.

▲ German doll's house by Morris Gottschalk, 19th century (£800-£1,200)

Although late 19th- and early 20th-century dolls' houses with little or no furniture can be found at auction for prices as low as £300, they command upper hundreds or several thousands of pounds if they include contemporary furnishings and contents.

DOLLOND, JOHN (1706- 61)

The best-known English optician had already had a career as a silk-weaver when he joined his son Peter (1730 - 1820) in a scientific instrument making business at 'The Sign of the Golden Spectacles and Sea Quadrant'

▼ Dollond astral telescope seen at Huddersfield Roadshow, c1840 (£250-£300)

in the Strand. Around 1760 he invented an achromatic lense, which reduced colour distortion in TELESCOPES. The business continues today as Dollond & Aitchison.

DOLPHIN

The dolphin is the king of 'fish', as the lion and the eagle are kings of beasts and birds. It was much used in classical art, as an attribute of Poseidon or Neptune, and it is also a symbol of Christ and the early Church– with an anchor it represents the Church guided by Christ. From the Renaissance onwards it served as a motif in many forms, appearing in feet and decorative masks for furni-

ture (by CHIPPENDALE and others) and silver, taps and spouts, supports for lamp standards and as an element in Baroque and ROCOCO scrollwork. A dolphin hinge is used on the fall front of a *secretaire*, and is, naturally, dolphin-shaped.

DORIC – SEE ORDERS

DOOR FURNITURE

The general term for knobs, handles, finger plates, escutcheons, which may be in matching sets, as well as the locks, latches, bolts and hinges that are used on doors.

DOUBLE DOMED

Two domes which make the top part of a bureau bookcase look like Siamese twin cupboards. It was a popular form in the early 18th century, and reappeared on Art Deco kitchen furniture.

▲ Detail of a double domed bureau bookcase in less than perfect condition

DOWER CHEST

A chest, generally large and oak, for storing clothes and household fabrics. It may or may not have started life in the 16th or 17th century as a container for a bride's dowry, as Victorian romantics thought.

£££-££££

DRAGON

Twenty-five distinct species of dragon are recorded in the medieval bestiaries. In general they have reptilian heads and bodies, eagles' or bats' wings, claws and powerful, perhaps barbed, tails. They may well spit fire. Dragons proper have four legs, but wyverns, such as the Welsh 'dragon', have eagles' talons for forelegs. A griffin, or gryphon, has the head, wings and claws of an eagle, the body of a

Doing the Lambeth walk

DOULTON

In the early 19th century, London's Lambeth riverfront was a centre for the manufacture of stoneware. In 1815 John Doulton bought an interest in one of these companies, and by the mid-1820s Doulton and Watts had become one of the largest LAMBETH potteries.

A few years later, John's son Henry joined and, under his guidance, the range expanded to include garden ornaments, architectural terracotta, drainpipes and sanitary fittings. Doulton was at the forefront of the sanitary revolution then sweeping through the world's major cities.

Inspired by John Sparkes, principal of the Lambeth School of Art, Henry Doulton set up an art pottery studio in the late 1860s to develop a new range of art stonewares. Initially small and experimental, this project

quickly succeeded, thanks to the abilities of the trained students drawn to it, such as Hannah BARLOW and George TINWORTH. By the 1880s the Lambeth studio was employing more than 200 men and women, many of whom were able to produce highly individual work in an industrial setting.

In 1877 Henry took over a Burslem-based manufacturer of domestic earthenwares. Under his dynamic leadership, this became a major producer of tablewares and ornaments in earthenware and bone china, establishing the reputation that Doulton enjoys today.

Finely painted porcelains, decorative figurines, Toby wares, printed Series wares and flambé wares were all part of the diverse range that made Doulton the leading pottery of the late 19th and early 20th centuries, and gave its products lasting appeal.

◀ Doulton stoneware jardinière with date mark, seen at Luton Hoo Roadshow, 8in high 1897, (£200-£300)

▲ Royal Doulton porcelain figure of Princess Badoura seated on an elephant, 1924. (£3,000-£4,000) Re-issued 1952 (£1,000-£1,500)

▶ Set of Doulton spirit flasks in original basket, 1881 (£250-£350)

lion and the beard of a goat. Although the dragon was a Celtic symbol of kingship, the Occidental creatures are almost always destructive and symbols of evil. Their Oriental counterparts are beneficent, representing strength, wisdom and fertility. The Chinese dragon may be even more mongrel, having a camel's head with demon's eyes topped by cow's ears and stag's horns; a snake's neck; clam's belly; carp's scales; eagle's claws; and tiger's pads. It may well clasp or play with the flaming pearl of wisdom, and is often accompanied by the Ho-Ho bird, or Chinese phoenix, when they represent pairs of opposites, usually the Emperor and Empress. The Imperial dragon most often has five claws, the common dragon four and the Japanese dragon three.

▼ **Detail of a dragon** on a Chinese Davenport, made for the European market, mid-19th century

DRAGON'S BLOOD

The bright red resin of the dragon-tree (*dracaena*), which was used from at least the 17th century to colour polishes and in JAPANNING.

DRAW TABLE

An extending, usually oak table in which end leaves slide under the central section when closed. Although known from the 17th century, they are most commonly met as Victorian and modern reproductions.

 £££-££££

DRESDEN

A name commonly used for the products of the MEISSEN factory which is nearby. Reject blanks were decorated at Dresden and it also housed numerous decorating shops painting on porcelain, including Helena Wolfsohn and Lamm. Many small-factories in the Saxony area made porcelain in the 19th and 20th centuries in Meissen style and these are lossely grouped under the Dresden name. Some used the city name on their products. J.F. BÖTTGER ran a faience factory there before his discovery of porcelain in 1708.

DRESSER

From the French *dressoire*, on which food was dressed. By the late 17th century, drawers were common beneath such sideboards, but only after about 1690 were superstructures added. These might have backboards and often had cornice friezes above, and carved below the drawers, with cabriole front legs. Low dressers continued to be made, remaining in dining rooms, while high ones migrated kitchenwards. Many regional variations exist, although Shropshire and other examples are often miscalled 'Welsh'. True Welsh pieces are usully oak. South Wales: 'pot board' shelves at floor level. Pembroke: 'dog kennel' between cupboards.

Yorkshire: central clock, up to 12 drawers below. Lancashire: similar drawers. Bridgwater: verticle sides made of single pieces of wood. Devon: panelled upper section doors. Suffolk: elaborate friezes, shelves and aprons.

£££-££££

▲ **Lady's fitted dressing** case with bottles and secret drawer, late 19th century (£1,000-£1,200)

DRESSING BOX

A small box, measuring perhaps 8in by 12in by 7in high with compartments for jewellery, cosmetics and toilet accessories, and a small looking-glass fixed inside the lid. They are known from Elizabethan portraits. Pepys noted in 1667 that he took little Betty Michell 'over the water to the cabinet makers and there bought a dressing box for her for 20s'. Large examples are sometimes miscalled glove or lace boxes.

£££-££££

DRESSING TABLE

Originally a small table with two or three drawers, the dressing or toilet table for both ladies and gentlemen became more elaborate during the 18th century. The glass, either swinging or folding down, became an essential, and in the 19th century the three-panel glass started to be usual. DRESSING CHEST or dressing commode were terms used by CHIPPENDALE and SHERATON for small chests of drawers, with the topmost drawer 'divided into conveniences for dressing'.

Sometimes, according to Sheraton, the top was hinged, with the dressing part in a well beneath it rather than a drawer, and the glass hinged in its turn. In this case there might be a wash basin. A dressing stand was a late 18th-century term for a compact,

◄ **19th-century kitchen dresser**

▲ Irish oak dressing table with cabriole legs and ball and claw feet, c1750 (£10,000–£12,000)

squarish dressing chest, containing a pot as well as a basin.

🗄️🪛🏰 £££–££££

DROP HANDLE

A drawer handle, or sometimes a door handle (especially for cupboards), shaped like a tear drop and suspended from a circular back-plate. They are usually hollow in cast-iron or brass. They were popular in the 17th century, and were often shaped like pears or acorns.

DROP-LEAF TABLE

A table with hinged leaves, which are supported by gate or other hinged legs or FLY BRACKETS.

DRUNKARD'S CHAIR

A Victorian name for an 18th-century type of chair with an unusually wide-fronted seat—perhaps 2ft 9in to a depth of 1ft 10in. They are often mahogany elbow chairs, and were made for the comfort of gentlemen wearing heavy, broad-skirted coats, irrespective of their lack of sobriety.

🗄️🪛 🏰 £££–££££

DUCHESSE AND DUCHESS BED

In his *Guide* (1788) HEPPLEWHITE illustrates a 'duchesse' day bed made up of two tub chairs with a matching stool between them. In 1803 SHERATON showed a similar arrangement, but below an elaborate canopy held up by posts attached to the backs of the chairs, and this he called a duchess bed.

🗄️🪛 🏰 R ££££

Way out front

DRESSER, CHRISTOPHER (1834–1904)

The most advanced designer of the 19th century began his career as a botanist and was a doctor of the University of Jena in Germany. On his rejection for the professorship at London in 1860 he turned to design full time, both writing and working for WEDGWOOD, MINTON, COALBROOKDALE and, from the mid-1870s, ELKINGTON.

Many early pottery and silver designs show Japanese influence. In 1876 he went to Japan via America, where he was appointed buyer for TIFFANY. On his return his work became much more abstract. He designed furniture for the Art Furnishers Alliance, silver and electroplate for HUKIN AND HEATH and James Dixon. Similar pieces in brass and copper for Benham and Froude and Richard Perry, pottery for LINTHORPE and Ault, and the Clutha range of art glass for James Couper.

He also produced textile and wallpaper designs. He is best known for his Hukin and Heath and Dixon's claret jugs, toast racks and so on, which make many Art Deco pieces look old hat and derivative.

Anyone coming fresh to a Dresser exhibition would find it hard to believe that one man could have produced such a range of designs with so many contrasts.

▶ Silver and glass claret jug designed by Dresser for Heath and Middleton, 1886 (£2,500–£3,000)

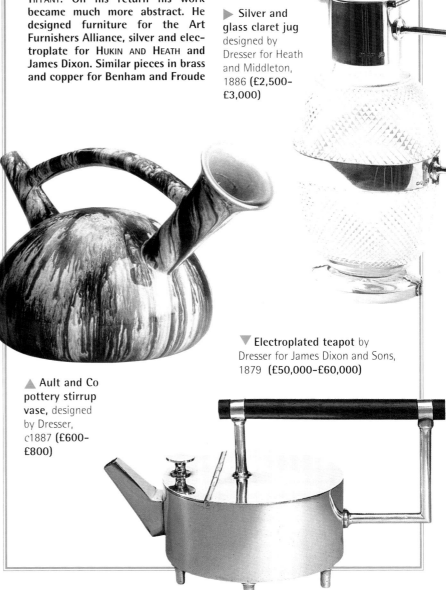

▲ Ault and Co pottery stirrup vase, designed by Dresser, c1887 (£600–£800)

▼ Electroplated teapot by Dresser for James Dixon and Sons, 1879 (£50,000–£60,000)

DUET TABLE

An unusual, but practical, piece of Regency furniture, also known as a composer's table. It has two adjustable slopes to hold books or act as music stands, together with a drawer for writing equipment, and various slides for candles. It is also practical for use by a music teacher and pupil, as the players sit opposite each other.

£££

◄ Duet table by W.W. Wright, seen at Basingstoke Roadshow, c1820 (£3,000–£4,000)

DUFOUR, JOSEPH (active 1805-36)

The great maker of scenic wallpaper during the French Empire and *Restauration* periods. His first known product, c1805, was made up of 20 rolls representing the adventures and death of Captain Cook, and later he produced brightly coloured views of Paris, Venice, London, Constantinople and the Bay of Naples. There were also patriotic papers showing Napoleon's campaigns, and romantic ones on themes from Scott or Don Quixote. They were as popular in Britain and America as in France, and his company, Dufour et Leroy, continued until 1860.

DUMB WAITER

A term coined in the 1720s for a movable stand with two or more tiers of circular trays on a central column mounted on a tripod base with castors. Some were quite elaborate, with cutlery drawers

▲ Pair of mahogany dumb waiters, c1780. The price is high because pairs are rare (£10,000)

and plate racks. They should not be confused with LAZY SUSANS, nor with American dumb waiters, which are service lifts from below stairs to the dining room.

££££

DUMMY BOARD

Cut-out pictures of men, women, children or animals painted on thin boards, which were used as fire-screens in the 17th and 18th centuries. The fashion probably originated in the Netherlands. They were usually placed so that they cast a flickering shadow on the wall. They spawned imitations in the 19th century and again in the neo-Georgian 1930s.

£££-££££

▶ Dummy board from 17th century. Two or three times the value of later examples (£4,000– £6,000)

DUTCH GOLD

An alloy which was used in the 18th century as a substitute for gold leaf. It was made up of 11 parts copper to two parts zinc, and was naturally much cheaper than the real thing. However, as a writer noted in 1758: 'With any access of moisture, it loses its colour, and turns green in spots; and, indeed, in all cases its beauty is soon impaired, unless well secured by lacquer or varnish.'

DWARF BOOKCASE

In the early 19th century this meant any small bookcase. By the 1830s it was a more specific term for a case with two rows of books below a *secretaire* drawer, and four more rows above. Later again, it meant a bookcase of roughly table height with glazed doors.

DWIGHT, JOHN (c1635-1703)

An ecclesiastical lawyer who became one of the most important figures in the development of English pottery. In 1671 he patented his 'Transparent Earthenware. Commonly knowne by the Names of Porcelain of China and Persian Ware, as also the Misterie of Stone Ware, vulgarly called Cologne Ware'. He set up a pottery in Fulham making BELLARMINES and stoneware bottles. Tea drinking was coming into fashion at this time and he also made redstoneware teapots. His masterworks were more ambitious figures which ranged from small statuettes to superb life-sized busts in salt-glazed stoneware. The ELERS brothers were ex-employees of Dwight whom he was obliged to sue in order to protect some of his patents.

EAGLE

Since ancient times, the eagle has been king of the birds and the attribute of the god Jupiter, lord of the heavens and god of rain, thunder and lightning. It was taken over by Christian iconography as a symbol of spiritual strength and as the attribute of St John the Evangelist, hence its popularity on lecterns. A double-headed eagle was the insignia of the Holy Roman Empire and imperial Russia. Single-headed eagles were adopted by Prussia, Poland, Nazi Germany, the USA and France under Napoleon.

▶ George III ebonised and giltwood console table with eagle base (£38,000)

EARTHENWARE

Unlike STONEWARE, earthenware remains porous after firing and must therefore be covered with a glaze. It is categorised according to technique and country of origin into DELFT-WARE, MAIOLICA, MAJOLICA, CREAMWARE and SLIPWARE.

EASTLAKE, CHARLES LOCKE (1836-1906)

A designer, architect and writer who was enormously influential in replacing the fussy, over-stuffed furniture and decoration of the Victorian era with a much simpler style. His two most important publications were *History of the Gothic Revival* and *Hints on Household Taste in Furniture, Upholstery and Other Details*. His designs, which included wallpapers, textiles, wrought ironwork, ceramics and furniture, were popular in America where the adjective 'Eastlaked' was coined for the new style.

EASEL AND TRIPOD CLOCKS

Chiefly associated with Thomas Cole (active c1835-58), a London maker of high-quality clocks. They are beautifully hand-engraved with flowers, and their silvered brass dials are lacquered and painted with numerals and a retailer's name. Cole's name and work numbers are often hidden within the case. Easels are about 5in high with oval or rectangular faces, loops for hanging, swivels for standing upright and hinged easel legs for standing at an angle. Cole tripods are taller, with barometers and thermometers in the base and a plumb pendulum above. Cole's elder brother, John Ferguson Cole, made the first English CARRIAGE CLOCK in the 1820s.

£££-££££

EASY CHAIR

Although the term was originally applied to WING CHAIRS in the late 17th century, it now describes almost any upholstered chair from the 19th century onwards. One of the most highly regarded makers of easy chairs is Howard. The company used the best possible grade of filling—white animal hair overlaid with black horse hair—which is why they have lasted so well. Howard chairs often have a pinky-red floral lining, and the back legs and brass castors are stamped Howard and Co, or Howard and Sons.

£-£££

TALKING ANTIQUES

EBENISTE

In France the furniture industry was divided into highly specialised crafts. An *ébéniste* was a superior craftsman specialising in veneered furniture, whereas a *menuisier* specialised in carved wood.

▲ Charles Eastlake oak daybed (£2,000-£2,500)

EBONY

A jet black, heavy, fine-grained hard wood, sometimes streaked with yellow or brown. It is native to Asia and Africa. See also COROMANDEL.

EDWARDIAN REPRODUCTION FURNITURE

Although there was a demand for 18th-century-style furniture at the end of the 19th century, it is generally referred to as 'Edwardian reproduction'. By the turn of the century reproduction CHIPPENDALE chairs were valued more highly than originals. Repro furniture-makers still practised the methods of their predecessors, which is not always true today. However, there is often a feeling of lightness to Edwardian 18th-century pieces.

EGG AND DART

A common classical moulding consisting of alternating egg and V shapes, used to enrich an OVOLO moulding. It is found as a detail on plaster, wood and stone mouldings.

EGG SCISSORS

A pair of scissors with circular spiked blades for decapitating a boiled egg. They appeared during the Victorian period and are sometimes found with the body in the shape of a cockerel.

     ££

EGGSHELL PORCELAIN

A porcelain so thin that it resembles an eggshell. It was made in China

▲ Saucer from a Japanese eggshell tea service, 1930s (£1 a piece)

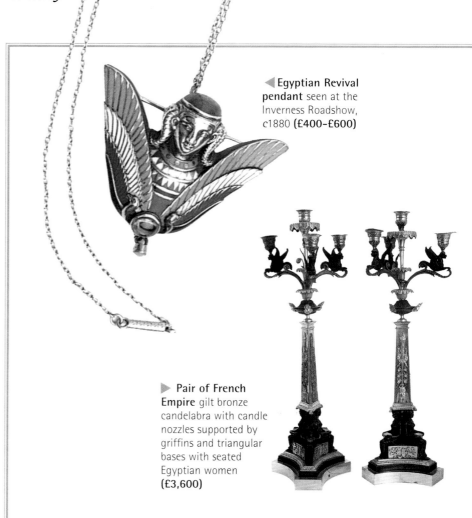

◄ Egyptian Revival pendant seen at the Inverness Roadshow, c1880 (£400-£600)

► Pair of French Empire gilt bronze candelabra with candle nozzles supported by griffins and triangular bases with seated Egyptian women (£3,600)

◄ Regency chiffonier with Egyptian monopodia decoration (£10,000-£15,000)

Exotic inspiration from the land of the pharaohs

EGYPTIAN STYLE

It was only after the middle of the 18th century that ancient Egyptian art began to make a serious impact on the West. Engraved sources gradually became more common and Egyptian motifs appear as an exotic ingredient in ROCOCO design. Piranesi used Egyptian decoration in the Caffè degli Inglese in Rome in 1769, but his understanding of it was limited.

Napoleon's Egyptian campaign resulted in the publication of the 23-volume *Déscription de l'Egypte* in **1809 and D. V. Denon's** *Voyages dans la Basse et la Haute Egypte* in **1803.** These provided an accurate source for designers and architects, and Egyptian-inspired forms and decoration began to appear on furniture, ceramics and metalwork, both in England, notably in the designs of Thomas HOPE and George Smith, and on the Continent.

Common motifs during the Regency period— although the style was never as strong in England as it was in France— are lion head terminals and paw feet.

Stylised ibis and scarabs also appear and there is considerable use of gilding. Often, legs have a band of opposed triangular stiff leaves.

One of the most extraordinary examples of the Egyptian style is the SÈVRES service made as a divorce present to Josephine from Napoleon. She rejected it and in 1818 it was presented to The Duke of Wellington. It is now in Apsley House, London. F. P. Robinson's Egyptian Hall in Piccadilly, 1812, and the interior of the Egyptian Hall at Stowe, c1800, are fine examples of the fashion for Egyptian architecture.

The discovery of the fabulous treasure buried in Tutankhamun's tomb in 1922 sparked another revival of Egyptian ornament, both on small-scale objects such as jewellery and textiles and on furniture and in the architecture of factories and cinemas such as Grauman's Egyptian theatre in Hollywood.

The British Empire Exhibition in 1924 featured a recreation of the tomb and numerous Egyptianesque commemoratives were produced including a Huntley and Palmer's biscuit tin.

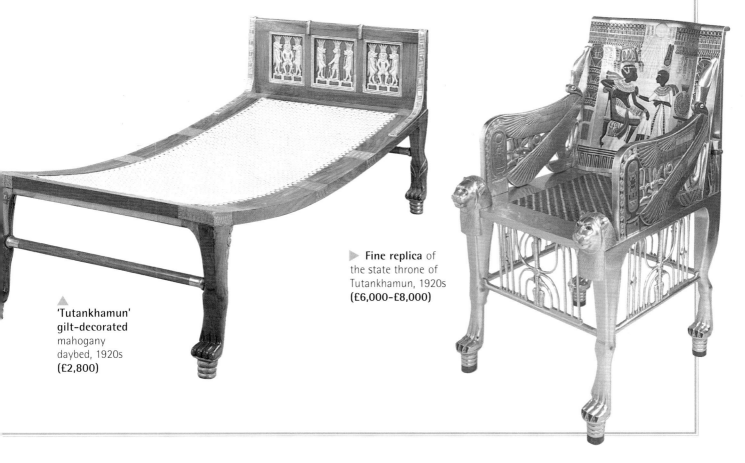

▲ 'Tutankhamun' gilt-decorated mahogany daybed, 1920s (£2,800)

▶ Fine replica of the state throne of Tutankhamun, 1920s (£6,000-£8,000)

during the Ming and Ching dynasties, but most came from Japan in the 1920s and 1930s.

 **£-££**

ELASTOLIN SOLDIERS

Elastolin was a compound of sawdust, resin and glue, which was moulded around a wire structure by German toy soldier manufacturers during the 1920s and 1930s. The best-known makers were Hausser and Lineol.

 £-££

ELBOW CHAIR

The 17th-century term for armchair from a set of dining-room chairs. It is now known as a carver.

ELECTRIC SHOCK MACHINE

In the 18th and 19th centuries static electricity provided a lot of fun. By 1780 Francis Hauksbee's original 1709 electrostatic friction generator had been considerably improved. A century later the most efficient model was produced by James Wimshurst, and sets of Wimshurst Tubes are often found in their compact mahogany boxes. Doctors believed electric shocks were good for certain conditions, but most generators were used as party entertainments.

££

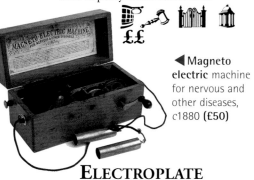

◀ **Magneto electric** machine for nervous and other diseases, c1880 (**£50**)

ELECTROPLATE

A silver coating deposited by electrolysis on to a base metal such as nickel alloy, BRITANNIA metal or copper. It is also known as electroplated nickel silver (EPNS). The process, patented by ELKINGTON in 1840, revolutionised the Sheffield plate industry, as it is faster and cheaper (using less silver) than the old rolled plate process. Worn objects can also be replated

Switching on in

ELECTRICAL DOMESTIC WARES

Electricity was catching on in the home by the late 19th century, and by the First World War the range of electrically-powered equipment for domestic use included cookers, heaters, kettles, clocks and vacuum cleaners. Other items, such as toasters, irons and hairdriers, soon followed, and by the early 1930s most of today's electrical goods existed, if in a rather rudimentary or primitive form.

Rarely very expensive today, such products have considerable appeal to the collector, thanks largely to their clearly defined period styling. Particularly popular are those with an Art Deco or 1950s flavour, such as streamlined, chrome-cased toasters, electric fires in maritime or architectural forms, Modernist clocks, BAKELITE-cased hairdriers and the famous bedside Teasmade, or those objects that can be associated with major industrial designers.

Inevitably, the most stylish and desirable are those made in the United States, the home of domestic and commercial Art Deco. As consumer

▲ Carron electric cooker, 1912 (£50-£100)

items, these pieces were often seen as fairly ephemeral and their survival has frequently been more by chance than design. For this reason they can be

cheaply. Sheffield plate that has been re-electroplated will have lost all crispness on details.

ELECTROTYPES

Three-dimensional 'castings' by electrodepositing were made from the mid-19th century to create replicas in copper of famous metalwork objects. They were then silver or occasionally gilded or enamelled. The finest lines were reproduced faithfully and pieces could be gem-set. The Victoria and Albert Museum became one of ELKINGTON's best clients, and between 1853 and the 1920s ordered more than

▲ 'John Company' elephant chess piece from a complete set

1,000 electrotypes from European collections. Many were in Russian collections, and during the Cold War electrotypes were the only means of studying the outstanding English silver in the Kremlin. Other makers in England included Signor Franchi, M. W. Johnson and Shaub and Son. Models commissioned by the V&A bear an official Science and Art Department mark, sometimes incorporating the name Elkington.

ELEPHANTS

When he conquered India, Alexander the Great used elephants, carrying wooden towers. The elephant and castle became a frequent medieval motif. Associated

the modern household

◀ **Dowsing patent fire** with Royal Ediswan elements, c1910 **(£30-£50)**

▶ **Machine** by the Eureka Vacuum Cleaner Co, c1920 **(£30-£40)**

▲ **German-made hairdrier,** c1935 **(£5-£10)**

bought more readily at car boot sales and antique markets than from specialist dealers.

Anyone using old or second-hand electrical products should remember that these items must be professionally checked first. Elderly wiring and worn-out components can be highly dangerous and in many cases it is illegal to sell appliances for use.

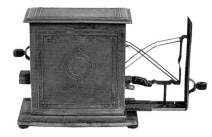

◀ **Universal toaster,** American-made, early 1920s **(£25-£35)**

---

also with Hannibal, the elephant was a symbol of victory and of chastity since it was believed to mate very reluctantly. Like the camel, another beast of burden, it was used as a decorative support for furniture and was popular in the later 18th and 19th centuries as a base for clocks, globes and lamps. SÈVRES vases were made with three elephant heads emerging in tripod form, their trunks forming candleholders. In the Victorian period, the elephant became associated with the Queen as Empress of India.

ELERS, DAVID AND CHARLES (active 1686-1700)

Brothers who began their careers as silversmiths in Holland and in 1686 settled in England, working for John DWIGHT in his Fulham pottery. From 1693 to 1698 they ran their own pot-

tery at Bradwell Wood, Staffordshire, making brown mugs and red stoneware teapots. Only a few pieces can definitely be attributed to them: mainly small mugs, teapots, canisters and cups of thin, fine, red stoneware, decorated with reliefs and very occasionally gilt or enamelling. They were much imitated.

ELKINGTON, GEORGE RICHARD (1829-36)

Trained as a gilt toy and spectacle-maker, in 1840 he patented the ELECTRO-PLATING technique, selling the licence to various silversmiths such

as Cristofle, and James Dixon in Birmingham. By 1847 he was producing huge quantities of tableware, especially for hotels and restaurants. He also made high-quality presentation and display pieces. Many of these were by leading French designers such as L. M. Ladeuil. His marks include E & Co in a shield and EM & Co with the firm's own date letter sequence.

◀ **Elkington electrotype** reproduction of a Renaissance cup and cover, c1850-70. Seen at the Taunton Roadshow **(£800)**

ELM

A coarse-grained, light brown timber used to make chair seats, table tops and coffins. The tree is a native of Britain, although most have succumbed to fatal disease in recent decades.

EMBOSSING

The technique of producing relief decoration by raising the surface of thin metal from the reverse of an object so as to form the design on the front. It is created using pressure and metal or stone dies, as opposed to REPOUSSÉ work, which is executed by hand.

▲Enamel tops and seats on French miniature furniture, c1890 (£700-£900)

ENAMELS

Enamels are glass-like substances, usually lead-soda or lead-potash based, with the addition of metallic oxide colorants which are fused to a base by heat in a kiln. The surface is hard and bright but has the same fragility as glass. Enamels are used on copper, brass or precious metals in CLOISONNÉ, CHAMPLEVÉ, CANTON, BATTERSEA and BILSTON wares coating the surface, or in PLIQUE À JOUR, where the enamel is used much as stained glass between metal supports. To compensate for the stresses set up between the metal and enamel the reverse surface is invariably also coated. Enamels are also the pigments, again metallic oxides, used by ceramic artists over the glaze and, as they are fired at a much lower temperature than those under the glaze, a wider range of colours is available. On soft paste porcelian bodies, the enamels sink into the glaze: on hard paste porcelain they remain slightly proud. In China, particularly in the 17th and 18th centuries, enamelling was executed on unglazed BISCUIT ground.

Fitted out in imperial splendour

EMPIRE STYLE

A French NEO-CLASSICAL style associated with Napoleon's ambitions for his new empire, which lasted from about 1800 to 1815. Its explicit classical references, such as palmettes, anthemions and winged lions, as well as Egyptian motifs intermixed with Napoleonic emblems including bees, giant Ns in laurel wreaths and eagles, were a propaganda attempt to identify France with the military prowess of ancient Rome.

The most important designers included C. Percier and P. Fontaine. Their influence is seen on furniture made by F. H. G. Jacob-Desmalter, silver by M. G. Biennais and J. B. C. Odiot, bronze and ormolu by P. P. Thomire and the silks woven at Lyons.

Exuberant tented draperies are a feature of the Empire style, and Jacquemart, Zuber and Bénard all designed wallpapers which imitate the effect. Emphasis shifted from handcrafted products for individual patrons to production on a semi-industrial scale. Jacob-Desmalter, Thomire and Biennais were all directors and factory owners who oversaw the production of their designs.

◄ Armchair from a suite of Empire giltwood seat furniture (single £2,000)

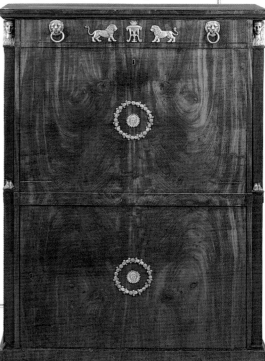

▼ South German ormolu-mounted mahogany secretaire (£5,500)

◄ One of a pair of Empire-style ormolu and bronze lamps in the form of Athéniennes (£20,000 the pair)

ENCAUSTIC TILES

Clay or brick tiles decorated with designs impressed from moulds into the damp clay and in-filled with a contrasting colour. They are then fired and can withstand considerable wear and tear. Encaustic tiles were made in the Middle Ages and are often found on the floors of cathedrals. The technique enjoyed a revival in the 19th century and was practised by architects such as A. W. N. PUGIN.

£-££

ENGRAVING

The technique of incising a metal surface with a sharply pointed steel tool known as a burin or graver. Metal is removed, leaving an indentation in the surface. The most common form of engraving was that done on copper or steel plates for printmaking, the print being the reversed image of the metal plate. But it was also employed as a technique for decorating silver and other metals, in particular with arms, monograms and commemorative inscriptions. Engraving was not done by a silversmith but was a specialist skill. One of the most famous engravers who decorated silver was the artist William Hogarth.

ENTRE-FENÊTRE

A narrow tapestry panel intended to hang between the windows but woven *en suite* with a set of larger figurative panels for the main walls.

▶ Aubusson entre-fenêtre, early 19th century (£3,800)

EPBM

Electro-plated BRITANNIA METAL. From the 1850s it was used as an alternative base to nickel silver for ELECTROPLATE, with the mark being found on objects after that date.

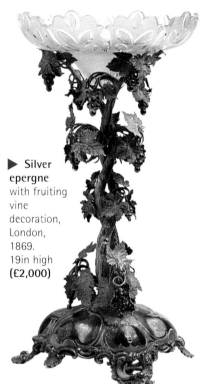

▶ Silver epergne with fruiting vine decoration, London, 1869. 19in high (£2,000)

EPERGNE

An elaborate table centrepiece which may support one single or several dishes or baskets hanging from branching arms. These were filled with fruits or bonbons. Some makers incorporated CANDLESTICKS. They were introduced in the 18th century and may be made of silver, plate, creamware, porcelain or glass.

£££-££££

ESCUTCHEON

In HERALDRY this is either the whole coat of arms or the shield on which the arms are painted. The word thus comes to mean anything shield-shaped, and small escutcheons are used as covers for keyholes on doors and furniture and as name plates.

ETAGÈRE

The French term for a WHATNOT.

ETUI

A small case fitted with miniature implements such as scissors, bodkins, needles, pencil and ivory writing tablet. It could either be hung on a CHATELAINE or carried in a pocket. Etuis were popular during the 18th century, came in various sizes and were often richly decorated with enamels and gilt hinges.

£££-££££

EWER AND BASIN

A tall, wide-mouthed jug and basin, decorated en suite and used for washing. Silver and porcelain examples were made for use in the dining room. Earthenware sets were made for the bedroom in the Edwardian period.

££-££££

▶ A French Empire ormolu-mounted opaline glass ewer and basin (£9,500)

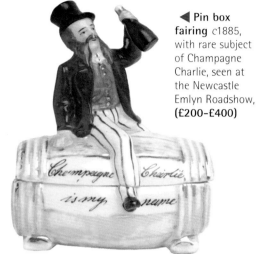

strongly influenced by the Venetian style throughout the 17th century.

◀ **Pin box fairing** c1885, with rare subject of Champagne Charlie, seen at the Newcastle Emlyn Roadshow, **(£200-£400)**

FACET CUT

The process of cutting gems, glass or metal so that the surface is completely covered with small, flat facets. In translucent materials it gives much greater brilliance as the amount of refracted light that escapes is greatly reduced. The technique was developed for cutting gemstones, especially diamonds which in a raw state have almost no sparkle. The rose cut, which has 24 facets, was introduced in the 15th century and was superseded in the 17th by the brilliant cut, which has 58 facets. Lead glass was ideally suited to this technique and in the 19th century was elaborately cut into sparkling prisms. Facet-cut steel was popular in the 18th and 19th centuries for buckles, buttons and even furniture made by the TULA factory in Russia.

FAÇON DE VENISE

Venetian-style glassware, made outside Venice but under the influence of Italian craftsmen, who by the late 16th century had set up glasshouses in France, Spain, Portugal, Bohemia, Germany, England and Scandinavia. While developing its own local characteristics, each one of the glasshouses continued to be

FAIRINGS

Small porcelain souvenir groups made at Pössneck, Saxony, in about 1860-1914, which were sold at country fairs and seaside stalls, hence the name. They often have a risqué or humorous content and inscriptions, mainly in English, inspired by popular songs. Made mostly for export, they were very popular in England but not in France or Germany. Little boxes were also made, decorated with humorous scenes and inscriptions. They are reproduced today but the modern ones are distinguishable by less crisp modelling and cruder glazes.

££-£££

◀ **Façon de Venise** goblet, 16th-century, seen at the Taunton Roadshow. **(£60-£80)**

▼ **'Come away do' fairing** inspired by a popular song **(£800-£1,200)**

◀ **Faenza** blue and white dishes. The one on the far left, c1650, is damaged (£1,000-£1,500). That on the near left is in good condition, c1580 (£5,000-£7,000)

Fancy that!

FAENZA-FAIENCE

Faenza. A group of Italian potteries, south of Ferrara, which produced excellent MAIOLICA from the mid-15th century. They used powerful colour schemes with dark blue, deep purple and orange predominating. The bold decoration has the mannered, sinewy vigour of contemporary Ferrarese painting. The early work is often confused with wares from DERUTA. After 1500 the contemporary ISTORIATO style was adopted, in particular by the Casa Pirotta factory. As this went out of fashion towards the end of the century, richly modelled wares with a thick white glaze, known as *bianco di Faenza*, were made. The potteries are still in production today.

Faience. Tin-glazed earthenware in maiolica style, especially that made in France, Germany and Scandinavia. The term is French and derives from Faenza pottery, which was especially popular in 16th-century France.

Faience patriotique. Generally fairly crudely potted wares made during the French Revolution from 1789 to 1794. They have patriotic inscriptions and revolutionary motifs such as flags or Phrygian caps. Genuine examples are rare and there are many later reproductions which are still being made today for the tourist trade.

◀ **Sicilian drug jar** seen at the Newcastle Emlyn Roadshow (£500-£700)

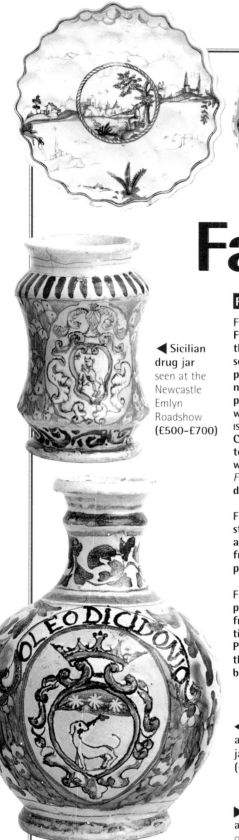

◀ **A fine maiolica armorial type jar,** also from Sicily (£1,500-£2,000)

▲ **Hanau faience** tankard, dated 1708 (£2,000-£3,000)

▼ **French hand-painted inkwell** made at Quimper, 20th century (£20)

▶ **Blue ground armorial tondinos** of Faience type, both c1600 (£1,500-£2,500)

▶ **Japanese Imari** bowl made in Canton within the last few years. Sold in high street shops (£20)

▲ **Nineteenth-century Coalport** copy of 18th-century Chelsea 'Goat and Bee' jug, seen at the Bridlington Roadshow (£60-£90)

▼ **Good Swiss watch** marked Breguet but not by him, c1825 (£1,200) If genuine £5,000 plus

▼ A reproduction **Van Cleef diamond, ruby and sapphire** bracelet (top), (£2,300). It is not as 'chunky' as the genuine article (below) (£60,000-£80,000)

Too good (or bad) to be true

FAKES AND FORGERIES

An object may be 'wrong' in a number of ways, and it is, therefore, important to be clear about the distinctions between terms.

FAKE: A genuine object that has been altered or converted, such as a wardrobe into a bureau-bookcase or an old map with later colouring. If an object is newly created in an attempt to deceive, it is a FORGERY. A REPRODUCTION is a copy or imitation of an earlier object or type with no intent to deceive — at least originally. Obviously this too can become a forgery, especially when 'DISTRESSED'.

Furniture: Since the 1960s, quantities of late 18th- and 19th-century style ORMOLU-mounted, marble-topped furniture 'by' Gouthiere and Beurdeley have been made in Paris, and appear even in reputable sales. Similar things are now being made in Poland, as well as 'Empire' wall lights and 'Louis XV' hall lamps with

one broken pane of glass and old wire, as if straight from an old house. Ormolu is one of the most difficult things for even experts to date.

Silver: Forgeries are rarely encountered because the strict silver laws have weeded out most of them. Forging HALLMARKS, or transferring marks from one piece to another, can incur a sentence of up to 10 years. Unmarked or wrongly marked pieces are unsaleable. Illegal alterations most commonly found are: tankards turned into coffee pots; christening mugs to cream jugs; 18th-century table spoons to APOSTLES.

Ceramics: A common problem is a class of porcelain made in China at the moment, probably at Guandong (Canton), and appearing on the market by the shipload. Most is heavily potted, vaguely reproducing FAMILLES ROSE and VERTE, Canton or Japanese IMARI. Designs are transfer-printed with matt black lines and hand-coloured. Marks are usually

▲ **Famille rose** teapot, 1770, seen at the Luton Hoo Roadshow **(£400)**

◄ **Fake Meerschaum pipe** made within the last ten years, of resin. Seen at the Blenheim Palace Roadshow **(£10-£20)**

'Canton', and often 'Qianlong'. These are acceptable as cheap decoration, but are not in antique shops or auctions. Another current Chinese line is 'Staffordshire' figures made of hard white porcelain rather than pottery, and stained with a black boot-polish-like pigment. They tend to be the more common late 18th- and 19th-century models, rather than rarities. The colours look authentic. A serious current deception is the later decoration of genuine porcelain to increase value.

Art Nouveau and Deco: While no one should mistake a Christopher Wray Art Nouveau lamp for the real thing, there are many serious forgeries of TIFFANY, GALLÉ, DAUM and LALIQUE glass — if a Tiffany lamp makes $1m, it is worth forging. Art Nouveau bronzes, and Art Deco bronze figurines are copied in resin, and Deco lamps in plaster, so be aware at fairs and boot sales. Clarice CLIFF forgeries are usually crudely painted, with unsteady borders and outlines, and the bottoms may have a patchy brownish glaze. Advertising material is now also being forged, including the large Robertson's Golly lamp and enamel signs. Modern copies of classic Art Deco telephones can also be deceptive.

Jewellery: Copies usually use cheaper methods than originals — casting rather than hand carving. The Art Deco period is a favourite with copyists in South East Asia, who use precious metals, diamonds and precious stones, so their work is difficult for a layman to spot. Really important pieces, by makers such as Cartier, are copied expensively,

but originals can be authenticated in the firms' stock books.

Automata: Forgeries may be made of period dolls' heads, old fabric and brand new mechanisms — with facsimile 19th century retailers' labels.

Dolls: New heads, marked with 'genuine' trademarks and mould numbers may be attached to old bodies and dressed in elderly clothes.

Mechanical money boxes: Copies of late 19th-century cast-iron boxes that were honestly stamped 'Taiwan' were made from the early 1970s. These may have been aged and their marks removed.

Scrimshaw: President Kennedy started a fashion for 19th-century whale teeth decorated by seamen, and copies were made in resin, to be labelled and sold through museum shops.

Teddy bears: Forgeries are made from old cloth and stuffed with imitation 'Excelsior' wood straw, as used pre-1930. Faces and proportions of limbs copy those of Steiff bears.

Militaria: A strong market in cap badges has resulted in reproductions of rarer examples. They have been made of brass and white metal, but are surprisingly easy to bend. However, the forgers are working on improving this, and they also distress their products.

General: The better the object you are looking at, the more likely it is to be wrong. Always be on your guard when making a 'discovery'. Ask yourself 'Why am I so lucky?'

FAMILLES JAUNE, NOIRE, VERTE AND ROSE

An arbitrary classification made in the mid-19th century by the French ceramic historian Albert Jacquemart to describe the enamel colour schemes used on Chinese porcelain from the reign of Kangxi (1662-1722) onwards. The type of decoration was on the showy side and intended mainly for the export market. Indeed, the Chinese term for the colour schemes translates as 'foreign colours'. It began as a fresh and free style, but by the 19th century had become rather laboured and overcrowded. The terms are still used to describe Chinese porcelain today. In *famille verte* the predominant colour is a brilliant transparent green enamel. The palette also includes iron red, blue, yellow, and aubergine purple. The earliest examples have underglaze blue, which on later examples becomes a blue enamel In *famille jaune*, a similar palette is used but with a dominant yellow background. *Famille noire* has a black ground washed over with transparent green enamel and decoration in the *famille verte* palette. *Famille rose* was introduced around 1720 and the best examples date from the reign of Yongzheng (1723-35). It is characterised by an opaque pink made from a pigment called purple of Cassius, which was introduced to China by Jesuit missionaries for use in enamels. (See CANTON ENAMELS).

▶ **Kangxi famille verte** wall cistern **(£2,500-£3,500)**

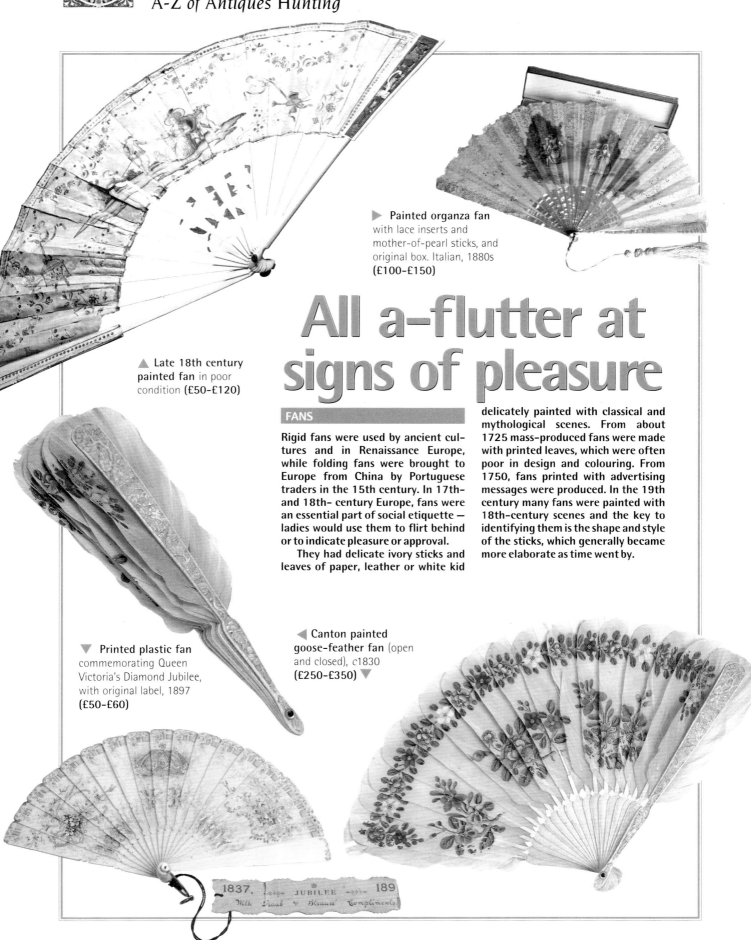

▶ **Painted organza fan**
with lace inserts and
mother-of-pearl sticks, and
original box. Italian, 1880s
(£100–£150)

All a–flutter at signs of pleasure

▲ **Late 18th century painted fan** in poor condition (£50–£120)

FANS

Rigid fans were used by ancient cultures and in Renaissance Europe, while folding fans were brought to Europe from China by Portuguese traders in the 15th century. In 17th- and 18th- century Europe, fans were an essential part of social etiquette — ladies would use them to flirt behind or to indicate pleasure or approval.

They had delicate ivory sticks and leaves of paper, leather or white kid delicately painted with classical and mythological scenes. From about 1725 mass-produced fans were made with printed leaves, which were often poor in design and colouring. From 1750, fans printed with advertising messages were produced. In the 19th century many fans were painted with 18th-century scenes and the key to identifying them is the shape and style of the sticks, which generally became more elaborate as time went by.

▼ **Printed plastic fan** commemorating Queen Victoria's Diamond Jubilee, with original label, 1897 (£50–£60)

◀ **Canton painted goose-feather fan** (open and closed), c1830 (£250–£350) ▼

FARTHINGALE CHAIR

A side chair with a broad seat, used in the 16th and early 17th centuries. The term was probably coined by the Victorians who thought that such chairs were made to accommodate hooped dresses or farthingales. See also DRUNKARD'S CHAIR.

 £££-££££

FASCES

A bound bundle of rods enclosing an axe, a symbol of the authority of ancient Rome. The rods denote the power to scourge, the axe the power to behead. It became a popular motif during the days of Edwardian classicism as well as giving its name to the Italian Fascist movement.

FASHION PLATES

Hand-coloured fashion plates, as opposed to prints of national costumes, were popular from the 1770s, and the heyday was between 1820 and 1890 when colour printing took over. For printing and artistic quality the best years were 1843-70 when illustrations were less stilted and more likely to be conversation pieces.

£-£££

FAVRILLE GLASS

TIFFANY'S name for hand-made iridescent glass. It was developed at his Corona glasshouse on Long Island, in

▼ Set of four watercolours of ladies of fashion, c1870s (£300-£500)

▶ Favrille glass vase from Tiffany (£1,600-£1,800)

collaboration with Arthur Nash who had worked for Thomas Webb of Stourbridge. The name is taken from the word 'fabrile', meaning hand-made or hand-crafted. The surface was made iridescent by treatment with hot white metallic salts, which were absorbed into the glass, creating a metallic lustre, which achieved dazzling colour effects. The various types of iridescent glass had names such as 'lava' glass, 'nacreous' ware and 'Cypriot' glass.

£££-£££££

FAZACKERL(E)Y COLOURS

Polychrome, painted flower decoration on Liverpool DELFTWARE in a palette of simple enamel colours— hues of red, blue, yellow and green with outline drawing in black. The pattern is named after two mugs made for Thomas Fazackerl(e)y and his wife Catherine around 1758.

FEATHERWORK PANELS AND PICTURES

Decorative panels of bird feathers were made, mainly by amateurs, in 18th-century England. They can be quite large and were used as wall hangings. In the 19th century feathers were employed to make realistic pictures, normally of birds.

£££

FENDER

A metal guard of iron or brass, introduced in the latter part of the 18th century to protect the floor and carpet from sparks. CLUB FENDERS, with padded seats, are particularly popular.

£££-££££

FESTOON

Loops of fruit and flowers were common in classical ornament and festoons became a key feature of Renaissance decoration, with intertwined rosettes, rings, lion masks and PUTTI. In the 17th century skilled carvers such as Grinling GIBBONS made fine, elaborately modelled festoons for interiors and furniture, and in the 18th century lighter and more delicate versions were a feature of ADAM-style ornament.

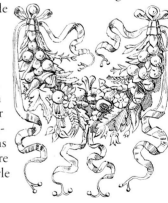

▼ Unique Liverpool delft shoe decorated in Fazackerly colours (£27,600)

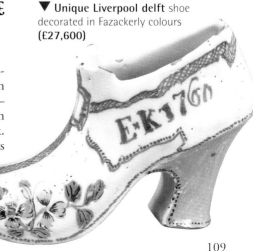

FIDDLE-BACK CHAIR

An 18th-century chair with a concave curve near the seat, giving it a waisted appearance resembling a violin. The spaces between the frame and the central splat suggested the sound holes.

 £££-££££

FIDDLE RACK OR BOARD

A board with holes cut to fit crockery and glasses. Used on board ship.

££-£££

FINIAL

An ornamental knob topping off lids or pieces of furniture. Common finials include acorns, vases, balls, flowers and pineapples.

FIRE IRONS

Sets of shovel, tongs and poker for tending the fire. They were made in iron as early as the 17th century. In the 18th century, sets in burnished steel, often with brass or copper ornaments were made to match fenders. Brass sets, frequently including a brush, were made in the 19th century.

££-£££

FIRE OR POLE SCREEN

A decorative panel, often of embroidery or painted wood, which moves up and down on a pole, generally with a tripod base. They were designed to protect delicate complexions. Also known as a pole screen.

£££

FIREBACK

Cast-iron panels at the back of a fireplace which radiate heat and protect the wall. In the 15th century they were made to fit large, open fireplaces. Later they became taller and narrower to fit smaller chimneys. In the 18th century, firebacks were made in one piece with the grate. Early decoration was simple: impressed initials, date or heraldic device. During the 17th century biblical, mythological or patriotic themes were common.

£££

The way they used to

Patterns for sets of cutlery were established in the mid-to late 17th century.

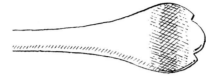

Trefid, 1660–1710. The earliest spoons (after apostles) have flat stems spreading at the top with two notches cut in the end. The bowls gradually lengthen and have a rat's tail along the back.

Dog nose, c1700. Forks were much rarer than spoons but were made to the same pattern with either three or four tines (prongs). Knives had round-ended cannon handles and steel blades.

The 18th-century elegance gave way to 19th-century elaboration, with a proliferation of complicated designs which are seldom used today.

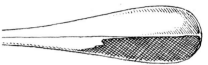

Hanoverian c1710–75. The most important 18th-century pattern. Top rounded, stem thinner and rounder. Earliest have ribs down the centre front. To 1730: rat's tails. Forks almost always three-pronged; knives pistol handled. Crests on reverse, as they were not laid the same way up as today.

Old English 1760–c1800. Ends turn down, instead of up. From then flatware laid as today, so crests appear on front. Forks tend to be four-pronged and knives straight.

FIRING GLASS

An English drinking glass with a large, bucket-shaped bowl, short stem and thickened foot for hammering on the table during toasts. Extremely popular in the 18th century, they were also known as bumping glasses.

 ££-£££

FITZROY BAROMETER

Lieutenant Fitzroy commanded the *Beagle* on Charles Darwin's voyage to South America in the 1830s. He rose to the rank of admiral and was appointed meteorological officer to the Board of Trade. He invented a BAROMETER with a printed paper scale, and 'remarks' on how to forecast the weather. Predictions to the left of the tube are based on rising pressure, to the right on falling pressure.

£££

FLATS

From c1850 until 1893 when BRITAIN invented a technique for hollow casting lead soldiers, they were flat, like cardboard cut-outs rather than fully rounded. Famous makers of these flat, painted figures were Hilbert and Stahl, Gottschalk, Wehrli, Mignot, Lucotte and HEYDE. They seldom appear on the market.

 £-£££

FLAT-BACK FIGURES

Made in the 19th century for cottage mantelpieces, flat-back pottery figures were mass-produced in cheap moulds. The backs are flat without any modelling, and the fronts usually decorated in underglaze blue and enamels. They were made mainly in Staffordshire but few can be traced to any particular factory. Popular subjects are royal, military, theatrical and sporting personalities and notorious criminals. The same moulds might be renamed for different characters, and many figures are now reproduced using the old moulds. (See FAKES)

 ££-££££

lay them

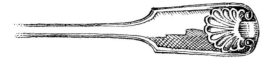

Fiddle. Introduced c1800. There are many variations on the basic pattern, the most common being fiddle and thread, and fiddle thread and shell (as above).

Albert. Named after the Prince Consort – who married Queen Victoria in 1840 and died in 1861.

King's pattern. This appeared in the early 19th century. Forks are four-pronged and knife hafts take their shape from the pattern. Often confused with King's, the Queen's pattern's shell is convex and the King's concave.

Pistol-handle. The basic shape for knives in the Hanovarian period. The pistol 'butt' can be much more elaborate than this, and is frequently turned into a full scroll.

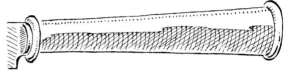

Cannon handle. Another basic design which could be elaborated in a number of ways

Forks
Italy is credited with the invention of the eating fork in the mid-15th century but it took over a century to catch on in the rest of Europe. By the late 17th century it was fashionable in France and drawings show the matching trefid-shaped spoons and forks ordered in large quantities by Louis XIV. Even by the 18th century the eating fork was by no means commonplace in Britain, and it spread only very slowly to the lower levels of society, where eating with spoon and fingers was still favoured. Fish knives and forks were not invented until the early 19th century.

▲ Pair of Staffordshire flat-back portrait figures of the preachers, Sankey and Moody, c1855 (£800)

FLOWER TABLE
A pedestal or four-legged stand in wood, metal or marble for supporting pots of flowers. Some are dual-purpose and have metal-lined containers hidden below removable table-tops.

          £££

FLÜGELGLAS
The German name for a goblet with a scrolled glass stem resembling the wings of a fantastic butterfly. It originated in 16th-century Venice and was imitated in northern Europe, with a revival in the 19th century.

          R ££££

FOLDED FOOT
Ring of doubled-over glass around the base of a glass, making it stronger.

FOOTWARMER
A small wooden box, perforated at the the top and sides, with a metal container for hot cinders. During the 19th century rectangular metal containers filled with boiling water were used on trains.

££-£££

FOOTMAN
An elegant 18th-century trivet on four legs, which was often made of polished steel or brass. It was used for holding objects such as kettles to warm by the fire.

          ££-£££

FOOTSTOOLS
These were introduced in the Middle Ages in conjunction with thrones. From the 17th century they matched armchairs, and in the 19th century some served a secondary purpose as a SPITTOON or salivarium.

FRANKENTHAL PORCELAIN
A hard-paste porcelain factory which flourished in 1755-99 and produced some of the best figure groups in Germany. It was founded by P. A. HANNONG. The products of the first 20 years are the best. An unusual hard paste was used, with a glaze which absorbed the enamel colours. Many of the figures were made after models by J.W. Lanz, who came from Strasbourg. More than 800 different subjects were produced, including the 'Music Lesson' after Boucher and a COMMEDIA DELL'ARTE series. Other

products include clock cases, mirror frames and chandeliers. The original-moulds were used in other German factories during the 19th century.

FRENCH COUNTRY FURNITURE

This was often a simplified version of Parisian styles, made of solid local woods such as oak or fruitwood. It varied from region to region, but the carving, often of animals and figures or geometric ornament, tends to be shallow. Seat furniture is seldom upholstered, and especially character-istic of provincial furniture are large ARMOIRES and cupboards with doors on the lower section and recessed shelves above. Hinges and keyholes are often of brass or steel and tend to be large and ornamental.

FRIGGERS

This is a glassmakers' term for decora-tive objects made in their spare time from left-over material. They are often brightly coloured and have novelty value rather than a useful function. Friggers include walking sticks, drumsticks, top hats, model ships and figures of animals.

▲ Apple-shaped fruitwood tea caddy, c1820. The value would be greater if it were in better condition (£700-£1,000)

FRUITWOOD CADDIES

Tea caddies, produced in the second half of the 18th century in the form of fruit. They were made of the appro-priate wood; apple and pear being most common. The bodies were hori-zontally divided a third of the way down, hinged to swing open and fit-

Toad in the hole

◀ Staffordshire blue and white mug, seen at Newcastle Emlyn (£40-£60)

FROG MUGS

Frog mugs first appeared in the late 18th century in Staffordshire and were an amusing way to shock a passing traveller.

Ale in those days was murky and, on draining his pint, the inno-cent abroad would discover a reptile lurking in the bottom. Some are double-handled and would be passed from hand to hand, each imbiber taking his share.

They are wheel thrown and the frogs hand-modelled. They are almost never marked.

ted with a lock and key to prevent ser-vants from stealing the precious tea. Larger and cruder versions date from the 19th century.

 £££-££££

FUDDLING CUP

A group of up to six small cups joined and connected internally so that one drinker could drain them all. They were made in England, Holland and Ger-many in the 17th and 18th centuries.

££££

FUMED OAK

A technique for finishing oak: it is exposed to ammonia in an air-tight chamber before polishing. This tones it to a greyish-brown colour which gradually fades to a yellowish brown.

FURNITURE BEETLE

The common furniture beetle *anobium punctatum* lays its eggs in the cracks of furniture. The larvae eat their way through the wood, boring holes before emerging as beetles.

Commonly known as woodworm, it can be treated by fumigation.

FÜRSTENBURG PORCELAIN

The factory was founded in Brunswick in 1747 but started mak-ing successful hard-paste porcelain only in 1753. Early wares have richly moulded ROCOCO scrollwork, often picked out in gold, and a series of vig-orous statuettes was made after models by Simon Feilner. The finest date from 1768-90: painted panels in elaborate Rococo frames, vases and table-ware decorated with delicate landscapes, figures and birds. After 1770 the influence of BERLIN and SÈVRES dominates, with busts of ancient and contemporary figures a speciality. From 1795 to 1814, the factory was managed by L. V. Gerverot, who had worked at Wedgwood. The neo-Classical style dominated and both BLACK BASALTES and blue JASPER WARES were made. Marks: F in blue; biscuit busts some-times have an impressed horse. Modern marks include A. a. M *aus alten Modell*, 'from an old model'.

▶ George III
mahogany
harlequin games
table (£7,500)

GALLÉ, EMILE (1846-1904)

An outstanding French glassmaker, famous for his ART NOUVEAU style and the establishment of a school of art glassmaking in Nancy, Lorraine. He was briefly apprenticed in Germany before returning to work with his father who had a glass and FAIENCE works in Nancy. His work was inspired by plant, insect and marine forms and he experimented with CAMEO GLASS, and subtle colour effects achieved by adding various oxides, veining and the use of metal foils. His pieces are flowing and often asymmetrical, never geometric. No two pieces are absolutely identical, since he deliberately exploited such imperfections as air bubbles and crazings. Pieces vary enormously from factory-made lines to those made by Gallé himself. Among the most famous items are his mushroom lamp and a surrealist hand, dripping

◀ Large Gallé cameo glass vase in foliate design, 28in high (£1,600)

in seaweed with shell encrustations. He also designed Art Nouveau plant form furniture, such as a water-lily table, often incorporating floral marquetry. The factory continued in production until 1914, and objects made after his death are carefully marked with a star beside the name Gallé.

££££-£££££

GALLERY

A small railing of wood or metal bordering the edge of a table, tray or cabinet top. Sometimes it looks like a miniature balustrade, but fretwork is more common.

GAMES TABLES

From the RESTORATION onwards, card playing was a fashionable occupation among the upper classes. Fortunes were won or lost and tempers raised over the gaming table. Samuel Pepys recounts his amazement at coming across the Queen playing cards on a Sunday. Card tables exist from the late 17th century. Generally of walnut veneer, they have folding circular tops, the back legs swinging out in support. In the 18th century the card table came into its own and a great deal of invention went into disguising it as a piece of occasional furniture. It might have a cleverly hinged top, and either a gate-leg or a concertina action. The two hind legs would be hinged to a folded section of the frieze which, when opened up, made a stable support for the unfolded top. Circular tops gave way to square ones with rounded corners to accommodate candlesticks and GUINEA PITS. By about 1730, square candlestands, giving distinctive 'ears' to the table, were a popular variation. Generally made of mahogany, tables could be plain, or adorned with elaborate carving to edges, borders and friezes. In the mid-century, satinwood, rosewood and harewood were also used. The triple-top card table had three cleverly hinged tops and served as a plain tea table, a baize-covered surface for cards or a backgammon and chess board. It could also perform as a reading or writing table once a reading slope was raised. In the late 18th century tables might be square, breakfronted, oval or serpentine, and decorated or painted. They often had a sliding panel forming the chessboard, which could be reversed or removed for backgammon. During the Regency period it was fashionable to combine games boards with work tables or sofa tables.

£££££-£££££

GARDE MEUBLE DE LA COURONNE

This was a French royal furniture store, one of which was attached to each palace and managed by a central department established in 1663. It is exciting—and valuable—to discover the stamps and inscriptions of the *garde meuble* on a piece of French furniture.

GARNISH

A set of vessels, usually pewter, for using on the table.

GARNISHED WITH NAILS

A charming term for the use of brass nails not just to fix leather or fabric to furniture, but to make ornamental designs. They were used by cofferers in the Middle Ages, and by upholsterers until the late 18th century. There have been revivals since.

▲ William and Mary trunk, hide garnished with nails, on later walnut stand (£5,500)

GARNITURE

A set of ornaments for the chimney-piece. In the 17th century it referred to porcelain vases. Later they could be silver or bronze. Clocks flanked by matching candlesticks were popular in the 18th and 19th centuries.

£££-£££££

In a garden of

GARDEN FURNITURE

Portland stone was the most commonly used material for 18th-century garden ornaments, but, due to the costs of quarrying, transport and carving, it was restricted to wealthy patrons with large country estates. As the century drew to a close, however, the emerging middle classes demanded less expensive garden furniture, and reconstituted stone, a type of cement, was used to produce everything from urns and statues to uncomfortable benches. Terracotta, seen in abundance on the Continent, became popular, but was prone to damage from careless gardeners and sometimes from harsh frosts.

In fact, a great deal of what passes for garden furniture would never have withstood outdoor conditions, even in southern Europe. Much was made for grottoes, orangeries and gazebos — the chairs below and the garden seat opposite, for example. All the masssive majolica wares made by Minton, George Jones and Wedgwood were not frost-resistant and were meant for indoor use.

Mass production in the late 18th century brought other stone-imitating ceramic manufacturers to the fore. The best-known was Mrs Eleanor Coade, who produced clay to a 'secret' formula.

▲ Garden lantern in blue and white Japanese porcelain, some chipping and bits missing, c1885 (£3,000-£4,000)

worldly delights

This clay was pressed into moulds to produce beautiful and (compared with carved stone) inexpensive ornaments and furniture. COADESTONE, as it is called, can be recognised by its pale yellow colour, and also by the factory mark, incorporating the word Coade, with which almost every piece was impressed. Two Coadestone NEO-CLASSICAL seats, each with a pair of sphinxes, can be found at Parham House in West Sussex. They are impressed with the LAMBETH mark. A modern process of mixing ground stone and cement and casting from originals produces convincing copies.

In the early 19th century, simple but elegant benches and seats were made from wrought-iron slats riveted together. As the Victorian period progressed, the new 'Iron Age', together with mass-production techniques, led to foundries experimenting with new products. The COALBROOKDALE foundry became the best-known, producing cast-iron garden furniture in wonderfully naturalistic designs. Benches and seats cast with entwined oak and ivy leaves, fern and blackberry, and the horse chestnut and water plant design by Dr Christopher DRESSER were among the most popular, and were copied by other factories.

They are now being reproduced (as are slatted seats) but original examples are easily identified by the the factory mark 'C. B. Dale Co', or 'Coalbrookdale', and can also be distinguished by the exceptionally high quality of the castings.

▶ French faience garden seat modelled as a monkey eating a cactus (£2,000-£3,000)

◀▶ Pair of gilt, silver, black and green-painted grotto armchairs (£5,500)

▼ Rare Coalbrookdale medallion-pattern cast-iron seat, (£2,400)

Firm that is good as gold

GARRARD'S

Robert Garrard was the driving force behind the establishment of Garrard's as one of the most prosperous 19th-century goldsmith's firms in Europe. It still trades under the family name from sumptuous Regent Street premises. His father, Robert Garrard I (1758-1818), went into partnership with John Wakelin in 1792 in a firm that had first been established by George Wickes in 1735. Wickes had entered his first mark in 1722, and from 1735 had supplied

Frederick, Prince of Wales. His most important products were designed by KENT.

On Garrard's death in 1818 the three eldest sons, Robert, James and Sebastian, succeeded him, trading as R. J. and S. Garrard. Although not a goldsmith by training, Robert was the most dynamic of the three, securing the patronage of the British aristocracy. At this period a somewhat confused style gripped the silver world. It mixed Rococo, late Baroque and naturalism and was known as 'Old French'.

In 1843 Garrard's were appointed Crown Jewellers, a title which the firm still holds, and they have maintained the Crown Jewels ever since. A prosperous business was established in

▶ William two-handled soup tureen and cover, 183. (£4,000-£6,000

useful tablewares, but the firm's reputation is mainly based on the spectacular presentation pieces that were shown with maximum publicity at the INTERNATIONAL EXHIBITIONS of the period. Its most talented modeller was a sculptor, Edmund Cotterill, who designed elaborate concoctions such as a table-centre including portraits of Queen Victoria's favourite dogs, and numerous horse-racing cups including the Ascot Cup of 1842, which showed an incident from the Battle of Crécy. They also made the America's Cup. Like most retailers of the period they also dealt in secondhand plate.

By the 1850s, silver sculpture of Arabs fighting in the desert was Cotterill's

particular speciality. The company also supplied a range of rich jewellery, some of it such as 'ancient' brooches and 'Gothic' bracelets, on historical themes.

In 1952 the firm merged with the Goldsmiths' and Silversmiths' Company, taking over the latter's premises on Regent Street but keeping the name Garrard and Co.

Various marks have been used by the company: IW/RG for Wakelin & Garrard in 1792; RG for Robert Garrard from 1802; SH for Sebastian Henry Garrard in 1900. As crown jewellers they had been entitled to place a crown above their mark from 1822, but in 1901 this was dropped as it could be confused with the Sheffield hallmark.

▼ Sculptural centrepiece by Garrard's, 1861 (£13,000)

▼ Pair of silver salts with gilded interiors, made in 1857, copying a 16th-century style. Seen at the Wrekin Roadshow (£500)

▲ **Gothic-style** 18 light brass gasolier with flying buttresses **(£6,500)**

GASOLIER

Although gas was used to illuminate factories from the early 19th century, it was not really welcomed into the home until the mid-century. From then on a wide range of gas light fittings was made. Gasoliers were the equivalent of hanging chandeliers, with six or so branches for burners fitted with glass shades. They were often elaborately decorated and made from a variety of materials, ranging from bronze to glass. Mechanisms involving a simple waterslide with balance weights enabled the height of the fitting to be adjusted.

 ££££

GATE-LEG TABLE

A drop-leaf table. When opened, it is supported by swinging hinged 'gates' which can be either single or double. In use from the 16th century.

GAUDY WELSH

A 19th-century pattern of stylised flowers in dark blue and orange-red, sometimes with touches of lustre. It was used on domestic wares, particularly cups and saucers, that were very popular in Wales, but actually made in Staffordshire.

££

◀ **Typical Gaudy Welsh** coffee mug or 'can', c1890 **(£20)**

GEORGIAN

The period of just over 100 years spanning most of the 18th century and a bit beyond. The golden age of the English decorative arts, it covers the reigns of the Hanoverian Kings:

George I   (1714-27)
George II   (1727-60)
George III   (1760-1820)
George IV   (1820-30)

The years from about 1811 to 1830, —which include periods when George III was suffering from bouts of insanity—are also known as the REGENCY period. The term 'Georgian'

▲ **George I walnut** knee-hole desk **(£12,000)**

▲ **Early George III mahogany** knee-hole desk **(£3,800)**

▲ **Mid-Georgian mahogany** knee-hole desk with large gilt handles **(£2,500-£3,500)**

▶ **Pair of two-tier dessert stands** on fluted, domed feet, chased with shells, foliage and strapwork **(£6,500 the pair)**

is used particularly to describe furniture, and covers a very wide range of styles. The early period was still dominated by Queen Anne types which were gradually displaced by the influence of the Italian BAROQUE and the designs of William KENT. In the reign of George II the ROCOCO influence spread from France. It was seen first in silver, but spread to furniture through the designs of Matthias LOCK, Thomas Johnson and Thomas CHIPPENDALE, who developed an English variant of the Rococo style known as Chinese Chippendale. The reign of George III was dominated first by the GOTHIC REVIVAL and then by the all-pervasive NEO-CLASSICAL influence of Robert ADAM and George HEPPLEWHITE. This in turn gave way to the flashier and more robust forms of the Regency,

epitomised by the designs of George SMITH and Thomas HOPE, which refer to antique prototypes rather than merely being decorated with antique motifs.

GERMAIN, THOMAS (1673-1748)

The best-known French ROCOCO silversmith and a superb craftsman. He was the son of Pierre Germain (1645-84), who worked for Louis XIV but none of whose pieces survive.

Thomas studied in Rome before returning to France, becoming a *maître* in 1720 and *orfèvre du Roi* in 1723. His designs reflect the most extreme excesses of the Rococo. A pair of wine coolers, 1727-28, are modelled like organic tree trunks encrusted with vines and snails. His most spectacular dinner service, made in 1733, includes bulging tureens with boars' head handles and covers decorated with three-dimensional hares, shellfish and vegetables. The most famous of all is the Portuguese centrepiece made in 1729 with its finely modelled greyhounds, hunting horns and swirling Rococo foliage. His son, François Thomas Germain (1726-91), took over his workshop on his death, as well as his royal appointment. He worked in a similar style to Thomas but far more of his work survives.

GESSO

A mixture of plaster of Paris, gypsum and animal glue, which has been left to soak for several days. It was used on wooden panels as the base of tempera paintings and for painted and gilded furniture from the Renaissance onwards. Put on in several thin layers, it provides a smooth surface to which gold leaf can be applied, but it might also be built up to a considerable thickness and then carved to improve crispness and detail. It is also frequently moulded in picture and mirror frames.

GILDING

A thin coating of gold leaf or gold dust applied as decoration to furniture, base metal, lacquer, glass and ceramics. There are many different types, the most common of which are water gilding, where gold leaf is applied on a film of water to dry animal glue on a GESSO surface, and oil gilding where

All that's carved is not Gibbons

▲ Carving by Gibbons, framing a Madonna and Child painting in the chapel at Belton House, Lincs

GIBBONS, GRINLING (1648-1721)

An Englishman born in Rotterdam, Gibbons came to England at 19. He had trained as a sculptor and was to become the greatest naturalistic woodcarver of the BAROQUE age. He also worked in marble, stone and bronze, but it is for his wonderful limewood festoons of flowers, leaves, fruit and animals that he is best remembered.

Perhaps his *tour de force* is a 'lace' cravat at Chatsworth. Other superb work by him is at Windsor Castle, Hampton Court, Kensington Palace, Luton Hoo, Petworth House, St Paul's Cathedral and Trinity College, Oxford.

John Evelyn, who introduced him to Sir Christopher Wren and Charles II, called him 'the most excellent in his profession not only in England but in the whole world'.

Carvings attributed to him do appear on the market occasionally, but all is not Gibbons. The efforts of 19th–century imitators were known as 'Gibbonwork'.

A fine form of furniture

GILLOW'S

One of the finest and best-documented of all English furniture-makers, the firm survived until recently as Waring and Gillow. The business was founded in Lancaster around 1695 and established securely by Robert Gillow I (1703-73), who was made a Freeman of the City in 1728.

At that time Lancaster was still a port, trading in timber, including mahogany, from the Americas. Robert was joined by his sons Richard, who took over the Lancaster end of the business, and Robert II, an architect who moved to London in 1776 to take over the branch established in Oxford Street in 1761. The family continued to be associated with the business until 1817.

The Gillows were Roman Catholics and built up a following among their co-religionists and the gentry and aristocracy of the North and Scotland, many of whom had Jacobite leanings. By the Regency period they had clients throughout the country, and were exporting furniture to the Baltic and the West Indies. They kept up with fashion and executed individual commissions which became popular successes, such as the DAVENPORT. They supplied pieces to PUGIN's Gothic designs for the Houses of Parliament, and in the 1870s used Bruce Talbert for more, very detailed, Gothic furniture, with much inlay, low relief, carving and spindles.

At the end of the century, they opened a Paris factory to make EDWARDIAN REPRODUCTION FURNITURE. They were the first English firm to stamp their work, from the 1760s, and their records from 1731 are in the Victoria and Albert Museum.

▲ **Gillow cabinet** with ivory inlay, seen at the Luton Hoo Roadshow, c1880 **(£10,000–£12,000)**

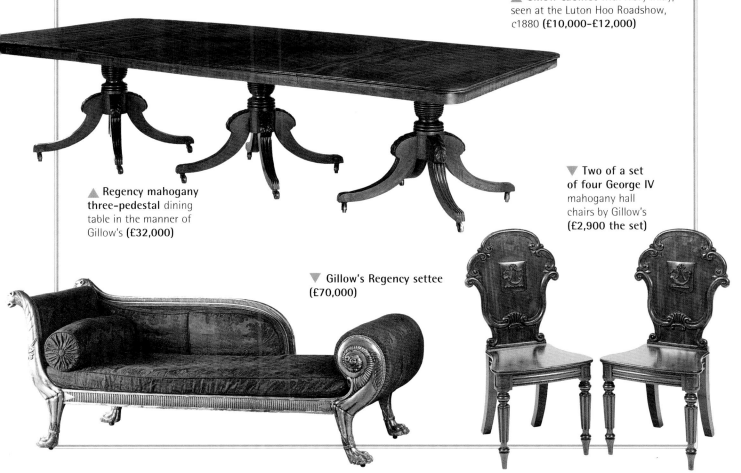

▲ **Regency mahogany three-pedestal** dining table in the manner of Gillow's **(£32,000)**

▼ **Two of a set of four George IV** mahogany hall chairs by Gillow's **(£2,900 the set)**

▼ **Gillow's Regency settee (£70,000)**

▲ Caughley jug decorated in the 19th century with a copy of a 1772 Giles pattern. A genuine Giles might be worth 10 times as much (£300–£400)

leaf is fixed with a mixture of linseed oil, gum arabic and mastic. On ceramics and glass, gold leaf was ground with honey or dissolved in mercury, painted on to the surface and then fixed by firing.

GILES, JAMES (1718–AFTER 1780)

A freelance decorator of porcelain and glass. He painted Bow, Worcester and Chinese porcelain in his London studio, as well as opaque blue and white glass. He never signed his work, but vessels enamelled and gilt with flowers or landscapes may be attributed to him.

£££–££££

GIRAFFE PIANO

An early 19th-century upright piano with a very tall, vertical case. It is lopsided and neck-like, the height gradually diminishing with the wires as the pitch of the keyboard rises.

R £££££

GIRANDOLE

An elaborately carved wall sconce with branches for holding candles. There is generally a mirror or similar reflector to double the candlepower, and in the 18th century the girandole was often ornately carved and gilt, especially when the GOTHIC and CHINOISERIE styles were in fashion.

£££–££££

When London started swinging

THE 'GIRL IN A SWING' FACTORY

The mystery of the 'Girl in a Swing' factory intrigued collectors for more than 60 years. CHELSEA porcelain divided neatly into different periods, but a range of ornaments apparently made at Chelsea just did not fit in. Peculiarities in the colouring and style suggested that a group of figures, scent bottles and bonbonnières were made by a single factory, but there were no clues to identify the maker. The distinctive modelling was typified by a figure group in the Victoria and Albert Museum of a girl seated in a swing. There was little doubt that it was made in London in the 1750s. Similar pieces came to be known as 'Girl in a Swing' pieces.

It was not until 1993 that the mystery was solved by the discovery of a document in France. This referred to Charles Gouyn making 'very beautiful small porcelain figures' at his house in St James's Street, in 1759. Gouyn was a jeweller who developed an interest in porcelain-making, probably as a proprietor of the Chelsea concern. He founded his own factory in about 1749 and continued for at least 10 years. His initial attempts to make porcelain figures were not successful, but mostly white groups, such as the girl in a swing herself, have considerable charm.

Through his experience as a jeweller, Gouyn found a ready market for precious metal-mounted trinkets, so-called 'toys', seals and other small china galanterie ware. Distinctive, painted features, oversized, flat leaves and a certain style of flower painting made 'Girl in a Swing' figures more appealing than the more sophisticated products of Chelsea, and they are highly collectable today. Some were also made at Gouyn's factory, and the few identified examples are among the most valuable of all 18th-century porcelain items.

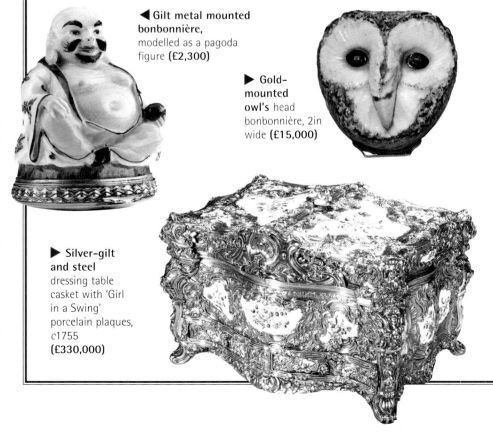

◀ Gilt metal mounted bonbonnière, modelled as a pagoda figure (£2,300)

▶ Gold-mounted owl's head bonbonnière, 2in wide (£15,000)

▶ Silver-gilt and steel dressing table casket with 'Girl in a Swing' porcelain plaques, c1755 (£330,000)

GLASS

The origins of glassmaking are obscure. There is evidence that glass beads were being made in the Middle East in the third millennium BC, and glass vessels a little later in Syria and Mesopotamia. But the best of early glass comes from Egypt, where the industry flourished around 1500BC, producing beads, scarabs, amulets and decorative vessels. Knowledge of glass production spread to the Mediterranean basin, and arrived in Rome in the late 1st century BC, developing into a productive industry which flourished for four centuries.

'Roman glass' embraces the products of the whole Empire, which extended to most of Europe and the

▶ Roman **glass flask** from the 5th century AD **(£4,000)**

Near East. Much Roman glass still exists, ranging from domestic vessels to decorative pieces such as the famous Portland vase and cage cups. The most significant development was the invention of glass-blowing, an improvement on the earlier techniques of casting in moulds, and core-forming, which allowed lighter, less expensive vessels to be made more efficiently.

After the decline of the Roman Empire glassmaking developed slowly in Europe. Fine artistic glass was still made in the Middle East and the examples brought home by

▶ **Irish George III** cut glass bowl **(£600–£750)**

Crusaders contrasted greatly with the primitive European glass. Nothing comparable was made in Europe until the 15th century, when the industry in Venice began to flourish. A clear, thin soda glass called *cristallo* could be decorated with diamond point engraving, or drawn out and pincered into elaborate shapes. This style, known as FAÇON DE VENISE, was widely imitated.

The addition of lead oxide created a brilliant, less fragile glass suitable for engraving and cutting. This was George RAVENSCROFT's achievement in the late 17th century, and paved the way for Britain to dominate domestic glass manufacture. Styles developed from simple, plain forms to enamelling, engraving and gilding. Lead glass also lent itself to cutting and this dominated decoration until the early 19th century.

▶ **Large Austrian glass bowl** in silver mount, 1905 **(£1,500)**

During the mid-19th century colourful Bohemian glass became fashionable, decorated with enamelling or cut through layers of colour. Later there were revivals of ancient techniques, including CAMEO GLASS. Artists such as Emile GALLÉ and TIFFANY developed glass as art. After the First World War, the French took the lead with their ART DECO creations. More recently, the Scandinavians and Italians have revitalised the glass industry.

◀ **Girl in a Swing candlesticks** figures modelled as a fisherman and companion (below), 5in high **(£85,000 the pair)**

◀ **A Bohemian stained ruby** goblet and cover engraved by August Böhn, *c*1840 **(£12,000)**

Around the world in different ways

◀ Newton's pocket terrestrial globe with shagreen case, 1818. Seen at the Huddersfield Roadshow (£800-£1,200)

GLOBES

By the 3rd century BC the Greeks not only knew that the Earth was a sphere, but had worked out its circumference almost exactly. They made both terrestrial and celestial globes; one of the latter is part of a marble statue of Atlas in the Uffizi Gallery, Florence. The oldest surviving globe of the world was made by Martin Behain of Nuremberg in 1492: this just missed Columbus's discoveries of that year. The earliest English globe (1592, at Petworth House) shows Drake's circumnavigation. By this time the Dutch (aided by Jews who had been expelled from Spain) had established a lead in globe-making which lasted until the 18th century, the best-known names being Gemma Frisius (c1536), Gerardus Mercator (1512-94) and Willem Janzs Blaeu (1571-1638).

In the 18th century British globe-makers caught up, helped by the fact that many navigators and explorers were British. Thus the tracks of Anson's, Cook's and Vancouver's voyages are often marked. It became usual for globes to be sold in pairs for libraries, with celestial globes showing constellations, matching the terrestrial ones. South Sea exploration led to the discovery of new constellations, which were given scientific rather than mythological names, so Fornax Chemica and Machina Electrica shine in the southern skies.

The best-known British makers were the CARYS. Among those who produced pocket globes — an English speciality — were Joseph Moxon (1690s), R. Cushee (1730s) and Nathaniel Hill (1750s). From the late 19th century the French took a large slice of the market for mass-produced schoolroom globes.

◀ Terrestrial globe in original stand, 1816. Seen at the Truro Roadshow (£8,000-£10,000)

▶ Library globe on original fruitwood stand. Published in Rome in 1744 with 16th-century cartography by Mercator (£7,500-£8,500)

▶ Pair of Regency miniature wooden globes with leather cases, c1800 (£20,000)

▶ **Goldscheider porcelain** female figures of varying heights **(£300-£1,000 per piece)**

GLASTONBURY CHAIR

A 19th-century folding chair, often found in country churches. The design is supposedly based on a chair used by the last Abbot of Glastonbury, who died in 1539.

GOBELINS

The most famous French tapestry factory got its name from a family of dyers who established a workshop on the outskirts of Paris in about 1440. The Gobelins factory was bought for Louis XIV in 1662 and turned into a workshop for supplying the royal palaces with magnificent furnishings. Under the direction of Charles LE BRUN, more than 250 tapestry weavers, painters, furniture-makers, bronze-workers, gold and silversmiths were employed. The factory closed in 1689 after Le Brun's fall from favour for being the protégé of a disgraced minister, and because of the King's financial difficulties. It reopened, as a tapestry workshop only, in 1699. Throughout the 17th and 18th centuries it produced some of the most exquisite tapestries ever made. Early on, the tapestries were designed by Le Brun, the most famous series celebrating the life of Louis XIV. After the reopening, designs were commissioned from many of the leading French artists, and sets of these tapestries were ordered by noble families all over Europe. The factory is still in production, but now works only for the French State.

GOFFERING IRON

A specially designed pair of iron tongs used for crimping neck ruffs. The tongs were heated and the material pressed between an upper convex and lower concave blade. Another, more common type is an iron rod mounted on a stand over which the material is stretched and pulled.

GOLDSCHEIDER

A Viennese pottery started in 1885 and still in production. Around the turn of the century it specialised in large (up to 3ft) figures of Neapolitan urchins and the like, patinated to give them the appearance of bronzes. At the time it employed about 30 modellers. Later it made smaller figures of ART DECO dancers, rather like versions of PREISS or Chiparus statuettes and, later still, figures of pretty girls in frocks.

Fore-runners

GOLF

In 1754, when the Royal and Ancient Golf Club of St Andrews was founded, a golf ball cost several times the price of a club. The first balls were made of wet leather, sewn together, and stuffed with boiled goose feathers to produce a hard ball, between 1in and 1½ in diameter. These 'feathery' balls are keenly sought after: an early 19th-century example might be less than £2,000; a ball by the most famous feathery maker, Allan Robertson, might sell for more than £10,000.

At the end of the 1840s, GUTTA PERCHA, a rubber-like substance from India, was used to make golf balls. At first they were smooth, but patterns improved the ball's flight. Smooth balls can fetch up to £2,000, and an early red gutta percha, for use in snow, can sell for up to £3,000. Look out for signs of cracking, and handle it like an egg to maintain its condition and value.

Early clubs had long shafts, and the long, narrow heads had a length of horn to prevent premature wearing. Early woods had scared (pronounced 'scarred') heads – grafted onto the shafts and then bound with twine. Many clubmakers stamped their names on pieces. Those to look out for include Hugh Philip, Robert Forgan, Tom Morris, Douglas McEwan and Willie Park. The best early clubs can fetch several thousands of pounds.

Although not reaching the high prices of long-nosed woods, mid-19th-century irons, usually made by blacksmiths, can fetch around £500 or £600. Examples of early 18th-century irons, which are exceptionally rare, have also been known to fetch considerable sums.

▲ A Brown's rake iron, c1900 **(£3,000)**

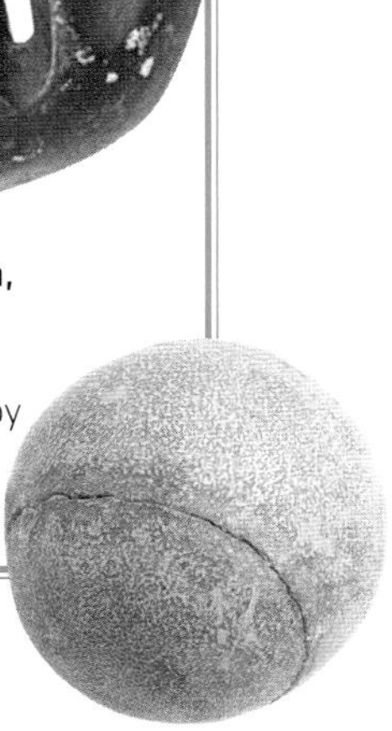

▶ Feathery golf ball by Robertson, c1835. **(£10,000-£15,000)**

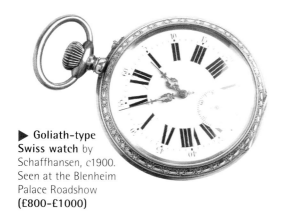

▶ **Goliath-type Swiss watch** by Schaffhansen, c1900. Seen at the Blenheim Palace Roadshow (£800-£1000)

GOLIATH

A popular name for a Swiss watch of extra large size, dating from c1900. They often ran for eight days.

££££

GOSSWARE

William Henry Goss (1833-1906) founded his Stoke-on-Trent factory in 1858 but it was not until the 1880s, under the influence of his sons Adolphus (1853-1934), Victor (1865-1913) and Huntley (1867-1947), that it began to produce its famous white-glazed souvenir models with their heraldic coats of arms. Executed in Parian ware and decorated with enamel colours, Gossware models included a whole range of local symbols and curiosities—animals such as the Warwick bear and the Aylesbury duck and copies of monuments and cottages. With the opening of the railways and the introduction of public holidays, the craze for collecting these souvenirs swept the nation. More than 90% of Edwardian homes owned some Goss china, and during the First World War tanks, guns, shells, dreadnoughts and dug-outs were made, still painted with town coats of arms. At the peace they were joined by war memorials. A League of Goss Collectors was founded in 1906, becoming the International League in 1918. In the economic depression of the 1930s the factory began to struggle, and by 1940 it had ceased production. Cupboard-loads of Gossware were consigned to the dustbin, but in the late 1960s it again became immensely collectable, and in 1970 a modern Goss Collectors' Club was founded.

Nearly all models have a description inscribed on the base and bear the Goshawk crest with W. H. Goss printed underneath. In the last 10 years of production, quality fell dramatically. Models made after 1931 also have the word England below the mark, and so are easily identified. Some very early models have an impressed W. H. Goss mark.

££

GOTHIC REVIVAL

This began in the late 19th century and was a much more genuine response to Gothic architecture than GOTHICK had been. Accurate recordings of buildings and their details were made, and the movement was concerned with reviving authentic Gothic detail in an historically accurate manner, rather than with decoration. From architecture it spread to embrace all the decorative arts, since suitable furnishings had to be made to fit the Gothic-style churches and public buildings being built. One of the leading designers of the style was A.W.N. PUGIN. Gothic Revival tiles were produced by MINTON, furniture, wallpapers and fabric by the Crace brothers, and metalwork by John HARDMAN.

▲ **Gothic-style armchair,** 1860s (£400-£500)

▲ George III mahogany display cabinet in Gothick style (£12,000-£18,000)

GOTHICK

The final 'k' is not always used but is useful in distinguishing between the first and second revivals. Gothick describes the 18th-century English ROCOCO taste for delicate Gothic decorative detail which preceded the Gothic Revival. It was used in architecture and interior decoration, often to give mansions a theatrical air of ancient lineage. The most famous examples were Horace Walpole's Strawberry Hill in Twickenham, which gave its name to Strawberry Hill Gothic, and William Beckford's massive Fonthill Abbey in Wiltshire, which collapsed because it was so feebly (and unauthentically) built. Batty Langley's *Gothic Architecture Inspired and Improved* was one of the first pattern books for the style. Fan vaulting, decorative buttressing, elaborate plasterwork, mantelpieces and Gothic-style bookshelves, chair backs, lanterns and clocks were all employed in the Gothick interior.

GOUTY CHAIR & STOOL

A self-propelled easy chair on wheels for people unable to walk because their legs were swollen by gout. Mid-18th-century gout stools were adjustable, and so, in HEPPLEWHITE'S words, 'particularly useful to the afflicted'. Later, non-adjustable stools were generally angled, with support at the end.

                    £££

GRACES, THE THREE

A group of three naked females with their arms around one another's shoulders which symbolised beauty in the classical world. In the Italian Renaissance they were interpreted by the high-minded as Chastity, Beauty and Love, but they also did duty as a conventional sign for a brothel.

▲ Part of a 'Brunswick' dessert service by Grainger's, c1835-40 (£100 per piece)

GRAINGER'S

One of the three WORCESTER factories, it started in 1801 and changed its name several times. It was taken over by Royal Worcester in 1889, work continuing until 1902.

                    ££-£££

GRAINING

The highly-skilled painted imitation of the grain of more expensive wood. Exceptionally fine graining was done on panelling in the 17th and 18th centuries, but in the 19th century it was used on some of the cheapest furniture as well as for doors and cupboards in fairly low-grade housing.

GRANDFATHER CLOCK

This popular name came into use only in 1878, the year after Henry C.

It's the same old song

GRAMOPHONE

The phonograph, the gramophone and the telephone are cousins, using vibrations on a membrane to transmit sound. The phonograph, invented by Thomas Edison in 1877, used cylinders, while the gramophone, invented 10 years later and marketed as a toy, used discs and needles. Edison's New Duplex and Concert phonographs (1888) were electric at first and then clockwork. The most common Edison models are the Standard and the smaller Gem.

The first gramophone records were vulcanised rubber; shellac followed in 1895. In Britain the Gramophone Co, founded in 1898, had sold 5,000 discs by 1900 when it changed its name to the Gramophone and Typewriter Co Ltd. In 1907 it became HMV. Its machines have been described as 'both the Rolls-Royce and the Morris of the British market' as they were not only high-quality but cheap, and G and T models are much sought

▶ **Tin-horn gramophone** with wooden case and no maker's mark, c1910 (£400-£600)

after. The most common horn model is the HMV Junior Monarch.

Between the wars, internal horns became usual and cloth covered picnic gramophones were made by the thousand. Automatic changers were introduced in c1935, as were radiograms. The introduction of electric record players in the 1940s ended the manufacture of wind-ups.

Prices are governed as much by visual appeal as by rarity. When buying always check that the needle goes fully to the middle of a record.

▶ **Edison Gem** phonograph, popular in the USA at the turn of the century (£300-£400)

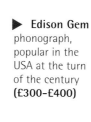

A-Z *of* Antiques Hunting

Work composed the song *My Grandfather's Clock*. Before this they were referred to as LONGCASE CLOCKS.

GRANDMOTHER CLOCK

A modern name, probably originating in America, for a longcase clock only about two-thirds as high as usual. They are fairly rare, most dating from 1690 to 1730. Some have a device for telling the time in the dark. When a cord is pulled, the clocks will strike the previous quarter, followed by the last hour, which suggests they may have been used in bedrooms.

££££

GRANNY WATCH

Ladies' small pocket watches, mass-produced near Geneva until the wristwatch took over in around 1910. Cases are usually engraved with flowers and are mostly in silver. These are worth about £50. Gold cases—in nine, 14 or 18 carat—are worth from £80 to £200.

££-£££

GRATE

An iron basket for burning wood and coal. Grates were first introduced to hearths in the 16th and 17th centuries, when coal became commonly available, and they were supported on fire dogs. In the 18th century fitted cast-iron grates were made with hobs on either side of the opening, often decorated with ADAM-style motifs. Free-standing grates with highly polished brass or steel fronts were also fashionable. By the Victorian period, fireplace design had become so

▲ Regency steel, brass and cast-iron grate in the manner of Bullock **(£8,000)**

Apogee of ancient pottery

GREEK POTTERY

Pots were an intrinsic part of daily life in Ancient Greece, used for storing food, water, wine and cosmetics, and for eating, drinking and performing ritual oblations. Thousands upon thousands were hand-crafted, using the local clay decorated in the familiar red and black figure forms, the only known decoration that could withstand the heat of the furnace. The earliest European pots are Cypriot, dating from the Neolithic period, about 4500BC to the later Bronze Age around 800BC. Cypriot vessels, figures and groups can be very sophisticated, often with distinctive geometric and circular decoration.

Next come the products of the Minoan and Mycenaean civilisations of Crete, roughly 2000-1200BC. These are fairly crude, a creamy ground decorated with black lines and patterns. The geometric period follows from about 900 to the early 7th century BC, with the centres of production shifting to mainland Greece. Shapes became more sophisticated and decoration included humans and animals in carefully arranged geometric patterns. The fully-fledged black-figure style first appeared in Corinth in about 675BC. These pots are in a different league. Derived from Oriental inlays, the designs are delicately drawn, with detail added in red and white pigment.

In the 6th and 5th centuries BC it was the Attic wares that represented the supreme achievement of the Greek potter's art. The decoration — naturalistic and perfectly balanced against the shape of the pot — depicted complex narrative scenes that were often highly entertaining (particularly those on wine vessels). In about 550 BC the red-figure style was introduced, giving the painter greater fluency. The background was filled in with slip, and details were painted rather than incised.

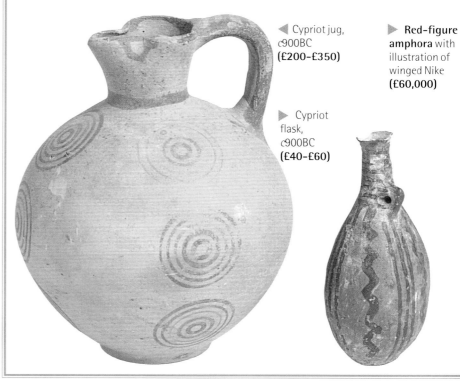

◀ Cypriot jug, c900BC **(£200-£350)**

▶ Red-figure **amphora** with illustration of winged Nike **(£60,000)**

▶ Cypriot flask, c900BC **(£40-£60)**

126

▲ **Attic red-figure** pelike from a collection of important Greek vases (£130,000)

advanced that a wide range of patented, fitted, cast-iron grates was available. Despite clean-air regulations, smokeless fuel is not suited to Victorian grates. It burns too hotly and cracks and warps them.

GREEK KEY

A classical motif of interlocking right-angled and vertical lines, usually applied in a continuous flow, like joined-up waves or swastikas. Common in Greek, Roman and Chinese art, it reappears throughout history in classically inspired ornament.

GREEK REVIVAL

A form of neo-Classicism which began in the 1750s and lasted for a century. It was inspired by the rediscovery of ancient monuments in Greece and southern Italy, and had a major influence on architecture in America and on the Continent. In the decorative arts Greek forms of furniture such as KLISMOS chairs and daybeds, and vessels such as kraters and wine jugs, together with Grecian oil lamps and Grecian jewellery, became fashionable. Thomas HOPE and the sculptor John Flaxman produced illustrations and designs in the Grecian style which were very influential.

GREENWOOD, FRANS (1680-1762)

A glass engraver of English descent working in Holland, who developed a technique of STIPPLE ENGRAVING his popular landscape, mythological and love-making designs with a fine, diamond-point graver.

R ££££-£££££

▶ **One of a pair** of Empire ormolu griffins (£8,000 the pair)

GRIFFIN

A fantastic beast with the head and wings of an eagle. Its hind legs and tail are those of a lion, and its front legs and talons those of an eagle. Used in Greek and Roman ornament, it also appears as a decorative motif, especially on furniture, from the Renaissance onwards.

GRISAILLE

Decorative painting in tints of grey, often used for mural decoration and painted reliefs.

▲ **Greek revival** mahogany klismos-type chairs, c1815 (£10,000–£15,000)

GROTESQUE

The name given to fantastic and monstrous carved ornament as well as to a fanciful type of decoration, inspired by Roman painting, which was popular during the late Renaissance. It combined human figures, sphinxes, monkeys and decorative motifs into whimsical and playful compositions. The word comes from the 'grottos' among the excavated Roman ruins in which the original wall paintings were found.

GUÉRIDON

A candlestand or small circular table for holding a candelabrum. It is normally a pedestal or column topped by a tray. The name may come from an African torch-bearer in an early 17th-century ballet. Certainly guéridons were often made in the form of the gilt and painted figures holding trays or candlesticks, which are also known as Moors or Blackamoors.

▲ Table-type, ormolu-mounted guéridon, stamped M. Ohneberg (£11,000)

The universal tram

GUNTHERMANN TOYS

Tinplate toy manufacturers, founded in Nuremberg in 1877 by Siegfried Gunthermann and famous for their well-made tinplate horse-drawn vehicles, fire engines and aeroplanes. The tram above is unliveried and so could be sold in several different countries without appearing 'foreign'. The firm ceased trading in the Second World War. Trademarks: SG, AW.

GUILLOCHE

A scroll pattern made by two or more bands twisted together like a plait. It orginated in Greece, was simplified by the Romans, and used to decorate furniture and metalwork from the 16th century onwards.

GUINEA PITS

The 18th-century name for the depressions at the corners of card tables for holding chips and money.

GUTTA PERCHA

The gum from various trees growing in Malaysia. In the 17th century English botanists thought it a wood, and in the mid-19th century tables were made of it. More practically it was used to make moulds for casting.

GUTTAE

These are the small, protruding wedges found as a decorative band on the cornice of the Doric ORDER. They are thought to symbolise the wooden pegs which once supported the entablature.

GYROSCOPE

A scientific instrument whose rotating fly wheel maintains a stable axis independent of surrounding movement. It was known as a children's toy but was reinvented by the Frenchman Jean Bernard Léon Foucault (1819-68) as an apparatus for demonstrating the rotation of the earth. It had no other practical use until the 1920s when German scientists realised it could be used in the guidance system for a rocket they were designing.

◀ Brass gyroscope from the 1880s (£2,000-£3,000)

HADLEY WARE

This is porcelain designed and made by James Hadley (1837-1903) at the Royal WORCESTER factory from 1875, and at his own factory from

► One of a pair of Worcester figures modelled by Hadley, 1887 (£2,000-£3,000 the pair)

1896 to 1905. The business was then bought out by the Worcester factory.

 ££-£££

HAIR JEWELLERY

In the 17th century a rather morbid custom arose of wearing the hair of a loved one set under crystal as MOURNING JEWELLERY. Rings were later specially adapted to hold a lock of hair, and in the mid-18th century it became fashionable to wear mourning brooches and lockets filled with plaited hair. Sometimes these were of funeral scenes, tombs or a weeping widow (or willow), with hair combined with paint. In the 19th century the custom became less morbid, with hair jewellery being given as love tokens. Hair-plaiting businesses were established in France and England, with horsehair sometimes added to human to give a firmer finish. More cheerful hair brooches were made, too, often with elaborate flower designs, incorporating gold wire thread and small pearls.

££-£££

► Georgian woven hair chandelier drop earrings, c1795 (£80-£100)

HALL CHAIRS AND BENCHES

Hall chairs are armless side chairs made of carved mahogany, and later oak, and hall benches are long, either with low, carved backs, or rails at the ends. Often decorated with the family coat of arms, such chairs were placed in the hall for servants and visitors to sit on. They were not made for comfort, with hard, flat seats, but the backs are often fanciful and decorative. They date from the mid-18th to the late 19th century.

£££

► Victorian hall chair in oak, c1860 (£100-£200)

HALLMARKS

England's oldest form of consumer protection started in 1300 with the appearance of the leopard's head hallmark on gold and silver of the required standard. From 1363 every maker of silver had to use his own registered mark. Originally these were symbols, but by the early 15th century, initials had begun to replace them. In 1478 a date letter system was introduced, enabling the assay master who passed the piece to be identified, should the standard of the piece be questioned at a later date. This enables almost every piece of British silver to be dated. As there are only a limited number of letter shapes available these are repeated, and the shape of the shield is vital when dating. When Henry VIII took over control of the Assay Office in 1544, the lion passant was

A-Z of Antiques Hunting

◄Leopard's head, the London Assay mark, 1876

◄Date letter, new sequence in this font started in 1876

◄Lion passant. Fully marked Sterling standard silver after 1544 should carry this

◄Monarch's or Sovereign's head, here Queen Victoria

struck. Although royal control ceased in 1550, this mark quickly became the recognised mark for STERLING standard. London-marked sterling standard pieces today have modern versions of these four marks, possibly with certain other marks. The mark of a monarch's head was used from 1784 to 1890 to show that tax had been paid. In 1697 a higher standard, the BRITANNIA, was introduced. Except for the years 1697-1720, gold was marked in the same way as silver until 1798, when numbers representing the carats were introduced. Until 1975 a crown was used in combination with the carat numbers 18 and 22 only, but today it is used with all carat numbers.

HANAU

A large German FAIENCE factory established near Frankfurt-am-Main by two Dutchmen in 1661. It continued in production until 1806. A

characteristic of the factory is the white background often sprinkled with blue dots. Marks: incised crescent, HVA or Hanau.

HANCOCK, ROBERT (1730-1817)

English engraver who pioneered the transfer-printing process on porcelain. He developed the process at the BATTERSEA enamel factory and in 1757 moved to the BOW porcelain factory. In the same year he began supplying transfer prints, notably his portraits of Frederick the Great, to the WORCESTER works. From the late 1770s he appears to have been supplying prints, often of rustic English scenes, on a freelance basis.

HAND COOLER

Marble, crystal and glass eggs used by 18th-century ladies to keep their hands cool.

£-££

HAND WARMER

This was a small object which could hold hot water or embers without scorching the hands. The inner container was surrounded by an outer casing, often made of decorative pierced metal.

££-£££

HANNONG FAMILY

Charles-François Hannong (1669-1739) was the founder of an

▼Rare brass hand warmer, 18th century, seen at the Derby Antiques Roadshow (£500-£700)

▲ Detail of stained glass window in St Mary's, Beverley, Yorks, designed by A.W.N. Pugin in 1850 and made by Hardman

important family of FAIENCE and porcelain factory managers. He started the Strasbourg and Haguenau factories later run by his son Paul-Antoine (1700-60), who went on to became the proprietor of FRANKENTHAL. In turn, his son Pierre-Antoine (1739-after 1794) began as manager of the Strasbourg factory and then moved to France, setting up factories at Vincennes in 1765, the Faubourg Saint Denis, Paris, in 1771, and at Vinovo in 1776. He returned to Alsace before ending up as director at SÈVRES in 1794.

HARDMAN, JOHN (1811-67)

A well-known metalworker who, with his partner William Powell, founded the firm of John Hardman & Co in Birmingham. They made domestic and ecclesiastical plate to designs by A.W.N. PUGIN, and later those of his pupil John Hardman Powell (William's son), in the GOTHIC REVIVAL style. From the 1840s they executed other types of church furnishings, including brass

Catch of the day

HARDY FISHING REELS

Hardy Brothers was founded in the 1870s at Alnwick, Northumberland, by William Hardy and his brother John. They sold sporting guns and knives, but soon expanded to make and sell split-cane fishing rods of the finest quality. When Forster, the third brother, joined the firm a few years later, they put the same commitment into the manufacture of fishing reels.

Two patents taken out in Forster's name, in 1888 and 1891, were for a new and literally revolutionary design which included ball bearings in Hardy reels to ensure a smoother rotation of the drum. These ball bearings were made of brass, but on the two smallest reels they were of steel. Like most fishing reels, the Hardy Brothers products came in various sizes. These ranged from 2 ¼in to 5 ¼in, the largest costing about 70 shillings, which was quite a sum in the 1890s.

The ball-bearing reels were the now famous Hardy Perfects, early examples of which have sold for many thousands of pounds. The continuing use of the name Perfect has, however, caused many disappointments, and it must be emphasised that only the first examples from the early 1890s are worth the highest sums. As a rule of thumb, Perfects made from brass and with an anodised finish are worth looking for.

Advances in production techniques can be an aid to dating Hardy reels with approximate accuracy. Ivory reel handles were used until about 1893, when ivorine was found to be an acceptable replacement that was less prone to cracking and breaking. Alloy Perfects made their first appearance in the 1897 catalogue, and from around the turn of the century alloy went into most reels. Horn was used in certain early reels, but also on some 20th-century ones.

The Hardy Brothers trademark, depicting a hand holding a fishing

▲ A rare Hardy 'Field' model, made for the angling editor of the *Field* magazine, c1900 (£150–£250)

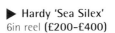

► Hardy 'Sea Silex' 6in reel (£200–£400)

rod, was stamped onto many of the early reels, and the company stopped using it in about 1905. The bracket which fixes the reel to the rod was plain and smooth until the early 1920s, when it was made ribbed with several rows of grooves. However, some later reels, too, have a plain bracket.

During the First World War, Hardy Brothers had the idea of making reels with interchangeable parts, and a later catalogue describes the Perfect, Special Perfect, Bougle, St George, St John and Uniqua reels as having common parts; reels bearing the words Mark I or Mark II fall into this category.

► A rare Hardy brass 3in Perfect reel (£3,000–£5,000)

► Hardy 'Zane Grey' game fishing reel, adjustable star drag and check catch, in case with screwdriver and Hardy's grease gun, c1928 (£1,500–£2,500)

▲ **George III** mahogany
Harlequin Pembroke table
(£800–£1,200)

work, embroideries and stained glass, and were employed for many of the furnishings for Barry and Pugin's Houses of Parliament. In the later 19th century the firm specialised only in stained glass, which, as John Hardman Studios, it still produces.

HARD-PASTE

This is true porcelain as invented by the Chinese. Made of china clay (KAOLIN) and china stone (petuntse), it is fired at a very high temperature at the gloss stage so that the glaze and body fuse into a single, vitreous, glass-like substance. It may be difficult to distinguish from SOFT-PASTE, but has a much harder, glass-like appearance and cannot be filed. When chipped, it appears uniform, unlike soft-paste, which has a granular appearance.

HARDWOOD

Botanical term for the timber from broad-leaved trees as opposed to softwood from conifers. In fact, much of it is not hard.

HAREWOOD

Sycamore or maple which has been dyed to a soft brown-grey. Used for the inlay on furniture. An alternative 18th-century name for it was silver-wood.

HARLEIAN BINDING

Eighteenth-century book bindings of red morocco, decorated with wide, tooled borders. They were made originally for the libraries of Robert and Edward Harley, the first and second Earls of Oxford.

 £££

HARLEQUIN TABLE

A dual-purpose table designed in the latter part of the 18th century. The folding, hinged top opens outwards and the interior is fitted as both a writing desk and a dressing table, with a hidden mirror and various drawers and pigeonholes. On other versions the interior fittings rise from the table-top when a catch is released.

R£££–£££££

HARRACHOV GLASS

A major Bohemian glass factory founded in 1712. It is well known for glass made in the BIEDERMEIER style, and in the late 19th century became one of the most important producers of luxury glass in Europe.

HAT OR HALL STAND

These were Regency innovations which became common in the mid-19th century. A hall stand could accommodate hats, coats, umbrellas and occasionally had a small drawer for clothes brushes. The first were mahogany, with upward, sabre-curve arms; Victorian versions might be cast iron or oak, and followed more elaborate, complicated designs. The independent hat stand made of BENT-WOOD, which is still a familiar sight, was probably first designed for restaurants and hotel lobbies, also in the mid-19th century.

£££–££££

▲ **Early Victorian** mahogany
hall stand (£4,500–£5,000)

▲ 3rd Dragoon Guards,
1871pattern (£2,000–£2,500)

▲ 12th Lancers
1856 pattern
(£3,000–£3,500)

▲ Scinde Horse, c1865
(£1,500–£2,000)

Get ahead, get a helmet

HELMETS

Helmets are almost as old as warfare and all ancient civilisations displayed rank and power through military headdress. With the advent of gunpowder, full armour and great battle 'helms' were gradually abandoned, but headdress continued to be flamboyant, as it is at ceremonial parades today. There follow a few 19th- and 20th-century examples and some maintenance hints for collectors.

The 3rd (Prince of Wales's) Dragoon Guards trace their origins back to 1685. Their battle honours for the Peninsular War (1808-14) are Talavera, Vittoria and Albuhera. The helmet shown here is of the last pattern, introduced in 1871. In post-First World War amalgamations the regiment joined the Carabiniers (6th Dragoon Guards), and in 1928 they became the 3rd Carabiniers (Prince of Wales's Dragoon Guards).

The 12th (Prince of Wales's Royal) Lancers. Formed in 1715 as Dragoons, they were converted to Lancers in 1816, remaining as such until after the Second World War when, with the 9th, they became the 9th/12th Lancers. They served through the Peninsula, Waterloo, Crimea and South Africa. The correct name for a lance cap is *Czapka*, often spelt 'shapka' in English. It comes from the Polish lancers who achieved fame with Napoleon's army. Originally the *Czapka* was far larger and more impressive, with a large square top

Indian Army — The Scinde Horse came into being at Hyderabad in 1838, and in 1841 Lieutenant John Jacob of the Bombay Artillery took command — a tough commander in a tough unit. After seeing much action in various places, the Scinde Horse took part in suppressing the Indian Mutiny. The helmet shown was worn until 1882 and, curiously enough, the men do not seem to have suffered from the sun, but they were allowed a scarlet cloth pugaree when needed for protection.

Prussian Garde du Corps. The headquarters was at Potsdam. They were the elite heavy cavalry regiment of the imperial German army and personal bodyguard to the Kaiser. They wore a breast and backplate (cuirass) and the helmets were made of tombac (an alloy of zinc and copper), with a lobster-tail back and the star badge. The metal rosette, or cockade, on the side carried the colours of the German empire. The silver flying eagle was worn only on full dress parades; at other times it was replaced by a spike finial. It was worn until the First World War.

The 9th (Queen's Royal) Lancers. Formed as a Dragoon Regiment, they became Lancers in 1816. In 1830 the regiment was adopted by William IV's Queen Adelaide. The lance cap badge bears her royal arms and interlaced and reversed cipher. On full dress parades a black and white cock's feather plume would be worn, and for undress, black and white horsehair.

◆ Never store helmets in a warm or damp attic.
◆ For storage over long periods place in polythene bags, extract air with a vacuum cleaner and seal.
◆ Leather-covered headdress should be wiped with a thin film of Vaseline before storage, especially any patent leather parts such as chinstraps. Do not touch cloth areas.
◆ Wash horsehair plumes in warm, soapy water and dry thoroughly. Comb out before drying.
◆ To clean dusty and lightly soiled feathers, place in paper bag, add fine salt, shake vigorously.
◆ Use only a bristle clothes brush on plumes and cloth.
◆ Ammonia can improve gilt on badges and metal parts (but remove from headdress if possible). Apply with a toothbrush, neutralise afterwards with water, and dry thoroughly.
◆ A badly soiled headdress should be professionally cleaned.
◆ Whatever you attempt to improve or clean, try a small area first.

▲ German Garde du Corps, *c*1900 (£5,000-£6,000)

▲ 9th Lancers, 1856 pattern (£3,000-£3,500)

Deep breaths of fresh air

HEAL'S

The well-known furniture business of Heal and Son was founded in 1810, at first as a mattress and featherbed manufacturer. By the late 19th century it was among the leading London furniture-makers and retailers.

The defining characteristics of Heal's furniture, as established by AMBROSE HEAL from the 1890s, were reticent quality and good-mannered gentility. Lightly fumed and waxed oak was a favourite material, sometimes inset with pewter, ebony or other ornamental panels. Gradually these lines weaned the British middle classes from their insistence on reproduction 18th-century furniture designs.

Heal's Simple Bedroom Furniture, and the equivalents for other parts of the house, were breaths of fresh air for those who felt stifled by the Victorian and Edwardian obsessions with the past. As the 20th century progressed, Heal's offered ART DECO, without going to extremes, and from 1930 produced a 'signed edition' series of furniture as well as beginning to stock chromium-plated and tubular steel items.

At this time the ARTS AND CRAFTS dominance was replaced by a flirtation with Continental designers such as Ruhlmann. Steel, aluminium and leather were common materials. Heal's was not limited to furniture. They were retailers for some of the most avant garde works of art of the time, selling ceramics by PILKINGTON's, Hans Coper and Lucie RIE and glass by leading designers. It was Ambrose Heal's advice that was sought by Stevens & Williams before taking on the influential Keith Murray who also worked for WEDGWOOD and whose pots were also sold at Heal's. They then won an excellent reputation for stocking the best modern furniture and fittings.

The range of Heal's fabrics, begun in the 1940s, was commissioned from such eminent designers as Roger Nicholson and Lucienne Day. By 1965 the store had grown to more than 21 departments. The company was sold to Sir Terence Conran in 1983, and in 1990 was the subject of a management buyout.

◀ Inlaid oak table, c1900, designed by Ambrose Heal. At the Geffrye Museum, London

◀ Dining table in limed oak, 1940s (£2,000–£3,000)

▲ **Special edition**
corner writing table
and chair in limed
oak, designed by
Ambrose Heal, 1931
(**£2,500-£3,500**)

◀ **A selection of**
trade catalogues
from Heal's

▲ **Twin pedestal** writing
desk, 'signed edition', 1931
(**£2,000-£3,000**)

▲ **Böttger Hausmahlerie** coffee pot,
probably painted by Elizabeth Wald (**£4,000**)

HAUSMAHLER
The term comes from the German for 'home painter' and means an independent decorator of porcelain, glass and enamels. These outworker craftsmen and women flourished in Germany, Austria and Bohemia, obtaining undecorated wares from the factories.

HEAL, SIR AMBROSE (1872-1959)
The leadership of Sir Ambrose Heal, who joined the family firm in 1893, turned Heal's into a flagship for modern British design. He issued his first catalogue of plain oak furniture in 1898, and thereafter employed the most talented young designers. From 1913 he organised exhibitions in the Mansard Gallery at the top of Cecil Brewer's new Heal's building, and commissioned writers and designers to produce booklets and posters about his products.

HEREND
Hungarian porcelain and pottery factory, founded in 1838. It produced from the 1870s. It made good quality reproductions that are often mistaken for SAMSON It flourishes today, making ornamental pieces and tableware.

HEROLD, JOHANN GREGOR (1696-1775)
One of the outstanding German porcelain painters who produced

All in the best possible taste

HEPPLEWHITE, GEORGE (d. 1786)

He probably never made any furniture himself, but became famous for a style of furniture based on his designs, published posthumously in 1788 in *The Cabinet Maker and Upholsterer's Guide* (shown below).

The Hepplewhite style became increasingly popular towards the end of the 19th century. Pieces are elegantly proportioned with curved seat rails and sofa backs, delicate tracery, carved fretwork and square, tapering legs. Mahogany and satinwood, often inlaid with marquetry, painting, lacquering and gilding, and NEO-CLASSICAL decorative motifs such as the husk, lyre and ACANTHUS were used.

It is because he published a successful book of designs that, together with CHIPPENDALE and SHERATON, he became a household name, and that his manner was so copied and imitated in late Victorian and Edwardian times, when even the names of many other eminent cabinetmakers of the period were forgotten.

▶ One of a set of five George III chairs after a design by Hepplewhite (£2,800 the set)

▲ Harewood and satinwood demi-lune side cabinet in Hepplewhite style, 1775 (£10,000–£15,000)

exquisite decoration on MEISSEN wares. He joined the factory in 1720 and was able to produce colours which maintained a faultless surface texture during firing. His most distinctive work is in the CHINOISERIE style with fantastic spidery figures, trees and buildings. Other designs include landscapes, harbour scenes, flowers and birds. Few pieces are signed, and he may have spent much of his time supervising the studio, rather than with brush in hand.

HEROLD, CHRISTIAN FRIEDRICH (*c*1700–79)

He may have been JOHANN GREGOR's cousin. A less noted porcelain painter, he was also employed at MEISSEN and is best known for his harbour scenes.

HEYDE

Georg Heyde began making toy soldiers in Dresden in about 1872, just after the Franco-Prussian War. The business was closed by the bombing of the city in 1945. His soldiers were 'full-round' and solid, and although they were often clumsy, misshapen and inaccurate, they came in a wide variety of true-to-life poses and were expertly marketed. Like his later competitors BRITAIN'S, Heyde produced armies of many nations, but unlike theirs, his products are not marked, and his cataloguing was perfunctory. This laid him open to the pirating of his designs, and to confusion with those of other makers such as Haffner, Heinrichsen and Spenkuch.

££–£££

▼ Heyde military cyclist from a set of 10 in original box, some damage (£800–£900)

▶ **Sheffield plate** soup tureen, c1830, with flamboyant family crest. Seen at the Blenheim Palace Roadshow (**£800–£1,000**)

◀ **Worcester saucer,** c1770 painted in the James Giles London studio, with the arms of the Worshipful Company of Plumbers (**cracked £100**)

◀ **Tables of consanguinity** between Queen Marie de Medicis and Henri IV of France, by genealogist Pierre d'Hozier (1592-1660) (**£3,500**)

Heeding the call to arms

HERALDRY

Many works of art, particularly ceramics and silver, have in the past been dignified by the owner's coat of arms or crest. If the piece can be tied to a particular individual or family, then the interest and value will be increased.

Despite the claims of salesmen, arms cannot be adopted by anyone with the same name. No two living persons are entitled to exactly the same arms. The basic shield of a family will be 'differenced' for various members, but a crest may be common to all.

Mottoes — the inscription, often in Latin, beneath the arms — are the easiest to check, but they, like the crest, may be shared by numerous families. In fact, the crest and motto are not always enough on their own to pin-point a family.

Heraldry is a hugely complicated subject, but books can guide one through the complexities. Failing that, a letter to the College of Heralds in London may be the solution. This may fail if the arms are of even a quite prominent Continental family or, as often, the arms were never properly owned or recorded.

A combination of motto, arms and the chain of the Order of St Patrick enabled experts at the Luton Hoo Roadshow to identify a fine damask linen tablecloth as being made for Lord Zetland, Lord Lieutenant of Ireland, 1889-92.

HINGES

Hinges evolved from iron straps into elaborate adornments in the 16th century in either butterfly or H form, known as a cockspur. They then shrank again, were made in brass and followed the current styles until, by the late 18th century they were mostly hidden.

HIRADO

Japanese porcelain factory outside Arita, founded in about 1760 and

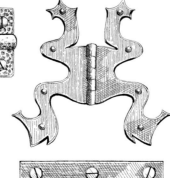

sold to Fukagawa in about 1900. They made mostly small scale wares decorated in underglaze blue in a fine white body. Pieces are rarely marked.

£££-££££

HISPANO-MORESQUE

A style in which European and Islamic elements were fused as a result of the Moorish conquest of Spain in

▶ **Hispano-Moresque** copper lustre and blue armorial charger (**£11,000**)

the 8th century. Hispano-Moresque pottery was made from the 13th to 15th centuries. It combined glazing and lustre techniques, as well as eastern motifs, KUFIC inscriptions and boldly painted animals with Gothic motifs and even heraldry. In the 15th century, striking silks were also produced with a similar combination of Islamic and Gothic motifs.

HÖCHST

A pottery and porcelain factory founded near Mainz in 1746. Initially it made FAIENCE wares in exotic forms such as tureens in the form of pug dogs, boars' heads and turkeys, painted in bright enamel colours, alongside more conventional wares. In 1750 it began producing porcelain, the best products being finely modelled figure groups including COMMEDIA DELL' ARTE figures, and a large centrepiece of a Chinese emperor. Marks: a six-spoked, or an impressed, wheel.

HO-HO BIRD

A mythical bird that eats nothing living and is a symbol of fire. In some ways it is the Chinese equivalent of the phoenix. It has a long

◀ Ho-ho bird: detail from a large giltwood Rococo pier mirror

beak, crest, claws, flowing tail and curving neck. Found on 16th-century grotesque ornament, it came into its own in the 18th century as a CHINOISERIE motif on woodwork

▼ Höchst figure of Daphnis, modelled by Taube, 1775 (£1,500–£2,000)

(especially LOOKING GLASSES), plasterwork and ceramics.

HOLLY

A hard, coarse, greenish-white or ivory-coloured wood, used for inlay in cabinetmaking. It was a favourite with George BULLOCK.

HONESTY BOX

A brick-shaped brass tobacco dispenser as used in 19th-century public houses. It has a handle in the middle and a coin slot at one end. The drop of the coin released the lid at the other end—leaving it to the honesty of the smoker how much tobacco he took.

££-£££

HONITON LACE

The earliest and best English lace, made from Antwerp thread in floral designs from 1620 to 1725. From the mid-19th century, machine-made lace was produced at Honiton. Handmade lace was later revived as a craft art.

HOOD

The movable part of the wooden case of a LONGCASE CLOCK, it surrounds the dial and encloses the mechanism. On early longcase clocks the hood slides upwards to expose the winding, but by the early 18th century hoods had grown in height and were fitted with doors.

HOOF FOOT

Cloven or solid hoof feet were used on furniture in ancient times. The device was popular in Europe during the 18th and 19th centuries.

Arbiter of Regency taste

HOPE, THOMAS (1769–1831)

A member of a Scottish banking and mercantile family that had settled in Amsterdam, he travelled as a young man in the Near East, Greece, Spain, Portugal and France.

In 1795 the French occupation of Holland forced him to move to London, with much of his wealth intact, and he became widely influential as a collector, patron, architect, furniture designer and arbiter of taste in Regency society.

His large collections of antique vases, works of art and sculpture were shown in his town and country houses, together with his own Grecian and Egyptian-style furniture. His approach to design was that of a purist, which can lead to the discomfort of anyone using his chairs.

His pieces make great play with classical features such as lion MONO-PEDIA, VOLUTES, ANTHEMIONS, winged or crouching lions, hieroglyphs and the like. His most influential publication was *Household Furniture and Interior Decoration*, 1807, and his designs were adopted and adapted by many British cabinetmakers, who were usually rather less pedantic than he was.

▲ One of a pair of Regency ormolu bacchante masks by Hope (£4,600 the pair)

▼ Regency simulated rosewood and parcel-gilt stool, after Hope (£13,000)

▼ Regency gilded mahogany stool by Hope (£34,000)

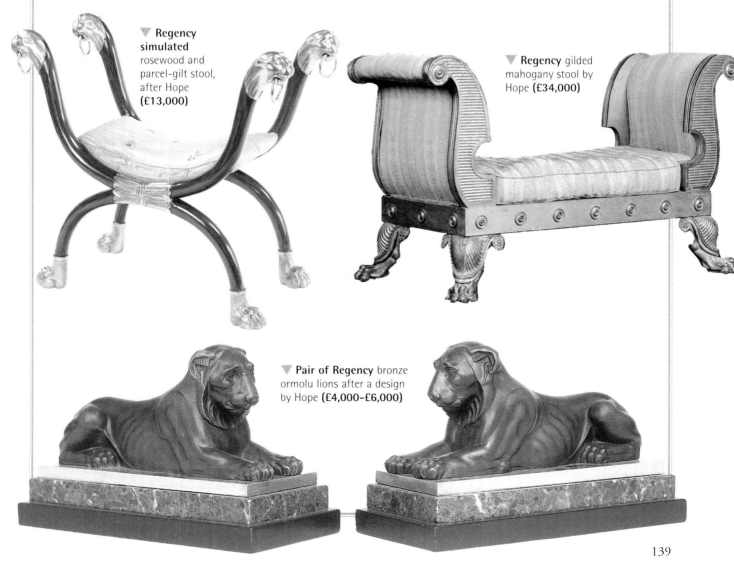

▼ Pair of Regency bronze ormolu lions after a design by Hope (£4,000–£6,000)

When trains ran on the right lines

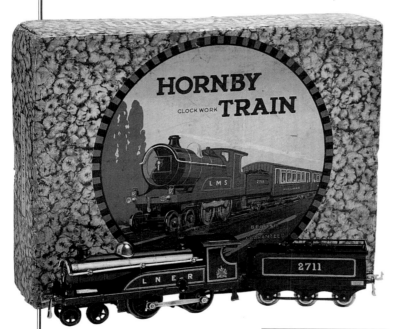

▲ Barely used 1925 train set in mint condition with box (£750–£1,000)

HORNBY

The most famous British toy train manufacturer was Meccano Ltd, founded by Frank Hornby in 1901. Hornby was convinced he could make a train that would compete with those of the German manufacturers. He researched and developed them carefully, using many of the standard pieces of the Meccano set,

so his early trains were bolted together.

He felt the large gauges of the German sets were too big for the average modern house, and so developed the '0' gauge which equals a track gauge of 1.25in. This was later reduced to '00' (0.625in).

In 1925 he produced his first electric train, and throughout the 1920s and 1930s brought out a vast range of locomotives, tank engines, Pullman coaches, brake vans and wagons.

The most desirable are the magnificent '0'-gauge trains such as the Princess Elizabeth and the LMS (London Midland and Scottish Railway) locomotives which will make £1,500–£2,000. Among the rarest and most valuable in the '0'-gauge are trains in the Caledonian livery. Pre-war trains were marked as Hornby Series, and the less collectable post-war ones as Hornby Trains.

During the Second World War, production was switched to the war effort but it resumed soon

after, as it did at DINKY toys. After the Second World War, production of the '00' gauge was seen as being the way forward, and production of the '0'-gauge range ceased in the early 1960s.

In 1938, after Frank Hornby's death, the company introduced a range called Hornby Dublo, accompanied by miniature vehicles known as Dinky Dublo models. After Lines Bros bought out Meccano in 1964, the trains were made in plastic rather than being die-cast, and these lines do not have the same collectability.

As so often with toys, condition is critical, as is the presence of the original box. However, there is a strong demand for complete layouts already fixed to baseboards and fitted with appropriate buildings, equipment and background landscapes.

▶ Two rare pre-war Dublo train sets. The top is clockwork, (£800–£1,000); the bottom electric (£400–£600)

▼ An '0'-gauge train, the 'Riviera Blue' (with original box £500–£800)

◀ **Hornby electric** locomotives from a mixed collection **(£300–£400)**

▲ **Hopvine decoration** on Beilby enamelled beer decanter, *c*1775 **(£6,000)**

HOPVINE DECORATION

A popular motif in 19th-century cast-iron work and plasterwork where it could trail across ceilings. It also appears as an ornament in public houses and on ale flutes and beer glasses. Sometimes the only way one can judge whether a glass was intended for beer or for wine is by the hop or grapevine decoration.

HORN FURNITURE

Furniture made from antlers became popular in the mid-19th century. The main centre of production was Frankfurt, but it was also made by the London firms of Messrs Silber and Fleming and Messrs Yetley. It was especially popular for furnishing Victorian shooting lodges, where presumably the evidence of sporting prowess was valued over and above comfort—or even after-dinner safety!

£££–£££££

▶ **Very unusual carved** mahogany 'buffalo' chair with real horns and hooves **(£30,000 a pair)**

HOUSEHOLD EFFECTS
Term to cover everything that cannot be slipped into the 'antiques' category — often the lots at the end of a house contents sale, which the auctioneer may not have catalogued in detail. Optimistic bidders hope to find bargains among the towel racks, chamber pots, broken toys and riding boots, with the result that they very rarely do.

HORSE
The horse is not only a servant of man, but a symbol of nobility, military prowess, and kingship. It also represents Europe among the continents. In its own right it may symbolise speed and strength, and it has appeared in art since the first cave painters. Among the proudest representations are the great pottery horses of the Tang dynasty, which escorted Chinese nobles in their graves. Furniture-makers, however, saw things in a more prosaic light. Just as the more humble donkey, *ezel* in Dutch, gave its name to the easel, 'horse' became the term for a four-legged frame acting as a support such as a clothes or towel horse.

▼ Large Chinese pottery figure of a horse, 30in high, AD618-906 (**£90,000**)

HORSE BRASSES
Horse brasses do not hold the appeal that they once did. Originally brasses were to protect draught horses from the evil eye, and they decorated martingale chest straps, and bridles. Simple suns, stars and the like, from before about 1815, should have hammer marks on the back. Cast versions appeared around 1835, and from 1870 copies were made in machine-stamped rolled spelter (commercial zinc). These are lighter and cruder in detail. Brasses should be on their straps, and pseudo-straps are known from as early as the 1870s. Large numbers of modern copies now flood the market

 £-££

HORSEHAIR
A material woven from the mane and tail of horses, popular for upholstery in the 19th century. Unwoven horsehair was also used. Restorers still use it in preference to the synthetic fireproof substitutes of today.

HORSE MEASURE
Horses are measured in hands to the shoulder, and the simplest measures for this are rulers with folding arms. Others are spirit levels with plumb lines, while some telescope into walking sticks.

 **££-£££**

HORSESHOE TABLE
A table with flaps which could extend to form a half-circle. It was ideal for drinking parties, as the guests sitting around the outer circumference could be served from the inner side. When not in use the flaps were folded back.

 ££££-£££££

HU
Chinese Bronze Age wine vessels which may be gourd- or moon-shaped, flat or square.

£££££-££££££

HUAN
A Chinese ritual jade object. It is a flat disk with a circular hole in the centre, and its significance is unknown.

£££-££££

HUKIN AND HEATH
A firm of ELECTROPLATERS and silversmiths established in Birmingham in 1855. The original partners were Jonathan Wilson Hukin and John Thomas Heath. Hukin retired in March 1881 and the company continued as Hukin and Heath with a new partner John Hartshorne Middleton. It is best known for its silver and electroplated goods produced in the 1870s and '80s to designs by Christopher DRESSER. It also made a whole range of domestic items in many styles and continued to encourage young designers through the 1920s and '30s before closing in 1953. The mark found on the firm's electroplate is a bird with spread wings.

▲ Brass horse measure, c1890, seen at the Newcastle Emlyn Roadshow (**£60-£80**)

▼ Claret jug, 1901, by Heath and Middleton, seen at the Blenheim Palace Roadshow (**£1,200-£2,000**)

Important George I two-handled wine cooler by David Willaume, 1718 (£120,000)

Standard raisers

HUGUENOTS

These were French converts from Roman Catholicism, whose numbers swelled following the spread of Protestant beliefs from Switzerland in the mid-16th century. Fierce opposition from the Catholics culminated in a massacre on St Bartholomew's Eve 1572, but the situation was calmed to an extent by the Edict of Nantes of 1598,

◄ Silver candlesticks by David Willaume, from a set of four (£15,000–£25,000)

which, with various conditions, allowed religious toleration for the Protestants in France. In 1685, however, the Edict of Nantes was revoked and those Huguenots who had not already left fled France to the Protestant countries of Europe. An estimated 50,000 of them eventually arrived in England. The goldsmiths, cabinetmakers and other craftsmen mostly settled in the developing suburb of Soho in London, apart from the weavers, who made their homes in Spitalfields.

The Huguenots were the finest craftsmen of the day. To succeed, they had to be as good as their Roman Catholic rivals and, given the prejudice against them, able to undercut the Catholics on price. Not only did they have to be superb craftsmen, they had to be extremely efficient businessmen.

Certainly they forced the English craftsman to raise his standards, and it is perhaps not unreasonable to attribute some of the high standards of 18th-century English craftsmanship to

▲ Queen Anne silver-gilt cup, cover and salver (detail above) by Philip Rollos (£150,000 the pair)

this 'shot in the arm' from the Huguenots. The casting of silver was one area where the improvements were radical.

And where would 18th-century English goldsmithing have been without names such as Pierre Harache, David WILLAUME, Philip Rollos, Peter Archambo I, Pierre PLATEL, Paul DE LAMERIE, Nicholas SPRIMONT (who went on to produce Chelsea porcelain), Anne Tanqueray and Paul Crespin?

◀ 18-carat gold hunter watch, *c*1825, seen at the Colchester Roadshow (£1,000)

HUNTER WATCH

A mid-19th-century watch with a hinged cover to prevent the glass from being broken. A half-hunter case has a chapter ring engraved or enamelled on the cover around a glass so the hands can be read without the lid being opened.

 £££-££££

HUNTING CHAIR

An early 19th-century overstuffed armchair with mahogany legs and a sliding frame extending beyond the seat. The cushions from the chair-back rest on the extended seat so that those exhausted by a day in the saddle can recline with their feet up.

£££-££££

HURDY-GURDY

A stringed musical instrument with a mechanical bow, used in Europe from the 11th century. It has a large, fiddle-shaped body with three strings and a peg box. The right hand turns a crank-handle which vibrates the strings: the left hand plays a row of finger-keys.

£££-££££

HUSK MOTIF

Stylised representation of a corn husk used in BAROQUE and NEO-CLASSICAL silver and furniture.

HUTCH

A small larder for meat or grain in the form of a wooden box on legs with doors of metal gauze.

◀ Hand-coloured hunting print, *Sweeping a Brook* by Henry Alken, from a set of six, 1831 (£3,800 the set)

Fit for the chase

HUNTING

The chase is far older than man, and even if hunting were ever abolished, an instinctive fascination would remain. As soon as hunting became more than a matter of mere survival and the satisfaction of hunger, it began to attract ceremonial. Each variety developed its language, uniforms and ritualistic equipment. Death was to be dignified. Hunting on horseback, in particular, became a way in which the military spirit could be fostered in case of need, and sublimated when not needed.

The great hunts of England, France and elsewhere have provided collectors with many relics of different kinds, from coats and BUTTONS, by way of horns and STIRRUP CUPS, to a wealth of paintings and prints. Buyers of hunting prints should remember that the best sets, such as those by Henry Alken, were frequently reissued, and late editions may be from worn-out plates. Colouring may also be modern, but if it is tactfully done, this may not detract greatly from value.

One of the more unusual items associated with hunting must be the chamber exercise horse. This was intended to help those who had over-indulged to get into some sort of shape before mounting a real horse.

▼ Hunting and other items from the estate of Siegfried Sassoon (£110-£350 each)

▶ Early 19th-century hunting coat (£100-£150)

144

IDEAL TOY AND NOVELTY COMPANY

The company founded by Morris MICHTOM in 1903 is credited with the invention of the teddy bear—although STEIFF would dispute it. After a newspaper photograph had appeared of the American President with a bear cub, Michtom wrote to Theodore Roosevelt asking permission to name a toy bear after him. The mohair teddy, with his shorn muzzle, wide ears and glass eyes, caught on, and under Morris's son Benjamin the company became the USA's largest toy manufacturer. The bear is still in production. Early bears are especially eagerly sought after. They are not usually marked but have a distinctive, barrel-shaped body, much wider than a German bear's, and a pointed hump at the back of the neck. The early bears were made of short mohair; later ones have longer fur. There are plenty of forgeries so be suspicious of bears in good condition, which have clearly never been loved.

£££££-£££££

ILLUMINATION

Strictly speaking, illumination means decoration including metallic gold or silver, which reflects and sparkles when it catches the light. In fact the term is applied to the lavishly deco-

▲ **Illuminated capital letter** from an alphabet by Ruth Rowland commissioned for this *Antiques Roadshow* publication

rated books which were produced by hand in Europe from the 6th century to the early years of the 16th. After this, most books were produced on a printing press, although luxury editions were still printed and then illuminated by hand. By the 1st century AD, bound books had evolved from the scrolls of antiquity, and vellum (specially prepared animal skin) had replaced papyrus as a more durable support. Among the earliest illuminated manuscripts to survive are the great Celtic monastic books such as the Lindisfarne Gospels, produced in Northumberland and Ireland while most of Europe was engulfed in the Dark Ages. From the 9th century the court of Charlemagne, which modelled itself on classical traditions, was a major centre of book production. Books were also being made in monasteries all over Europe. By 1200, the monastic tradition had largely died out and the new scribes and illuminators were professionals supplying the needs of the universities, the new centres of learning. In the 15th century the French and Burgundian royal families were famous patrons of illuminated books, but with the rise

of the middle classes the demand for books, both ecclesiastical and secular, seemed almost unlimited. Illumination had a final flowering in the Renaissance when a whole new generation of humanistic collectors was swept up in the excitement of rediscovering the classical texts of antiquity.

IMARI

The European name for a type of Japanese porcelain made at ARITA for export from the late 17th century and shipped through the port of Imari. It is very richly decorated with underglaze blue, red enamel and gilding. Imari patterns, such as the floral 'brocaded Imari', were adapted and widely used by English porcelain factories, including DERBY, MINTON, SPODE and WORCESTER.

◄ **One of a pair of Imari** vases from the Arita kilns, seen at the Newcastle Emlyn Roadshow, 25in high (£1,500-£2,000)

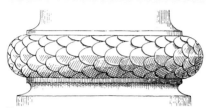

IMBRICATED ORNAMENT
Carved ornament that represents formalised fish scales.

IMPERIAL DINING TABLE
The furniture company GILLOWS
gave this name to a Victorian dining
table that could be lengthened by
inserting loose leaves.

£££££-£££££

INCUNABULA
Derived from the Latin word *cunae*
meaning a cradle, incunabula are
books produced from the invention
of printing, *c*1440, until the year
1500. Such works are not as rare as
one might think. Most survivors were
printed in Latin in Venice and
brought learning to an eager public
throughout Europe.

£££-£££££

INCISED ORNAMENT
Decoration which has been cut or
carved into the surface—be it silver,
wood, ceramic, stone or lacquer.
In the case of the latter, layers of
different colours may be built up
which show stripes when cut.

INDIAN ROSEWOOD
Also known as Bombay blackwood,
this is a dark, purplish-black wood
which is exceptionally tough and used
for furniture and piano cases.

INDIANISHE BLUMEN
Literally meaning 'Indian flowers',
this is the German name for formalised flower motifs taken from

▲ **Fine Anglo-
Indian** ivory-
inlaid rosewood
cabinet on
stand, late 18th
century
(£10,000)

▼ **Workbox
decorated** with ivory
and porcupine quills,
made in India for the
European market,
1835-55. Seen at the
Guernsey Roadshow
(£150-£200)

◀ Corporation of the East India Company 1808 (£1-£3)

▶ Cartridge which helped start the Indian Mutiny seen at the Basingstoke Roadshow

Mutiny and the bounty

INDIAN GOODS AND STYLE

In the early 18th century the term covered every variety of produce imported from the Orient, not just India but also China and Japan. 'Indian shops' grew up to suppply the demand for textiles, porcelain and other decorative objects. They were stocked from quayside auctions held by the East India Company.

With the decline of the Mogul Empire and the rise of British influence in India in the late 18th century, a picturesque version of the Indian style became much in vogue in British architecture and design. William Hodges's *Selected Views of India* (1785-88) and T. and W. Daniell's *Oriental Scenery* (1795-1808) were important sources of ornament, which was translated into porcelain designs. Imported Indian cottons had a strong influence on British textile design, particularly the famous PAISLEY pattern.

Nabobs of the East India Company, such as the first governor-general, Warren Hastings, built houses incorporating Indian elements on their return home, and Thomas HOPE had an Indian drawing room in his Duchess Street mansion. The exterior of the Prince Regent's Brighton Pavilion is in Hindu style. In the mid-19th century India re-emerged as an important influence in decorative arts.

Following the Great Exhibition of 1851, an enormous number of Indian objects were purchased for the Victoria and Albert Museum. The Indian Mutiny (1857-58) kept the sub-continent in the forefront of the public mind, and once Queen Victoria was declared Empress of India in 1877, the style was even more in vogue.

A relic of the Mutiny, which turned up at the Basingstoke Roadshow was a reminder of the part played in it by artists' cartridge paper. This was used as casing for cartridges, and it was the Hindu troops' belief that the paper was greased with cow fat that sparked the revolt.

The tea planters and administrators brought back INDIAN IVORY FURNITURE , boxes, CHESS SETS, inlaid steel armour and dishes. Among the most sought after Indian works of art are the 'Company School' paintings executed by European-trained local artists who specialised in the flora and fauna of their area. Popular too then, as they are today, were inlaid marble tables. Particularly sought after are miniature paintings depicting the Maharajas, religious and folk stories.

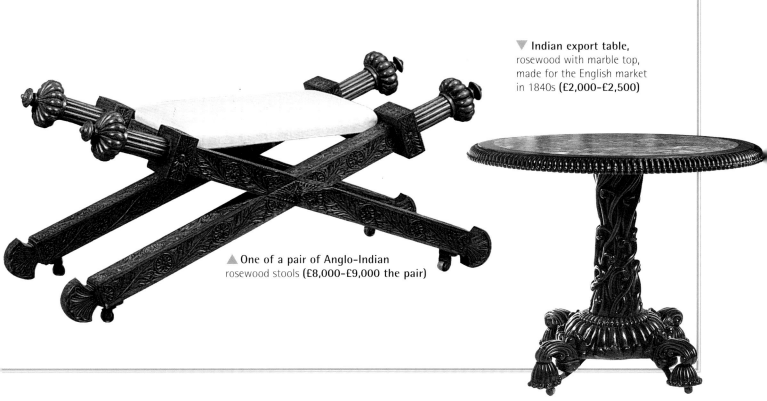

▼ Indian export table, rosewood with marble top, made for the English market in 1840s (£2,000-£2,500)

▲ One of a pair of Anglo-Indian rosewood stools (£8,000-£9,000 the pair)

Oriental porcelain. The petals are firmly outlined and filled in with simply graded colours. They first appeared on MEISSEN porcelain in c1725 and were copied throughout Europe.

INDIAN IVORY FURNITURE

As the British began to colonise India in the mid-18th century, they started to demand European-style furniture, and turned to local craftsmen and materials to interpret their designs. The coastal station of Vizagapatam, and Murshidabad, the capital of Old Bengal, became important centres for furniture in the Anglo-Indian style. Built around a core of wood such as padouk, sandalwood, satinwood or teak, it was either inlaid with ivory or completely veneered with ivory sheets. Distinctive Indian designs were used for decoration, and ivory pegs for jointing and veneering. Lacquer, blackened by the addition of iron sulphate, was applied to ivory to highlight the decorative motifs. Some of these magnificent pieces were brought home by returning dignitaries, and more generally there was a flourishing trade in portable items such as sandalwood and ivory boxes, frames and mirrors well into

◀ **Japanese inro,** showing the way the different compartments are held together, c1860 **(£2,000-£3,000)**

the 19th century. There are important suites of Anglo-Indian furniture at Powis Castle in Wales, Kedleston Hall in Derbyshire, Buckingham Palace, and Osborne House, Isle of Wight, where Queen Victoria created a Durbar Room as a showcase for her Indian collections, many presented after she was proclaimed Empress of India in 1877.

INGLENOOK FURNISHINGS

In the 17th century the large, open inglenook fireplace with its deep, hooded chimney was the centre of family life and the place where most of the cooking was done. Furnishings, mostly in cast or wrought iron, included fire backs and dogs, spits for roasting, jacks for turning spits, kettles and kettle tilters to hang them on, flat gridirons for grilling, and a whole range of ladles, hooks and trivets. 'Inglenook' literally means the fireside corner, and the inglenook seat was a high-backed wooden settle which fitted into the sides of the fireplace. In the Edwardian period the inglenook was revived to become an essential feature of cottage-style architecture.

INRO

These are small, beautifully decorated Japanese lacquer boxes made up of compartment trays strung together, one on top of the other. The inro hangs by a cord from a carved NETSUKE which is pushed up under a sash to sit on top of it, since Japanese clothes had no pockets. The compartments were for seals and medicines.

£££-££££

INLAY

Ornamenting the surface of an object by inserting a contrasting material in a decorative pattern. Mahogany is often inlaid with lighter-coloured woods or tortoiseshell, and mother-of-pearl and silver with contrasting metal alloys or NIELLO.

INTARSIA

A type of pictorial Italian marquetry found especially on Renaissance choir stalls. Architectural perspectives were especially popular, and intarsia panels were designed by artists as famous as Piero della Francesca and Uccello.

INTARSIO WARE

Hand-painted earthenware art pieces, produced after 1896 by the SHELLEY pottery factory and others.

££-£££

◀ One of a pair of Indian polychrome ivory-veneered chairs in the Regency style, c1830 **(£22,000 the pair)**

▶ **Intarsio ware vase** by Wileman and Co, c1905. Seen at the Taunton Roadshow **(£250-£350)**

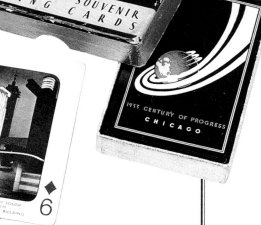

◀ **Souvenir silver card case** of the Great Exhibition, sold through the early 1850s **(£500–£600)**

▶ **Pack of playing cards** with views of different scenes from the Chicago World's Fair, 1953 **(£30–£50)**

Roll up, roll up for the greatest show on earth

INTERNATIONAL EXHIBITION

The Great Exhibition of 1851 was the brain-child of Prince Albert, Queen Victoria's consort, and the Crystal Palace built by Joseph Paxton to house it in Hyde Park caught the imagination of the world. The event was a great success and spawned a series of imitations which still continues in the modern World Fairs. Ceramics, glass and all sorts of commemoratives abound, as do items celebrating local art and industry fairs. The major international exhibitions have included:

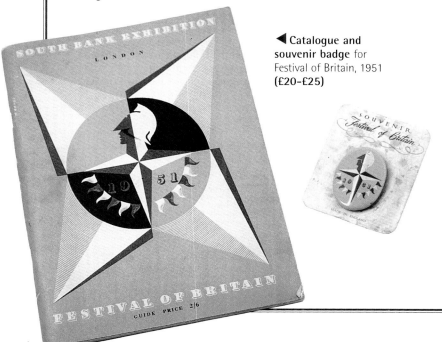

◀ **Catalogue and souvenir badge** for Festival of Britain, 1951 **(£20–£25)**

London	1851
Paris	1855
London	1862
Paris	1867
Vienna	1873
Philadelphia	1878
Sydney	1879
Melbourne	1880
London	1886
Melbourne	1888
Paris	1889
Chicago	1893
Paris	1900
Buffalo	1901
St Louis	1904
Liège	1905
London (Franco–British)	1908
Brussels	1910
Panama	1913
Pacific	1915
Wembley (British Empire)	1924–5
Paris	1925
Brussels	1935
London (Festival of Britain)	1951
Chicago	1953
Brussels	1958
Montreal	1967
Osaka	1970
Vancouver	1976
Seville	1992

Centuries–old treasures from the Emerald Isle

IRISH FURNITURE

Little survives from before the mid–18th century, but thereafter Irish furniture is distinctive. From c1740 to 1775 there was a vogue for hearty carving, especially of animal heads, masks, scallops, scrolls and baskets of flowers on the aprons of tables. Cabriole legs often had acanthus above claw, paw or pad feet. Dark woods, notably bog oak and mahogany stained to look like it, were popular until NEO–CLASSICISM brought in satinwood and harewood in the 1780s. Card tables, commodes, cabinets and PIER TABLES are often semi–eliptical rather than semi–circular as in England. The long, oval, gateleg 'WAKE' or COFFIN TABLE, as seen at the Newcastle Emlyn Roadshow, is Irish, although it was used for everyday dining as well as wakes. There are also a number of particularly Irish characteristics to 18th–century chair-backs, such as vase-shaped splats with two top rails, and corkscrew terminals on top rails.

In the mid–19th century the romantic popularity of Killarny inspired a local tourist industry making furniture and decorative objects of arbutus wood with inlays and carving of such local plants as shamrock, arbutus and bracken. Sometimes there is further pokerwork decoration of local views. The principal makers were Jeremiah O'Connor and James Egan.

Unlike many English contemporaries, James Hicks of Dublin (1866 - 1936) was no slavish copyist of 18th century designs. He was a 'cabinet-manufacturer, collector and restorer of CHIPPENDALE, ADAM and SHERATON furniture,' who was born 150 years late. He also made Irish furniture which is very hard to tell from its ancestors.

▲ Silver dish ring, or 'potato ring', mid-18th century

IRISH SILVER

Traditions of goldsmithing go back at least 4,000 years in Ireland, with a 'golden age' from the 8th to the 12th century. Thereafter, little remains until the 17th century. In 1605 the Dublin City Council reorganised the Goldsmiths, requiring them to have a maker's mark and to submit pieces for testing and marking. It was not, however, until the Charter of 1637 transferring power from the Council to the Goldsmiths that standards really improved.

A year later date letters were introduced in addition to the crowned harp and maker's mark. From then it should be possible to date exactly any Dublin marked pieces. It was common, however, in the 18th century to omit marks. In 1731 a tax was imposed on silver. To show this had been paid the Hibernia mark was added and this has been retained. In 1807 the monarch's head mark first appeared, lasting, as in England, until 1890.

Many of the best surviving pieces date from the first half of the 18th century when top goldsmiths such as Bolton, Williamson, Hamilton, Walker and Calderwood were at work.

By the mid-18th century certain distinctly Irish characteristics and shapes are apparent: a rustic ROCOCO incorporating farmyard and rural scenes; helmet-shaped cream jugs; sugar bowls; some flatware; Freedom boxes; and of course, DISH RINGS. Often incorrectly called potato rings, these were to keep hot dishes from scorching table tops. Irish provincial silver is well worth looking out for, with the Cork mark the most likely to be found.

▲ Irish mid-Georgian yew-wood card table (£32,000)

IROKO

A heavy, strong and durable tropical wood that varies from light yellow to deep gold and dark brown, and takes on a good polish. It is sometimes used as a substitute for teak.

IRONS

These basic pieces of home equipment come in a range of sizes and forms that alter through the years. They were either heated in the fire or had hot bricks or charcoal put in the 'box'.

£-£££

▲ Victorian cast-iron box iron, seen at the Manchester Roadshow (£30-£50)

IRONSTONE

A tough, heavily potted form of porcellanous stoneware, a variant of which was patented by Charles James MASON in 1813. Ironstone, opaque china, opaque porcelain and other variants were made by numerous STAFFORDSHIRE manufacturers but none, despite the patent, contained the claimed ironstone slag. It was ideally suited for large dinner services as well as massive vases and fire surrounds. Considerable quantities were exported to the US and there is a flourishing market there.

ISLAMIC CERAMICS

The glazed earthenware made in the Middle East from the 9th to the 17th centuries was an enormous influence on the development of European ceramics. The human figure is very rarely depicted, and decoration consists of stylised leaves, birds and animals, and may show Chinese

▼ Iznik pottery tile, *c*1560 (£4,000-£6,000)

▲ Fine Islamic black and white jug from Nishapur 10th century (£9,000)

influence. It was probably an attempt to imitate the purity and whiteness of Chinese porcelain which first led to the invention of tin-glazed earthenware in 9th-century Baghdad. An independent school also flourished in eastern Persia, making wares with a pink or buff body decorated in a thick clay slip. In the 12th and 13th centuries soft-paste porcelain was made at Rayy and Kashan. These wares were decorated in monochrome to resemble Chinese celadon wares. The technique of LUSTRE painting is a 9th-century Islamic discovery; developed in Kashan, it was later transmitted to Spain, appearing on HISPANO-MORESQUE pottery. After the 13th century Mongol invasion of Persia only Kashan continued to flourish as a pottery centre. In the 15th century imported Chinese porcelain was copied in Syria and Persia, and by the early 16th century IZNIK was established as the most important pottery centre in the Middle East.

ISTORIATO

A type of decoration found on Italian MAIOLICA. Pots were covered with historical, biblical or mythological scenes, and were intended more for decoration than for actual use.

ITALIAN WALNUT

A hard, finely grained, light brown wood occasionally streaked with gold or stripes of darker brown.

IZNIK

Pottery made from 1490 to c1700 at the Ottoman pottery of the same name. It is decorated in rich colours of cobalt blue, turquoise, green, purple, red and black, on white clay slip and covered with a brilliant clear glaze. The decoration is abstract with stylised flowers and long curling leaves and combines the influence of Chinese porcelain with arabesques and KUFIC inscriptions. By the 17th century the quality had declined but it had considerable influence on 19th-century potters such as William de Morgan, and it is still produced for the tourist industry today.

££££-£££££

Toothy products of the carver's art

Strictly speaking, ivory is the tusk of an elephant, but the tusks and teeth of narwhals, walruses and hippopotamuses are also included under the term.

Since it is only available in comparatively small pieces, it is ideally suited for making delicate and intricately carved objects or small statues. It takes on a smooth, shiny surface when polished and is translucent when thinly carved.

Some of the finest carvings date from the late classical and early Christian periods. Exquisite ivories, many of ecclesiastical subjects, were made in the Middle Ages, especially in France. During the BAROQUE period some of the finest figurative carving was done by known masters such as Christof Angermair and J. M. Maucher. For a long time Dieppe was a major centre of the craft, as was Maastricht which specialised in ivory pistol butts carved as Turks' heads and the like. The 19th century saw a great revival of ivory carving; many objects were imitations of earlier works, some of fine quality.

The Chinese have carved ivory for thousands of years, most of their work being of Buddhistic significance, although quantities of pierced ivory concentric balls, card cases and fans were made for the export market. It was in Japan in the late 19th century under the influence of the Tokyo school that some of the most breathtaking figures were carved. These immortals, warriors, peasants and fisherman seem imbued with life and they are highly regarded both in the West and in Japan.

There is no reason why there should be any hesitation about owning old carvings and the market has not been affected by recent international Wildlife Protection Acts. However, in Britain, as in many countries, the trade in all modern ivory is banned, but objects over 100 years old may be imported and exported, provided a licence is obtained from the Department of the Environment. A certificate of authenticity from the British Antique Dealers' Association must accompany the licence. There is, however, an increasingly strong lobby to impose a total ivory trade ban.

◀ Late 19th-century Japanese carved ivory tusk (£1,500-£1,800 per pair)

◀ Ivory toothpick case with brass inlay (£40-£60)

▼ Beautifully carved ivory peapod needle case of unknown origin, late 19th century. Seen at the Newcastle Emlyn Roadshow (£100-£150)

Tokyo school **carving** of a Bijin (beautiful woman) c1900 **(£1,500–£2,500)**

JACOBEAN

The period covered by the reigns of James I and Charles I (1603-49), although the latter is strictly speaking Carolean. Jacobean ornament tends to be more restrained than Elizabethan and includes geometrically ornamented panels, strapwork, arcading, balustrading and herm figures (see CARYATID). Furniture is generally oak and richly carved, often with heraldic and emblematic motifs. Flowers and plant forms were popular on textiles, and often furniture is richly upholstered in CREWELWORK.

JACOBITE

Objects which commemorate the Old and Young Pretenders of the Stuart dynasty, James Edward (1688-1766) and Charles Edward (1720-88) and the uprisings of 1715 and 1745. The principal Jacobite emblem was the rose, representing the English crown, but almost any symbol was attributed to the

Jacobite cause in the late 19th century: oak leaves, star, bee, butterfly and forget-me-not as well as Jacob's ladder foliage, carnation, daffodil and Prince of Wales plumes. Some symbols have local Jacobite significance, such as the dolphin, which was a badge of the Sea-Serjeants Society in Wales. They were mainly engraved on drinking glasses for toasting the 'King over the seas', sometimes with inscriptions such as *Fiat* (let it be done), *Redeat* (may he return), *Revivescit* (he grows strong again). Jacobite glasses often date from just after the failure of the cause at Culloden. Be wary as they were widely faked in the 19th century and in the 1920s. Recent research has cast doubt on much so-called Jacobite engraving which was executed in the late 19th century

◀ **Wine glass** with, possibly later, Jacobite emblems and motto, 18th century. Seen at the Derby Roadshow **(£450–£500)**

JACQUARD LACE

Machine-made lace with a large and complicated pattern, popular in the 1830s and '40s. The Jacquard loom —capable of weaving textiles with intricate patterns—was invented by Joseph-Marie Jacquard of Lyon in 1805. The mechanism was adapted to lace-making first in France, and then in Nottinghamshire.

JADE

The term covers various hardstones including nephrite and jadeite. Nephrite ranges from white to shades of brown and green. The most highly prized in China is the white variety known as 'mutton fat'. Nephrite, which has been worked by the Chinese since ancient times, is so hard it cannot be scratched even by steel but it can be ground away. Carvings are difficult to date, although during the QING period they became elaborate, with deep undercutting. Jadeite is dark green or emerald and was carved only from the 18th century onwards.

JAPANNING

Imitation Japanese lacquer-work, introduced into England in the 17th century. The essential ingredient of lacquer, the resin *rhus vernicifera*, was not available in Europe, so imitations were made, using gum-lac, seed-lac or shell-lac, applied in layers and dried by heat. Large pieces of furniture, boxes, brush handles and trays were japanned in black, dark green and sealing-wax red. The decoration was outlined in gold size and built up with a composition of gum arabic and saw-dust, polished and gilded with metal dust. It can be difficult to distinguish from true lacquer but the decoration, generally CHINOISERIE, and the Euro-peanised forms of the furniture give it away. (See PONTYPOOL JAPANWARE.)

From the land of

JAPANESE SWORDS

The Japanese sword has a reputation for quality that no other edged weapon can match, and although many Shinto blades can be found, few swords made before the 14th century, have survived, and when they appear can fetch huge sums today.

Whilst many secrets died with the master swordsmiths, the actual method of producing the steel remained basically the same. Iron, in the form of fine sand, was collected and smelted in large pits to form a mass of irregularly shaped iron. This was broken up, re-melted, and formed into brittle flat plates of metal. Broken by hammers into coin sized pieces, it was placed into a rectangular pile about four by six inches in size. This was reheated to a workable temperature, beaten to about twice its length, and then folded back to its original size. This was repeated, and it was during this stage of constant re-heating, hammering and folding, that the carbon level (controlling the metal's hardness) was adjusted.

The optimum number of folds was found to be around 15, giving over 32,000 layers. This hard steel was needed for the edge, but would make the blade very brittle, and so a softer steel, folded perhaps 10 times, was used for the core, making the whole blade exceptionally durable.

Of the many methods of combining the different steels to make a finished blade, one of the best was to laminate four pieces of hard steel around a softer core. When the newly forged blade had been inspected for flaws, it was coated in a thin layer of clay, which, when nearly hard, was partially scraped away along the edge. It was then heated, the clay causing the edge to attain a higher temperature than the body of the blade, and then quenched in water.

Only Samurai were allowed to carry two swords, the *wakizashi* and the *katana*, but when the Emperor Meiji regained power in 1867 the wearing of swords in public was outlawed. Many swordsmiths, lacking work, turned to making utility items or bronzes. There are many collectors of sword fittings, which are an artform in their own right. TSUBA, the decorative hand guards at the bottom of the hilt are especially prized.

Although many Europeans obtained swords during the Second World War from captured Japanese officers, these were usually mass produced. Blades should never be handled, and if finger-prints occur they must be wiped off straight away with talcum powder and a soft dry cloth. Inspection for a signature involves the removal of the hilt, and should be carried out by an expert. Never use metal objects to dis-mantle a sword, and under no circumstances should the blade be pol-ished by anyone other than an experienced professional, and then only if absolutely necessary.

JAPANESE ARTS AND CRAFTS

Ceramics. Japanese ceramics is a vast subject, covering about 7,000 years, from the cord–pattern wares of the neolithic Jomon period (c 4500-200BC). Later, especially in the 8th century, Tang influence reached Japan by way of Korean potters, but from then until the 17th century, when porcelain was introduced, Japan went its own way. Tea wares, especially low-fired RAKU pots represent a most important tradition, in which asymmetry was

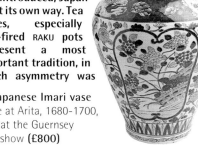

▶ Japanese Imari vase made at Arita, 1680-1700, seen at the Guernsey Roadshow (£800)

▲ Japanese sword with elaborate silvered metal fittings engraved with dragon and cloud designs (£5,000)

the rising sun

judged a virtue. The coming of porcelain coincided with the arrival of the Portuguese and the Dutch, and the start of the export trade. See also ARITA, IMARI, and SATSUMA.

Metal work. Iron rather than bronze was the Japanese metal, except for making Buddhist statues and sword fittings. However, after 1853 bronze figures and vases were made for export and some of the latter are superb. The best-known sculptor is Miya-o, who used gold and silver inlays.

Wood-block prints. In Japan the technique of printing from wood blocks dates back to the 8th century, when it was introduced from China. These prints were in black and were mainly Buddhist subjects for devotional use. It was not until the late 17th century that there was an explosion of interest in wood-block printing. Using separate printing blocks for different colours was a natural development, introduced around 1740. At first only pink and green were covered, a full palette appearing in about 1765.

The artists whose 'signatures' appear were not responsible for the engraving, which was done by specialist carvers. The printmaker brought the print to life by the way he brushed on the colour, wiped areas clean or merged the inks. All prints were supposed to be presented to a censor, whose role was merely to prevent the circulation of seditious prints.

Landscapes gained in popularity from the beginning of the 19th century, reaching their high point with the prints of Katushika Hokusai and Ando Hiroshige. From Hokusai comes the most famous print of all: towering waves with Mount Fuji in the background.

The value of prints depends on the fame of the artist, the subject, the colour and the condition, including the width of the margins. Prices can range from a few pounds to tens of thousands.

▼ **Japanese iron tea kettle** with a jadeite finial, cast with a carp with golden eyes, c1900. Brought into the Newcastle Emlyn Roadshow **(£100–£150)**

▲ **One of the best known** of all Japanese prints: *Fuji from the Wall of the Great Wave off Kanagawa* by Hokusai, **(£100,000 for a rare early impression)**

JAPONAISERIE

In 1854 America negotiated trading rights with Japan, ending two centuries of isolation and unleashing a flood of Japanese artefacts on Europe. Artists and designers were amazed by the prints, textiles, bronzes, metalwork and ceramics which became available for the first time. They were particularly prized as the products of a non-industrialised, craft-orientated society. The simplicity of the prints with their two-dimensional nature and unconventional perspective was enormously influential on painters. A craze for all things Japanese swept Victorian England, and was fed by companies such as LIBERTY which imported cheap goods designed for the Western market. Christopher DRESSER, Louis-Comfort TIFFANY and Thomas Jeckyll were just a few of the designers who fell under the Japanese influence.

JARDINIÈRE

A table or stand with a metal-lined bowl or tray set in the top to hold flowers or plants. They have been made in a huge variety of styles and materials, and were especially popular in the 19th century.

£££-££££

JASPER

A vitreous stoneware body developed and named by Josiah WEDGWOOD in 1774. It is most commonly pale blue and sprigged with white reliefs, but other colour combinations are not uncommon. It was copied by other manufacturers.

JENNENS AND BETTRIDGE

This was the leading firm of PAPIER-MÂCHÉ manufacturers. From 1816 to 1864 their Birmingham factory produced a whole range of OBJETS DE VERTU and household wares, from snuffboxes, CARD CASES and caddies, by way of screens, trays and picture panels, to chairs, DAVENPORTS and tables. They generally have black, red or dark green backgrounds with designs in a variety of colours, and are inlaid with materials such as MOTHER-

▲ **Jardinière on stand** in the Japanese style by Christofle of Paris, 1874 **(£10,000)**

OF-PEARL. Leading designers and artists, such as Richard Redgrave, RA, were commissioned, but the name stamped or painted on panels is usually that of the firm rather than the artist. Larger pieces, where strength was required, were often reinforced: chairs have lacquered wooden legs, and beds with *papier-mâché* head and footboards have lacquered iron supports.

£££-££££

JENSEN, GEORG (1866-1935)

The son of a knife grinder, he was apprenticed to a goldsmith in Copenhagen and later studied sculpture at Denmark's Royal Academy of Art. After travelling in Europe, he returned to Copenhagen and worked as a silversmith for Mogens Ballin, a leading advocate of Danish ART NOUVEAU. In 1904 he opened his own workshop and in 1905 began experimenting with silver hollow-ware (that is, not cutlery). Although strongly influenced by Art Nouveau, Jensen's work has none of the fussy embellishments of other designers. Decoration is restricted to finely modelled finials, and his pieces rely on clarity of form, curvaceous contours and subtle decorative effects, achieved by gently hammering oxidised

▲ **Jennens and Bettridge** papier mâché work box, c1850 **(£250-£350)**

silver surfaces. Until the 1921 Depression, Jensen's products were exported throughout Europe and America. The company is still in production using many Jensen designs.

JEWISH ARTEFACTS

The market in Judaica or Hebraica is vast, Covering Hebrew and Yiddish literature and manuscripts, paintings and maps, as well as ritual objects in silver. A number of these are to do with Torah scrolls, and indeed plain scrolls without their silver holders are held in some suspicion, since they may not be kosher. There are also Torah shields, finials, crowns and pointers. Hannukah lamps, spice towers and Etrog boxes, too, come onto the market.

JIGSAWS

Jigsaw puzzles date back to the 1760s, but the earliest versions are usually known as 'dissected' puzzles, since they consisted firstly of squares, and later simple figures and shapes cut out from the backgrounds. They were the invention of John Spilsbury, engraver, cartographer and drawing master at Harrow School. Other London makers include Newbury, taken over by John Harris in 1802, William Peacock around 1850, and Raphael Tuck & Sons from about 1870. Many jigsaws were produced from the second half of the 19th century using lithographic prints by the German makers of toy bricks. The Americans also have a long tradition of making puzzles.

££-£££

▲ **Jigsaw map of England and Wales**
in original box, 1860-80 **(£80-£100)**

JOHN HILL AND CO

The company was founded in about 1900 by an ex-employee of BRITAIN'S, and continued trading until around 1967. It made hollow-cast lead soldiers and, from 1956, plastic ones. They were inferior to Britain's, and fail to fetch comparable prices. Various trade names include John Hill, J. Hillco, Jo Hill and Johilco.

£-££

JOINER

A craftsman who handled woodwork that was more highly finished than the structural work executed by a carpenter. He specialised in interior fittings such as staircases and panelling, and his skill was based on firmness and accuracy of the joints, and in the smoothing of surfaces.

JONES, OWEN (1809-74)

An influential designer and writer, who was involved with Henry Cole in launching the 1851 Great Exhibition. Their belief was that 'ornament must be secondary to the thing ornamented', and Jones's *The Grammar of Ornament*, 1856, was widely influential in popularising such sources as the Islamic, HISPANO-MORESQUE, Oriental and primitive arts. He was a forerunner of both William MORRIS and ART NOUVEAU.

JUGENDSTIL

This was the name given to the ART NOUVEAU style in Germany, after the magazine, *Jugend*, published in Munich 1896 -1914. It was influential in Germany, Austria and Scandinavia, the most important designers being Otto Eckmann (1865-1902) and Richard Riemerschmid (1868-1957).

JUMEAUS

These bisque-headed French dolls are most highly regarded by collectors. The business was founded in 1842 by Pierre Jumeau, whose son Emile took over in about 1875. They made a wide variety of dolls of exceptional quality with beautifully painted heads, including 'portrait Jumeaus', supposedly modelled on real children. The dolls were remarkable for the superb dresses and accessories. After 1899 the company began to import cheaper German heads, and quality was compromised by more crudely painted faces. Apart from the very earliest, the Jumeau dolls are usually marked on the head. After the company won the Diplôme d'Honneur in 1885 the dolls' bodies were stamped 'Diplôme d'Honneur' in blue.

£££-££££

JUMP-UP

This was a mid-19th century term used by chair-makers in High Wycombe for children's table chairs. These are chairs that stand on a low table that has a raised rim to prevent the legs sliding off. When the chair is taken down, the table is the right height for a child.

£££-££££

▲ **Jump-up chair**
on its original base,
early Victorian
(£300-£450)

saluminium silicate formed from decomposed granitic rocks. It was known in China from the 7th century. The first samples were brought to Europe by a Jesuit missionary in 1712. (See COOKWORTHY).

◀ **George III console table** in the style of Wiliam Kent (**£15,000-£20,000**)

KENT, WILLIAM (1685-1748)

He was the first known British designer to make individual pieces of furniture to match specific interiors. Although Kent began as a painter, under the influence of his patron Lord Burlington he turned to architecture and interior design. His interiors are sumptuous and elaborate, rich in stucco-work and carved and gilt wood, with vast marble chimneypieces. This BAROQUE effect was in striking contrast to the restrained PALLADIANISM of his exteriors. The designs of Inigo Jones (1573-1651) were an important influence on his work, and he published a volume of Jones's designs. His own were published by John Vardy in 1744. Kentian furniture is strongly derived from Italian sources. It is solid and deeply carved with thick scrolling supports. Curling foliage, classical masks, shells and PUTTI are favourite motifs. PIER TABLES and pedestals are supported by strongly sculpted members in the form of eagles, dolphins and cherubs. Furniture by Kent is far too rare to come on the market. The best examples are at Kensington Palace, Houghton Hall in Norfolk and Chatsworth. However, Kent-inspired pieces do turn up.

KAKIEMON

Traditionally, a class of Japanese enamelled wares have been called Kakiemon after an early potter. Actually, both Kakiemon and the early enamelled 'Kutani' wares hailed from ARITA and were made in more than one kiln. Kakiemon is thus a style rather than the output of an individual. Japanese porcelain was not developed until about 1620, when a number of Korean potters arrived in Japan. By the last quarter of the 17th century superbly painted dishes, bowls, vases and figures were appearing in Europe. Subjects were flowers, landscapes, birds, animals and occasionally, figures. Kakiemon became most sought after in Europe at the turn of the 18th century. Many of the early factories, such as MEISSEN and CHELSEA, copied it and it is now widely collected. With pieces fetching £100,000 or more, Kakiemon has become the target of fakers, who add decoration to undecorated blanks. Reproductions are also known

KAOLIN

The name given to the 'china' clay which forms the essential ingredient of HARD-PASTE porcelain. It is a white

▼ **Kakiemon dragon vase** c1660-80 (**Restored £4,000-£5,000**)

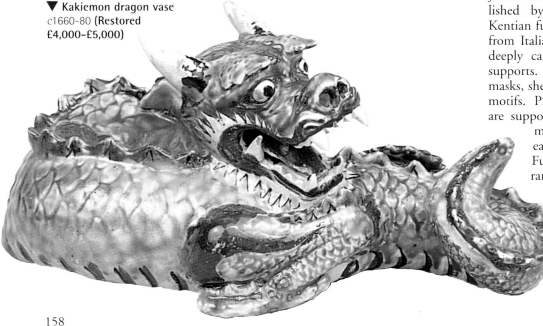

158

KEYS

As well as being vital for the protection of property, keys have long had a symbolic value as giving access to power and information. In the Middle Ages the giving up or a city or fortress was symbolised by the surrender of its keys. Roman keys were made of bronze, and pierced apertures operated on levers within the lock. In the Middle Ages keys were made of wrought iron, and the lock mechanism consisted of simple springs and bolts attached to a flat plate. Many of these keys were highly elaborate with pierced quatrefoils and delicate fretwork. The larger, more elaborate ones would have been made for cathedral treasuries. About 1500 the development of better springs allowed for heavier bolts, and lock mechanisms became more complicated, set in a square box and operated with a precision key. In the Renaissance, figurative ornament and finely chiselled work and engraving were popular, and during the 17th century both France and England were important centres of lock-making. English keys were often made of brass, the finest of gilt brass and blued steel. By the 18th century great technical developments had taken place, and in that century keys became light and delicate to match ornate cabinets. Towards the 19th century the simple latch key, ancestor of the modern house lock, was developed, and in the 20th decoration became secondary to function.

  £-£££

KEY PATTERN

A geometric ornament of intersecting horizontal and vertical lines, repeated to form a band. Also known as a fret.

KEY PLATE

The mount, often in brass, which surrounds a keyhole. Very elaborate ones are known as ESCUTCHEONS.

KICK PLATE

A strip of wood attached to the base of a LONGCASE CLOCK to prevent damage from brooms. Also, metal plates on swing service doors so they may be kicked open by waiters.

If you can't stand the heat

KITCHENALIA

Early wooden and iron cooking implements, such as MOLIQUETS, three-legged skillets, and kettle-tilters — hooks to hang a kettle over the fire — are occasionally to be found, but most collectables date from the 19th or 20th century.

Acording to Mrs Beeton, the most important item in a Victorian kitchen was the saucepan. The best-equipped 19th-century kitchens sported *batteries de cuisine*, long rows of graduated copper saucepans with tightly fitting, handled, lids. However, copper pans needed constant relining with tin, and in the middle of the century many cooks changed to cast iron. From about 1830 copper jelly moulds became common, but they can also be found in earthenware, BRITANNIA metal, tin and later in glass. Elaborate copper examples can fetch hundreds, but smaller, decorative moulds are quite cheap. Beware of reproduction copper jelly moulds which are usually lighter in weight, with tin linings lighter in colour.

Stone jars range from Dundee marmalade pots and ginger beer bottles to large containers for cider.

Reasonably priced items include butter pats, cutlery boxes, carving knives, strainers, pastry cutters and jiggers, lever-action tin openers, salt and spice boxes, toasting forks and sugar nips.

Bread boards are particularly popular in America, and there are collectors of machinery, such as coffee mills, mixers, clockwork bottle-jacks, scales, marmalade cutters and whisks. On a larger scale are kitchen tables, spice cupboards, and butchers' blocks.

French china storage jars, and classic kitchen pottery such as T.G.Green's banded Cornish ware are always popular, and antiques markets are full of French enamel saucepans and utensil racks. It is still possible to find Victorian stone pestles.

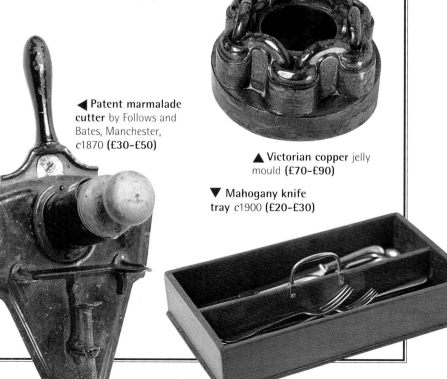

◀ Patent marmalade cutter by Follows and Bates, Manchester, *c*1870 (£30-£50)

▲ Victorian copper jelly mould (£70-£90)

▼ Mahogany knife tray *c*1900 (£20-£30)

A-Z *of Antiques Hunting*

KIDNEY TABLE

An 18th-century table whose top was shaped like a kidney, often used for ladies' work or dressing tables. Some have a rising desk in the centre and tiers of drawers on either side. HEPPLEWHITE designed a kidney library desk, which was reproduced in the late 19th century.

KINGWOOD

Dark purple, hard and close-grained, its main use is for banding and inlay.

KLISMOS

A classical Greek chair with sabre legs. The front legs curve forwards, the rear ones backwards and the back has a concave yoke-rail. It was very popular during the GREEK REVIVAL of the 18th and early 19th centuries.

KNEADING TROUGH

A fairly crude piece of country furniture made of oak or pine. It looks like a chest on legs, with the body splaying outwards. Inside it is divided into compartments for dry flour and for kneading dough.

                     £££

KNEEHOLE

The central space below the top of a desk, dressing table or bureau. It was introduced in the early 18th century for reasons of comfort. George I and II bureaux generally have recessed cupboards in the kneeholes.

KNIFE BOXES AND CASES

The most common type of knife box has a sloping top and curving front, and was made of mahogany or covered with SHAGREEN (see SHERATON). Interiors should be fitted with slots to hold spoons as well as knives, but often they have been gutted. During the ADAM period knife boxes were made in the shape of urns.

           £££-££££

KNOLE SOFA

A sofa with a high back and straight-sided, hinged arms which drop down. It is so called after a unique early 17th-century example at Knole in

Celtic craftsman

KNOX, ARCHIBALD (1865-1941)

A leading ARTS AND CRAFTS silversmith, he was born on the Isle of Man and studied in 1878-84 at the Douglas School of Art, and probably in Baillie Scott's Isle of Man office. In 1897 he moved to London and worked for LIBERTY, designing their popular 'Cymric' silverware and 'Tudric' pewter range in 1899 and 1900. These designs had a strong influence on the widespread CELTIC Revival style. In 1904-12 he designed carpets, textiles and jewellery for Liberty — and even Arthur Lasenby Liberty's tomb in 1917.

◀ Liberty silver and enamelled copper vase attributed to Knox (£1,500-£2,000)

▶ Silver and enamelled vase designed by Knox, c1930 (£3,000-£3,500)

Kent. The type became immensely popular in the 1920s and '30s.

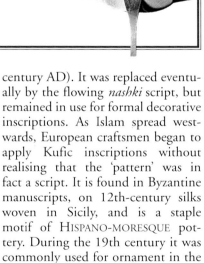   £££-££££

KNOP

This is a swelling, most commonly found ornamenting the stem of a glass. Knops come in a huge variety of forms, including eggs, balls, cushions and acorns. In ceramics and metalwork they also form the handles of lids and the FINIALS of early spoons.

KNURL FOOT

A scroll foot where the scroll is formed on the inside of the leg and so cannot be seen from the front. It is found on mid-18th century chairs.

KUFIC

A script in general use during the first centuries of Islam (from the 7th

century AD). It was replaced eventually by the flowing *nashki* script, but remained in use for formal decorative inscriptions. As Islam spread westwards, European craftsmen began to apply Kufic inscriptions without realising that the 'pattern' was in fact a script. It is found in Byzantine manuscripts, on 12th-century silks woven in Sicily, and is a staple motif of HISPANO-MORESQUE pottery. During the 19th century it was commonly used for ornament in the Moorish and Turkish styles.

KYLIN

A Chinese mythological animal with a single horn on its head, flaming shoulders, the body and legs of a deer or stag, and a bushy tail. It is found on Chinese ceramics and metalwork and was copied in designs at the WORCESTER factory.

▲ Chinese lacquerwork lady's workbox, 1820s (£250-£300)

gilding, particularly work tables and cabinets were imported from China and, during the 19th century, boxes from Japan.

LADDER-BACK CHAIR

A country-made chair introduced in the early 18th century. The back is formed by horizontal slats between the uprights. The style was later adopted by more fashionable chair-makers who modified it, sometimes introducing decorative, wavy slits in the slats or, in the ART NOUVEAU style, hearts.

£££

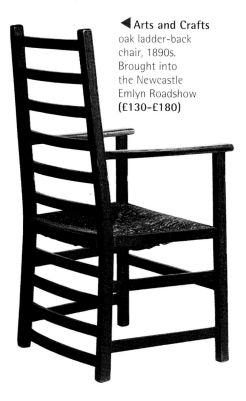

◀ Arts and Crafts oak ladder-back chair, 1890s. Brought into the Newcastle Emlyn Roadshow (£130-£180)

▲ Detail from *The Lacemaker* by the Victorian artist, George Smith. Seen at the Truro Roadshow (£3,000-£5,000)

LACE AND LACE BOBBINS

There are two ways of making lace: needle lace, dating from the late 15th century, is made with a single needle and thread, using buttonhole stitch. This is built up on an outline structure of thick threads tacked onto a sewing pillow. Bobbin lace is made with a variable number of threads, wound on bobbins and joined by plaiting and weaving, following a design marked out by a series of pricked holes. Straight lace is made in one run, and part lace in sections of pattern. Until the invention of machine-made lace in the early 19th century, lace was a luxury and centres of production shifted according to fashion and economics. The 1930s JACQUARD attachment was responsible for a huge expansion of the industry. Lace was an essential garment trimming, and lace shawls, curtains, bed covers and furniture drapes were all available. With the 20th century, fashion changed and the industry collapsed. Lace bobbins were made of bone, wood or ivory turned on a lathe, weighted with beads and occasionally inscribed and dated.

LACQUER

True lacquer comes from the sap of the *rhus vernicifera* tree, indigenous to China and introduced to Japan. The grey, syrupy juice is strained and heated, and applied in dozens of thin coats to wood, fabric, metal or leather. When exposed to air, it forms a hard, durable surface which can be carved to reveal a different colour underneath. By the 4th century BC, the Chinese had perfected the technique for small objects. From about 1600 lacquer became enormously popular in Europe. The secret of making true lacquer, however, was not known in Europe and as a substitute JAPANNING was developed (see VERNIS MARTIN). In the late 18th century large quantities of wooden or *papier-mâché* objects decorated with painting and

Glass that set the tone

LALIQUE, RENE (1860-1945)

The French jeweller, glass-maker and designer whose jewellery pioneered the ART NOUVEAU style, and whose glass set the tone of ART DECO. In 1885 he established his own workshop in Paris, supplying jewellery for Samuel Bing's shop, L'Art Nouveau.

His jewellery has elaborate, sinuous mounts with curving, asymmetrical detail incorporating such Art Nouveau motifs as peacocks, dragonflies and limp female nudes. Stones are of secondary importance and are often semi-precious, and horn was a commonly used material. After 1902 he concentrated on designing glass, which is now highly collectable.

He began with cast objects, using the LOST WAX technique. He established his own glasshouses in 1909 just outside Paris and began mass-producing glass scent bottles for François Coty in a wide range of designs, eventually more than 300. The success of the scent bottles led to other objects: light fixtures, statuettes, car mascots and delicately etched glass screens, many of them for luxury liners.

Most typical are the vases, dishes and drinking glasses in blue-tinted opalescent glass, but he also produced a number of other colours, including greens and yellows.

Most pieces were blown into moulds or press-moulded, usually in clear or tinted metal, but occasionally white between two layers of colour.

After his death the factory continued, as it does today, but the mark changed in 1945 from R. Lalique to Lalique in script. However, 16 marks were used at the factory and dating Lalique glass can be difficult. Generally, the earlier clear glass has a greysih tint while postwar glass is clearer.

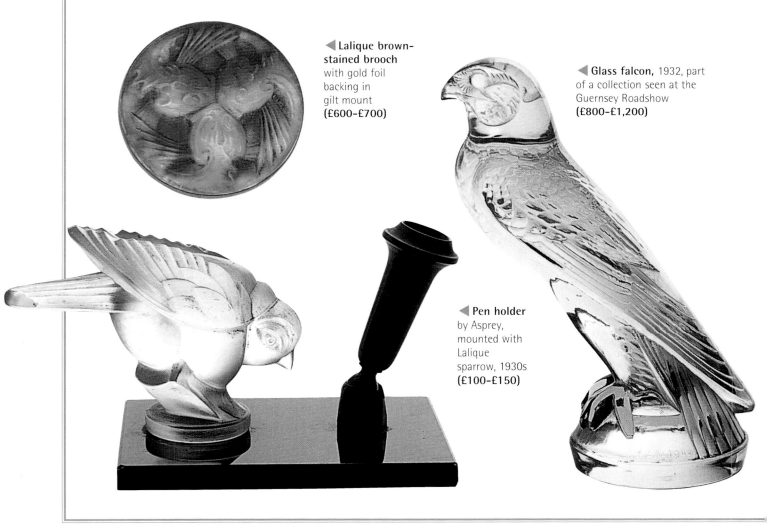

◀ Lalique brown-stained brooch with gold foil backing in gilt mount (£600-£700)

◀ Glass falcon, 1932, part of a collection seen at the Guernsey Roadshow (£800-£1,200)

◀ Pen holder by Asprey, mounted with Lalique sparrow, 1930s (£100-£150)

◀ **Pouilly glass,** 1931. Value depends on size (**£40–£120**)

▲ **Lalique green glass pendant** moulded with dragonflies and signed (**£800–£1,200**)

◀ **Black glass seal** in the form of an eagle's head (**£600–£700**)

◀ **Blue-stained Ceylan vase,** post-1924 (**£1,800–£2,000**)

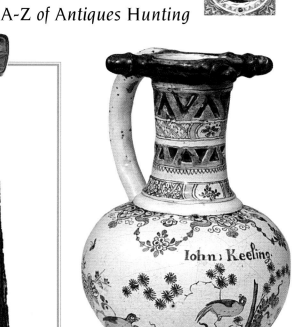

▲ **Lambeth delft** puzzle jug, dated 1742 (**£30,000**)

LAMBETH DELFTWARE

Tin-glazed earthenware was produced at Lambeth in London from the early 17th to the late 18th centuries. The earliest pieces have a softly pinkish glaze and the later a greener tinge. A wide variety of forms was made, from plates, bowls, candlesticks and vases to salt cellars, water bottles and pharmacy wares. Decoration is both blue and white and polychrome, with CHINOISERIE motifs appearing in the 18th century.

 £££-£££££

LAMBREQUIN

The French name for a stiff pelmet. It was introduced into England in the late 17th century. The edges were generally scalloped and trimmed with fringes or tassels, and thus the name was given to 'lambrequin ornament' of symmetrical decorated scallops, often imitating a woven fabric. In fact this had appeared much earlier on 16th-century Dutch metalwork and carving. The Victorians later revived the word for a shaped panel of fabric pinned to a mantelpiece.

A prince among potters

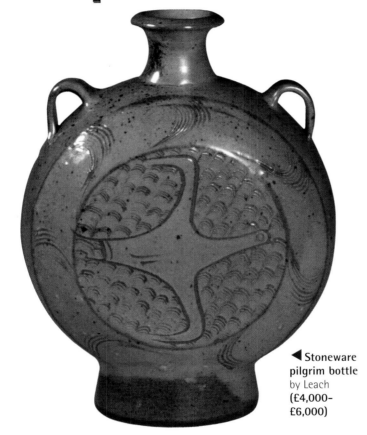

LEACH, BERNARD (1887–1979)

The most influential British studio potter of the first half of the 20th century, Leach first visited Japan in 1909, staying in the Far East for 11 years, and on his return he founded his own pottery at St Ives, Cornwall.

According to Michael Cardew, it was 'an attempt by an artist potter to discover and re-apply standards of craftsmanship largely forgotten in the passage from traditional hand methods to large-scale production'.

The Japanese potter Shoji Hamada worked with him for three years and, in 1956, Leach married Janet Darnell, a pupil of Hamada. Leach's sons David and Michael and grandson John continue the family potting tradition, and there have been many famous studio potters who were his pupils.

The worthy, oatmeal efforts of some of his disciples should not blind critics to the strength and beauty of Leach's own work. His great influence was as a teacher. He produced many superb pots but also a large number of domestic utilitarian wares of no great merit. Numerous acolytes have found it all too easy to imitate his pots.

◀ Stoneware pilgrim bottle by Leach (£4,000–£6,000)

LAMINATED WOOD

This is built up from thin layers of the same or alternating materials as in plywood or plywood faced with metal or plastic sheets.

LANTERN CLOCK

A typically English, weight-driven, brass wall clock developed from the beginning of the 17th century to the first quarter of the 18th. The design follows that of the GOTHIC clock with a square pillar frame, going train in front, striking train behind and a bell in the canopy. The area below the bell may be decorated with heraldic motifs in pierced brass fretwork. The circular dial usually has a single hour hand and extends beyond the width of the frame. The name 'lantern' is supposed to have come from the shape of ships' lanterns at this period.

The best-known makers include Thomas TOMPION and Joseph Knibb.

 £££–££££

LAPIS LAZULI

A semi-precious stone, deep ultramarine blue in colour. During the Renaissance it was highly prized and, when ground, was widely used for the pigment known as ultramarine. It is also found in inlay and *pietra dura* and was used for ornamental wares, especially by Russian craftsmen in the late 18th and early 19th centuries.

LARCH

A deciduous conifer native to Europe. It is a hard, strong wood, varying in colour from reddish brown to pale yellow. It was used for the carcasses of case furniture and for rustic furniture.

LAUREL WREATH

In ancient times, outstanding achievements were celebrated with the presentation of a crown of laurel. As an evergreen, it also signifies eternity and is used on memorials. Bands of it have been used to decorate furniture, silver and porcelain, especially during the NEO-CLASSICAL period.

LAZY SUSAN

A mid-19th century American term for a revolving condiment tray, mounted on a heavy base and placed in the centre of the dining table.

 ££–£££

LE BRUN, CHARLES (1619-90)

A French painter and designer, who was the first director of the GOBELINS factory and founder of the Académie Royale des Beaux-Arts. He was an important propagandist for LOUIS XIV, designing magnificent tapestries and overseeing the goldsmiths, furniture-makers and bronze-workers who supplied furnishings for the palaces.

LEAD GLAZE

Lead has been used in ceramic glazes for hundreds of years because of its availability and low melting temperature. It gives a yellowish tinge to clear glazes and helps to produce strong colours. It poses no health risk, although strong green lead glazes should not be used with acidic foods.

LEEDS POTTERY

Established in 1750, the company began with WHIELDON imitations, but was best known for the production of creamware from the 1780s, when it was known as Hartley, Greens and Co. Similar to those of WEDGWOOD, the wares have a less even glaze and a yellow or pale green tinge. Moulded decoration, and pierced fretwork borders for plates, are common and wares were decorated in enamel colours or transfer-printed in red and black. Much was decorated in Holland. The firm also made PEARLWARE, which had a slightly bluish glaze. In the late 19th century, Slees Modern Pottery began reproducing 18th-century patterns, often from the original moulds. These are slightly lighter in weight and have a more lustrous, even glaze. Genuine Leeds pottery is rarely marked but sometimes has the name impressed.

▼ **Leeds creamware,** pierced-rim side plate, chipped **(£170–£200)**

Beauty that is skin deep

LEATHER

Fragments of leather book bindings survive from the 4th century AD. From the 8th century, Córdova (see CORDWAINING) became famous for the production of very fine leather which, later, was elaborately decorated with hand punches and painting. Most of the surviving 'Spanish' leather was in fact produced in the Netherlands under the influence of Moorish craftsmen who emigrated from Spain in the 14th century. In the 16th and 17th centuries fine embossed leather wall hangings were enormously popular.

Leather was widely used throughout the 17th and 18th centuries for seat covers, desk tops, book bindings, clothes and shoes. Motoring and flying gave a further boost in the 20th century.

The tanning process has remained largely unchanged up to the present day and can still be seen in many towns in Morocco.

▲ Second World War leather despatch rider's coat, in need of re-sewing **(£40–£50)**

▼ Mill worker's leather clogs, from Lancashire, c1930 **(£40–£70)**

▲ Used 20th-century notebook, rolled morocco, blind stamped, gilt on top board, spine gilt stamped with raised bands **(£10–£20)**

▼Lehmann tinplate cockerel coach driven by a rabbit, with missing ear. Seen at the Huddersfield Roadshow (£700-£900)

LEHMANN

A German tinplate toymaker founded in Nuremberg in 1875. While the older MÄRKLIN and BING were the leaders for trains and battleships, Lehmann made a name for novelties such as clockwork ostrich and zebra carts driven by clowns and cowboys, tricycles ridden by ladies with parasols, a 'Baker and Sweep—a Study in Black and White', animals like 'Nina the Cat', and figures such as the 'Heavy Swell'. However, once established, they competed directly with cars, ships and aeroplanes. The monoplane 'Ikarus', with its paper wings, may not have been wisely named, but it would have commanded the nursery in around 1912. By the 1920s and '30s vehicles such as the Luxus limousine sported electric headlights.

£££-££££

LENCI

A firm of felt dollmakers set up in Turin by E. and E. Scavini in 1920. Signora Scavini, the main designer, had great style and flair: her dolls have eyes which glance to the side, and often have a slight pout. The middle fingers of each hand are joined together, and the dolls wear elaborate and beautifully made clothes. Ethnic and national costume was a speciality, also harlequins and pierrots, and long-legged ladies, sometimes in huge skirts, frills and crinolines with felt flowers or bows. They are marked on the soles of the feet, and should also have a label or button attached to the body. Lenci dolls are still made, but they have been extensively faked and copied, even though they tend not to be as expensive as BISQUE or painted-head dolls.

££-££££

Rare felt Lenci doll, with applied felt lips and shoe button eyes, c1925 (£400-£500)

Lenci cloth doll with open/closed mouth, glass eyes, mohair wig, c1931 (£2,000-£3,000)

LESNEY

The east London firm launched an assault on the success of DINKY in the 1950s with the immensely appealing MATCHBOX series of small die-cast vehicles in boxes based on the famous Bryant & May design. This was followed by their Models of Yesteryear series of vintage vehicles, from 1956. The firm closed in 1987.

£-££

LESSORE, EMILE AUBERT (1805-76)

Originally a pupil of Ingres, Lessore turned from painting to the decoration of pottery and porcelain. He is best known for his work for the WEDGWOOD factory, painted in a free style as if working on canvas. After his return to France the factory continued to ship him cases of undecorated wares.

LETTER RACK

A small, hanging rack for letters or cards, which is divided vertically into hinged sections. It appeared in the mid-18th century, was often pierced with Gothic or Chinese frets and may have been the forerunner of pigeon-holes. Early examples are expensive.

££-£££

LETTER BOX

From the 19th century many country houses had letter boxes for the use of guests. Some are small versions of pillar boxes, others caskets with a slit in the lid. They are generally wooden.

££-£££

▼ Regency ebony letter box inlaid overall in brass (£700-£1,000)

Highest hopes for British style

LIBERTY, ARTHUR LASENBY (1843–1917)

Arthur Liberty had high aspirations, believing he could mould the taste of a nation. He began as an importer of exotic Oriental goods, notably textiles, just as aestheticism was in the ascendant. Decorative painters loved his products, and the wealthy and fashionable followed their lead to the shop he established in Regent Street in 1875. Gradually his business emphasis shifted from importing to originating and retailing, in a style that was outside the mainstream of late Victorian design, but consistently fashionable and advanced.

Unlike William MORRIS and the true ARTS AND CRAFTS MOVEMENT, Arthur Liberty saw nothing wrong in aligning industrial techniques to good design. Many products were mass-produced in the Liberty studios; others were specially commissioned. They included not only the famous textiles and Liberty prints but also furniture designed by architects such as Voysey and Godwin, silver and pewter, notably the famous Cymric and Tudric ranges by Archibald KNOX, and jewellery and pottery, in particular MOORCROFT and Brannam Barum ware. Metalwork was inspired by Celtic ornament, and lines of fabrics grew from flower motifs woven into abstract patterns. The furniture had tapering outlines and elaborate hinges and mounts. In Italy 'Stil Liberty' is still a synonym for ART NOUVEAU.

By the 1920s the company had acquired a warren of little shops in Regent Street. Faced with Sir Reginald Blomfield's designs for the rebuilding of the whole of Regent Street, the Liberty directors believed the character of the shop

would be lost if it became 'one of those lofty, marble, gilt department stores'. To them contemporary shop design was anathema; hence the extraordinary Tudor building they designed behind the Regent Street façade which is the Liberty flagship. A shop on a human scale, it emphasised the traditional values of craftsmanship that had inspired its founder.

Modern Liberty's is unashamedly a retail outlet, stocking brand names from all over the world and giving individual floor space to companies ranging from Karl Lagerfeld to Issey Miyake. Economies of scale now make it impossible for it to have its own studios or to commission original Liberty brand products. Liberty of London Print Ltd is an entirely separate company reproducing historical Liberty prints alongside original designs.

Where books do the talking

LIBRARY FURNITURE

Furniture which was specially designed for use in libraries became enormously popular in the REGENCY period, with designs appearing in both George SMITH's *Cabinetmaker's and Upholsterer's Guide* and SHERATON's *Cabinet Directory*. Sets of library steps and the familiar pedestal library tables or desks, wide enough for two people to sit facing one another, were common.

More ingenious devices included the METAMORPHIC library stool, which had a padded, hinged lid opening to reveal a set of library steps. Steps were also fitted into chairs and stools and even into PEMBROKE tables.

A library firescreen was a small, free-standing bookcase with a sliding side which, when raised up, doubled as a firescreen protecting the user from the heat of the fire.

BREAKFRONT library bookcases are also found that have a surprise — a folding bedstead — contained in the lower part of the break front. Mahogany library wheelbarrows with shaped sides and curved handles were used in particularly large libraries.

◀ Regency library chair, c1820-30, with a possibly later reading stand. Seen at the Colchester Roadshow (£800-£1,000)

◀ Set of George III mahogany metamorphic library steps (£3,000-£4,000)

▲ Regency mahogany library desk (£15,000 – £20,000) because of its poor condition

LIGNUM VITAE

An extremely hard wood imported from central America. Dark brown or greenish-black, it is used where an enormous amount of wear and tear is expected. It owes its name 'wood of life' to the mistaken belief that it was a cure for venereal disease—shavings were sold to the credulous.

LIME

An easily worked wood, creamy white in colour, used for turnery and carved decoration.

LIMEHOUSE PORCELAIN

Recent research has established that wares previously attributed to William Reid of Liverpool were actually made at the short-lived Limehouse factory in London which advertised from 1747-8.

LIMOGES ENAMELS

There were two schools of enamels at Limoges. The first, established in the Middle Ages, was centred on monasteries making religious objects in *champlevé* enamel. These generally have a blue ground with multi-coloured designs similar to those of the MOSAN school. In the 16th century Limoges emerged as a centre for the newly developed technique of painted enamels. A few families monopolised the craft, jealously guarding its secrets. Vividly coloured plaques were inspired by religious and Renaissance subjects and miniature portraits. Towards the end of the 16th century, enamels painted in *grisaille* became popular, with production ceasing 100 years later. Limoges enamels were widely reproduced in the 19th century by many factories, including SAMSON. They are difficult to tell from the originals and may fool even experts.

£££-££££

LIMOGES POTTERY AND PORCELAIN

The main source of china clay in France is at Saint-Yrieix, near Limoges, and from 1736 this was being quarried for use at the SÈVRES factory. The availability of the raw

Strike a light

LIGHTERS

For centuries the most common form of obtaining a light was by the tedious method of striking a flint with sharp steel. At the end of the 19th century the Austrian scientist Auer von Welsbach discovered that, when struck with a sharp object, a metal alloy with a 30 per cent iron content will produce a spark within a fraction of a second to ignite a flammable substance such as a petrol-soaked wick.

Welsbach patented his revolutionary invention on October 1, 1904. The striking action was soon replaced by the still familiar wheel, and lighters were produced in a whole variety of shapes, sizes and materials. In 1947 the invention of the gas lighter meant the wick could be replaced by a miniature valve and in 1961 the French Criquet plastic disposable lighters were introduced. Among the most lavish lighters were those by Boucheron and Cartier in tooled gold, sometimes encrusted with precious stones. Another important French manufacturer was Dupont.

In England Dunhill launched the Unique in 1922, with a twin-wheel action which remained in use for half a century. The most famous American makers were Ronson, who were especially known for their large table lighters, and ZIPPO. The familiar rectangular brass Zippo lighter, launched in 1932, remained unchanged for half a century.

◀ Lacquered Rollagas lighter by Dunhill, gold plated with simulated ivory, discontinued in the 1980s (£50)

▲ Limoges enamel and gilt copper crucifix, 13th century (£7,000)

material encouraged the establishment of a hard-paste porcelain factory at Limoges under the auspices of the Comte d'Artois (the future Charles X) in 1771. In 1784 this became a royal factory financed by Louis XVI to produce plain white ware for decoration at Sèvres. The arrangement did not work well, and in 1796 the factory closed. After the Revolution many factories sprung up in the town, which soon became the main centre for porcelain production in France. It is still known for its creamy tableware, decorated with flower sprigs, and for delicate boxes. Even more factories were opened in the early 19th century, including Haviland & Cie (founded by an American, David

A-Z of Antiques Hunting

Style was their signature

LINNELL, WILLIAM (c1703–63) AND JOHN (1729–96)

Like CHIPPENDALE and HEPPLEWHITE the Linnells did not stamp their furniture, so little can be attributed to them without the evidence of a bill, an inventory or John's designs, many of which are in the Victoria and Albert Museum. Unlike Chippendale and Hepplewhite, however, the Linnells published no book of designs, so their name is relatively little known.

At the Duke of Beaufort's Badminton House in Gloucestershire is a set of furniture, including a very splendid bed, made in about 1753 to John's design in his father William's Berkeley Square workshop. It would be unfair to call this 'Chinese Chippendale', since the Linnells' CHINOISERIE predates Chippendale's.

Later John was a follower of furniture fashions, from ROCOCO to ADAM, for whom he worked. The Linnell workshop produced superb craftsmanship, and like their most successful competitors they were carvers and upholsterers as well as cabinetmakers. Rather surprisingly, they do not appear to have been related to the great 19th-century landscape painter John Linnell.

▶ One of a pair of George III black and gilt japanned open armchairs by Linnell (**£150,000 the pair**)

Hamilton), which made porcelain mainly for export to the USA and went on to produce some of the best French art pottery. FAIENCE was also made at Limoges from as early as 1736 but not much has been identified. On the few marked examples that are known, the tin glaze has a tendency to crack. Porcelain marks include Cd incised or painted, or Cd with Sèvres mark and painter's initials. Porcelaine de Limoges is sometimes added in red.

 **£–£££££**

LINENFOLD

A type of decoration used mainly for late 15th-century panelling, where vertical mouldings terminate in folds. The name suggests it was inspired by cloth hanging in folds on the walls. However, there is no evidence that linen was ever used in this manner.

LINEN PRESS

A device comprising two boards compresed by a screw for pressing linen (see NAPKIN PRESS), or a cupboard for storing clothes. Most have shelves behind doors above and drawers below.

LINOLEUM

Made from oxidised linseed oil, ground cork and resin, it is used mainly on floors, although certain types were also produced for wall coverings. Linoleum was first made by Frederick Walton, who took out a patent as early as 1860. Patterned and coloured examples were being made by various companies in Europe and America by the early 20th century.

LION

In ancient cultures, the lion is regarded as king of the beasts and symbolises strength, courage, pride and majesty. Christian legend suggests he sleeps with his eyes open, giving him the attributes of spiritual watchfulness. A winged lion is the symbol of St Mark the Evangelist, and thus of Venice. Crouching lions formed the base of medieval pulpits and coronation thrones. Lions became popular again in the REGENCY period, taking on the cat-like appearance of the Egyptian form. The British Lion entered the Victorian caricaturist's repertoire as a stereotype, especially that of John Tenniel, personifying the Empire and British power.

LITHOGRAPHY

Literally meaning 'stone drawing', lithography was invented in 1798 by Alois Senefelder. It is based on the fact that grease and water repel each other. A drawing is made on a suitable surface (originally stone, but later zinc or aluminium) in a greasy medium. The surface is dampened with water, which is repelled by the grease, and printing ink is then rolled over it. The ink adheres only to the drawn marks, the water repelling it from the rest of the surface. Finally the ink is transferred to paper by running the block through a press. The process revolutionised printing, allowing much greater freedom in designs and subtler modelling effects. It can be difficult to tell a lithograph from an original drawing.

LITHOPHANES

These are panels of biscuit porcelain with pictorial scenes, often after Old Masters, moulded in *intaglio*. Such scenes become visible against the light. The technique was patented in Paris in 1827, and lithophanes were made at MEISSEN and BERLIN, and in England by Grainger Lee and Co. From the 1850s they were sometimes tinted by the addition of metal oxides.

 £££

◄ Liverpool group, 'La Nourrice', 1760 (£3,000-£4,000)

LIVERPOOL POTTERY AND PORCELAIN

By 1760 there were some 12 factories in Liverpool making tin-glazed earthenware similar to LAMBETH and BRISTOL. A great deal of their production was exported directly to the colonies. Large punch bowls, painted with ships on the insides, were a speciality. Some wares were decorated with FAZACKERLEY colours. Flowers, birds and seascapes were all common,

and after 1750 transfer-printed tiles were made. Among the most important factories were those run by Samuel Gilbody, Richard Chaffers and the Penningtons. One, founded by Richard Abbey, was then taken over by Worthington, Humble and Holland and named Herculaneum. The factory flourished until 1841, producing cream-coloured earthenware and lustreware. Herculaneum wares were marked with the name impressed, or after 1833, painted.

££-£££££

LOBMEYR GLASS

One of the most outstanding firms of Viennese glass decorators, it was founded by Josef Lobmeyr (1782-1855) and is still flourishing. His son Ludwig (1829-1917) played a major part in the firm's development, commissioning designs from leading artists. Most of the glass was made in southern Bohemia, the most interesting examples being elegant drinking glasses and decanters. Early in the 20th century the company became associated with the artists of the Vienna Secession, including Josef Hoffmann who became a co-director in 1910.

▲ Lobmeyr glass circular dish, engraved by Kal Pietsch (£38,000)

TALKING ANTIQUES

'LOADED' (OR 'FILLED')

Items made from sheet silver — such as candlesticks, knife handles and dressing table brushes — may be loaded with pitch or plaster of Paris to give weight and strength. This frequently breaks down with time.

LOCK, MATTHIAS (active 1724-69)

A furniture-maker who was the most important exponent of the English ROCOCO style. Firmly attributed pieces are very rare, although there are a few examples of his work in the Victoria and Albert Museum. Lock is best known for his many published designs. Three pattern books date from around 1746, and in the 1750s he published another two, including *A New Book of Ornaments in the Chinese Taste*. His designs, including sconces, console tables, looking glasses and chimneypieces, abound with 'C' scrolls, masks, birds, winged dragons, trellis work, scroll terms and CHINOISERIE elements, all combined in the most delightful and elegant Rococo manner.

LOGWOOD

A bright red wood from central America, used chiefly as a dye for staining other woods black.

LONGTON HALL

The first porcelain factory to be established in Staffordshire, it ran from 1750 to 1760, making wares in a heavy soft-paste similar to CHELSEA. A speciality of the factory was useful wares made of simulated overlapping leaves. Early figures are heavy and are often confused with those made at DERBY. When the factory closed it is supposed that William Duesbury acquired the stock and machinery for Derby.

 £££-££££

LOO TABLE

A circular or oval card table with a central pillar supporting the top, which rests on a base with three or four feet. Introduced in the late Georgian period, it was designed for the round game of cards known as lanterloo. In the *Cabinet Directory* of 1803 SHERATON shows a loo table that has a large, rectangular top hinged so it can stand against a wall.

 ££££

Hickory, dickory

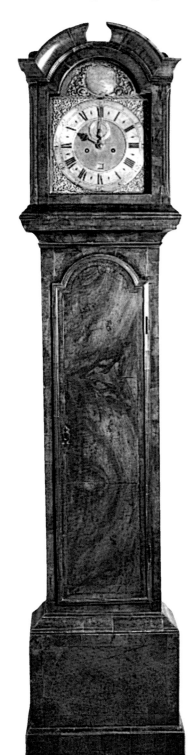

LONGCASE CLOCK

The correct name for a 'grandfather' clock. The tall, narrow case was devised as a direct consequence of the introduction of the pendulum to clocks by Christian Huygens in 1656. In the following year his fellow Dutchman Salomon Coster made the first 'Hague' clocks under the Huygens patent, and the London-based Ahasuerus Fromenteel sent his son over to learn the craft.

The anchor escapement was developed for pendulum clocks c1670, and this, with the seconds-beating pendulum, made for great accuracy. However, pendulums and weights required housing — thus the longcase was introduced.

The great period for English clock-making was 1660-1720. The Fromenteels were succeeded by Joseph Knibb (d.1711) in Oxford and London, Thomas TOMPION (1638-1713) and his nephew George Graham (1673-1751) and Daniel QUARE (1649-1724), all in London.

The cases of the earliest examples were oak veneered with ebony, or ebonised pearwood, and were classically architetcural in form. The hoods were pushed up for winding, and were wider than the trunks. This meant that clocks had to be screwed to the wall, since they were top-heavy when the weights were wound up. By the mid-1670s, walnut with pearwood inlays or veneers was usual. Clocks became still taller — up to 6ft 6in, and after 1700, up to 7ft or more. Dials were 10in square from 1675 to1690, 11in until 1700 and 15in thereafter.

Mahogany was introduced later than for other types of furniture, from about 1750. The early flat-topped hoods gave way to pediments, often broken, with brass finials. From about 1730 dials were arched and trunk doors followed, and during the Regency period round dials came in.

During the 18th century every country town had its longcase clockmaker, but most stopped making them in the 1830s, about 10 years after London.

◀ English walnut and boxwood inlaid ongcase clock, needing some attention, c1730 (£7,000-£8,000)

dock

► English marquetry long-case clock, c1705, with quarter striking movement on six bells. Seen at the Colchester Roadshow (£10,000)

LOOKING-GLASS

'Looking-glass' and 'mirror' are now interchangeable, both meaning a reflective glass in a decorative frame. Originally, 'mirour', derived from French, referred to small, polished-metal, or occasionally crystal, hand-held mirrors, before the manufacture of flat glass. The word 'looking-glass' may have originated to distinguish polished-steel and crystal. It appears in a French royal inventory of 1532 . The Venetians are credited with the invention of flat mirror glass in about 1460. Backed with an amalgam of tin and mercury, this was highly reflective. The secrets of glass-making were jealously guarded, but leaked out with emigrant Venetians. In the late 17th century the French glasshouse of St Gobain revolutionised the industry by introducing plate glass, whereby looking-glasses of much greater size and evenness could be produced. Since reflective glass was highly prized it was elaborately framed in carved and gilt wood, composition or gilt bronze. During the 18th century PIER glasses and overmantel mirrors were an essential decoration. More practical types were the CHEVAL GLASS and the toilet glass.

LOOS, ADOLPH (1870-1933)

A leading Austrian architect and designer who advocated simple functional furniture, glass and household objects. He settled in Vienna where his theories were directly opposed to Josef Hoffman and the Wiener Werkstätte. In his most famous article, published in 1908, entitled *Ornament and Crime*, he denounced the use of any ornament, including curves.

LOPERS

These are the sliding rails which pull out from a bureau to support the fall.

LORGNETTE

Hand-held spectacles popular in the 19th century. The handle often ends in a loop to hang from the wrist. Many have a spring action so the lenses can be doubled over to use as a magnifying glass. They were made until about the First World War.

££-£££

◄ Steel and gilt metal lorgnette, c1900, (£35-£45)

Royal patrons of Baroque and Rococo

LOUIS XIII, XIV, XV & XVI

The great period of French decorative arts lasted from about 1661 until the Revolution of 1789-99. The lavish patronage of the kings and the strict rules of the French guilds resulted in outstanding craftsmanship. Under Louis XIII a late BAROQUE style, heavily influenced by immigrant Italian craftsmen, predomi-

▲ One of a pair of giltwood Louis XV open armchairs by J.-B. Lebas, with some restoration (£4,500 the pair)

nated. Louis XIV took an unprecedented interest in the arts, personally supervising the decoration of his royal residences. He established a native school of French craftsmen whose designs influenced the whole of Europe.

The rapid spread of the style was partly due to the Revocation of the Edict of Nantes, 1685, which exiled the Protestant Huguenots, many of them highly skilled craftsmen. The style is rich, heavy, and sombre, reflecting the formal grandeur of Louis's court. Costly materials were favoured, such as Oriental lacquer, tortoiseshell, especially BOULLE, PIETRA DURA, gold and silver, the last for massive furniture, none of which

has survived. Symbolic motifs, including Apollo's head, sunbursts, the LL monogram, dolphins and thunderbolts were used for royal pieces.

Louis XV's reign was the great age of French ROCOCO, which ran from about 1700 to 1750. The phase from around 1710-30 is known as the *Régence* because for much of it (1715-23) the King was a minor. Furniture still retained the grandeur of Louis XIV, but the Louis XV style was frivolous and intimate, reflecting the vogue for smaller rooms and the informality of the court, where Madame de Pompadour ruled.

For all of the preceding reigns, the use of ORMOLU mounts on furniture and works of art was, along with superb veneers, a unifying factor. Furniture and porcelain were delicate and elegant, delighting in S curves. The serpentine commode came into its own and exquisite flower decoration adorned FAIENCE, SÈVRES and the silks woven at Lyons.

Louis XVI's style was a NEO-CLASSICAL reaction against the ROCOCO, which had already set in by 1750. The great cabinetmakers OEBEN, Reisner, Weisweiller and also ROENTGEN, Carlin and the bronze-worker Gouthière epitomised the best of it. Their work was calm and restrained, with curves and scrolls ironed out. Greek and Roman motifs, such as the PALMETTE, ANTHEMION and BUCRANE were favoured, as well as classical architectural features.

The reigns of Louis XV and Louis XVI saw the dominance of the market by the *merchant merciers*, dealers who sold works of art both old and new, mounted oriental porcelain and took commissions for furniture. Madame de Pompadour, mistress of Louis XV was a frequent buyer from such dealers. She was a strong supporter of the Sèvres factory, founded by Louis XV and owned by Louis XV and XVI. The artistic excesses of the court, such as Madame de Pampadour's spending the equivalent of £2million on Sèvres flowers, fuelled the Revolution.

The RESTAURATION covers the reigns of Louis XVIII and Charles X. It was basically a continuation of the EMPIRE style of Napoleon but coarser and heavier. Napoleonic motifs disappeared and Bourbon symbols were also avoided. Colours were brighter and gaudier, and swans, lyres and acanthus scrolls were all favoured motifs. The romanticising 'troubadour' or GOTHIC REVIVAL style made its appearance.

Louis-Philippe style is an even more bourgeois version of the Restauration, and the troubadour style was replaced by more accurate imitations of Gothic and Renaissance furniture.

Louis XIII (1610-1643)
Louis XIV (1643-1715)
Régence (1715-23)
Louis XV (1715-74)
Louis XVI (1774-92)
Restauration (1815-30)
Louis XVIII (1814-15, 1815-24)
Restauration (1815-30)
Charles X (1824-30)
Louis-Philippe (1830-48)

▲ Louis XIV ebony
and boulle marquetry
Mazarin bureau
(£85,000)

LOST WAX PROCESS

Also known as *cire perdu* this ancient
method for casting metal is still used
today. A plaster or clay core is made
and covered with a layer of wax. This
is then finely modelled, covered with
clay and heated in an oven until the
wax melts away. Molten metal is then
poured into the mould, replacing the
wax. When cooled, the mould is
cracked open, the core broken up and
the hollow metal object emerges.

▶ Rare Lowestoft cat,
c1780. Seen at the
Colchester Roadshow
(£3,500-£4,000)

LOWESTOFT PORCELAIN

Founded in 1757, the factory made
SOFT-PASTE porcelain with a high
bone-ash content, similar to BOW. The
decoration is inspired by Worcester
and Chinese models in underglaze
blue or transfer-printed. Many pieces
have inscriptions or the name of a
child or owner. The factory closed
c1800, but its owner, Robert Allan,
continued as a porcelain painter.

    ££-££££

▲ One of a pair of
Louis XVI ormolu-
mounted, painted
and parcel-gilt
corner consoles
(£20,000 the pair)

▶ Lowestoft
cylindrical
mug, inscribed
with a motto,
c1790
(£250-£300)

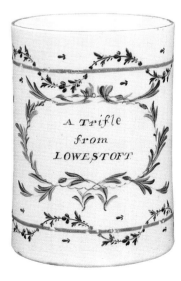

A Trifle
from
LOWESTOFT

◀ **Ludwigsburg coloured parrot,** a rare example, 1765 (£20,000)

LUDWIGSBURG POTTERY AND PORCELAIN

Founded in 1758 by J. J. Ringler under the auspices of Duke Carl Eugen of Wurttemburg, the factory was housed in the ducal palace until 1793. Its most remarkable products were the ROCOCO and NEO-CLASSICAL figures modelled by the chief painter G. F. Riedel and rendered in the factory's greyish-coloured paste. The tablewares were undistinguished, decorated after MEISSEN models. In the 1790s models were provided by the neo-Classical sculptor Johann Heinrich Dannecker. A FAIENCE factory, established at the same time, merged with the porcelain factory in 1795. By 1800 the factory was in decline and it closed in 1824. Marks: (1759-93) crossed Cs, sometimes with coronet above; (c1790-c1810): stag's antlers.

£££-£££££

LUSTREWARE

Pottery with an iridescent metallic surface. A glazed surface is painted with metallic oxides, mixed with fine ochre and refired at a low temperature. Silver, gold, copper or platinum produce varying shades of pink, purple, dark red and a pale yellow. Islamic lustreware and later HISPANO-MORESQUE pottery appeared in the Middle Ages. During the Renaissance the main European centres were Deruta and Gubbio in Italy. Large quantities of popular wares were produced by WEDGWOOD and at LEEDS, SUNDERLAND, SWANSEA and Tyneside during the 19th century, and the technique as an art form was revived in the later 19th century by William DE MORGAN.

▲ **Copper lustre mask jug,** c1850 (£40-£70)

LUSTRE

The French name for a CHANDELIER, which in the 16th century was decorated with rock crystal drops. From the late 17th century these were replaced by cut glass and the term came into English to mean a cut-glass pendant. It is now used to describe any type of chandelier or candlestick decorated with cut glass.

LYRE-BACK CHAIR

This is an open chair-back with a pierced splat resembling a Greek lyre. It was introduced by Robert ADAM in about1775 and is also found in the designs of HEPPLEWHITE, SHERATON and Duncan Phyfe in America.

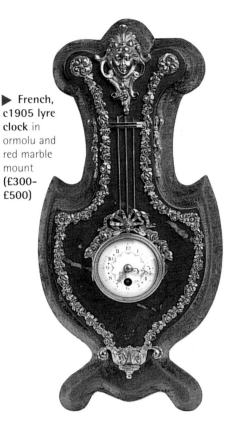

▶ **French, c1905 lyre clock** in ormolu and red marble mount (£300-£500)

LYRE CLOCK

A table or mantel clock in a lyre-shaped case, popular during the reign of Louis XVI. It made its way across the Channel soon after.

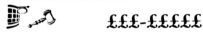

£££-£££££

LYONS SILK

In the 18th century Lyons boasted the most famous silk factories in Europe and their patterns were copied all over the Continent. In 1466 Louis XI set up his own silk industry there and by 1660 there were more than 3,000 master weavers at work, producing BAROQUE patterns similar to those woven in Italy. In about 1730 these were superseded by the naturalistically shaded designs of fruit and flowers for which Lyons became famous. The fabrics designed by Philippe de Lasalle, who worked for the Pernon factory, were among the most exquisite ever made. They were eagerly sought after by both the Empress of Russia and the Sultan of Turkey. The industry had a big revival under Napoleon, and with the introduction of the JACQUARD loom. Lyons still produces some of the best silk woven in Europe.

the background remained still. Fades, dissolves, superimpositions and other 'modern' techniques were also used. Accordingly, prices vary hugely. An 18th-century example, or a good 19th-century triple lantern with accessories, could be worth thousands, while a commonplace one can still be had at £50-£100. Phantasmagorical effects, as on some lanterns by the toymaking firm George Carette & Co, are much collected. In the same way, slides range from a pound or two upwards, with sets of unusual subjects—such as ballooning—or moving slides priced in the hundreds.

££-££££

MAHOGANY

There are several varieties of mahogany (*swietenia mahagoni*). All are very hard, smooth woods with a close grain and curly 'figure' or natural ornamental markings. When polished, mahogany has a deep, rich red colour. It was first used extensively for furniture in the reign of George I, and it became *the* wood of the 18th century. The most common source was Jamaica. Merchants there also bought mahogany from Cuba and the Bay of Honduras ('baywood') and shipped it to England. In the second quarter of the 19th century African mahogany began to be imported.

MACASSAR EBONY

A deep brown wood with dark, almost black stripes, which was used as a veneer on cabinet work, especially in the 1920s.

MACASSAR OIL AND ANTIMACASSAR

Oil extracted from the macassar tree, which was used by sailors on their pigtails and as a general Victorian hair oil. An antimacassar was a small piece of cloth placed on chair backs to protect against smears.

◀ Nursery magic lantern by Ernst Plank, with a collection of slides, 1890-1900. Seen at the Huddersfield Roadshow **(£300-£400)**

MACRAMÉ

A fringe of knotted thread or cord similar to that found at the end of Turkish towels—the Turkish word for towel being *macrama*. Since it became an English craft, countless unwanted presents have probably been made in macramé.

MAGIC LANTERNS

Magic lanterns and slides were first popular in the 18th century, when candle-power or oil lamps were used. They enjoyed a renewed craze in the later 19th century, with acetylene and electric lanterns, and are now enthusiastically sought out by the Magic Lantern Society of Great Britain and other collectors. There is a huge variety, from standard tinplate and brass lanterns and common slides, such as the text of the Lord's Prayer or the picture of a very grumpy Queen Victoria, to elaborate specialised equipment. Even in the early days attempts were made to simulate movement, by means of slides with moving parts which revolved while

Man who drew the line at nothing

MACKINTOSH, CHARLES RENNIE (1868–1928)

An outstanding Scottish architect and designer, Mackintosh was an important influence on the development of Modernism. He earned little respect in his own country but gained popularity on the Continent, especially in Austria and Germany.

His work has far more in common with the ART NOUVEAU of the VIENNA SECESSION (he was a close friend of Josef HOFFMANN) than with the more rustic ARTS AND CRAFTS movement and the William MORRIS tradition.

Born and educated in Glasgow, Mackintosh qualified there as an architect. His early work was done in close collaboration with his wife, Margaret Macdonald, her sister Frances and her husband Herbert MacNair. 'The Four' as they became known, established the Glasgow style, and their designs for interiors, textiles and stained glass reflected influences as diverse as CELTIC and JAPANESE art and ART NOUVEAU. So disliked were their designs that they were christened 'The Spook School'.

Mackintosh's revolutionary Glasgow School of Art, 1897, now considered a brilliant example of proto-Modernism, complete with its furniture and fittings, still stands as a monument to his principles of design and architecture.

Other major commissions, such as Windyridge at Kilmalcolm, Hill House, Helensburgh, the interiors for Miss Cranston's tea rooms and her own house, Hous'hill, underlined his commitment to total design, from furniture and wallcoverings to cutlery and light fittings. His interiors are sparsely furnished, often in cool colours.

Furniture, which today sells for outstanding prices, is architectural and geometric, based on straight lines and gentle curves. His chairs often have straight, elongated backs. Although sometimes using the natural effects of wood, Mackintosh favoured painted furniture: black, white or decorated in gem-like colours in intricate designs.

There were also designs for silver and flatware, and for metalwork, particularly fittings for cabinets and hinges, textiles, posters and fabrics. One motif which occurs frequently in the Glasgow school design repertoire is a stylised rose.

From 1923 Mackintosh lived at Port-Vendres on France's Catalan coast, where he concentrated on his watercolour painting. It was only in the 1930s that his designs began to be re-evaluated. He is now regarded as one of the founders of the Modern Movement and is particularly venerated in Japan.

Some of his furniture is now in production again, and interior schemes designed by him have been rescued and put on display in Glasgow.

◀ Rare ebonised oak ladder-back chair, re-upholstered in modern fabric, 1903 (£15,000)

▼ Two chests in ebonised pine with inset aluminium squares, c1905 (£5,000–£7,000)

◀ **Stained oak armchair** made for the Argyle Street Tearooms, Glasgow, 1896 **(£5,000)**

▲ **Oak writing desk** attributed to Mackintosh, c1905 **(£1,500-£2,500)**

▲ **Maiolica drug jar** from Castel Durante, c1590. Seen at the Basingstoke Roadshow **(£6,000-£7,000 a pair)**

MAIOLICA

This Italian term was originally applied to Spanish lustre pottery imported via Majorca. but, from the 16th century it described tin-glazed earthenware made in Italian factories from the 13th century onwards. The main factories were at BOLOGNA, Cafaggiolo, CASTEL DURANTE, Castelli, DERUTA, FAENZA, Florence, Gubbio, Mon- telupo, Padua, Turin, Urbino and Venice. The term is some-times applied to all European tin-glazed earthenware but strictly speaking should refer only to Italian wares or direct imitations.

MAJOLICA

A corruption of the term MAIOLICA, this is a type of earthen-ware introduced by MINTON in 1851. It was richly modelled and the biscuit body was dipped in tin-enamel glaze, then decorated with clear glaze coloured with metallic oxide. It was used for a wide range of decorative and useful objects includ-ing JARDINIÈRES and umbrella stands, fountains and tiles.

▶ **Majolica umbrella stand**, c1880, seen at the Wrekin Roadshow **(£2,000-£3,000)**

MAJORELLE, LOUIS (1859-1926)

The son of a cabinetmaker, he became the leading producer of ART NOUVEAU furniture in Europe. After training as a painter, he returned to Nancy to run the family workshops, which made 18th-century reproduction furniture, when he fell under the influence of GALLÉ. He mechanised his workshop and turned out luxury furniture at affordable prices. His designs lack the inspiration and fantasy of Gallé's but the forms are well thought out and the carved decoration seems to grow organically out of them. One of his most characteristic pieces is his limpid water-lily table with its sculptural bronze mounts emphasising the sinuous forms. After the First World War he returned to Nancy and adapted his designs to the new fashion for Modernism, using straight lines, circles and squares.

 £££-£££££

MALACHITE

A very bright green veined mineral which is a hydrous carbonate of copper and mined mainly in Russia. Solid pieces were used to make small decorative objects, especially by Fabergé, but it was also used as a thin veneer on a base of copper or stone to make large objects such as table tops and ornamental vases. The Malachite Hall in the Winter Palace at St Petersburg is decorated with columns and a fireplace faced with malachite.

MALLING JUGS

These are English tin-glazed earthenware jugs made (probably in London) in the 16th century. Decorated with silver mounts, they were given speckled blue, purple and brown glazes in imitation of Rhenish stoneware. The name comes from the church of West Malling in Kent, where an example was found.

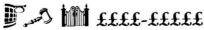 **££££-£££££**

MANDARIN DRESS

In 1766 the Manchu Emperor issued a series of strict dress regulations. Blue became the dynastic colour, replacing

▼ Late 19th-century Chinese painting of a fifth rank military mandarin. Seen at the Taunton Roadshow (£1,500)

the red robes of the Ming dynasty. Only the imperial family wore yellow. Everyone else wore blue, even down to peasants in indigo-dyed cotton. The ranks of the mandarins, both civil and military, were proclaimed by a highly sophisticated dress code from which it was forbidden to deviate. Those of the first, second and third ranks had nine four-clawed dragons embroidered on their robes. The fourth to sixth ranks had eight dragons, and the seventh to ninth five dragons. The type of girdle clasp and the button at the apex of the hat also showed rank as follows:

First rank: clasp, jade set with rubies; button, transparent ruby. **Second**: gold set with rubies; opaque coral. **Third**: worked gold; transparent sapphire. **Fourth**, worked gold with opaque lapis lazuli; silver. **Fifth**: worked gold with transparent crystal; plain silver. **Sixth**: mother-of-pearl; opaque jade. **Seventh**, silver; plain gold. **Eighth**: clear horn; worked gold with *shou* characters (representing good luck). **Ninth**: buffalo horn; worked gold with two *shou* characters.

The Manchu also adopted the Ming system of lavishly embroidered squares sewn to the backs and fronts of robes. Military ranks were indicated by animals and civil ranks by birds:

First rank, lion (military); crane (civil)
Second, lion; golden pheasant
Third, leopard; peacock
Fourth, tiger; wild goose
Fifth, bear; silver pheasant
Sixth, panther; egret
Seventh, rhinoceros; mandarin duck
Eighth, rhinoceros; quail
Ninth, sea-horse; paradise flycatcher.

▲Chinese punch bowl decorated in mandarin palette, c1760 (£1,800–£2,000)

MANDARIN PALETTE

The colours used on Chinese export porcelain decorated in Canton, including figure subjects in panels of underglaze blue. The palette, particularly the distinctive purple pink was copied in the 18th century by WORCESTER, amongst others.

MANTEL CLOCKS

Mantel clocks were first developed in France under Louis XV. Unlike the earlier bracket clock—designed to stand on a bracket screwed to the wall—mantel clocks were designed to stand on furniture. By the later 18th century they had arrived on mantel-pieces, often flanked by garnitures of candelabra or pot-pourri vases. Early French mantel clocks have circular enamel dials and the movement is in a drum canister. Sometimes the clock is borne on the back of an animal such as an elephant or incorporated into an exotic CHINOISERIE figure. ORMOLU cases were common in the 19th century, often with porcelain plaques. In the mid-Victorian period it seemed as if black BELGIAN 'MARBLE' clocks were on virtually every middle-class mantelpiece.

◄Gilded brass French mantel clock with enamel plaques, 1878. Seen at the Wrekin Roadshow (£3,000–£4,000)

Don't lose your marbles

MARBLES

The game of marbles is one of the oldest and most universal of all human amusements. Palaeolithic cave dwellers in Austria, Ancient Egyptians, Greeks, Romans, Incas and Chinese, and schoolboys everywhere, have played it in much the same way. The earliest balls were made of coloured clay, nuts or polished stone rather than glass, and many of the later, glass types still imitate marble or agate. From the 15th century, glass marbles were made in Venice and Bohemia, doubtless as by-products.

China marbles were introduced in around 1800, and remained popular throughout the 19th century. Although stone, agate and marble marbles continued to be made, glass really took off as a marble material once German glassblowers had produced special marble shears, by the middle of the century.

A great number of colours and patterns were devised, many of which acquired local names among players. In many parts of the British Isles, for instance, the best marbles are known as 'alleys', while the actual 'shooter' may also be called a 'taw'.

Clay marbles were mass produced on both sides of the Atlantic from about 1870, and in the 1890s machines were introduced to make glass ones. However, machine production did not really take hold until the First World War, when the American market was cut off from traditional European sources.

Marbles are still made all over the world from all the different materials mentioned above, but glass remains the most popular of these. However, the days of the hand-made marble could soon be at an end as it seems there is only a handful of makers left.

Of course, the more marbles have been played with and the more battered they are, the less valuable they become.

◄Collection of glass marbles, including some from the late 19th century (£5–£10 each)

▲ George III Manx table
(£5,000-£6,000)

MANX TABLE

A tripod table with the three feet carved to represent legs with knee breeches and buckled shoes.

 R ££££

MAPLE

A light, yellowish brown wood with dark brown lines, growing in Canada and the eastern USA. It has a very decorative figure known as bird's eye which consists of a series of small spots linked by undulating lines. It remains highly prized by cabinet-makers as an ornamental veneer.

Have tin, will travel

MÄRKLIN

Theodor Freidrich Wilhelm Märklin founded 'W. Märklin and Co' with his wife, Caroline, in 1859. Their first products were dolls' cooking utensils. Theodor died in 1866 and the firm passed into the hands of Caroline and her two sons. The company was renamed, 'Gebruder Märklin' and the business thrived.

In 1891 they exhibited the first 'system' railway at the Leipzig Trade Fair, and bought up another tin-toy manufacturer, Lutz. They were quick to adopt modern methods and mass production, and are particularly famous for their transport toys — trains, cars and wonderful ocean liners. Their pre-Second World War train sets are especially sought after. Most remarkably, the firm managed to survive both World Wars, and today it proclaims itself the world's oldest toy train manufacturer. The early GM mark, in various styles, was superseded by 'Märklin', combined with a speeding locomotive.

▼ Large tin-plate liner by Märklin, 1920 (£2,000-£3,000)

MARBLING

Painting inferior stone or wood to imitate marble. The technique was used on furniture and in interiors from the 17th to the 19th centuries, and is popular again with interior decorators. Paper can also be marbled.

MARBLED WARE

This is pottery which looks like heavily veined marble. It is made either by wedging (mixing) tinted or coloured clays or by colouring the glaze with different metallic oxides. It was made in China during the Tang dynasty and by WEDGWOOD and others to resemble marble, porphyry, malachite, lapis lazuli and onyx.

MAROT, DANIEL (1663-1752)

A Huguenot refugee, Marot was a key figure in the dissemination of the Continental BAROQUE style to England. He is believed to have worked in BOULLE's *atelier* before fleeing to Holland where he was employed by William of Orange to design the interiors of the palace of Het Loo. He followed William to England and was employed at Hampton Court. His numerous published designs for furniture and interior decoration were enormously influential. They included all kinds of furniture, curtain designs, toilet services and even silver andirons.

'MARRIAGE'

A piece of furniture made of two period pieces which did not start life together, is known as a marriage. For example, a bureau bookcase might be created by adap– ting an ordinary low bureau to take a period bookcase. Although such objects can be attractive, they do not have anything like the value of an integrated example See 'Made up'.

dolls which included the popular 'Dream Baby'. There were also Oriental and Negro heads, which are now amongst the most sought after. The most prolific of the German manufacturers, he supplied bisque heads to a number of other companies, but these are considered of poor quality with crudely painted faces.

£££

▲ Serpentine bureau with marquetry decoration, c1760. Seen at the Derby Roadshow (£5,000)

MARQUETRY

Although the term originally meant a comparatively simple inlay of wood in wood, by the time of Charles II it was used for a far more elaborate form of decoration on furniture. Patterns, often floral or arabesques, were cut in a sheet of veneer, and then filled with thin slivers of decorative woods, IVORY or MOTHER-OF-PEARL. The resultant sheet was then glued to the carcass of furniture. The technique was often used with PARQUETRY, a geometrical mosaic made from slices of decorative woods.

MAROTTE DOLL

A doll's head mounted as a glove puppet, with a baton concealed by the dress. When twirled it plays a tune. Marotte dolls were made from the late 19th century.

£££

MARROW SCOOP

A long, thin implement used to extract marrow from a marrowbone. One end is channelled in the form of a long, narrow scoop; the other end can be either a narrow, elongated bowl or a grooved channel of a different width. Silver scoops, often by good smiths such as DE LAMERIE, were used in England from the late 17th century.

££-£££

MARSEILLE, ARMAND (active 1885-1930)

Born in Russia, he moved to Thuringia where he assumed control of a porcelain factory near Sonneberg, then the toymaking capital of Europe. In 1884 he bought a toy factory from Matthias Lambert and by 1890 began to produce bisque

▲ Musical marotte doll, c1900, brought into the Huddersfield Roadshow (£150-£200)

▲ Marsh and Jones satinwood and marquetry bureau cabinet (£12,000)

MARSH AND JONES

A long-established firm based in Leeds and London, which became one of the most prominent Victorian furniture-makers when bought by John Marsh and Edward Jones in 1864. They are especially well known for their elaborate GOTHIC REVIVAL pieces designed by Bruce Talbert and Charles Bevan. Later they made furniture in the ART NOUVEAU and ARTS AND CRAFTS styles, the latter to elegant designs by W.R. Lethaby, and in 1907 Edwin Lutyens was designing for them. Their pieces are often labelled with the name of the craftsman as well as the firm. They are generally of excellent quality.

££££-£££££

Feathers fly at the fantasy factory

THE MARTIN BROTHERS

The major pioneers of art and studio pottery in Britain were the eccentric but highly original Martin brothers, Robert Wallace, Charles Douglas, Walter Fraser and Edwin Bruce. They set up a small pottery at Fulham in 1873, making a wonderfully idiosyncratic range of saltglazed stonewares. Inspiration came from the medieval world and from the grotesque side of natural life, with echoes of the fantasy worlds of authors such as Lewis Carroll.

They insisted upon being responsible for all stages of production, from preparing the clay to selling the finished wares, and their standards were remarkable,

▶ Grotesque Martin Brothers bird, 1902, mounted on ebonised wood base (£3,000–£,4000)

considering the technical difficulties of the process.

Modelling and incising were their favoured techniques, and they are probably best known for the series of grotesque birds, with detachable heads and astonishingly varied expressions, that were the creation of Wallace Martin. Marine motifs and reptiles were also popular – along with floral decoration often based on Japanese art.

In 1878 they moved to Southall and continued to produce from there until the early 1900s, using refined decorative techniques that reflected their command of the technology and their increasingly sophisticated interpretations of Oriental styles.

They were taken to the Paris Exhibition of 1900 where the gourd-form wares of the French potters inspired them. The

high prices asked by the French, compared to their small returns was eye-opening. Edwin produced many miniature vases once they returned and these are among the most original of their products. Each piece was unique. The popularity of the birds is amply demonstrated by the biscuit tin shown under ADVERTISING.

Charles ran the shop in London where he was known for refusing to sell to prospective purchasers. When the shop burned down in 1903, large quantities of the best pots were found hidden under the floorboards and Charles's sanity, never strong, was lost forever. Robert Wallace, the eldest brother, died in 1923 but the pottery continued under his son Clement and a Captain Butterfield. These late wares are generally of poor quality.

◀ Diamond section vase in matt dark green decorated with dragons, 1889 (£400)

◀ Triangular section vase in brown glaze with stork and pelican decoration, 1898 (£900)

▼ Globular vase with cylindrical neck, glazed in dark green. Handles modelled as grotesque hounds (£400–£500)

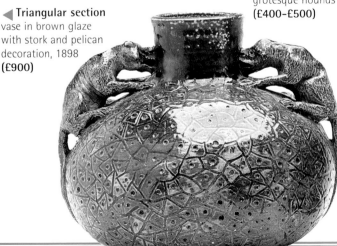

▲ **Martin Brothers vase** with writhing, globular body. Handles modelled as snakes (£1,500–£2,500)

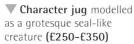

▼ **Character jug** modelled as a grotesque seal-like creature (£250–£350)

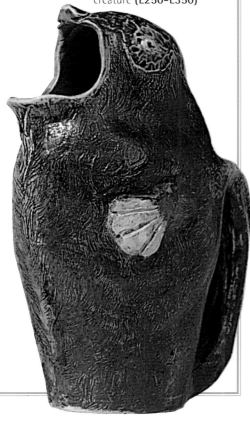

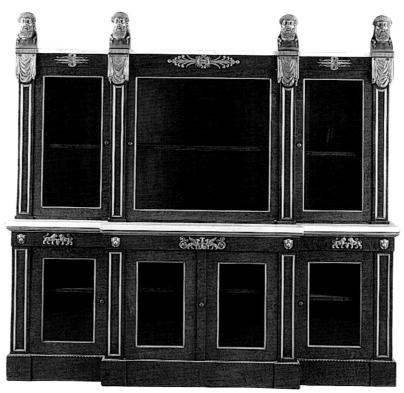

▲ **Marsh and Tatham** ormolu-mounted breakfront bookcase with a later marble top (£150,000–£200,000)

MARSH AND TATHAM

William Marsh (active 1775-1810) was a cabinetmaker who was joined in 1785 by George Elward, by Edward Bailey in 1793, and in 1798 by Thomas Tatham (1763-1818). From 1803 the firm was known as Marsh and Tatham. It was one of the most influential REGENCY cabinetmakers, making stylish pieces in the Anglo-French mode for the Whitbread family seat at Southill, Bedfordshire, JAPANNED furniture for the Prince Regent at Brighton Pavilion and Grecian library furniture for his CARLTON HOUSE. Henry Holland may have provided many of the designs, as well as Charles Heathcote Tatham, Thomas's brother, who was employed by the Prince Regent. The firm was in business up to 1840.

£££££-££££££

MARTHA GUNN

She is the female version of the Toby jug. The original for the model was a celebrated bathing-machine attendant, who is shown seated, wearing a voluminous dress and Prince of Wales feathers—signifying her 'royal appointment' to the Prince Regent at Brighton.

£££

MARTIN, GUILLAUME (d.1749)

One of four French brothers who invented the finest type of European JAPANNING, known as VERNIS MARTIN. In 1730 they were granted a monopoly for making imitations of Chinese and Japanese lacquer in relief, but they are best known for their own lustrous, gold-dusted vernis Martin. It was developed from a varnish known as cipolin, and ranged in colour from pearl grey through lilac to a strong Prussian blue, built up in as many as 40 coats, each of which had to be separately polished. They worked for Madame de Pompadour and Louis XV and decorated the panelling of the Dauphine's apartments at Versailles. They also made many smaller decorative objects, including fans, ÉTUIS and snuffboxes.

MASON'S IRONSTONE

George Miles and Charles James Mason took out their patent for ironstone china in 1813, and produced it in the Staffordshire pottery established by

Dogged defiance

MASONIC SIGNS

England's first grand lodge was established in 1717, after which freemasonry spread rapidly through 18th-century Europe. As the Roman Catholic church disapproved, excommunicating masons in 1738, masons began to use cryptic signs, such as the pug dog. Masonic items range from glasses engraved with set square, triangle and other symbols, to the superb MEISSEN tankard brought in to the Brussels Roadshow. Later in the century, at least in Germany, the Catholic authorities became less critical.

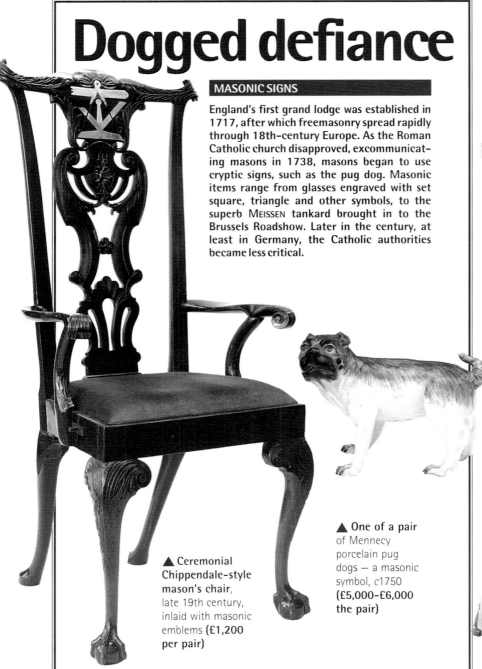

▲ Ceremonial Chippendale-style mason's chair, late 19th century, inlaid with masonic emblems (£1,200 per pair)

▲ One of a pair of Mennecy porcelain pug dogs — a masonic symbol, c1750 (£5,000-£6,000 the pair)

▲ Glass match holder with silver rim and ribbed sides for striking non-safety matches, 1930s (£30-£40)

MATCH HOLDERS

No Victorian or Edwardian smoking room was properly furnished without match holders, such as Loysel's Patent China Lucifer Match Ignitor, which might cost no more than a shilling, or even Fabergé's silver-mounted brick, which cost very much more. The most usual kind is a thick glass vase sometimes with a silver collar holding non-safety matches. The sides are ribbed so that matches can be struck against them.

£-££

▲ Matchbox Riley saloon from the late 1950s (£20-£50)

china in 1813, and produced it in the Staffordshire pottery established by their father Miles (d.1822). The body was perfectly suited to dinner wares and even large-scale pieces, including chimneypieces and garden seats. It is decorated in bright colours, often in the IMARI palette. The firm was taken over by Ashworth in 1848. Marks include: 'Mason', 'Mason's Patent Ironstone' and the Royal Arms.

MASSIER, CLÉMENT (c1845-1917)

££-£££

French potter, the son of a potter at Vallauris. He had a studio at Golfe-Juan, near Cannes, where he made 'Persian' and other wares, decorated with lustre glazes.

MATCHBOX TOYS

The most famous line of the LESNEY toy factory. The first little die-cast cars on a scale of 1:25 were issued in their Bryant & May-like boxes in 1953, and were immediately popular, as they are today. The firm ceased its UK operations in 1987.

£-££

Boxes that were up to snuff

MAUCHLINE WARE

During the first quarter of the 19th century, the Smith family of Mauchline set about developing the Scottish wooden box industry that had grown rapidly in the late 18th century to meet a dual demand for snuffboxes and Robert Burns souvenirs. The first boxes they produced were hand-painted or drawn with pen and ink, and are much sought after today, fetching hundreds of pounds. Coloured sporting scenes are generally the most decorative and valuable, but boxes bearing ink portraits of 'the Ayrshire bard' and objects decorated with tartan are also popular. The preferred wood was sycamore, which had a close grain and, when seasoned and varnished, a beautiful, golden yellow colour.

The foresight of the Smith family kept them consistently one step ahead of their competitors, and in 1829 they opened a factory in Birmingham to cope with the ever-increasing demand. In the early 1830s transfer printing, hitherto used on ceramics, was introduced as an improvement on the previous labour-intensive production methods. When the decline in snuff-taking drove many Scottish firms out of business, the Smiths of Mauchline varied their wares, offering a variety of objects from razor strops and string holders to card cases and pin cushions. As the firm's popularity grew in the second half of the 19th century, so did overseas demand for its wares, and it is common to find transfer-printed objects showing fashionable Continental tourist spots.

Towards the end of the 19th century, cheaper foreign products were causing such a decline in orders that the factory was in danger of closing. An attempt to revive the business was made by introducing 'fern-ware', a method of decoration in which real fern was applied to boxes and varnished. Later, ferns were used in a type of stencilling process, which was successful for a while. But after a major fire in 1933 the business was never the same again, and the outbreak of war in 1939 saw its final demise.

▲ Mauchline ware sycamore money box, transfer-printed with view of a Scottish house, c1890 (£30-£50)

▲ Transfer-printed snuffbox, c1900, seen at the Huddersfield Roadshow (£40-£50))

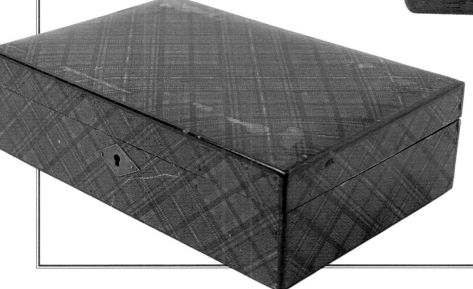

◀ Victorian tartan souvenir box, in poor condition and without an illustration on the lid (£35-£45)

Cranking out melodies on the music machine

▲ Portable barrel piano automaton, with animated dancers and a choice of eight tunes, c1850. Seen at the Colchester Roadshow (£6,000-£8,000)

MECHANICAL MUSIC

Attempts to make music without musicians have been known since ancient times. In late medieval times clock towers often played a melody by means of a cylinder with revolving pins, which led to the development of musical boxes.

The barrel organ first appeared in the 18th century. This was a horizontal wooden barrel, fitted with pins in a wooden case and turned by a crank handle. The pins engaged with valves attached to small pipes and the air chamber was supplied by bellows worked by the same crank handle.

The 19th century was the great age of the barrel organ, when free rods replaced the pipes. These were sounded by a revolving perforated card attached to valves. The early 19th century saw the birth of the cylinder musical box, originally developed by the watch-making industry in Geneva. Here a pinned brass cylinder plucked the teeth of the tuned steel comb as it revolved, driven by a clockwork mechanism. Some cylinders could be shifted to enable several tunes to be activated and larger machines had spare cylinders. The earliest musical boxes were wound by a key, this being later replaced by a lever. In most cases a list of tunes was stuck on the underside of the lid. Generally, the larger the number of tunes the higher the value. Mechanisms slowly became more complex with added drums, often beaten by butterflies, triangles and so on.

By the end of the century the disc musical box had been introduced, which used an interchangeable steel disc producing a clear, strong tone. The advantage was the ease with which tunes could be changed, the robust nature of the discs and the small storage space compared to cylinders. Large machines were installed in public houses and activated by a penny. America, Germany and Austria were the main centres of production. Large fairground organs were combined with percussion instruments to imitate the sound of a full-blown orchestra.

Mechanical pianos known as pianolas or phonolas did not appear until the 19th century. The mechanism used pins on a cylinder to press levers to engage the hammer. At first they were operated by foot, but a pneumatic mechanism was later introduced. Later still came the electric piano, with its amazing range of pitch and fingering. Mechanical violins, or violinas, were also experimented with but never entirely successfully. By 1920 the GRAMOPHONE had largely superseded mechanical devices.

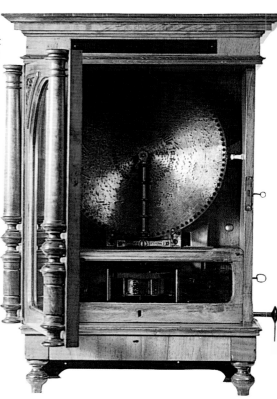

▶ Symphonium disc musical box 19⅛ in. German c1900 (£2,500-£3,500)

▲ **Disc mechanical box** made in Germany, c1895. Brought into the Derby Roadshow (£450-£600)

▲ **Paper roll organette**, called a Cabinetto, plays hymns and popular tunes of the day (£3,000-£4,000)

▲ **Gilt and enamel** singing bird box. The bird rotates, flaps its wings and opens its beak (£1,000- £1,500)

MATCHLOCK

The first firearms appeared in Europe in the 14th century, the earliest piece with a mechanical action being the matchlock musket in the late 14th or early 15th century. Long, heavy and cumbersome, it was operated by firing a trigger which caused an arm (the serpentine) to swing forward, to press the glowing tip of a piece of cord (the match) into a pan full of priming powder mounted at the side of the barrel. The flame passed through the touch hole in the side of the barrel, firing the main charge inside. It was highly unreliable, dependent on humidity and the weather.

 R£££££

MAZARINE

A pierced plate dish which fitted into a dish for holding food, such as fish. They were made in silver, Sheffield plate and ceramics including Staffordshire blue and white.

£££-££££

▲ **Mazarine and serving dish** from large Chinese dinner service, second half of 18th century (£7,000-£9,000)

MAZARINE BLUE

English name for the dark-blue underglaze ground colour known as *gros bleu* at SÈVRES. It was first employed by the Chelsea factory in about 1755 and was also used at Worcester from around 1769.

MAZER

A shallow wooden bowl with silver mounts, used as a drinking vessel from the 13th to the 16th century in Europe. Particularly grand versions were made of maple, the best mounted in precious metals. Complete silver bowls are later.

▲**Yarn gauge and balance** from Yorkshire mills, mid 19th to early 20th century (£20-£80)

MEASURES

Many trades and industries have evolved weights and measures to suit their specialised needs. From the Middle Ages merchants needed to weigh coins, to see if they had been clipped or 'sweated', and portable balances became common. In 1775 a waistcoat pocket version was produced by Anthony Wilkinson. From 1840 letter scales came in with the Penny Post. While these are widely collected, many more specialised balances and gauges are of real interest only to those with connections to the business that used them, Such industrial measures as the yarn gauges seen at the Huddersfield Roadshow were made and used until comparatively recently. Another collecting field is official measures for commodities such as corn, wine and beer.

MECCANO

One of the most famous British toy companies, it was founded by Frank HORNBY at the turn of the 20th century. The Meccano construction kit was an unrivalled success for six decades. Hornby went on to produce the Hornby assortment of clockwork and electric trains and shortly before his death launched the DINKY range which was originally sold as lineside accessories to the train sets. Dinky remained the mainstay of the company's fortunes until 1964 when it was taken over by TRI-ANG.

 £-£££

Gongs struck for gallantry

▲ Waterloo campaign medal, issued in1816 (£300-£400)

MEDALS

There are three sorts of medal: the commemorative, celebrating an individual, usually a ruler or an event; campaign medals relating to a particular military operation; and medals for gallantry. Until recently commemoratives were only found in European cultures.

The modern history of medals begins with the Renaissance, when Roman coins bearing heads of the emperors inspired imitation. The leading exponent was the painter Pisanello, who from the 1440s made exquisite medals for Italian princes including the D'Estes and Gonzagas. They were portable, durable and often exchanged as tokens of friendship.

In northern Europe, Albrecht Dürer also designed outstanding medals, as did Nicholas Hilliard in England, but it is the goldsmith and sculptor Benvenuto Cellini (1500-71) who is regarded as the outstanding Renaissance medallist. Medals abound from the English Civil War, when both sides needed tokens of loyalty.

The 19th century saw a revival of interest in medals – not only under Napoleon, who never missed an opportunity to identify himself with the ancient emperors, but also in Victorian England, where artists such as Alphonse Legros, Alfred Gilbert, William Wyon and Sir Edward Poynter all turned their hands to medals that were often highly sentimental.

The first campaign medal to be awarded to all ranks was that for the Battle of Waterloo issued in 1816. During the reign of Queen Victoria it was decided to honour veterans of previous Napoleonic battles (1793-1814) by issuing the Naval General Service medal and

▲ Victoria Cross (far left) and group of medals awarded to Private H. May of The Cameronians, 1914 (£18,250)

the Military General Service medal. There was a twist in the tail: the claimant had still to be still alive in 1849 when the medals were struck.

Further medals were awarded throughout Queen Victoria's reign for various wars in Africa, Canada, China, Egypt, India and the Crimean War – when the Victoria Cross was instituted to become the highest award for valour.

Campaign medals issued to any fighting man who took part in the First and Second World Wars are worth only a few pounds. Gallantry medals, preferably those accompanied by documentation, grip the imagination, particularly when they have been won in

and glory

▲ **Crimea medal** with three bars, 1854-56 (**£150-200**)

a famous battle or awarded for a deed of great heroism.

There is considerable interest in medals awarded to sportsmen and women, particularly Olympic golds, or those issued for celebrated football matches.

Collectors should avoid re-named medals, which can be identified by a worn, rounded rim which is thinner than at the centre. Never split groups of medals or discard old, worn ribbons. If you must use a cleaning fluid never leave it on for too long: keep neutralising its effect by washing it off under a tap.

▼ **Memorial medal** struck for the death of James II, 1701, by James Dassier (**£25-£30**)

MECHLIN LACE

Mechlin in Flanders is supposed to have been one of the best centres for the production of lace in the 17th century. No examples can be traced so the term is now applied to a very popular type of pillow lace made from the 1720s with ROCOCO designs outlined in a flat thread heavier than that used for the rest of the fabric.

MEDAL CABINETS

Cabinets, with shallow drawers to contain coins and medals, made for collectors from the mid-18th century. They vary in size and ornament. Some are tall and narrow with drawers protected by doors, others mounted on carved stands with drawers and cupboards. A simplified form of coin cabinet known as a WELLINGTON was designed soon after Waterloo. It had little or nothing to do with the Duke, but his name was good for sales.

£££-££££

MEDICI FAMILY

The family of bankers who dominated the Republic of Florence from 1434, when Cosimo de Medici was appointed Signor, or chief citizen. His son Lorenzo the Magnificent ruled from 1469 to 1492 and was one of Europe's greatest patrons of the arts. The family was expelled between 1494 and 1512 and again in 1527-30. In 1569 they became Grand Dukes of Tuscany, ruling until 1737. They also produced three Popes: Leo X (1513-21), Clement VII (1523-34) and Pius IV (1559-66) and two Queens of France, Catherine who married Henry II in 1547, and Marie who married Henry IV in 1600.

MEDICI PORCELAIN

This was the first European factory to produce SOFT-PASTE porcelain of which examples survive. It was in production in Florence between 1575 and 1587. Set up by Grand Duke Francesco I, the factory used white clay from Vicenza, white sand, powdered rock crystal, calcined lead and tin. A creamy thick lead white glaze was applied after the pieces had been biscuit fired. Medici porcelain looks more like opaque glass than true porcelain and is decorated in underglaze blue in styles derived from 16th-century Chinese porcelain. It is very rare: only 59 pieces have been identified. Marks: the six balls of the Medici arms; a drawing of the dome of Florence cathedral.

MEDICINE CHEST

A large version of a DISPENSARY. Although often referred to as 'apothecaries' cabinets', these were more often the ancestors of the domestic bathroom cabinet. In Britain in the late 18th and 19th centuries they were made by specialist cabinetmakers in the same way as TEA caddies. They derive from military and naval chests and are either for allopathic (orthodox) or, from the early 19th century, homeopathic medicines. The most popular British shape was the trunk, with one or more drawers below, but cylinders and front-opening door models are also known. Until about 1720 they are likely to be oak, or SHAGREEN-covered; to around 1820 mahogany; thereafter perhaps rosewood, walnut or coromandel. An elaborate 1850s example might contain more than 50 items.

▲ **Domestic medicine chest**, mid-19th century (**£400-£600**)

Now say 'aaah'

MEDICAL INSTRUMENTS

Silver has the unusual property of being self-sterilising — bacteria cannot survive on its surface — so, for centuries, it has been preferred for medical instruments, except cutting ones.

A barber surgeon's instrument case survives from about 1500, but most instruments today are from the 18th century onwards, with surgeons' ÉTUIS containing bloodletting knives being fairly common. Tongue depressors are among the more decorative items as the 'blade' is often attractively pierced. Other small instruments encountered are spatulas, tweezers, forceps, scissors, directors and probes. Less desirable are catheters of which a good number survive from the late 18th century onwards.

Ear trumpets are found in an extraordinary variety of sizes and shapes. Since they were used socially, they are much more likely to be decorated than other medical

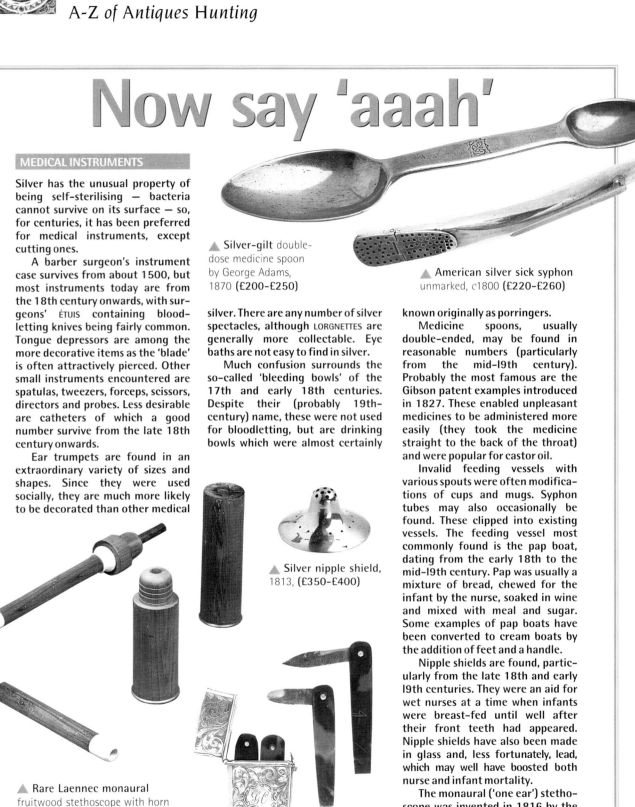

▲ Silver-gilt double-dose medicine spoon by George Adams, 1870 (£200-£250)

▲ American silver sick syphon unmarked, c1800 (£220-£260)

silver. There are any number of silver spectacles, although LORGNETTES are generally more collectable. Eye baths are not easy to find in silver.

Much confusion surrounds the so-called 'bleeding bowls' of the 17th and early 18th centuries. Despite their (probably 19th-century) name, these were not used for bloodletting, but are drinking bowls which were almost certainly

known originally as porringers.

Medicine spoons, usually double-ended, may be found in reasonable numbers (particularly from the mid-19th century). Probably the most famous are the Gibson patent examples introduced in 1827. These enabled unpleasant medicines to be administered more easily (they took the medicine straight to the back of the throat) and were popular for castor oil.

Invalid feeding vessels with various spouts were often modifications of cups and mugs. Syphon tubes may also occasionally be found. These clipped into existing vessels. The feeding vessel most commonly found is the pap boat, dating from the early 18th to the mid-19th century. Pap was usually a mixture of bread, chewed for the infant by the nurse, soaked in wine and mixed with meal and sugar. Some examples of pap boats have been converted to cream boats by the addition of feet and a handle.

Nipple shields are found, particularly from the late 18th and early 19th centuries. They were an aid for wet nurses at a time when infants were breast-fed until well after their front teeth had appeared. Nipple shields have also been made in glass and, less fortunately, lead, which may well have boosted both nurse and infant mortality.

The monaural ('one ear') stethoscope was invented in 1816 by the Breton René Laennec, and early turned fruitwood examples, which resemble elegant clarinets, are well worth looking out for. The familiar stethoscope was invented in 1856 by George Cammanon of New York.

▲ Silver nipple shield, 1813, (£350-£400)

▲ Rare Laennec monaural fruitwood stethoscope with horn and ivory extension, early 19th century (£3,000-£4,000)

▼ Metal telescopic ear trumpet, c1860 (£350-£400)

▲ Silver lancet case with four lancets, 1843 (£350-£400)

▼ **Meerschaum pipe** portrait of a Grenadier, amber stem, velvet case, probably made in Vienna, c1880 (**£500-£700**)

MEERSCHAUM

The Turkish white stone from which meerschaum pipes are carved resembles spume or sea foam, which is what the German word means. The centre of the 19th-century industry was Vienna, where the elaborate bowls were fitted with amber mouthpieces. The more the pipe is smoked, the more the warm brown colour permeates the stone. Meerschaums were still being carved in the early 20th century, and more recently resin FORGERIES have been made.

££-£££

MEIGH

A Staffordshire pottery established by Job Meigh in about 1780. His sons Job and Charles succeeded him and Job the younger invented a new type of glaze for the interior of cooking vessels as ordinary lead glaze could dissolve in vinegar and poison the food. Charles Meigh produced highly successful GOTHIC REVIVAL and neo-Renaissance pieces in stoneware, winning a medal at the Great Exhibition.

££-£££

MEIPING

A tall, baluster-shaped Chinese vase which is narrow at the bottom and rises to a swelling curve at the shoulder. The neck is usually short and narrow. These vases were popular from the 13th to the 18th century.

MEISSONIER, JUSTE AURÈLE (c1693-1750)

An Italian, he spent most of his life in Paris working as a designer, architect and goldsmith, succeeding BÉRAIN in 1725 as *architecte-dessinateur de la Chambre et du Cabinet du Roi*. He developed a highly flamboyant ROCOCO style, but very little of his work survives, his fame rests on 120 engraved designs for architecture, interior decoration, furniture, silver and bronze, which gave inspiration to others.

◀ **Mennecy figure** of a Chinese boy, c1740 (**£8,000-£12,000**)

MÊNE, PIERRE JULES (1810-70)

After Barye he is the best known of the French ANIMALIER sculptors. He received some instruction from René Compaire but was largely self-taught, establishing his own foundry in 1838. He had a thriving business, winning several prizes at the International Exhibitions. His bronzes were also reissued by founders such as BARBEDIENNE.

▲ **Bronze model of a retriever** by Pierre Jules Mêne (**£1,000**)

MENNECY

A porcelain factory founded in Paris in 1734 and transferred to Mennecy in 1748. Its production was restricted by laws to protect the royal VINCENNES factory and gilding was forbidden. It produced fine-quality SOFT-PASTE porcelain, brilliantly painted in enamels, often with a characteristic purple-rose. Early work was inspired by KAKIEMON, later pieces were more in the style of Vincennes with delicate flowers. In 1773 the factory closed in favour of new works which were set up at Bourg-la-Reine. Marks: DV in red, black, blue or incised.

At the sign of the crossed swords

MEISSEN

The Meissen factory, some 20 miles outside Dresden in Saxony, was the earliest in Europe to produce true or HARD-PASTE porcelain, first made by the alchemist Johann BÖTTGER in 1708-10.

The earliest pieces were, in fact, of stoneware, polished and engraved like contemporary glass (see AUGUSTUS THE STRONG). By 1720 porcelain production was in full swing generally with CHINOISERIE decoration by J. G. HÖROLDT and his workshop. In the

▲ Part of a complete Meissen tea service decorated with deutsche Blumen, c1740-50. Seen at the Taunton Roadshow (£10,000 the set)

▼ Pair of Meissen vases c1850-70, 30in high but not in good condition. Brought into the Newcastle Emlyn Roadshow (£10,000-£15,000)

1730s this gave way to European harbour scenes, often with Turkish merchants, armorial wares and pieces directly inspired by the KAKIEMON porcelains of Japan.

At the beginning of the 1730s the modeller J.J. KÄNDLER produced some large white animals for his patron Augustus III of Saxony. These were technically very difficult to produce, but gave rise to numerous smaller, coloured birds and animal figures which were modelled over the next 20 years. The late 1730s and '40s saw the first of the famous Italian Comedy figures of Harlequin, Columbine and other characters, a theme which was to be taken up by almost every European porcelain manufacturer. Among his finest groups are a series of 'Crinoline' subjects depicting ladies in wide-panniered skirts together with their admirers and attendants.

He also modelled figures of miners, and others representing the different nations of the Levant. Kändler designed the Swan service, too, consisting of over 2,000 pieces, for Count Brühl. Water was the theme — Brühl means marsh — and the plates are moulded with swans amongst bulrushes. Not only was it perhaps the largest service ever made, but it is now among the more expensive: individual pieces regularly sell for more than £30,000.

After 1750 the factory became much less successful, although some fine NEO-CLASSICAL pieces were produced by Michel Acier, a French modeller who succeeded Kändler.

The 19th century saw a repetition of the great models of the previous century, usually with insensitive use of colouring. Large vases, chandeliers and mirrors encrusted with flowers were popular and have remained desirable.

In the 20th century there was a renewal of inspiration at MEISSEN with fine figures by Max Esser, who renewed the tradition of animal figures, Paul Borner, Paul Walther and Paul Scheurich, who returned to Italian comedy. All their work is collectable. The factory is still in production making good quality useful and decorative wares, figures continuing to play a part.

The factory mark since 1723 has been the crossed swords of Saxony in blue. On early pieces they are small and straight. They have gradually grown larger and less carefully drawn. The 19th-century pieces are also marked with an incised (scratched) model number. Mid-18th century figures often have a flat base and the mark is on the side at the rear rather than underneath, and it may bear the impressed number of the 'repairer' who assembled the piece. In addition, the finest vases are marked with an AR monogram for AUGUSTUS REX. This is probably the most imitated mark in the history of German ceramics. Genuine pieces are few and far between.

Meissen has been an inspiration for most factories that followed, and a great deal of what appears to be Meissen, including marked pieces, was made elsewhere.

▲ Model of a street cryer, 1740s. seen at the Truro Roadshow (£1,500-£1,800)

MERCURY GILDING

A technique for gilding metal and ceramics, used from the Middle Ages onwards. An amalgam of gold and mercury is applied as a paste and the object fired at a low temperature so the mercury is driven off, leaving a thin film of gold. The process can be repeated several times, producing a thick layer of gold which can be burnished to a lustrous hard brilliance.

MERCURY TWIST GLASS

An air-twist glass stem which has a brilliant silvery appearance and is found in English wine glasses from about 1760. It actually has nothing to do with mercury, but occurs in glass with a high lead content, giving it a greater brilliance.

£££

MERRYMAN PLATES

Sets of six London delftware plates, each painted with a line from 'What is a mery man/Let him doe all what he kan/To entertayne his gess/With wyne and mery jest/But if his wife doth frown/All meryment goes downe'. The earliest are possibly the work of an immigrant Dutch potter, and dated examples are known from 1684 to 1742.

££££

► One of a set of six Merryman plates (£38,000 the set)

MERRYTHOUGHT TOYS

Teddy-bear makers at Ironbridge since 1930. Their first bears were in mohair plush, with glass eyes and swivel joints. In one ear should be a button proclaiming 'Hygienic Merry-thought Toys. Made in England' and displaying a wishbone symbol. After 1950 cleanliness was dropped in favour of geography: 'Merrythought, Ironbridge, Shrops. Made in England.'

Fantasy furniture that changes shape

METAMORPHIC FURNITURE

Metamorphosis: a transformation, change of form or structure, appearance or character by natural development or by magic. Magic furniture conjures up a wonderfully romantic image of automated doors and fairy dust. In reality furniture-makers did create very ingenious pieces that had more than one use. The most common is the folding library chair, which opens into a step ladder to reach books on the top shelf. Made in the Regency period, around 1810, by Morgan and Sanders, these solid mahogany chairs realise about £5,000 at auction.

Thomas SHERATON's designs are full of fanciful magic that can be difficult to put into practice. One that was made was a HARLEQUIN pembroke table that has a pop-up book section, operating by pulleys and springs. The Victorians adapted this in the better DAVENPORTS, one of which was valued at £3,000 at the Derby Antiques Roadshow.

The Victorians adored making something do two jobs at once. Often the dual purpose was for reasons of space and economy. Grand Rapids, furniture-makers in the Chicago area, made beds that folded away during the day into piano cases (unfortunately the pianos were not playable!). Chairs could be converted into bath tubs, and tables concealed mangles.

Few survive today but there is a lot of simpler metamorphic furniture available. There are dining tables that extend lengthways — among them the complicated late-Georgian Cumberland table and the circular Jupe's Patent table, which accepts curved and segmental leaves.

French designers during the reign of Louis XV had a craze for the DUCHESSE Brisée — a large and a small BERGÈRE chair fitted together either side of a tabouret or stool to form a sumptuous daybed. Hundred-year-old copies can be bought for £1,000-£2,000 today.

▲ Oak metamorphic chair/steps, c1880 (shown closed, above, and open, below) seen at the Brussels Roadshow (£800-£1,200) ▼

▼ Mahogany metamorphic dining table, c1835, which opens out to take extra leaves (£2,000-£3,000)

▲ **Mickey Mouse rocker**, made by Tri-ang, 1930s. Seen at the Huddersfield Roadshow **(£2,000-£3,000)**

MICKEY MOUSE

Mickey Mouse's first appearance was in 1928 when he starred in the Walt Disney 'silent' cartoon *Plane Crazy*. In his third cartoon (actually premiered first), *Steamboat Willie*, Mickey was given a voice and the film was an immediate success. Disney copyrighted the image of Mickey which meant that all products using his likeness had to be licensed. Early Mickey Mouse toys show him with 'pie-crust' eyes (like a pie with one slice missing) and sometimes teeth, making him less the winsome creature we recognise today. Some of the most sought-after Mickey Mouse collectables are wrist watches, first made by Ingersoll in 1933. Worth looking out for are early soft toys by Charlotte Clark and DEANS Rag Book and tinplate toys by Distler and other German makers. Celluloids ('cells') used in the animation process for Disney films are highly prized.

MICROMOSAICS

Using tiny pieces of coloured stone, the art of micromosaic originated in the Vatican workshops in around 1720, when it replaced the decaying altarpieces of St Peter's with enduring mosaic pictures. As they are executed in brilliant colours and fantastic

▲ **Micromosaic of Rome** with St Peter's in background, late 19th century **(£4,000)**

detail, at a distance it is difficult to tell the best micromosaics from a painted image. They were so admired that the technique was adapted to make elaborate table tops from the late 18th to the mid-19th centuries. The finest examples were produced in the Vatican workshops as diplomatic gifts, but workshops sprang up all over Rome to supply the demands of souvenir-hungry travellers on the Grand Tour. The subject-matter frequently included classical themes, views of Rome and Italy and stories from mythology.

 £££-£££££

MICROSCOPE

The two-lens compound microscope and the single-lens pocket version were invented by Dutchmen, *c*1590, but Britain was the major centre of manufacture for the next two centuries. Most 18th-century models such as the Culpepper, were fixed upright, so the user had to stand. Towards 1800, W. and S. Jones added a ball-joint to their 'Jones Most Improved Model' which was popular with desk-bound scientists. The CARYS introduced a boxed microscope which could be screwed to the lid of its case and, in 1830, J. J. Lister adapted DOLLOND's telescope lenses to microscopes. The first binocular microscope was produced in the 1840s. In Germany, ZEISS was in production from 1875. Most common at Roadshows, however, are mass-produced school microscopes. These are well made but inexpensive.

££-££££

MICHTOM, MORRIS

Maker of the first American 'Teddy' bear, *c*1903. He was inspired by Clifford Berriman's cartoon of President Teddy Roosevelt refusing to shoot a bear cub on a hunting trip. STEIFF was, of course, already making bears, and gratefully seized on the name.

MIHRAB

In architecture this is the prayer niche or arch in a

mosque which shows worshippers the direction of Mecca. It is a fundamental motif on prayer rugs, differing in design between regions.

MILLEFIORE

Meaning 'a thousand flowers', this is a type of glassmaking where canes of coloured glass rods are arranged in bundles so that in cross-section they form decorative patterns. Known in ancient times, the technique was revived in Venice in the 16th century and again in 1840, especially for paperweights and larger doorstops. These were imitated almost immediately by the French glasshouses.

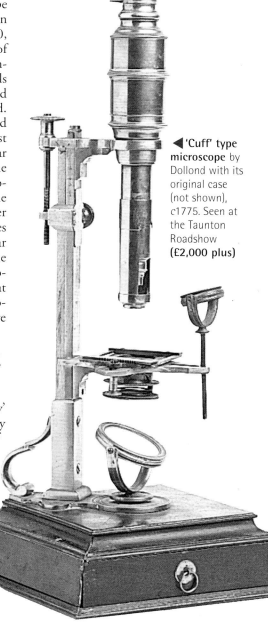

◄ **'Cuff' type microscope** by Dollond with its original case (not shown), *c*1775. Seen at the Taunton Roadshow **(£2,000 plus)**

From battledress to officer's mess

MILITARIA

Armour survives from Renaissance times and occasionally from antiquity but most such pieces are now in museums. The first collectable militaria is that of the English Civil War period, which was when Cromwell formed the basis of the British Army. But the availability of Royalist or Parliamentarian artefacts is strictly limited.

Apart from lobster-tail HELMETS, cuirasses, pikeman's pots (helmets) and body armour, there is little else for the collector. This field of collecting does not really get started until the Napoleonic Wars and then continues throughout the 19th and 20th centuries.

The many specialist areas include: headdress, UNIFORM, accoutrements including shoulder belt and waistbelt plates, and helmet, shako and cap badges and MEDALS. As to ephemera, collections can be made of postcards, cigarette cards, diaries, letters and documents. And of course, libraries can be formed on various subjects.

When the British Army went to war in 1914, the general wear of the scarlet coat was lost forever and with it the glamour and glitter of the British soldier. Apart from the Household Cavalry and the Brigade of Guards, it is today only the regimental bands that wear what has become known as the ceremonial dress. Nevertheless, the collector can still find plenty of eye-catching militaria on the market through specialist auction houses and dealers.

First World War collectors like to acquire khaki officers' tunics showing the rank on the sleeve, also the original Tommy's tin helmet (the Brody pattern) and general equipment, not forgetting soldiers' diaries. Apart from cap badges, First and Second World War collectors seek cloth regimental shoulder titles and divisional signs.

One area with a very strong following is Nazi material, particularly with the swastika insignia. Here, as with other military material one must be on one's guard: forgeries are being turned out in increasing numbers. The important part played by the RAF in the Second World War has led to considerable interest in flying jackets, helmets and goggles.

It is rare that an enthusiast collects anything and everything. Many pursue a single regiment while others collect a specific category.

Apart from early armour, the highest prices are paid for JAPANESE SWORD blades which may date back 500 years, Most commonly found are those from the Second World War and these are £60 or so.

▼ The actual sample of khaki serge for uniforms which replaced red jackets, approved by the Prince of Wales in 1900 (literally priceless)

◄ Civil War cavalry trooper's breast plate (as excavated). Seen at Blenheim Palace Roadshow (£150-£200)

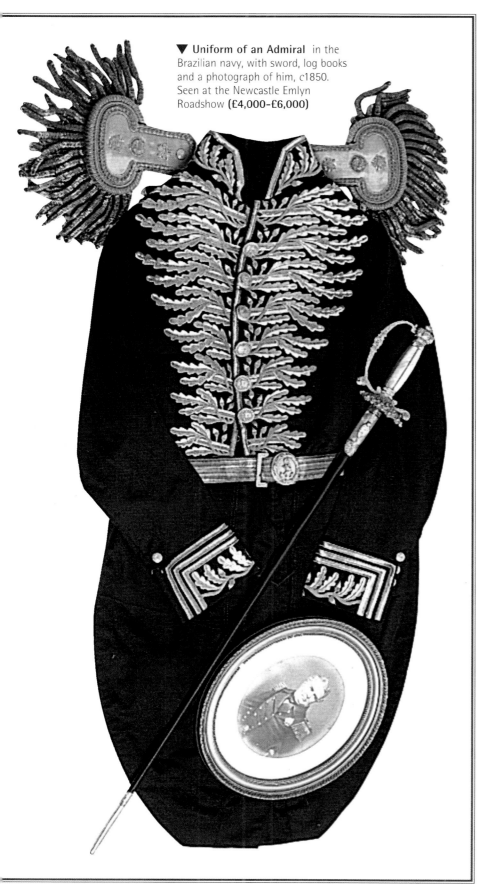

▼ **Uniform of an Admiral** in the Brazilian navy, with sword, log books and a photograph of him, c1850. Seen at the Newcastle Emlyn Roadshow (£4,000-£6,000)

MILLS, NATHANIEL II (active 1836-52)

A Birmingham silversmith who entered his mark in 1836. His father was active from the 1770s. He was one of the most prolific 19th-century vinaigrette and snuffbox makers, a notable line being fox and eagle head boxes with crisp, realistic fur. He also produced fine cast and chased card cases, *aides-mémoire*, and cased for small MEDICAL INSTRUMENTS.

MING

The native dynasty which ruled CHINA from 1368 to 1644, between the Mongol Yuan and the Manchu QING dynasties. Perhaps because it produced the first porcelain to reach the West in large quantity, Ming is sometimes taken to be synonymous with the best of Chinese craftsmanship, but this is not always the case. The general characteristics were repetition of designs and techniques, and increasing elaboration of decoration. The period excelled in LACQUER and *cloisonné,* and Ming furniture set the standards of purity to which all subsequent Chinese furniture-making has aspired.

MINIC TOYS

An innovative line of thin tinplate clockwork vehicles produced by TRI-ANG from 1933 to 1971. Pre-war examples should have white, not black, tyres, and many have Shell petrol cans mounted on their running boards. As with all toy cars, condition and having the original boxes determine prices.

 £-£££

MINIATURE

Made more often for adults than children, miniatures are frequently exact copies of the full-sized object. Despite popular belief they were neither samples nor APPRENTICE PIECES.

▼ **Pearl-handled gilt metal** miniature revolver, 1880s. Seen at Blenheim Palace Roadshow. Shown lifesize with a 50p coin (£500)

Making quality wares for the top table

MINTON

Founded in 1793 by Thomas Minton, this Staffordshire company soon developed a reputation for high-quality tablewares in earthenware and bone china, in both simple and more florid REGENCY styles. Unusually, many original design books are still extant and have enabled umarked pieces to be attributed.

From the mid-1820s Thomas's son Herbert took control and, under his direction, Minton rose to become Britain's leading ceramics manufacturer. As well as leading the market in tablewares, figures and ornaments, often in 18th century French styles, Minton pioneered the pro-

duction of encaustic floor and decorative wall tiling, PARIAN porcelain, MAJOLICA glazes, PÂTE-SUR-PÂTE and much else.

Well known for the quality of its products and the skills of its artists, many of whom came to Stoke from France and other European countries, Minton took part in all the major displays from the Great Exhibition of 1851 onwards, winning medals and acclaim. The celebrated majolica St George fountain made for the 1862 Exhibition was over 20ft high.

Design inspiration came from China, Japan, the Middle East, the Renaissance, the Classical world, naturalism, the 18th century and contemporary

art, resulting in a diverse range of products that appealed to most sectors of the market. Among the most successful influences was that of SÈVRES in the 1860s and 1870s and oriental *cloisonné*, much designed by Dr Christopher DRESSER, whose originals have survived in the factory archives.

The Royal family were important customers, along with many crowned heads of Europe, while links with the South Kensington Museum (now the Victoria and Albert) led to the setting up, in the 1870s, of the Minton Art Pottery Studio, a training ground for the next generation of artists and designers.

On Minton's death the company passed to his

nephew, Colin Minton Campbell, who expanded further its Victorian reputation. Minton remained under family control until 1968 when it joined the Royal DOULTON Group, by which time it had left behind its Victorian exuberance and reverted to its roots as a maker of high-quality tableware. Collectable, Minton products are generally well marked, and often dated. There is an impressive museum and archive at the factory in Stoke-on-Trent.

Apart from the early wares, the factory was careful to mark its wares including, from 1842, an impressed date code. A further aid to dating is the addition of a final 's' in 1872.

▼ Large stoneware mask jug, impressed 'Minton', 1830s (£120-£150)

◄ Pink bordered plate decorated with the most famous of J. F. Herring's blacksmith scenes, 1850-70 (£500-£700)

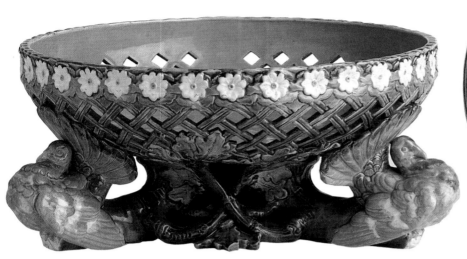

▲ **Large Minton majolica dish**, 12in wide, 1865-70. Seen at the Colchester Roadshow **(£2,000-£3,000)**

◄ **Minton spill vase**, c1875. Brought in to the Huddersfield Roadshow **(£600)**

▶ **Minton vase** decorated by Henry Steel, 1887 **(£600-£1,000)**

▶ **Rare Minton** cabinet watering can, or violeteer, c1820 **(£300-£500)**

◄**Edwardian hand mirror** shown to experts at The Blenheim Palace Roadshow **(£10-£20)**

MIRROR

While the terms 'mirror' and 'looking-glass' are now entirely interchangeable, it appears that the word mirror originally applied to small, hand-held mirrors of polished metal or crystal before the invention of large sheets of flat glass. The Mexicans used polished obsidian for mirrors from 4000BC, and by 3000BC gold, silver and bronze as well as glassy rocks were in use. The Greeks used polished metal, sometimes overlaid with platinum or bronze, the handles being cast bronze, and they developed the small standing mirror. There are references to Roman glass mirrors backed with a layer of zinc. In the Middle Ages most were still polished metal or speculum (a silvery-white alloy including rose-copper and tin). They were often in carved ivory frames.

Glass convex mirrors were made at Nuremberg in the 15th century, their shapes being decided by the size of the bubble from which they were blown.

MOCHA POTTERY

Earthenware made to resemble moss-agate, a milky-coloured stone with mossy markings in green and reddish-brown. It was made in England from brown, blue-green and black pigments

▶ **Early 20th century** dressing table hand mirror decorated with pewter and coloured stones, damaged **(£5-£15)**

mixed with an infusion of tobacco or hops and applied with a blow-pipe or trickled over the surface to achieve the feathery plant form. It was used on the more humble STAFFORDSHIRE earthenware and is found in horizontal bands on mugs and jugs.

 ££

MOLIQUET

A turned wooden handle with a cog-like head which was used as a mill or whisk for eggs and chocolate. It was introduced to British kitchens from France in the late 17th century. Early silver, Sheffield plate or ceramic chocolate pots have central holes in the lids so that a moliquet could be swizzled between the hands to froth the mixture.

 £-££

MOLITOR, BERNARD (d.1833)

Born in Germany, he settled in Paris, becoming one of the best-known directoire and EMPIRE furniture makers. He first tried to establish himself in Paris by advertising a remedy for furniture bugs and a new type of foot warmer, masquerading as a pile of books, for use in churches and theatres. He became a *maître* in 1787, receiving several royal commissions, and after the revolution worked for Napoleon. His best work is typically Empire in style but is seldom stamped and thus difficult to identify. Alas, the Paris Metro station is named not in his honour, but for a much less distinguished Marshal of France.

MONOPEDIUM

An animal or human head on a leg and foot, which was originally a Roman chair or table support. It was taken up again by NEO-CLASSICAL designers, such as Thomas HOPE.

MONSTRANCE

Used to display the Host on the altar, it is usually an elaborate variation on the basic form of a glass case supported on a stem. The custom of

Looking after the pennies

MONEY BOXES

First manufactured in the late 1860s, money boxes became more complicated and amusing over the years.They often incorporated a spring drive or mechanical action, which was triggered when a coin was deposited, thus encouraging savings through entertainment. The early money boxes, generally made of cast iron, were often produced by makers of goods such as cooking stoves and ploughs, who found this a profitable adjunct since they could charge high prices for amusements which contained relatively little raw material.

Still more profitable lines were produced after the First World War, with the introduction and popularity of pressed tinplate money banks. These were generally 'still' (that is, they had no mechanical action). Their appeal lay in their decoration: they were brightly lithographed or handpainted with fine details.

There is a well-developed international market for money boxes, with thousands of pounds being paid for the rarest examples. At the Antiques Roadshow at Beaumaris on Anglesey in 1994, a sought-after mechanical bank in the form of a reclining Chinaman appeared. A similar bank fetched £3,910 at auction in November 1994.

▲ **Punch and Judy mechanical bank,** lacking grille to base, (£700-£1,000)

▲ **Rare cast-iron pillar box bank**, 1880s. Not in the best condition (**£300**)

▲ **Rather battered** cold painted spelter money box, c1900 (**£150**)

reserving the Host originated in the Low Countries in the mid-13th century and spread to the whole western church. Monstrances are generally silver, with a crystal or glass cylinder in the centre to hold the Host, and often lavishly decorated with precious stones.

MONTEITH

A large silver bowl with a notched and scalloped rim. Filled with ice, it was used for cooling wine glasses, placed bowl down with the feet held in the scallops. Later examples have detachable rims and so could be used as punch bowls. They first appeared in England in the 17th century and were supposedly named after a Scotsman who wore a cloak with a tattered hem.

🪆 ⚔ 🏛 **££££-£££££**

MONKEYS

In the Middle Ages a monkey represented the devil and later, with an apple in its mouth, the fall of man. It then became a general symbol of luxury and vanity, satirising mankind's follies. It returned to popularity in the 16th and 17th centuries, appearing in grotesque decoration, and is an essential feature of 18th-century CHINOISERIE decoration, where it is often depicted in human activities. This idea was developed in paintings of the second quarter of the 19th century, when costumed monkeys aping humans were an immensely popular subject. They were known as *singeries* in France, and 'monkeyana pictures' in Britain. They were given a further boost by Darwin's *Descent of Man*.

▶ **Austrian terracotta monkey**, c1875, with cold painted decoration (**£350-£500**)

MOONFLASK

A full-moon, disc-shaped Chinese vase with a pair of handles flanking a long, straight neck. It is a more sophisticated version of the European pilgrim flask.

MOORCROFT, WILLIAM (1872-1946)

The son of a Staffordshire china painter, Moorcroft started by designing for the MacIntyre & Co pottery. He set up his own pottery in Cobridge in 1913, taking all his

▲ **Typical Moorcroft vase**, 1920s. Seen at the Huddersfield Roadshow (**£300-£400**)

original designs and many former employees with him. All his wares were wheel-thrown, slip-trailed and decorated with rich, glossy glazes fired at very high temperatures. In 1913-20 he made many new patterns and experimented with glazes, lustres and flambés, producing pottery with a lustrous brilliance in deep hues of purple, crimson and olive green, the decoration inspired by floral motifs and Oriental carpets. Even the factory's everyday line, which was known as Moorcroft blue because of its deep eggshell-blue glaze, was hand-thrown. William's son Walter and Walter's half-brother William John both joined the firm. In 1990 it became a limited company and it is still in production today. Marks: decorative wares are signed William or W. Moorcroft; and are impressed Moorcroft.

MORDAN, SAMPSON

In the 19th century propelling pencils were known as 'Mordans' whether or not they had been made by Sampson Mordan of London (1790-1843). He himself gave the credit to his former partner J. I. Hawkins, and they had a joint patent for improvements in 1822. Mordan was a favourite apprentice of J. BRAMAH, and his company made pen cases and patent locks as well as pencils from 1822. Under his sons and successors, it expanded into all sorts of other fancy goods to do with writing, printing, smoking and toiletries until 1941, when the factory was bombed. Its various patents were then in production with another manufacturer, Edward Baker, until 1952. Among Mordan's exhibits at the 1851 Great Exhibition, were a bright steel fire-proof jewel-box decorated with ORMOLU; a large frame containing an assortment of gold pens and pen-holders; and a combination copying and seal press, a little like the COPIER seen at the Newcastle Emlyn Roadshow.

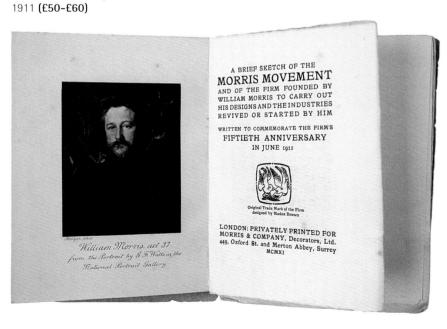

▲ Silver telescope pencil by Sampson Mordan, (£250-£300)

MOROCCO

Fine red leather which originated from Moroco and was especially popular for bookbinding.

MORTAR

One of the oldest of all kitchen implements. Stone, wood, cast-iron and bronze mortars, which are used with pestles for grinding and pounding food and medicines, survive from the 14th century onwards. A hanging pestle and mortar was the recognised shop sign for an apothecary, and it was thanks to these items that it was apothecaries who supplied artists with the first commercial powdered pigments.

££-£££

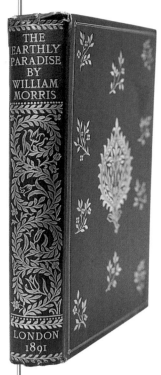

▼ Popular 1891 edition of *The Earthly Paradise*, by William Morris (£20-£30)

▲ Morris and Co embroidered wool portière designed by Henry Dearle, 1910 (£35,000)

▼ Booklet published to commemorate the 50th anniversary of Morris and Co in 1911 (£50-£60)

A BRIEF SKETCH OF THE
MORRIS MOVEMENT
AND OF THE FIRM FOUNDED BY
WILLIAM MORRIS TO CARRY OUT
HIS DESIGNS AND THE INDUSTRIES
REVIVED OR STARTED BY HIM

WRITTEN TO COMMEMORATE THE FIRM'S
FIFTIETH ANNIVERSARY
IN JUNE 1911

LONDON: PRIVATELY PRINTED FOR
MORRIS & COMPANY, Decorators, Ltd.
449, Oxford St. and Merton Abbey, Surrey
MCMXI

William Morris, aet 37 from the Portrait by G. F. Watts in the National Portrait Gallery

Artist who had a hand in everything

▲ Bronze plaque of Morris by Alfred Adrian Wolfe, 1918. In the William Morris Gallery

MORRIS AND CO.

One of the leading figures of the late Victorian decorative arts, William Morris (1834-1896) began as an architect before taking up painting. He became involved with the Pre-Raphaelite painters and while designing the interiors for his house, built by Philip Webb at Bexleyheath, realised that 'all the minor arts were in a state of complete degradation'.

This led him to set up a firm producing high-quality decorative objects with assistance from Webb, Burne-Jones, Rossetti and Ford Madox Brown. Known as Morris, Marshall, Faulkner and Co, it became Morris and Co in 1875, moving out from London to Merton Abbey.

Morris's early commissions were mainly for stained glass, tiles and pottery designed by DE MORGAN. His wife Jane Burden, the Pre-Raphaelite model, and his sister-in-law ran the the embroidery workshop. In 1862 Morris began designing wallpaper. His textile and wallpaper designs are most frequently reproduced today, although he also designed carpets, embroideries, tapestries and some furniture.

He had a genius for flat pattern, evolving floral and foliage designs in dense luxurious schemes inspired by 16th- and 17th-century textiles as well as by Oriental carpets.

Morris's hostility to mechanisation and his belief that real art had to be hand-made — the creative process imbuing it with a special significance for both maker and user — made him the precursor of the ARTS AND CRAFTS Movement. It meant, however, that his output was limited, and while his teachings and philosophy did have an effect on the care with which ordinary houses were designed and decorated, only the wealthy could afford his products. This was somewhat in conflict with his socialist leanings.

He was a prolific author, of political tracts as well as novels and poetry, many of which were printed at his Kelmscott Press. This he founded in 1891, and it produced beautiful and expensive hand-printed books with Morris himself designing several typefaces.

The most renowned book was his Chaucer, completed in 1896, with more than 600 illustrations by Burne-Jones. It can lay claim to being one of the finest books ever published.

The output of his factory was small, and original textiles and carpets by Morris turn up only rarely, when they fetch enormous prices.

Morris was a polymath whose multiple talents and enormous energy made him a difficult partner but he left a body of work, any section of which would have been enough on which to found a reputation.

▲ Cupboard in Morris's Red House, Bexleyheath with wallpaper designed by him

▶ 'Minstrel with cymbals' stained glass window, designed by Morris in 1868 (£8,500)

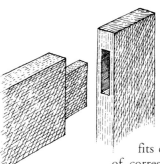

MORTISE AND TENON
The basic technique for making English furniture. A glued projecting tenon (or end of a piece of wood) fits exactly into a hole of corresponding size and the joint is then tapped home.

MORTLAKE TAPESTRIES
English tapestry factory which was established on the instructions of James I in 1619. It employed 50 immigrant Flemish weavers and flourished particularly under the patronage of Charles I in 1625-35, when its products rivalled Flemish and German works. Its tapestries were woven from cartoons by Rubens, van Dyck and Francis Cleyn, the most famous being the Acts of the Apostles woven from the tapestry cartoons by Raphael, acquired by Charles I in 1623 and now in the Victoria and Albert Museum. Other favourite subjects include the History of Vulcan, Hero and Leander, the Five Senses and the Twelve Months. The standard of weaving declined during the Protectorate and the Restoration, and the factory could no longer compete with the GOBELINS, Beauvais and Brussels. The factory finally closed in 1703. The Mortlake mark, a white shield bearing a red cross, is also found on tapestries woven by ex-Mortlake weavers who left to establish smaller factories.

R £££££-££££££

MOSAN ENAMEL
The first great school of European enamels flourished in the Meuse valley during the 12th century. It used the CHAMPLEVÉ technique derived from

◀ Franco-Flemish Mosan roundel enamelled in silver frame (some damage), late 14th century (£5,000)

Byzantium. Unusually for the Middle Ages, two named artists, Godefroid of Huy and Nicolas of Verdun, are known. Output was almost entirely religious, with magnificent objects and reliquaries being made for the great monasteries of Europe. Figures are expressive and the favourite colour scheme is blue and yellowish-green with a great deal of white. They were extremely popular in the 19th century and many high-quality forgeries have been made.

MOSER, KOLOMAN (1868-1918)
An Austrian ART NOUVEAU designer who, with Josef Hoffmann, Gustave Klimt and Josef Olbrich, broke with the Vienna Academy to found the 'Secession'. He had studied at the Academy, and at the School of Arts of which he was appointed director in 1900. He and Hoffmann set up the Vienna Werkstätte ('workshop') in 1903, designing silver, furniture and jewellery. His work as a painter, illustrator and graphic designer combines geometric patterns with abstract floral and naturalistic motifs. His textiles contain interlocking patterns of birds and foliage and his furniture tends to be rectilinear, and can look 20 years ahead of its time.

MOTE SPOON
A spoon with a pierced bowl and a long, thin handle with a sharpened point. The bowl was used to skim off floating tea leaves and the handle to unblock the spout of a tea pot.

££-£££

MOTHER-OF-PEARL
This is the pearly substance which lines the shells of the pearl oyster and the abalone. It is polished to bring out the colour and then cut and used for furniture, inlay and marquetry. It was especially popular during the Renaissance and the 17th century, and so (naturally) again in the revivalist 19th.

▶ Mote spoon dated 1720 with later feathering. Seen at Blenheim Palace Roadshow (£50-£60)

Photographs courtesy Robert Brooks Auctioneers

▲ Original Monaco Grand Prix poster, 1930 (£2,500-£3,000)

▼ Ceramic teapot decorated with illustrations by Mabel Lucie Atwell (£300-£400)

MOULD-BLOWN GLASS
Glass vessels made by being blown into a mould. The technique was known in Roman times and became enormously popular in the 19th century for cheap domestic hollow-ware. Two- and three-piece hinged moulds were developed, allowing deeper cut-glass-like effects to be achieved.

MOURNING JEWELLERY
In the 16th and 17th centuries mourning jewellery was primarily a 'memento mori' to remind wearers of their own death. These were generally in the form of skulls, coffins and skeletons. Later jewels came to be worn in memory of specific individuals, especially after the

How to drive a hard bargain

MOTORING MEMORABILIA

This covers an enormous range of material from badges, mascots and motoring art to spare parts, accessories such as lamps and horns to picnic sets and presentation trophies, books, magazines, maps and ephemera.

The most collectable items are from the first years of motoring 1895-1905, with vintage spare parts as much in demand as more decorative items. Objects relating to the most famous marques, Rolls-Royce, Bugatti, Ferrari, Alpha Romeo and Mercedes Benz are also the rarest and most valuable.

As motoring gathered momentum and more and more cars were produced the range of accessories and associated advertising blossomed. Specially designed picnic sets were made by companies like Coracle and Drew and Sons and a whole range of vanity units which included drink holders and car vases.

Several artists specialised in motoring art from its earliest days, among them Frederick Gordon Crosby who is best known for his racing scenes. Artists and designers also turned their hand to car mascots; those by the glass maker René LALIQUE, especially the fox, are considered among the finest ever made. Some were fitted with a special base which illuminated to light up the mascot at night.

▲ Pre-war enamel garage advertising signs (£150–£250 each)

▼ 'Speed god' car mascot, c1925 (£350–£500)

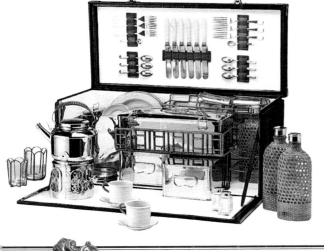

◀ A good six-person fully-fitted picnic set by Asprey and Co., c1930 (£2,000–£3,000)

◀ Victorian black enamel mourning brooch (£20)

execution of Charles I when Royalists wore rings and brooches with the initials CR or enamelled portraits of their monarch. Mourning rings were given at funerals, the hoop engraved with the name of the deceased. From the 18th century hair jewellery was worn. Skulls and coffins disappeared in favour of sentimental depictions of romantic grief. Weeping willows, broken tombs and angels were enamelled on brooches and medallions. Jet from Whitby in Yorkshire became popular in Victorian England and after the death of Prince Albert Queen Victoria insisted it should be worn by all ladies presented at court. Irish bog oak was another suitable material.

££–£££

MOUSTACHE CUP AND SPOON

A cup with a little shelf just inside the rim to prevent the moustache from getting wet while drinking. It was invented by the ever-ingenious Victorians. The spoon has a similar guard, to protect mustachioed invalids from stickiness.

££

MOUSTIERS POTTERY

One of the most important groups of French FAIENCE factories established north-east of Marseilles. The earliest wares date from about 1680-1710 and were simple shapes with underglaze blue decoration. The best years were 1710-40, when elaborate vessels decorated with designs after BÉRAIN were produced. After 1740 high-temperature polychrome decoration was introduced, and in the 1770s wares decorated with enamel colours were made. Moustiers continues as a centre for faience production today.

MUCHA, ALFONSE MARIA (1869-1939)

A popular ART NOUVEAU graphic artist and designer who published

▲ One of a set of four posters
by Alfonse Mucha, advertsing
chocolate (**£3,000**)

numerous postcards, posters and prints. Born in Czechoslovakia, he was trained in Munich, Vienna, and Paris. His fame was established by his 1894 poster of the actress Sarah Bernhardt. He designed the Paris jewellery shop of Georges Fouquet and collaborated with TIFFANY. He exhibited carpets, jewellery and textiles and designed the Czechoslovak pavilion for the 1900 Paris exhibition. He returned to Czechoslovakia in 1910 but he continued to travel. His favourite themes are sinuous young women and flowers.

MUDGE, THOMAS (1715-94)

A watch and clockmaker who was apprenticed to George Graham before setting up on his own in 1751. He is famous for inventing the forerunner of the lever escapement used in almost all pre-battery watches and travelling clocks today. He made mainly watches and from 1776 was watchmaker to George III.

MUFFINEER

A type of small caster. Usually vase-shaped with a domed cover and no handle. They are believed to have been used to sprinkle sugar and cinnamon on to muffins, hence the name.

£££

MUGHAL ART

The art of the courts of the Moslem rulers of India, who established control of the subcontinent in 1526, derived from both Islamic and Hindu art and relied mainly on leaf and flower motifs rendered with jewel-like intensity. The reigns of Akbar (1556-1605) and Shah Jehan (1628-57), who built the Taj Mahal, saw the greatest imperial patronage and produced the best-quality work. This includes jade carving, textile weaving and metalwork as well as the exquisite Mughal miniatures, and carpets which were woven under Persian influence in a royal factory employing Persian weavers in 1580.

MULBERRY

Native to Europe, mulberry is a hard, heavy wood varying from golden to reddish brown with dark streaks. It was used occasionally for cabinet work as a veneer or for small articles.

MULE CHEST

A chest invented in the mid-17th century which had two or more drawers fitted into the plinth. It was the forerunner of the chest-of-drawers, and the name is comparatively recent.

£££

MULL

A type of snuffbox which originated in Scotland. It was usually made of horn but sometimes of silver or lignum vitae and the hinged lid is often set with a cairngorm (a variety of rock crystal). The table mull is a much larger version, sometimes made of an entire ram's head, the horns set with cairngorms. It was passed from

▶ Snuff mull with an agate and
silver mount, c1790. Seen at
Blenheim Palace Roadshow
(**£250-£300**)

diner to diner in the same way as the port. The term 'mull' is the local dialect for mill, and the name came about because some of them also had an apparatus for grinding the snuff.

£££-££££

MÜLLER, BERTHOLD

A silver manufacturers' agent whose mark is often found on German silver imported into Britain from about 1892 to 1911, when he died. His son Berthold Herman (who politically changed his name to Miller in 1915) carried on the business until 1922. Many of their imports, including such grand table decorations as knights with ivory faces, copied from 16th- and 17th-century originals, were made by Neresheimer of Hanau, and others by Dutch and Austrians.

MUSICAL GLASSES

Different-sized glasses mounted in a wood and felt frame, played by rubbing the rim with a wet finger—also known as glass harmonicas. Invented by Benjamin Franklin, Haydn and Mozart composed for them.

£££-££££

MUSIC PLATES

Dessert plates of blue Dutch DELFT-WARE decorated with the score and verse of a song, presumably to be sung by diners at the end of a meal. Common in 17th-century Holland, they were made in Delft and reproduced at Moustiers and Milan. Many were reproduced in the 19th century.

£££-££££

MYSTERY CLOCKS

These were made in the 19th century to conceal the connection between hands and motion. They took various ingenious forms. In one a turtle floating in a basin of water might be carried round by the pull of a magnet on a rotating arm. In another the clock dial might be in the base of a pendulum swung from the outstretched hand of a figure.

▲ So-called 'vomit pot' (actually a spittoon) from the Nanking Cargo, c1750 (£3,500 in 1986)

NACRE

The French word for mother-of-pearl, the lustrous, iridescent interior surface of many seashells, widely used to decorate metalwork, jewellery and furniture.

NAILSEA GLASS

A distinctive range of glass produced for about 100 years from around 1790. Although there was a glasshouse at Nailsea near Bristol, which made domestic as well as window glass from about 1788, the name is now given to glass in the Nailsea style, wherever it was made. Nailsea includes bottles, jugs, vases and dark green bowls, flecked or striped with white and red enamel. From around 1845, there are opaque white flasks, bells, pipes and other fancy items (known as 'friggers'), decorated with brightly coloured zig-zags or wavy lines. Particularly well known are glass walking sticks with colourful

◀ Typical Nailsea-type glass walking sticks (£100–£300)

twisted filigree decoration running along their length—these are definitely not for use.

                            £££

NANKING WARE

An old term (occasionally Nankeen) current in the 19th century, for blue and white porcelain made at Jingdezhen but shipped via Nanking by the East India Company. The term still has currency in America where it describes a pattern of a chain-link border with a landscape including a pagoda. It was revived for the sale by Christie's in Amsterdam of the cargo of the Dutch vessel *Geldermalsen* which went down in the South China Seas in 1752. The ship's cargo, including gold bars, was raised and the porcelain included 171 dinner services, 578 tea pots, 9,735 chocolate cups, 19,535 coffee cups and saucers, and 63,623 tea cups and saucers. Many had survived for 230 years on the sea-bed, with no more than the odd barnacle and a slightly clouded glaze—partly because the tea was used as protective packaging. Prices were reasonable for ordinary wares in large lots, and many people were able to buy a souvenir of this treasure trove. Unusual items went for much higher prices than they would today.

NANTGARW

A small south Wales factory set up in 1813 by the famous porcelain painter William Billingsley and in operation until 1822. It made mainly plates, dishes and small vessels and is renowned for the quality of its painting—usually wonderful floral designs. Some are impressed with 'Nant garw', but so are most forgeries, although some have red painted marks.

NAPKIN PRESS

Otherwise known as a LINEN PRESS, this is a device for pressing napkins and other linen. It comprised flat boards between which folded, damp linen was placed, and pressure applied by a spiral screw. The presses were of table height, or smaller. They were used in the 17th and 18th centuries.

£££

NAPLES ROYAL PORCELAIN (AND GIUSTINIANI)

The Naples royal porcelain factory was established in 1771, after the earlier CAPODIMONTE works in Naples had closed. It turned out beautiful NEO-CLASSICAL services, vases in classical style and groups in white biscuit-ware (including an enormous masterpiece 5ft high). Most successful were the wares decorated with views and eruptions of Vesuvius. Also making pottery and porcelain in Naples was the Giustiniani factory, which opened in 1760, but flourished particularly in the late 18th century and continued after the royal factory closed in 1820. Its strength was the reproduction of antique forms and decoration, with biscuit copies of antique statues, and dinner services in Etruscan designs. Later in the 19th

Living out their escapist fantasies

NAPOLEONIC PRISONER-OF-WAR WORK

The main objects made by French prisoners-of-war in Britain during the Napoleonic Wars (1793-1815) were items made of bone, and boxes decorated with applied designs in straw. During this period, many thousands of French prisoners were held in hulks (prison ships), castles and the first prison camps.

To supplement meagre rations, those who were able created artefacts to be sold or bartered at the prison markets. Many of the prisoners were conscripts from northern French coastal towns, particularly Dieppe, where the tradition of carving (usually in ivory) was strong. So, despite having little to work with apart from the bones from their meals and straw from their beds, they set about it. Before long, they became sufficiently successful to send out for the materials they needed.

Most highly prized are the bone SHIP MODELS, often of meticulous accuracy, complete with hair or thread rigging, and metal details. Even at the time, such pieces could command substantial prices — there is a record of £40 being paid for a warship, which had taken two prisoners six months to construct.

Articulated toys include many 'spinning jennies':
women in Breton bonnets at their spinning wheels, sometimes surrounded by other figures, plus the family cat or parrot. When a handle is turned, the wheel goes round, the women nod and even the cat may twitch.

More gruesome are working model guillotines. Frequently the scaffold platform is highly ornate, and details include heads rolling into baskets and specially applied 'blood'. Turn a handle and the blade comes whistling down — a great entertainment. Workboxes, cribbage boards, games boxes, watch stands, mirror frames and chessmen were among other PoW artefacts from the Napoleonic period.

The other material readily available to the prisoners was straw from their palliasses. This they dyed, wove or cut into short lengths and glued to carcasses of boxes and cabinets. They also made tea caddies, face screens, pictures and fans. The vegetable dyes they used have now faded from their former glory except where protected from light on the insides of drawers and doors. To achieve high prices condition is all-important.

Anyything which could fall into this category is given the PoW name since romance helps saleability but there is no doubt that much was commercial work made by sailors or simply the output of hobbyists.

◀ **Bone, book-shaped** box, containing a set of dominoes. Made by a French PoW, *c*1800 **(£150-£200)**

▶ **Bone model** of the 74-gun French ship *Hercule*, *c*1800 **(£10,000-£11,000)**

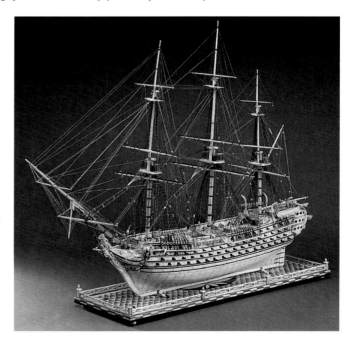

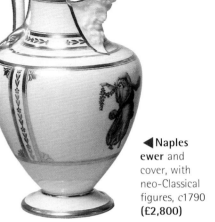

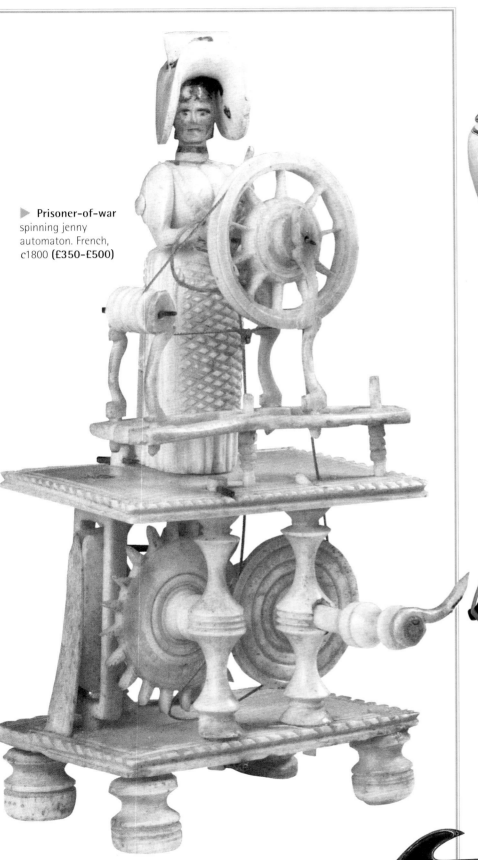

► **Prisoner-of-war** spinning jenny automaton. French, *c*1800 (**£350-£500**)

◄**Naples ewer** and cover, with neo-Classical figures, *c*1790 (**£2,800**)

century, imitations of Renaissance MAIOLICA were made. The crowned N is one of the most forged of all marks.

NAUTILUS CUP

Cup made from a pearly nautilus shell (like a flattened, very large snail shell), mounted in gold or silver and often bejewelled. The best were made in Germany in the late 16th and early 17th centuries.

£££-£££££

▲ **Silver nécessaire** (shown closed), London, 1870. Seen at the Taunton Roadshow (**£200-£300**)

NÉCESSAIRES

Beautifully crafted, pocket-sized cases containing a microcosmic array of accoutrements for personal use when travelling. They are usually small, rec-

▼ **Item as above**, open with contents

tangular boxes, made in a variety of materials including enamel and sha-green, and varying in shape from slanting-topped miniature knife boxes to little caskets, or even real walnuts, mounted, lined and fitted. Inside would be all manner of implements, from pencils to ear-wax spoons, toothpicks, rulers, sewing accessories, scent bottles and bodkins. They were particularly popular in the mid and late 18th century; later, some larger, less pocketable examples were made.

£££

NEEDLEPOINT

As well as being a type of lace, this name is given to all kinds of needle-work on canvas, where the stitching is governed by the canvas, rather than free-hand embroidery. It could there-fore be said to include the kind of work we wrongly call 'tapestry' today, stitched in wool on canvas. But it is more correctly applied to finer work, carried out in tent stitch, such as the 'petit point' seen on 18th-century cushions and chair covers.

▼ Continental silver nefs. The larger has import marks for 1897 (**£8,000**). The smaller one is also late 19th century (**£3,500**)

TALKING ANTIQUES

NECKING AND NOSING
Necking is a term for a band of moulding around a verti-cal, such as a table leg. Nosing applies to a rounded, projecting edge, such as found on a step, or stair tread.

NEF
A silver table decoration in the form of a ship, sometimes mounted on wheels to glide over the table. It was first made in the Middle Ages, and it is thought that the idea originated from a silver model of a ship dedicated by Queen Margaret (wife of Louis IX) in thanksgiving for surviving a storm at sea. They were extremely grand objects, reflecting the glory and wealth of their owner. Within the hull were compartments for spices and salt, and even a knife and spoon. By the 16th century, they were used merely as table decorations. Those made in Germany and Switzerland were especially elaborate, often with detailed rigging and a crew of little sailors. Many copies were made in Germany during the 19th century, and these include the majority seen in Britain. They usually have BERTHOLD MÜLLER's import marks.

££££

NEKOLA, KARL AND JOSEPH
Father and son who worked in the painting shop at the Fife Pottery in Scotland, which became famous for its WEMYSS ware, produced from the 1880s until 1930. Karl Nekola came from Bohemia and joined the pottery in about 1882, introducing the big, blowsy roses, which became charac-teristic of Wemyss ware, and other decorations. Typical products include large pigs, toilet sets and jam pots. After the pottery closed, Joseph Nekola moved to the Bovey Tracey pottery and continued to work in the same style until his death in 1942.

£££

NELME, ANTHONY AND FRANCIS
Father and son, both goldsmiths working in London: Anthony (active c1680-1722), and Francis (active 1719-59). Anthony, son of a Here-fordshire yeoman, is revealed by the surviving examples of his work to have been the finest of English gold-smiths. His early pieces were in the florid, ornate RESTORATION style, but he is particularly admired for his later, understated Queen Anne pieces such as candlesticks and teapots, which have a grace of their own. Larger works included Chatsworth's massive Pilgrim Bottles. His son Francis joined him shortly before his death, and followed his style.

NELSON CHAIR
The furniture designer THOMAS SHERATON gave this name to designs for chairs he published in 1806 to celebrate Nelson's victory at Trafalgar. Not his most successful or elegant designs, they feature anchor-backs, and dolphins masquerading as front legs.

£££-££££

Matchless marvels in miniature

NETSUKE

This is a small carving, usually of wood or ivory, but also of other materials, serving as a toggle. A cord passes through the base and from this hangs a pouch or a small nest of boxes called an INRO. The netsuke is pushed up under the sash, or *obi*, and sits on it, preventing the pouch or *inro* from falling to the ground. It dates back to the 17th century and developed into miniature sculpture. Despite its small size (usually only 1in or 2in), a whole world of birds and beasts, humans and immortals, the amusing and the grotesque, could be encapsulated by the Japanese carver.

Huge supplies of redundant netsuke flooded the West when the Japanese adopted the suit and its pockets in about 1870. At the turn of the century, they were sold for a few pence as novelties in stores such as Liberty's. Today's collector is still spoilt for choice, so will probably opt for a particular carver or subject. He will look for compactness — the netsuke was a functional object and any protruding parts could have snagged the kimono. The design of a good netsuke still makes sense from whatever angle it is viewed. The cord holes will be placed so that they do not interfere with the meaning and indeed may form part of it — the paws of a monkey, for example. Netsuke are not always signed and the absence of a signature does not mean that they are earlier or less valuable than signed examples. Prices have risen greatly over the last few years and the record now stands at £140,000 for the horse by Tomotada shown below.

Collectors should beware of poor-quality Japanese-style carving coming from Hong Kong — elephants are being killed to produce it. Another danger area is reproductions in resin: realistic as to weight, colour and detail as they are cast in a flexible latex rubber mould which picks up every detail of the original. Although the resin reproductions are sold perfectly honestly in museum shops as souvenirs, the problem comes when they escape to the antiques market in fairs, car boot sales and country auctions.

▲ **Wood netsuke** rabbit, by Sukenaga of Takayama, 19th century (£4,400)

▲ **Ivory netsuke** of Chinese general Kanyu, unsigned, 18th century (£2,600)

▼ **Ivory netsuke** of wild boar and young by Masanao of Kyoto, 18th century (£85,000)

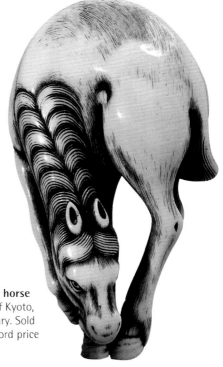

▶ **Netsuke of horse** by Tomotada of Kyoto, late 18th century. Sold for a world record price (£140,000)

▲ Neo-Classical
guéridon, with
centaur monopedia
supports (£4,800)

NEO-CLASSICISM

This is the name given to the mid-18th-century revival of the classical taste, a return to formality after the florid and flippant excesses of ROCOCO. It began to emerge in the 1750s and was established in Europe and all areas of the decorative arts by the 1770s. Typical characteristics are geometric forms, linear decoration and quiet, restrained colouring. Ornaments were derived from ancient Greek and Roman designs, recently discovered at Pompeii and Herculaneum, and published by archaeologists. The neo-Classical style encompassed architectural features such as capitals, arches and pillars but also simple shapes such as vases and urns, and fantastic beasts like griffins and sphinxes. On the whole, 18th-century craftsmen took ideas and inspiration from classical antiquity, rather than making exact copies of Greek or Roman forms. Particularly influential was the architect and designer Robert ADAM, who gave his name to one aspect of the style. Another influential figure in the spread of neo-Classicism was the potter Josiah WEDGWOOD, whose simple designs inspired a generation of vases and tablewares. Of obvious neo-Classical inspiration was his famous blue and white jasperware.

NESTS

Sets of small tables, each slightly less wide and high than the last, so that they may be stacked one inside the other, are known as nests of tables. When the set comprises four, they may be called quartetto tables, a name adopted by THOMAS SHERATON. In the 17th and 18th centuries pigeonhole-like structures of shelves or drawers (as seen in old chemists' shops) were also called nests.

 £££-£££££

NEVERS GLASS

The glasshouse at Nevers in France became famous in the 17th and 18th centuries for making figures and toys, as well as *façon de Venise* pieces. The figures and toys were produced from glass rods, softened with a lamp and blown or pincered into shape. Figures, often representing religious scenes, were mounted in elaborate landscapes with trees and flowers. Such pieces are known as *verre de Nevers*, but similar tableaux were made in other parts of Europe.

£££ £

NEVERS POTTERY

A group of potteries which, in the first half of the 17th century, worked in the Italian MAIOLICA style, making wares including ewers, pilgrim bottles and istoriato dishes. Later in the century their wares became more characteristically French, and they also made careful imitations of Chinese vases, finely painted in soft colours, as well as blue and white. Another style, Bleu Persan, was painted in light colours on a dark blue ground, and was much imitated. By the end of the century, the Nevers potteries were no longer leading the fashion, but they continued to be productive, making tablewares decorated with pictures of saints and, later, with revolutionary emblems. Nineteenth-century copies were made of 17th-century pieces, and pottery is still made in Nevers.

£££-£££££

▲ New Hall cup and saucer, pattern No 241, c1790 (£80-£120)

NEW HALL

A porcelain factory in Staffordshire which was set up in 1781-82, and initially made hard-paste imitations of Chinese export wares, featuring elaborate groups of mandarins, later moving to simple, restrained designs with isolated sprigs of flowers. Typical New Hall shapes were based on silver: straight-sided teapots and helmet-shaped cream jugs, for example. From about 1814, the factory made tea, coffee and dessert sets in bone china, decorated in a wide variety of colourful designs, with good-quality gilding. Although the spriggy Chinese export designs of the late 18th century, on tea and coffee wares, are typical of New Hall, other factories did make similar pieces, and not all is New Hall that looks it. The factory closed in 1835.

££-£££

NEWCASTLE GLASS

French and Italian glassmakers settled in Newcastle upon Tyne in the 17th century, introducing enamelling and engraving skills to the area, which has been known for its glass ever since. Enamelled Newcastle glass was made famous by William and Mary BEILBY. Newcastle gave its name to a type of mid-18th-century drinking glass, with multiple knopped stem and conical bowl. Newcastle flint glass was also ideal for engraving, and was exported to Holland for the purpose. As well as table glass and ornaments, Newcastle manufactured a lot of window glass. In the 19th century, Newcastle specialised in pressed glass and made full use of the new technique.

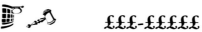 ££-££££

The enigmatic jeweller

▼ **Brooch/pendant by Mrs Newman** with a moonstone surrounded by translucent enamels and multi-coloured sapphires, c1900. seen at the Guernsey Roadshow (£2,500-£3,500)

It is often surprising how little has been recorded about certain people who must have been notable figures in their day. When this brooch by Mrs Newman appeared at the Guernsey Roadshow, it proved difficult to discover much about its maker.

She was a 'manufacturing goldsmith and court jeweller' with her own London shops, in first Savile Row and then New Bond Street. However, she hardly makes an appearance in any of the reference books.

Her full name was Charlotte Isabella, Mrs Philip Newman, and it is known that she trained at the South Kensington Schools in the 1860s.

After working as assistant to another jeweller, she set up her own business in about 1884, and was a fashionable name in the West End of London for the next 20 years at least. In 1985 Sotheby's sold a group of more than 50 of her jewellery designs.

NIELLO

This is an ancient technique, employed on small precious objects, where a design engraved on silver is enhanced by filling the grooves with a black mixture of silver, lead, copper, sulphur and borax, making a high contrast and bringing out every detail. Once the substance has been fixed by heat, the surface is polished until the silver and black are flush. Niello reached its height in Renaissance Italy but is most commonly found in Russia in the 19th century.

NIGHT LIGHTS

In 19th-century nurseries the terrors of the night were dispelled by slow-burning candles in safety containers such as Price's Venus or Clarke's Pyramid. Clarke's lights could be used to warm an invalid cup on a stand. The slogan proclaimed: 'When nights are dark then think of Clarke, who's hit the mark precisely. For his Night-lights create Light-nights, in which you see quite nicely.'

£-££

NIGHT TABLE

The most useful of bedside tables, this concealed behind a demure drawer front a pull-out chamber pot, supported at a comfortable height off the floor. These tables are usually square, and have a wavy tray top, over a cupboard and/or drawers. They have frequently found their way to the drawing room these days, having on the way lost both drawer and pots.

£££-££££

NONSUCH CHESTS

Nonsuch was the boastful name given to Henry VIII's palace at Cheam. Representations of it can be seen on inlaid oak chests dating from the late 16th and early 17th centuries. It is thought that they are German, or the work of immigrant craftsmen, following late 16th-century drawings.

◀ **Clarke's Patent Pyramid** nightlight, with saucer missing (£25)

NOTTINGHAM ALABASTERS

Medieval carved panels, these depicted religious tableaux in high relief, for altarpieces. Some free-standing figures were also made. A type of alabaster particularly suitable for carving was quarried near Nottingham in the 14th and 15th centuries, and carved by local crafts-men. When first quarried, alabaster is soft and may easily be carved, hard-ening later to resemble marble. Common themes are the lives of the Virgin and saints, and Christ's Passion. Nottingham also had a par-ticularly successful line in heads of John the Baptist. Carvings were originally painted in bright colours, but now only traces remain. Many altarpieces were destroyed in the Reformation, although some were hidden and survived, and fragments occasionally turn up.

NOTTINGHAM LACE

Machine lace, this was produced from the mid-19th century in imitation of hand-made lace, with embroidered white decoration on a net ground. It was widely used for curtains by the Victorians. Despite the name, not all of it came from Nottingham.

NOTTINGHAM POTTERY

Although established in medieval times, the Nottingham potteries are famous for stoneware produced after about 1690. From a brown, smoothly salt-glazed body, they made mugs, jugs, teapots, and urns for flowers, as well as bear jugs with detachable heads for cups. Except for the bears, decoration was typically incised, or pierced through an outer surface of the vessel, but sometimes slip-paint-ing was used. The potteries declined in the late 18th century and closed around 1800.

NOVELTIES

In the 19th century, Staffordshire potters and silversmiths in BIRMINGHAM made countless novel-ties—'toys' and fripperies to amuse the newly rich middle classes. Functional items such as salt cellars, pepper casters, silver vesta cases, cigar

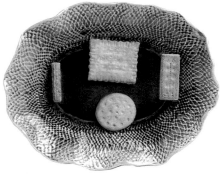

▲ **Bretby pottery** joke biscuit plate, seen at the Taunton Roadshow **(£50-£80)**

lighters and scent bottles were dis-guised as animals, birds, boats, harlequins and the man in the moon—the more outlandish the bet-ter. Joke and puzzle novelties in pottery also abound. This enthusiasm lasted well into the 20th century, and novelties are keenly collected. Most silver was made in Birmingham but London makers, including Sampson MORDAN, also made novelties. The most fertile collecting areas are scent bottles (such as silver-mounted birds' eggs, seashells and figures), vesta cases, vinaigrettes and small dining-table items—condiments and bells—as well as silver-mounted claret jugs in the form of owls, seals and the like, which were popular in the late Victorian period. The last were a spe-ciality of Alexander Crichton.

££-££££

NURSING CHAIR

An armless chair with a low seat, and occasionally a drawer in the seat. Early chairs and stools used by those nursing infants include basketwork examples, and simple, wide-seated stools with carved legs, both dating from the 17th century. Nowadays the term is mostly applied to ornate 19th-century upholstered chairs.

££-££££

NYON PORCELAIN

This Swiss porcelain factory, founded in 1780, made fine HARD-PASTE wares, usually decorated in imitation of Paris porcelain, often with sprigs of flowers, swags and medallions. It also imitated WEDGWOOD with cream-coloured earthenware and stonewares. The fac-tory closed in 1860.

▶ **Pair of Nymphenburg** white figures of the Virgin and St John, c1756 **(£30,000-£40,000)**

Double vision led to Rococo delights

NYMPHENBURG PORCELAIN

The enthusiasm for porcelian of AUGUSTUS THE STRONG was inherited by his granddaughter, Maria-Anna Sophia, who married Prince Max Joseph II of Bavaria. In 1747 he converted a hunting lodge at Neudeck, just outside Munich in Bavaria, into a porcelain factory which, after some years moved to Nymphenburg. Here it flourished from the vision of two men, Graf Heinrich von Heimhausen, the Elector of Bavaria's chief minister, and the modeller Franz Anton BUSTELLI.

In his very brief career, which ended in 1762, Bustelli created one of the most exciting series of ROCOCO figures ever made. Alone of the great porcelain modellers, he produced

models in wood in the tradition of Bavarian sculpture. His earliest work seems to have been a Crucifixion group dating from about 1756. This was followed by a series of delightful small Ovidian gods. Bustelli's COMMEDIA DELL'ARTE set of 16 characters is the most complex and skilfully articulated of any such series, conceived not as 16 individual figures but as eight pairs in which the attitude of one figure is clear only when it is placed beside the other. His charming CHINOISERIE models are the apogee of Bavarian Rococo. Those of Bustelli, like those of his rival KAENDLER at Meissen, are still in production.

Bustelli's successor Dominikus Auliczek produced some excellent groups of animals.

The decorator of Bustelli's figures, who must have worked in very close collaboration with the modeller, is as yet unknown. So, too, is the painter responsible for the factory's two great services painted for the Electoral court and for Heimhausen, each with butterflies skilfully shaded

to 'detach' them from the porcelain surface, and luxuriant flowers. During the EMPIRE period Nymphenburg, like other factories, made large vases painted with portraits or landscapes on elaborate gilt grounds. Its decoration also includes monochrome vignettes and *trompe l'oeil* engraved prints on *faux bas* grounds.

Still working, the factory has continued to repeat its 18th-century models, including precise imitations of the original decoration. It also acquired many of the moulds from the Ludwigsburg and Frankenthal factories,

which it continues to make.

The Nymphenburg mark has always been the shield of Bavaria impressed. On the earliest figures it is to be found not under the base but among the Rococo scrollwork that supports the figures. It is generally coloured and gilt like the figures. In the later marks the shield is always to be discovered under the base.

There is some difficulty in attributing Bustelli's figures as they continued in production until the 1770s. Many were left 'in white' and decorated later, some in the factory a century ago.

▶ Nymphenburg group of a Chinaman fighting a leopard, c1767 (£30,000–£40,000)

BOULLE, and became the best *ébéniste* of the mid-18th century. He worked for Madame de Pompadour and became an *ébéniste du Roi* in 1754. He specialised in concealing clever mechanical devices in his furniture, allowing for secret drawers and cupboards. An example is a writing-desk he devised, called a *bureau à cylindre*, with a semi-cylindrical closure at the top. The shutter on his finest example, for Louis XV, was so perfectly balanced that it rolled back as soon as the key was turned in the lock.

OGEE
A double-curve -shaped moulding, in section like a much flattened S shape. It is seen on furniture, picture frames and in architecture.

OAK
Perhaps our best-loved indigenous tree, the history of the oak stretches back to the Druids who held it in great veneration. Apparently more likely to be struck by lightning than any other tree (possibly because there were more of them), it was thought to be sacred to the god of thunder. Later, it played an important part in these islands' defence, with timber from about 3,500 oaks needed for each three-decker man-of-war. An oak sheltered a king, Charles II, thus providing a Jacobite symbol and many pub names. Oak's great qualities as a wood are hardness and durability, which are ideal for furniture-making. It is usually a pale colour, but darkens over time to a rich, dark brown, sometimes nearly black. It was used for furniture in northern Europe from the Middle Ages onwards, and much fine oak furniture still exists in this country from the 17th century.

OBVERSE
The side of a coin or medal that bears the head, as opposed to the tail or 'reverse'.

OCCASIONAL TABLE
This now refers to any small, reasonably portable table with no specific purpose, therefore free for use as occa-

sion demands. SHERATON was more specific, suggesting that occasional tables were chiefly for games, and usually had a concealed chessboard.

OEBEN, J.F. (*c*1721-63)
German cabinetmaker who arrived in Paris in the late 1740s, studied with

▲ Late Victorian ocasional table, in burr maple and ebony, boxwood, ivory inlay and metal mounts, c1885 (£3,500)

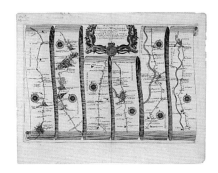

▲ Ogilby road map. Prices depend on the area covered (£95-£225)

OGILBY, JOHN (1600-76)
A man of many parts, Ogilby was born in Edinburgh, was master of revels in Ireland and died in London. He is best remembered as a geographer who published strip road maps, showing routes between large towns as a series of scrolls, with landmarks portrayed and compass bearings to aid the traveller. There is a central CARTOUCHE along the top, giving details of the route. These were the first maps to use the standard mile—until then, opinions had varied regionally about what constituted a mile, and Scottish and Irish measures differed until the 19th century, giving rise to jokes and bad temper.

££-£££

When small was beautiful

'Vertu', or 'virtu', is about virtuosity, meaning exceptional technical skill in the fine arts, and implies a love and appreciation of such skill. So 'objects of vertu' are not crucifixes and altar cloths but small, precious objects, made using a variety of materials, and valued for both the technical skills they represent and for their beauty.

The term today covers a vast range of exquisite pieces made from the 17th to the 19th centuries, although the golden period was from about 1730 to 1830. This was a time when craftsmanship was highly prized, and these skills coincided with the development of materials of great decorative potential — enamel, lacquer, porcelain and glass. It also coincided with the rise of the merchant class, which appreciated small, pretty objects on the lines of spectacularly glamorous (and expensive) French gold snuffboxes.

All manner of objects of vertu were made, most of them for personal use or adornment, some for display on desks, tables and in the boudoir. There were clever little NÉCESSAIRES and ÉTUIS, made of enamel, shagreen, glass, agate, silver — in fact almost anything beautiful — and often mounted in gold. Then there were seals, and the snuffboxes, patch boxes, and BONBONNIÈRES (for sweets). These ranged from humble but decorative PAPIER–MÂCHÉ to the most elaborate novelties, such as musical boxes and those with automated figures, birds or erotic scenes. Another area of objects of vertu comprises scent bottles and VINAIGRETTES. Superb porcelain examples were made in the form of figures and animals, but there are also many of great quality in silver, enamel and glass.

The craftsmanship that made objects of vertu so special was overtaken in the Victorian era by a lust for technical wizardry and novelties. A later flowering of comparable skills is the work of Carl Fabergé in the late 19th and early 20th centuries, with his astonishing Easter eggs and other treasures.

▲ Mother-of-pearl and gold mounted twin blade folding knife, French, 19th century (£600)

▲ Ivory bell push, hexagonal dome shape, with porcelain and seed pearl decoration, 19th century (£400-£500)

▼ Continental opera glasses, enamelled with rural scenes and mother-of-pearl eye pieces (£300-£350)

▶ William IV nutmeg grater in the form of a walnut. Made in Birmingham (£350-£400)

▼ Silver gilt mounted glass tapering scent bottle, French (£350-£400)

▲ Ivory grip in the form of a hound with glass eyes and silver collar, for a rosewood walking stick (£300-£400)

Living in the modern world

▲ Adam and Eve and the Serpent design by Vanessa Bell for the Omega workshops, 1913 (£8,000–£10,000)

▼ Design for a fabric by Roger Fry, c1913 (£1,000–£1,500)

▲ Writing case covered with Omega fabric designed by Roger Fry (£500–£750)

OMEGA WORKSHOPS

These were set up in London in 1913 by the art critic Roger Fry. The idea was to improve the standard of decorative design, applying modern art to daily living. Fry also wanted to encourage young artists such as Vanessa Bell, Duncan Grant and Wyndham Lewis. He believed the joy of the artist in creating was more important than perfection of finish. The Omega artists were therefore generally decorators rather than concerning themselves with the structure of furniture or techniques of fabric printing, unlike the Arts and Crafts Movement.

Textiles and pottery were the most successful, but furniture was also decorated in characteristic style. Their textile designs and decorations on pottery are usually brilliantly colourful, sketchily drawn images, often involving vases of flowers, leaves and figures, as well as more abstract elements. Charleston Farmhouse, in East Sussex, where Grant and Bell lived from 1916, is an enchanting repository of Omega style that can be visited today. The Omega Workshops in London had two showrooms, the range including furniture, screens, lamps, toys, bead necklaces, and hand-painted or printed curtains and cushions, not to mention dresses, fans, parasols, collage hangings and embroidered panels. Murals and stained glass could be commissioned.

Fry was not a great businessman, and the enterprise was undermined by the First World War, so the workshops closed in 1919, but not before they had introduced a new taste for gaiety, colour and spontaneous design.

▼ Ceramic cat designed by Henri Gaudier-Brzeska, with Omega symbol stamped on base (£8,000–£10,000)

OLIPHANT

An obsolete version of the word elephant, now used to describe a medieval ivory cup or horn carved from an entire tusk, often with highy decorative carving. Medieval and Renaissance originals were reproduced in 19th-century Germany.

  £££-£££££

OMBRE TABLE

Ombre was a card game, thought to have been brought to Britain by Catherine of Braganza, Charles II's Portuguese-born queen, and popular throughout the 18th century. A special small triangular table, with GUINEA PITS, was introduced, probably late in the 17th century.

ONYX

A variety of agate characterised by stripes of colour ranging from black to white but with brown predominating, frequently used in jewellery, especially for CAMEOS. It is of the same family as cornelian, bloodstone, jasper and chrysoprase. It can be dyed to produce other colours, particularly green. In this form it provides the bases for art deco bronze and ivory figures.

▶ **French clock**, *c*1900, in the form of a green onyx stand with a bronze and ormolu eagle holding a watch. Seen at the Truro Roadshow. Some damage **(£100)**

OPALINE

This is the name given to a slightly translucent type of glass, usually pastel-coloured or whitish, but occasionally darker. It was made in the 19th century, at French factories including BACCARAT, St Louis and Choisy-le-Roi, and also in America. In the 20th century it has also been made at Murano, Venice. Opaline glass appears most commonly as boxes, sometimes with gilt-metal mounts, but also as carafes, vases and candlesticks.

OPAQUE TWIST

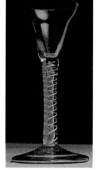

A form of stem for drinking glasses, with spirals of coloured or white glass enclosed within, this was seen particularly in English and Dutch glasses of the 18th century. Opaque and coloured twists were made from about 1760 to the mid-1770s.

£££-££££

OPERA GLASSES

Small, decorative binoculars became particularly popular in the 19th century, as theatres and opera houses became much larger. High-quality optical glass, originally developed for scientific and naval purposes, found a new application as a fashionable accessory. The best opera glasses were made in England, France and Germany, and are usually very decorative, the lenses cased in brass, decorated with enamel, MOTHER-OF-PEARL,

▶ **Unusual pair** of mother-of-pearl opera glasses, decorated in Japan, *c*1880 **(£150-£200)**

porcelain or leather. Some had telescopic lorgnette handles so that they could be propped on the nose.

££-£££

OPUS ANGLICANUM

This English ecclesiastical embroidery of the 13th and 14th centuries was thought to be the finest in Europe at the time. Several successive Popes sent to London for their elaborately embroidered vestments. The embroideries were worked on silk or satin, with couched gold thread as a background, and figures worked in silks in great detail. The designs are like the illuminations in contemporary English manuscripts.

ORMOLU

This gilded bronze, used for decorative mounts for furniture, clocks and other works of art, is particularly associated with French furniture of the 18th century. The term comes from the French *or moulu*, meaning ground gold, and implies bronze gilded by the mercury process. BOULTON was the most famous English maker of it. Modern ormolu is an alloy of copper, zinc and tin.

ORRERY

Named after the 4th Earl of Orrery who commissioned one in 1712, this is a working model of our solar system. The planets are held on arms of different lengths around the sun and, when a handle is cranked, they pursue their yearly round, aided by

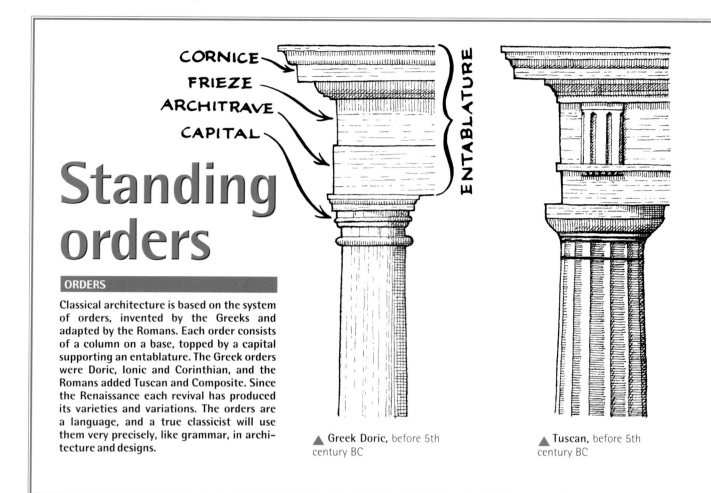

CORNICE
FRIEZE
ARCHITRAVE
CAPITAL

ENTABLATURE

Standing orders

ORDERS

Classical architecture is based on the system of orders, invented by the Greeks and adapted by the Romans. Each order consists of a column on a base, topped by a capital supporting an entablature. The Greek orders were Doric, Ionic and Corinthian, and the Romans added Tuscan and Composite. Since the Renaissance each revival has produced its varieties and variations. The orders are a language, and a true classicist will use them very precisely, like grammar, in architecture and designs.

▲ **Greek Doric,** before 5th century BC

▲ **Tuscan,** before 5th century BC

---

clockwork. Orreries were popular in the 18th and 19th centuries, and occasionally turn up in salerooms.

££££

OSIERS AND OZIER PATTERN

Osiers are flexible willow twigs, used in basket-making. The ozier pattern is a moulded imitation of basket-weave on the borders of plates. It was first introduced at MEISSEN in the 1730s, and much copied elsewhere.

OSLER'S CRYSTAL

In the 19th century F. & C. Osler were the world's leading glass-cutters, making fountains, furniture and clocks as well as drinking vessels, finger bowls, butter dishes and vases. The firm was founded in Birmingham in 1807, and, although it never really recovered after the First

World War, ceased trading only in the 1970s. The best-known creation was the glass fountain at the centre of the Crystal Palace for the 1851 Great Exhibition, but similarly elaborate pieces, not to mention chairs, tables, ÉTAGÈRES, chandeliers, gasoliers and CHEVAL mirrors, were made for shahs, maharajahs and khedives, as well as European royalty and nobility. Candelabras were supplied to Prince ALBERT, the Prince Consort, for Osborne House on the Isle of Wight, 'sun dishes' (gas lights, since electrified) for Windsor Castle, and gasoliers and very large chandeliers for Buckingham Palace. Osler's glass is one of the most characteristic products of the Victorian age, a blend of opulence, tradition and technical wizardry. It is never marked, although metal mounts may be stamped.

££-£££££

OSTRICH EGGS

These enormous eggs, once thought to belong to mythical beasts such as griffins and phoenixes, were elaborately mounted in silver as decorative cups in the 16th century, when, with curiosities such as coconuts and unicorn horns, they were prized above great paintings. Existing mounted examples are usually German.

££-£££££

OTTOMAN

As the name suggests, the ottoman is a Turkish sofa, usually an armless, sometimes backless, low, upholstered seat covered with cushions. It became popular in Britain and America in the late 19th century. A box ottoman has a hinged seat which lifts to reveal storage space.

££-£££

▲ **Greek Ionic,** Asia Minor, about 5th century BC

▲ **Corinthian,** end 5th century BC

▲ **Composite.** Rome from AD82

◀ **Victorian silver-mounted** ostrich egg and cover **(£500)**

OVERGLAZE

Decoration applied to porcelain or pottery on top of the glaze. It may be painted or printed.

OVERLAY

This technique for decorating glass involves two or more layers of differently coloured glass being fused together. The outer layer is called the overlay, and may be carved or cut into decorative designs, contrasting with the layer beneath. (See CAMEO glass.)

OVERMANTEL

An ornamental mirror over a fireplace. During the Victorian period, these became elaborate, with a smaller mirror and lots of shelves, the whole edifice sometimes extending from mantelpiece to cornice. They were often highly decorated, both with carving and turning, and with painted panels.

▶ **Bohemian glass vase** and stand with overlay panels, c1850 **(£1,300–£1,400)**

223

OVERSTUFFING

This is the thick, padded upholstery found underneath the cover material on chairs and settees, and attached to the wooden framework. It provides comfort, and also determines the shape of arms and backs. If the wooden frame is the skeleton, over-stuffing is the flesh.

OXFORD CHAIR

A Victorian upholstered easy chair, with a high back and open, uphol-stered arms. Alternatively, the name was used by 19th-century chair-makers around High Wycombe for different types of 'WINDSOR' chairs. They are usually in beech, but rarer examples can be found in yew. They tend to be heavily constructed but some versions are very elegant.

          ££-£££

◀ **One of a set of six** 'Windsor' chairs in Oxford style, 1840-70. Brought into the Blenheim Palace Roadshow (**£1,200-£1,500** the set)

OXFORD FRAME

A frame where the corners are not mitred, but project out to form a cross.

OYSTER VENEER

A thin slice of wood, cut as a section, across a branch. Laying these side by side creates a dramatic effect. It was popular in English furniture in the late 17th and early 18th centuries.

Not such a wise old bird?

OWL

A symbol of wisdom and learning, and an attribute of Athene or Minerva, goddess of learning, the owl is sometimes used in the decoration of writing tables and libraries. It is also associated with night and sleep. In Christian sym-bolism, the owl may also represent the Jewish people. Pottery or stoneware jugs were made in the form of owls, with detachable heads to act as the cup — perhaps for a nightcap. An image of an owl, blinded by daylight and being mobbed by other birds, is a moral tale, since it shows that even wisdom has its limits.

▲ **Original watercolour of a snowy owl** by Joseph Wolf, for Gould's *The Birds of Great Britain*, 1862-73 (**£30,000**)

▶ **Victorian silver owl** preserve pot by C.T & G. Fox, London, 1846 (**£5,000**)

PADOUK

A hard, heavy, golden to reddish brown wood with dark figuring. It was imported from the Andaman Islands and Bengal, and used in the 18th century for decorative fretwork, and for some chairs.

PAGODAS

Fanciful versions of Chinese towers, with their upcurved eaves and projecting roofs, became an important element in CHINOISERIE decoration. After publication of drawings in the mid-18th century, and the building of the spectacular Kew Gardens pagoda, furniture-makers were inspired to add pagoda-style roofs (with bells dangling from the eaves) to hanging shelves, cabinets and four-poster beds. Pagodas also appear on porcelain, textiles and silver. DELFT tulip vases were made in the form of tall pagodas.

PAISLEY PATTERNS AND SHAWLS

The well-known Paisley pattern takes its name from the wool-weaving town near Glasgow, but has a much more exotic origin. Its characteristic element is the 'boteh', in the shape of a teardrop with a curling point, said to be a representation of a pine cone, intricately filled in with flower heads.

It is thought to have originated in 17th-century India, and is widely seen in Moghul textile design. Wonderful shawls, woven or embroidered with this design, were made in Kashmir and were widely imitated in Europe, especially from the late

◀ Paisley shawl, 19th century. Price depends on condition and quality
(£100-£300)

18th century. Paisley itself became a major centre in the 19th century, making good-quality copies at a fraction of the price of the originals, thanks to innovative weaving technology. Paisley shawls may be double or single-sided, and vary in size from stoles to large rectangles or squares for wearing over crinolines. They are made of wool, or a wool/cotton mix, and in general are predominantly red. Paisley shawls went out of fashion around the 1870s, and weaving in Paisley ended around the turn of the century.

£££-££££

PALISSY, BERNARD (c1510-90)

A French potter and naturalist who so loved reptiles and slimy creatures that he portrayed them slithering over his dishes, plates and bowls. He developed suitably muddy glazes—blues, browns, greens and greys—and made dishes that were like small ponds alive with snakes, newts, crustaceans and fish. For greater accuracy, he even made casts of dead animals. Famous and imitated in his day, he ended his life in prison for heresy. Further imitations of his work were made in the 19th century.

PALMETTE

Fan-shaped decoration that looks like a formalised palm leaf or, in another version, the flower of a honeysuckle. It is seen in classical decoration and its revivals (see ANTHEMION).

PANELLING

From the 15th century onwards, it was fashionable to apply panels of wood to the walls of rooms, to help insulate them and to reduce draughts. Panels might have carved decoration (LINENFOLD), or be painted or inlaid. In 18th-century France, panels decorated with elaborate shallow-relief carving were used, known as *boiseries*.

▲ German **papier-mâché** snuffbox by Stobwasser, with maker's name inside and portrait on lid,1830-50 (£300-£400)

Stronger than the sum of its parts

PAPIER-MÂCHÉ

Paper mashed up with water and other stiffeners makes a thick paste which can be pressed and moulded into various shapes, and is known as papier-mâché. This is a lightweight material which can easily be decorated by lacquering and painting. The technique was introduced to France from the Far East in the 17th century, and was used in England from about 1750 onwards. Pretty trays and boxes made of decorated papier-mâché were popular in the 18th century, while in the mid-19th century there was a fashion for papier-mâché furniture. This was often embellished with inlay of MOTHER-OF-PEARL, gold leaf, coloured stones and tortoiseshell, as well as flowery painting, typically on a black background. Small tables and chairs were made, and even bedsteads. The best-known and most prolific British manufacturers were JENNENS & BETTRIDGE, and their competitors included Clay and Ryton & Walton.

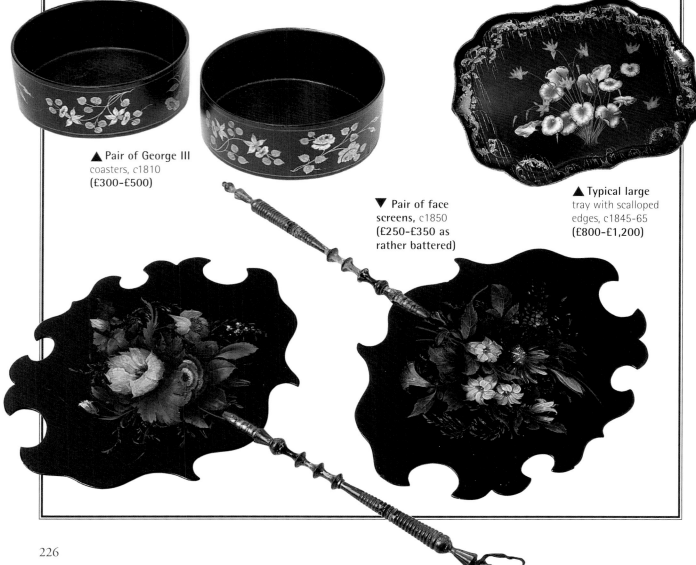

▲ Pair of George III coasters, c1810 (£300-£500)

▼ Pair of face screens, c1850 (£250-£350 as rather battered)

▲ Typical large tray with scalloped edges, c1845-65 (£800-£1,200)

PAP BOAT

A small, boat-shaped vessel, usually of pottery or silver, for feeding babies or invalids in the 18th and 19th centuries. Pap was a mixture of bread and wine. (See MEDICAL INSTRUMENTS.)

 ££-£££

PAPERWEIGHTS

Most collected and admired are the glass examples made in France in the mid-19th century, particularly those from the BACCARAT, CLICHY and ST LOUIS factories. The English also made paperweights in the 19th century. American makers included some unusual shapes, such as oblongs, squares and moulded fruits. Not all are so decorative—some were made of green bottle glass. This century has seen a revival of paperweights as works of art by individual craftsmen.

 £££-££££

▼ **Glass paperweight** as company promotional item, *c*1920 **(£20-£30)**

PARASOL

Sunshades in the form of umbrellas, made of delicate, decorative fabrics, were popular in the 19th century, and became particularly fashionable in the Edwardian era, many imported from Japan. Ladies would carry them ostensibly to protect delicate complexions, but also as accessories, perhaps trimmed to match a dress.

 ££-£££

▲ **Mid-17th-century folding parasol** **(£100-£300)**

PARCEL GILT

Style of decoration where a silver article is partly gilded

PARIAN WARE

In 1846 MINTON and COPELAND, working in competition, each developed a new ceramic modelling body. A kind of feldspathic porcelain, designed to remain unglazed and look like marble, became known as Parian, although there were other names, such as statuary porcelain. Ideal for detailed modelling, it had a similar relationship to sculpture as the print to the painting. Thanks to a patent reducing machine, developed in 1844, accurate, small-scale reproductions could be made of large sculptures in bronze, marble and other media. One of the sensations of the Great Exhibition of 1851, Parian achieved success in both artistic and commercial terms, and figures and busts noted after sculptors were soon gracing parlours. The leading makers were Minton, Copeland, WEDGWOOD, WORCESTER, ROBINSON & LEADBETTER and GOSS,

▶ **Parian ware** bust of Prince Albert by Minton, 1862 **(£400)**

but more than 100 companies were recorded as manufacturers. The best pieces are often based on works by contemporary sculptors. Tinted and decorated Parian was also produced, and the material was occasionally used for moulded tablewares.

PARLOUR FURNITURE

The name 'parlour' has at different times meant a dining or a sitting room. SHERATON gave the name to single chairs with upholstered seats. In the Victorian period 'parlour furniture' comprised upholstered chairs and settees, often in suites, for the middle-class version of a drawing room. The set usually consists of two large armchairs, four side chairs and a settee or CHAISE LONGUE. Often included are versions of EASY CHAIRS with no arms, to allow for ladies' voluminous skirts.

▲ **Louis XV parquetry** guéridon **(£6,500)**

PARQUETRY

A form of marquetry, where woods are pieced together in geometric patterns, relying on contrasting colours or grains to enhance the design. Used by British cabinetmakers from about 1660, and particularly fashionable in the 18th century.

PARTNERS' DESK

A large, flat-topped, knee-hole desk on pedestals, at which two people may sit facing each other, made from the mid-18th century. It has drawers and cupboards on each side.

£££-£££££

PARTRIDGE WOOD

A hard, heavy South American wood with a straight grain, resembling partridge plumage in its tones of brown and red. It was used in 17th-century PARQUETRY, and as a veneer in the 18th century. Partridge cane is one of the strongest for walking sticks.

PARURE

A matching set of jewellery made of the same stones, comprising perhaps a necklace, earrings, bracelet and brooch. A partial set is called a *demi-parure*. Parures were made in the 16th century, and became fashionable again in the 19th. Diamonds were used in parures for formal, and other stones for less formal, occasions.

PASTE

Imitation gemstones, made of glass, widely used in jewellery. They are usually colourless but may be tinted or backed with coloured foil. Paste jewellery became very popular in England, France and Spain during the 18th century, meeting a middle-class demand for cut-price glamour. Another factor may have been the prevalence of highwaymen. Similar factors make good examples very collectable today.

▲ Staffordshire cottage pastille burner *c*1835, damaged (**£300 undamaged**)

PASTILLE BURNER

Anything to disguise the awful smells of bad drainage was welcome in past centuries. Burning aromatic pastilles (the antique equivalent of joss sticks) was one such idea. Silver burners were made from Elizabethan times, and bronze in the 18th century, but in the 19th pastille burners were frequently made of pottery or porcelain, often in the shape of little houses. The scented smoke escaped through the chimneys and windows.

£££-££££

PATCHWORK

Originally developed for reasons of economy to get the last bit of use from a worn-out garment, patchwork developed into an art form. A winter pursuit, undertaken when outside occupations were either unattractive or impossible, it was widely used to make quilts, the patchwork design being worked first, then quilted by stitching through

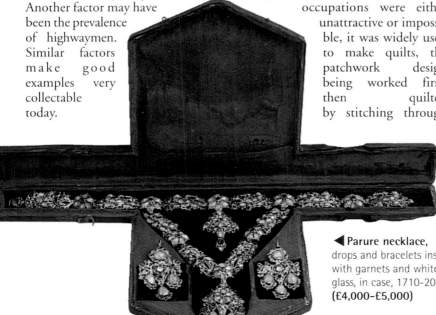

◄ Parure necklace, drops and bracelets inset with garnets and white glass, in case, 1710-20 (**£4,000-£5,000**)

wadding to a backing material. American patchwork is particularly famous and is typically made up of a number of 'blocks' of pattern. These are repeated, using brilliant colours and striking designs, which are often symbolic. English patchwork is more usually composed of geometrical patterns made up of hexagons. 'Crazy' work, made up of silks and velvets with embroidery, was favoured in the late 19th century.

PÂTE DE VERRE

Literally, glass paste, made by grinding glass to a powder and mixing it with a flux (to help it fuse) and water, and perhaps a colouring agent. It was then fired in a mould, and maybe carved. *Pâte de verre* is a long-used technique, known in ancient Egypt, but it enjoyed a revival in late 19th-century France, particularly for ART NOUVEAU ornaments.

PAW FOOT

Many an early or late 18th-century chair is supported on front feet modelled as the paws of a lion or bear. Sometimes the allusion extends to a hairy knee or hock further up the leg. This idea has roots in ancient Egypt, appearing in various cultures since. At the end of the 18th century SHERATON took it up.

◀ **Mintons** part dessert service, c1878, with turquoise-ground pâte-sur-pâte. Decorated by Desire Leroy (£2,000-£2,500)

Building a stylish image layer by layer

PÂTE-SUR-PÂTE

Developed in France in the mid-19th century, and widely used in Europe during later decades, pâte-sur-pâte was a new decorative technique for ceramics, based on the principle of building up an image in relief by the application of successive layers of liquid clay, or slip, generally in white on a coloured ground.

Highly skilled and painstakingly slow and expensive, pâte-sur-pâte was associated particularly with one man, Marc Louis Solon (1835-1913). He perfected the technique in Paris, working at SÈVRES, and then came to England in 1870 to join MINTON, remaining in Staffordshire until his death. Working together, Minton and Solon perfected the pâte-sur-pâte process, producing wares considered at the time to be the artistic apogee of creative ceramics and the perfect marriage of the fine and the applied arts.

Pâte-sur-pâte styles were highly varied, drawing for inspiration on Japanese art, the Renaissance and NEO-CLASSICISM. The technique was also used by other British potters such as DOULTON, and by leading manufacturers in France, Germany, the United States and elsewhere.

◀ **Blue-ground** pâte-sur-pâte porcelain vase decorated by Solon, 1893 (£3,000)

▶ **Two ormolu-mounted** pâte-sur-pâte porcelain lamps, 2nd half of 19th century (£1,450 the pair)

▲ **Slender** Mintons pâte-sur-pâte, oviform, two-handled vase, c1894, by Solon (£8,000)

The moving finger writes and then moves on

PENS

The ancient stylus gave way to the pencil, various brushes and the quill pen. Steel pens were made in the 17th century but the quill remained the most usual writing implement until well into the 19th century, when steel dip-pen nibs were mass-produced, particularly by Josiah Mason of Birmingham who developed James Perry's 'Patent Perryman System' during the 1830s and '40s. The fountain pen was the invention of Lewis Edson Waterman, patented in 1884. Pre-1910 Watermans are eagerly collected. They were made of hard black rubber, which might be covered in silver or gold. Other sought-after makes include Conklin, Conway Stewart, Mabie Todd, Mont Blanc, Schaeffer and Parker. Also much collected are Japanese Namiki fountain pens which are lacquer-covered. Prices depend on quality and the rarity of particular models.

PENCILS

Originally 'pencil' meant a fine brush, and one still uses 'pencilling' for fine black decoration on porcelain. But the lead pencil encased in a thin wooden tube — perhaps the most common and least noticed of human implements — was a new invention in the 1560s. In the 18th century some of the best, such as Middleton's, were made of Borrowdale graphite, and during the French Revolution the inventor Conté produced his ceramic leads. In 1843 the painter William Brockedon patented an artificial plumbago lead, which was developed commercially by MORDAN. Among the leading American manufacturers were the Thoreaus, while the world-famous German business of A.W. Faber was set up in 1761. By the mid-19th century inferior German makers were stamping 'Faber' on their wares. Few old pencils will ever be highly priced simply as pencils: they may be collected as commemorative or advertising material. Collectors of (and dealers in) old carpenters' tools often throw away the pencils in the boxes, even though they may be the oldest tools of the set.

PENKNIVES

As the name implies, these were originally for cutting quills. They evolved into multi-functional pocket knives. True penknives should have sharp steel blades but pearl-handled, silver-bladed pen- knives were used for cutting fruit and they are sometimes cased with similar folding forks. These were popular in the late 19th and early 20th centuries, and were intended for handbag or watch-fob.

▼ Part of a collection of fountain pens c1900 - late 1950s, seen at the Taunton Roadshow. Values range from £60 to several hundred pounds

▶ Waterman fountain pen, with retractable nib, 1910 (£100)

▲ Silver or steel bladed mother-of-pearl penknives, early 20th century (£10-£20)

▲ **Highly stylised peacock motif** on the back of a dining chair, c1888

PEACOCK

With its spectacular plumage, particularly the tail feathers with 'eyes', the peacock has appeared in ornament as far back as Roman times, when it was an attribute of the goddess Juno. It was a popular motif on Oriental textiles, and became much beloved of the Aesthetic Movement in the late 19th century. As peacock flesh was believed not to decay, it was used as a symbol of immortality. The tail feathers have been thought by some cultures to represent the evil eye, so are sometimes regarded as unlucky.

PEARDROP

A small, pear-shaped brass pendant handle seen in 17th-century furniture, on drawers or cupboards.

PEARWOOD

A hard fruitwood with a close-grained appearance, pink to pale yellowish in colour. It was sometimes stained black to imitate ebony. As well as country furniture, it has been used for inlay on Elizabethan and Jacobean furniture, for picture frames, and for elaborate, Grinling GIBBONS-style carvings.

PEARLWARE

A type of earthenware introduced by WEDGWOOD in 1779, to increase the whiteness and porcelain-like appearance of his creamware. The glaze is bluish-tinged, which can most clearly be seen where it pools around the foot-rim or base of a piece. It was adopted by several other potteries, including Spode and Leeds, and used particularly in conjunction with underglaze blue decoration.

  ££-££££

▲ **Scandinavian peg tankard**, late 18th to early 19th century (**£500-£700**)

PEG TANKARD

A tankard for communal drinking, ensuring fair shares by means of eight pegs or pins evenly spaced inside to mark the level to which each could drink. It usually held two quarts, so

▼ **Staffordshire pearlware** figure of musicians, dog and sheep (**£600-£900**)

everyone got half a pint. Introduced in the late 17th century.

£££-£££££

PELLATT, APSLEY (1791-1863)

A glassmaker whose father had bought the old Falcon glasshouse in Southwark. His most characteristic products are flasks, paperweights and tableware decorated with cameo-like busts and figures. These were made of a silvery ceramic mixture sandwiched in crystal and called sulphides. He also imitated Venetian and Islamic glass. His huge chandeliers at the Great Exhibition competed with OSLER's crystal fountain. Occasionally pieces are marked Pellatt & Green or Pellatt & Co.

£££-£££££

PEMBROKE TABLE

An elegant and versatile, small drop-leaf table, introduced in the mid-18th century, allegedly at the behest of a Countess of Pembroke. Typically it has two hinged leaves, supported by brackets, above a rectangular framework, usually with a drawer, and four straight, tapering legs. Early ones had fretwork stretchers until about 1760. Decoration is often pretty, and may include painting and MARQUETRY in NEO-CLASSICAL designs. Much heavier and less attractive examples were made in the Victorian period.

£££-££££

PENWORK

A late 18th and early 19th-century decorative fashion used on furniture, boxes, fans and other wooden objects. Usually a piece would be JAPANNED black, leaving areas which could be filled in with quill and black ink in fine detail. The overall impact is dramatic, although designs are often composed of delicate floral, Oriental and arabesque motifs. CHINOISERIE themes were particularly popular on REGENCY furniture.

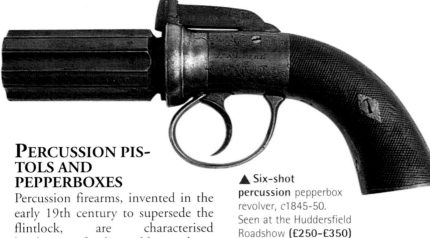

PERCUSSION PISTOLS AND PEPPERBOXES

Percussion firearms, invented in the early 19th century to supersede the flintlock, are characterised by the use of a disposable metal cap containing a small amount of gunpowder. When the cap is struck by the hammer, it ignites a powder charge. A pepperbox pistol is an early form of revolver which has several revolving barrels allowing the hammer to strike a fresh one each time the trigger is pulled. Most were made from about 1850, with a percussion mechanism.

  ££-£££

PERSIAN POTTERY

Some of the most beautiful Islamic pottery was made in Persia (now Iran), influencing ceramic development in both China and Europe. Particularly significant for the West were the lustre wares which flourished in Persia in the 12th to 14th centuries, and again from the late 17th century.

Blue and white faience was made from the 14th century, and may have preceded the Chinese

▲ Six-shot **percussion** pepperbox revolver, *c*1845-50. Seen at the Huddersfield Roadshow **(£250-£350)**

in this form of decoration. The importation of Chinese *kraak* wares through Persia led to the Persians copying the style and a small number made their way to Europe, the soft nature of the Persian body making their survival unusual.

PERSIAN RUGS

Some of the finest rugs and carpets ever made came from Persia, where this skill reached a zenith in the 16th and 17th centuries. In terms of design, colour and technique, Persian rugs span the widest possible range, representing not only the output of commercial workshops, sometimes working to special commissions, but also of nomadic tribal groups, and craftsmen working in remote villages, making rugs and textiles for domestic use as well as barter. Superb classical carpets were made for the courts, often using naturalistic floral designs, inspired by the Moslem idea of paradise as a garden. Examples of these carpets survive in museums, some of them probably representing the whole life's work of a weaver. After a decline in the 18th and early 19th centuries, the industry revived around the 1860s, and most of the decorative Persian carpets and silk rugs seen today date from after this. As well as the court carpets made at urban workshops, much was made by tribal groups, including not only rugs and kilims, but tent hangings, saddle bags and other animal trappings. These

◀ Fine Persian carpet, Kashan, 13ft 9in by 9ft 9in **(£900-£1,300)**

often bear vivid designs, which have symbolic meanings and representations. These tribal weavings are keenly collected today.

PETIT POINT

A type of embroidery using a fine, small, slanted or tent stitch on a woven canvas, its delicacy allowing considerable detail and shading in designs. It was used in medieval embroideries, but is particularly known today on 18th-century chair and cushion covers.

PEW GROUPS

Small pottery figures with round, doll-like faces and beady brown eyes, seated in twos or threes on a high-backed seat or pew. They are made of salt-glazed stoneware or earthenware and are usually uncoloured, except by brown slip. Sometimes the men are depicted as musicians, seated beside a lady. They date from about 1730 to 1745, and may have been produced by a single potter. Equestrian figures and females whose dresses form bells may come from the same source.

  ££££

▲ Child's picture bricks in box, with rare early motoring scene, probably Dutch or German, 1905-10 **(£40-£60)**

PICTURE BRICKS

Children's toys, dating from the 19th century. There are two types. Cubes of wood decorated with printed paper, showing individual pictures or letters on each face, could be both looked at and used as building blocks by a child. More complex are sets where each side of a block bears part of a picture. By assembling them correctly the child can see the whole view.

PIER GLASS OR TABLE

A pier is the narrow wall between two windows, and pier glass is the name for a tall, slender mirror designed to fit it, giving the illusion of space. They were particularly fashionable in the 18th century, and were often complemented by a small, free-standing pier table, also perfectly tailored to fit.

£££-£££££

▲ William IV giltwood table with Florentine circular pietra dura top surrounding a micromosaic (£39,000)

PIETRA DURA

The Italian term for hard and semi-precious stones such as agate, chalcedony, and lapis lazuli. It is also used to describe a mosaic of small, carefully shaped pieces of these stones and of marble, forming designs and pictures. Pietra dura, also known as 'Florentine mosaic', is built up painstakingly piece by piece, each fitting to the next, and glued onto a backing slate. Pietra dura panels were used to decorate cabinets and table tops. The technique was introduced during the Renaissance, and decorative panels are still made today.

Touchstone of domestic wares

PEWTER

An alloy, predominantly tin, hardened by the addition of copper or varying amounts of lead — the less lead, the better the quality. The working of pewter developed in the Middle Ages for domestic wares such as plates, bowls, drinking vessels and candlesticks, and these early pieces show little decoration. From the 16th century, a fashion arose in Europe for display pieces, which were decorated in relief (the decoration being cast in the mould as the piece was formed).

A complex system of marks, called touchmarks, has been applied to pewter, both here and on the Continent, which can help identify makers, but marking was not so consistently enforced as it was for silver. In the 19th century, the development of another, more silvery (and cheaper) alloy, BRITANNIA metal, and of ELECTROPLATE, put an end to pewter, apart from a brief revival at the end of the century by LIBERTY.

▶ Typical English 18th-century pewter plate with engraved coat of arms, 1730-40 (£20 each, £60 a pair)

▼ Late 19th-century pewter jugs (£30-£50)

PILGRIMS' BADGE

The 'I was there' T-shirts of their day, these lead badges were handed out to pilgrims at the major shrines of medieval Europe. They wore them in their hats to prove they had completed the journey. Pilgrims' badges were extensively forged in the 19th century, and were among the BILLIES and CHARLIES made by William Smith and Charles Eaton.

       £££££

PILKINGTON

A pottery factory near Manchester in production from 1893 to 1938 making largely LUSTRE wares painted on an earthenware body by a number of skilled artists. The dominant figures were the chemist William Burton and his brother Joseph. The artists invariably signed their work on the bases, and most pieces bear a date code. The firm also made large numbers of tiles and in later years, monochrome moulded wares. There is no connection with Pilkington's Glass Works.

       £££

PILLEMENT, J.B. (1728-1808)

A French painter and designer, who worked as far afield as England, Poland and Spain, as well as in France, Pillement is best known for CHINOISERIE designs, engravings of which circulated widely. His exotic flowers, and whimsical Chinamen gambolling around spindly pavilions, inspired textiles, porcelain, enamel and furniture-decorators throughout the ROCOCO period.

PINCHBECK

All that glisters is not gold, certainly not in the case of Christopher Pinchbeck. He was an early 18th-century London watchmaker who invented an alloy of copper and zinc which superficially resembled gold. It was used in the 18th century for watch-cases, snuffboxes, ÉTUIS and cheap jewellery, but was later superseded by rolled gold and gilded metal. The term is often wrongly used to describe any small item of gilt metal.

PINE

Although stripped pine enjoyed great popularity in the 1970s era of home-spun lifestyles, it must have shivered in its nakedness, as pine was never intended to be seen. In the late 17th and 18th centuries, it was used for carcasses of furniture that were to be veneered, although it is more liable to warp than oak. Its smooth surface also made it suitable for gilding. In the 19th century, it was used to make inexpensive painted furniture and it is this which has usually been stripped.

PINEAPPLE

This became a symbol of hospitality in Europe from the later 17th century,

▲ **Silver coffee pot** with pineapple finial, 1775. Seen at the Newcastle Emlyn Roadshow (**£3,000**)

which explains its prevalence as a finial on gateposts and in guest bedrooms. One of the royal gardeners, John Rose, presented Charles II with the first pineapple grown in England. In the early 17th century, German silversmiths made standing cups in the form of pineapples held aloft by a figure. Pineapples also form finials in ROCOCO furniture, and WEDGWOOD imitated their shape in green and yellow-glazed tea wares. Thus a plastic pineapple ice-bucket has an honourable pedigree!

PIPE RACKS AND KILNS

Pipe kilns are cages made of wrought iron hoops which are used for cleaning CLAY PIPES or 'churchwardens'. Used pipes would be laid within such cages (designs vary since they were blacksmith-made) and baked in a hot oven until all traces of tobacco juice were gone and the pipes were fresh to use again. This habit of recycling pipes was particularly common in pubs up to the 19th century. Wooden pipe racks were made for the storage of clays and, from around 1900, briars. These may be elaborate walnut or mahogany structures, either wall-hanging, sometimes with tambour fronts, or in the form of a 'smoker's companion' for a desk, with pipe holders arranged around a tobacco jar.

    ££

PIQUÉ

A technique of decoration involving the inlay of gold or silver into tortoiseshell (or, more rarely, ivory) to form patterns and decorative scenes. It was used mainly on small items such as snuffboxes, ÉTUIS and fan sticks. Said to have originated in Naples in the 17th century, it became fashionable in France and England as well through the 18th century and into the 19th. A design made up of dots is known as 'piqué point', while that using flat strips of metal (sometimes engraved) is called '*piqué posé*'.

You'll want to keep these close to your chest

PLAYING CARDS

Little is known about the true origin of playing cards, although various theories have them emanating from Persia, India or China. Some even believe that cards depicting chess pieces may have been carried by Crusaders while travelling.

One of the earliest references to playing cards is made in a document dated 1377, held by the British Museum. Designs were very different from those familiar today, and early Italian packs have suit marks of swords, cups, coins and batons, which were also taken up by the Spanish (who still use them). The court cards were all male: King, Knight and Jack. In Germany, which became a major producer of playing cards in the 15th century, cards were printed with wood blocks, and a variety of suit marks was used — lions, monkeys, parrots and peacocks, as well as hares, books, fishes and drinking cups. Eventually the Germans settled on hearts, hawk bells, leaves and acorns, and still use them today. The suit marks of hearts, clubs, spades and diamonds with which we are familiar developed in France, which became the leading card producer in the 16th century.

Both French and Spanish cards were imported into Britain, and a card-making industry soon sprang up here, establishing the familiar designs of court cards known today. The elaborate style of the Ace of Spades, with its complex pattern incorporating the maker's name, could only be acquired from the stamp office on payment of duty. Many novelty packs were made, the card value indicated at the top or in one corner of the card, the rest being a picture on some humorous, satirical, political or educational theme. These are now keenly collected, as are French cards from the time of the Revolution, showing Royalist or Revolutionary themes (sometimes court cards were doctored to remove crowns and royal insignia).

Very early hand-painted cards are hardly ever found and are worth huge sums. Eighteenth-century packs can still be found today, occasionally at auction or, if you are really lucky, at car boot sales. These can fetch hundreds or even thousands of pounds. However, most cards found these days tend to be 20th-century, and they may advertise anything from whisky to cruise liners. Sadly, most have little value.

▼ A pack of circular novelty cards, 1960s (£5–£10)

◀ 19th-century cards. Square cut corners and absence of numbers denote age (£20–£50)

PLATE BASKETS, BUCKETS, CUPBOARDS, WARMERS

To ease the problems of carrying a stack of plates down long corridors connecting the kitchen to the dining room, plate buckets or pails were designed in the 18th century. These are straight-sided wooden buckets, about 12in to 18in deep, with a slot in the side to allow removal of plates. Those of octagonal shape, with one of the vertical slatted or fretwork panels removed to form the slot, are sometimes called plate baskets. They were often made in pairs, and might be warmed by the fire. From about 1770, plates were also warmed in cupboards flanking a sideboard. A plate cupboard is an early term for a court cupboard, an open-shelved piece of furniture on which silver, glass and pewter were displayed.

£££-££££

PLYMOUTH PORCELAIN

The first English factory to make true HARD-PASTE porcelain, which has a greyish appearance, often with smoky patches, and a glassy, yellowish glaze. Typical wares include figures, mugs, sauceboats and seashell salts. They were decorated in underglaze blue or coloured enamels. The factory was shortlived, being founded by COOKWORTHY in 1760 and moving to Bristol in 1770. Eventually the patent for hard-paste porcelain passed to NEW HALL in 1781.

POKERWORK

A common form of decoration on small furniture in the late 19th cen-

tury. Designs of dots and grooves were scorched with a red-hot poker.

POLE SCREEN see FIRESCREEN

POMANDERS

Perfume containers intended to combat the smells of everyday life, and to ward off infection. Silver or silver gilt, they took the form of a ball, engraved and divided internally into segments. Each segment opened to take aromatic herbs or a sponge soaked in spiced vinegar or perfume. Pomanders might stand on a table, be suspended from a CHATELAINE, or from a chain around the wrist or neck. There were also perforated metal

Hello, hello, hello, what's all this?

POLICE ITEMS

Since their introduction in 1829, the police have adorned and equipped themselves with a range of insignia and paraphernalia which has become popular with collectors. Uniform was not standardised across the many different forces until the 20th century, so there are plenty of variants on a general theme. The top hat was worn for 34 years, 1829-63, after which a military, Prussian-style helmet was adopted, but instead of a spike, a rose or crest is usual. Another area of collecting comprises belt buckles, buttons and badges, from the second half of the 19th century onwards, and ranging from simple to intricate. Police truncheons, intended as defensive weapons, also served as a badge of office, and were decorated with the royal cypher or a coat of arms. Already used by elected constables, they became standard police issue. Other police items include bull's-eye lanterns, rattles, whistles and handcuffs.

Bull's-eye police lantern seen at the Manchester Roadshow, c1890 (£50-£60)

Rare Plymouth porcelain sauce boat by William Cookworthy, c.1765 (£400-£500)

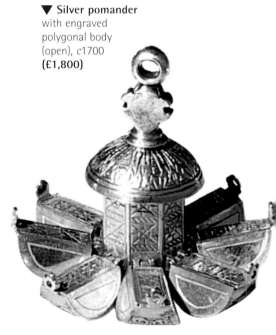

▼ Silver pomander with engraved polygonal body (open), c1700 (£1,800)

globes to take oranges stuck with cloves. Mostly made in Holland and Germany, they were in use only until the mid-17th century, and are rare today. Late reproductions in brass occur.

 **R £££-££££**

PONTYPOOL JAPANNING

The name Pontypool is often applied to any JAPANNED metalwares, but should be used only for those from the Pontypool factory in Monmouthshire, set up in the late 17th century. Domestic goods produced during the 18th century include trays, canisters, candlesticks, boxes, urns and vases. The wares are made of tin, decorated with CHINOISERIES, flowers or landscapes on red, green, yellow, and blue as well as tortoiseshell, black and white. Many layers of varnish make a hard, durable finish. The factory closed in 1820, but japanning continued in Birmingham. In French it is known as *tôle peinte*.

£££

PORCELAIN

A ceramic body which is usually white, translucent, hard and gives a musical note when struck. There are numerous variations to the formula but the commonest is the HARD PASTE body developed by the Chinese in the TANG dynasty. It was employed by the Koreans and in Germany, whereas in England and France a SOFT or hybrid body was adopted, usually replacing china stone with glass or bone ash. The ubiquitous BONE CHINA and PARIAN are both porcelains. Confusingly, STONEWARE, not regarded as a porcelain by the Europeans, is so in the East as it is fired at the same temperature

PORRINGER

A shallow bowl with one or two flat handles appllied to the rim. Usually silver or pewter, they were used from the 17th to 19th centuries and are commonly, but incorrectly, called bleeding bowls.

£££-££££

▲ **Wedgwood** black basalte Portland Vase, c1880 **(£1,000)**

PORTLAND VASE

The most spectacular example of CAMEO glass, dating from the Roman Empire. Dark blue, decorated with classical figures in white relief, it takes its name from a previous owner, the Duchess of Portland, and is now in the British Museum. Many copies have been made, in glass, in WEDGWOOD's Jasperware, and in plaster. Broken at least twice, once into more than 200 fragments, it has been expertly restored.

PORTOBELLO POTTERY

This applies to two distinct types of pottery. First, a group of delft or Staffordshire wares commemorating the naval victory at Portobello in Panama, decorated with applied or moulded ships and figures of Admiral Vernon (see BLUE AND WHITE). From 1786, factories at Portobello in Scotland made domestic and decorative wares, including figures of Scottish interest, mainly in earthenware and decorated in coloured glazes. Thomas Rathbone's factory ran until the 1850s, and another Portobello concern was run by the Cornwall family from 1826 until modern times.

POSSET POTS

Posset is hot spiced milk, curdled with ale or wine. A special vessel was made for it in the late 17th and early 18th centuries, which may be cylindrical or bucket-shaped, and usually has two or more looped handles and a lid and spout. They are made of slipware, stoneware or tin-glazed earthenware.

R ££££-£££££

▲ **An appropriate** illustrated card from the Bamforth 'Comic' series, 1926 **(£5)**

POSTCARDS

It is now a century since regulations first allowed picture postcards to be sent through the mail without an envelope, provoking a whole new industry. Linked to the development of tourism and advertising, postcards had become part of the British way of life well before the First World War, when they were already being collected. Today the interest is truly international. The appeal lies in the diversity and accessibility. The most common type is the topographical or view card. Of greater interest and value are those by named artists, such as the Bonzo cards by George Studdy, or the many comic series. Popular subjects are early aviation and motoring, railways, ships, show business and politics, especially movements such as the suffragettes. However obscure the subject, someone will collect it. Condition is all-important, and the message and the stamp are generally of secondary interest.

£-££

▼ **Posy holder,** gilt metal with mother-of-pearl handle, 1850-60. Seen at the Wrekin Roadshow **(£150-£200)**

POSY HOLDERS

Shaped like ice-cream cornets, these allowed ladies to carry posies of flowers without touching the stems or getting wet. They were very popular with the Victorians, and all sorts were made. Some could be attached to the finger by a ring and chain: others had tripod legs so the posy could be put down without crushing it. Many are engraved silver, but some are further embellished with beads, pearls, porcelain plaques or enamel. Porcelain posy holders were made at BERLIN and elsewhere. Inexpensive souvenirs in plate or brass were also produced.

 **££-£££**

POT LIDS

A pottery cover for a shallow pot originally containing potted meats, savouries, or bear's grease for dressing men's hair, decorated with transfer-printed pictures, including landscapes, buildings, bear dancing and portraits. They are highly collectable, irrespective of the pot base. F. & R. PRATT specialised in making them from 1846 to 1880, although other factories also made them. Early lids are flat, and often in black only, while later examples are slightly domed, and employ more colours.

 **££-£££**

▼ **Pot lids** made by F&R Pratt, late 19th century **(£10-£60, depending on condition)**

POT-POURRI VASE

A vase with a pierced top or neck, in which a mulch of aromatic petals and leaves is placed, so that fragrance may permeate a room. They were made in porcelain from the 18th century.

POUNCE BOX

Pounce is a fine powder used to fix ink, in the absence of blotting paper. Pounce boxes are usually silver, with pierced lids, and could form part of an inkstand.

POWDER COMPACT

Once it became acceptable rather than immoral to powder one's nose, this item was added to the paraphernalia of womanhood. Powder compacts were made from around the turn of the 20th century, and became increasingly decorative and sophisticated. They were produced in many different metals, sometimes decorated with enamel, and might include a lipstick holder and cigarette case.

 **££-£££**

POWDER FLASK

A container for the powder used in muzzle-loading guns. They were usually pear-shaped and made of leather-covered wood or metal, but few of the former survive. They might be decorated with inlaid silver or bone to match the gun.

££-£££

▶ **Powder flask,** 1850-75. They lose value if the patina is cleaned off **(£35-£125)**

▲ **Picture Post** 1952 for the 1953 Coronation, and 1935 Royal Jubilee souvenir **(£8-£12)**

▲ **Edwardian corset** shop window advertising card, c1900 **(£10)**

▼ **Swiss-made Turkish** cigarette pack, 1972 **(£1)**

Throw-away memories

PRINTED EPHEMERA

The development of chromo-lithography (colour print-ing) in the 1840s led to the birth of the modern poster, but it was not until the 1880s and 1890s that the potential was fully realised by French artists and designers such as Toulouse-Lautrec and Cheret.

From that time on the multi-coloured poster was an essential component of the street scene, with bright and decorative images being used to promote everything imag-inable, from books, plays and events to cigarettes, drinks, bicycles and all kinds of domestic products.

Starting in the early 1900s the travel poster became increasingly pop-ular, along with images used for political and military purposes. Over the last century many artists and designers have built their reputation upon the poster, and works by men such as Will Bradley, Cassandre,

Tom Purvis and Fougasse are particularly desirable (and expensive) today. Key areas for collectors are motoring, aviation and travel by train and ship, especially during the 1920s and 1930s when some of the most exciting images were produced, along with the propaganda posters of both World Wars.

Early ADVERTISING is also extremely popular, with famous designs by artists such as MUCHA, the Beg-garstaff Brothers and Hassall fetching large sums. However, most posters can still be bought for less than £500, and there are always discoveries to be made. Post-war material tends to be much cheaper, but as always condition is all-important. Auction houses hold regular sales of posters which have made the transition from ephemera to fine art.

Collecting ephemera in all its forms is bound up in our increasing fascination with the recent past and our

desire to preserve those ele-ments of it, however trivial, that survive. The particular appeal of printed ephemera lies in its diversity and its ability to bring to life a place or time. It started with stamps, posters and POST-CARDS, but these are now well established in their own right and so have moved away from the purely ephemeral.

Today the great attrac-tion lies in printed material that was not designed to outlive its immediate period or function, and whose survival is a matter of chance. The field includes material such as trade cards and book plates dating from the 18th and the early 19th centuries, but most items collected today are far more recent and often just beyond living memory.

The range is infinite, but popular areas for collectors include magazines and newspapers, packaging and labels for foods, drinks and other consumer products, tickets and related material,

especially transport adver-tisements and promotional brochures, catalogues and programmes, with theatri-cal and sporting subjects always attracting a lot of interest. Trade cards and stationery, political leaflets and pamphlets and even wrapping and bags are also well in the picture.

Newspapers of the 17th and 18th centuries have survived in surprisingly large numbers and often cost only a few pounds, although among the rarest ephemera are broadsheets dating from the mid-15th century at the dawn of printing. The Dr John Johnson Collection at Oxford is one of the largest of its kind and has scouts saving every scrap of printed material they can find.

All these and more have their devoted enthusiasts, part of the appeal being the accessibility and cheap-ness of much printed ephemera. Indeed, for today's throwaways the material is free.

◀ Religious motto chromolithograph, late 19th century (£5)

Collection of 35 British chocolate wrappers, 1950s (£100 in album)

◀ Soap bookmark (£1)

A-Z of Antiques Hunting

PRATTWARE

One of those unfortunate terms in the antiques world that has currency through long-term usage. It describes a class of lead-glazed CREAMWARE made in Staffordshire from about 1775, first probably by William Pratt, but much copied locally. Jugs and plaques, many of them commemorative, and figures were the main output, decorated in underglaze blue, green and a distinctive ochre-brown. F.&R. Pratt later made POT LIDS.

PRAXINOSCOPE

An optical toy, based on persistence of vision, invented by Emile Reynaud in 1877. It is an improved ZOETROPE, with a stationary mirrored drum in the centre of a revolving one. When the outer drum turns, figures seen in the mirrors seem to move. Elaborate versions were mounted with oil lamps.

£££

PREISS, FREDERICK (1882-1943)

A master of ART DECO sculpture, known for small figures of athletic ladies, usually striking dramatic poses, whether with golf club, javelin, or just in dance. The models were produced by Preiss-Kassler in Berlin. Most are 'chryselephantine', a combination of bronze and ivory also used by Chiparus in Paris, which was highly fashionable during the 1920s and '30s. (See FAKES.)

££££

PRESENTATION SWORDS

Swords inscribed for presentation to officers are among the most collectable of edged weapons, many dating from the 19th century. The Rolls-Royces of these are the blued and gilt bladed swords, presented by the Lloyds Patriotic Fund for acts of valour and heroism in the Napoleonic Wars—the Victoria Cross of their day. Inscriptions on antiques sometimes decrease value, but the importance of presentation swords is enhanced by their association.

££££

Gothic all-rounder

PUGIN, A.W.N. (1812-52)

The GOTHIC REVIVAL architect and designer was responsible for the furniture and fittings of the Houses of Parliament and for the Medieval Court at the 1851 Great Exhibition.

The son of a French refugee who had set up as a draughtsman and drawing master in London, at 15 he designed a set of chairs for Windsor Castle, and at the same time produced designs for the royal goldsmiths. Later he built a number of churches as well as private houses. He also designed jewellery, wallpapers, Gothic ceramics for MINTON, and church plate and stained glass for John HARDMAN, whose business he had co-founded. He made serious efforts to produce medieval furniture, rather than modern furniture with medieval ornamentation. His work is generally chunky and relatively plain, although he was more extravagant for the Houses of Parliament.

▼ Page from Pugin's book *Ornaments of the 15th and 16th Centuries* (£250-£350)

▲ Pugin-style desk, seen at the Bridlington Roadshow, 1855 (£2,500)

PRIE-DIEU

Furniture for the pious: early examples took the form of a praying desk to kneel at. In the 19th century, the Victorians came up with a prie-dieu chair, with a low seat on which to kneel facing the tall, straight back with an elbow rest on top.

£££

PRISONER OF WAR WORK

see NAPOLEONIC PoW WORK

PUNCH BOWL

Punch drinking became popular in Britain in the late 17th and 18th centuries, first as a convivial masculine activity and later in polite society. Punchbowls were made in porcelain, particularly Chinese export, delftware and silver. Glass was popular in the REGENCY period. Punch would be served using a ladle, which often had a silver bowl (possibly with a coin set into it) and an ebony, whalebone or ivory handle. Punch pots were an alternative to bowls from the mid-18th century, taking the form of very large teapots.

PUTTI

Chubby, naked little boys gambolling all over the post-Renaissance decorative arts, whether modelled, moulded or painted. Correctly, putti don't have wings, but they often find themselves mixed up with angels, who do, cherubs and seraphs, who have two, four or six wings but no bodies, and amorini, who are winged cupids.

QING

As the MING dynasty weakened, the Manchu began to establish control. They took Beijing in 1644, and their Qing dynasty ruled China until 1912. The sacking of Jingdezhen meant a distinct break with tradition and the Transitional style took over. During the reign of the Emperor Kangxi (1662-1722), it produced some of the finest Chinese porcelains ever made at the Imperial factories at Jingdezhen. Many of these were inspired by SONG dynasty pieces. Characteristic Kangxi wares include the rich ox blood or SANG DE BOEUF and the more delicate peach-bloom glazes. Blue and white wares were decorated with a radiant sapphire blue, and the FAMILLE VERTE palette and IMARI, copied from the Japanese also became established. The whole Qing period was influenced by the increased contact between East and West and the growing demands of Europe. At the very end of Kangxi's reign, the FAMILLE ROSE palette was introduced. Porcelain made after 1756, when Tang Ying, the last of the great supervisors, retired from the Imperial porcelain factory, never reached the quality of early Qing.

◀ Ivory,
japanned
longcase clock
by Daniel Quare
(£200,000)

QUADRANT

An instrument for measuring latitude by the angle of the sun above the horizon, developed *c*1750 by James Hadley in England and the Baradelle brothers in France. Although triangular, it is called a quadrant because it forms a quarter section of a circle. Originally of mahogany or ebony, from the end of the 18th century they were made of brass with silver or gold dividing scales.

£££

QUADRANT DRAWER

A drawer that is pivoted below a writing table or desk and swings outwards when opened. Often used by 18th-century cabinetmakers to hold ink and sand, it was a quarter section of a circle.

QUAICH

A shallow Scottish drinking bowl with two or, occasionally, three flat handles, made in wood, horn, silver or pewter, They were common in the 17th and 18th centuries.

£££

QUAKER CHAIR

Also known as a 'round back' chair. The origin of the description 'Quaker', which appeared in the mid-19th century, is unknown. With its open, round back, it was the commonest form of Victorian bedroom chair and is sometimes called a BALLOON BACK.

£££

QUARE, DANIEL (1648-1724)

Along with Thomas TOMPION, Quare was one of the most important English clockmakers. As a strict Quaker he was prevented from becoming clockmaker to the King but was received at court and was well connected with the nobility. He was admitted as a brother to the Clockmakers' Company in 1671, and in 1708 he was Master. He is credited with inventing the repeating watch, which repeated the hour and quarter at one push of a button, receiving a

▲ **Appliqué quilt** of the early 19th century. Shown to the experts at the Blenheim Roadshow (£600–800)

patent from James II. Quare was also important in the development of the equation clock, which had a separate dial to measure the difference between solar time, as shown by a sundial, and mean time. Previously this had been calculated by a table, often pasted inside LONGCASE CLOCKS. His output included longcase clocks, bracket clocks and watches. He also invented a portable barometer. Many fine examples of his work survive and are highly prized.

££££-££££££

QUARRY
The Old English term for a pane of glass was a Quarrell, hence the use of 'quarry' to describe a lozenge- or diamond-shaped lead-glazed pane. They were often used for the doors of bookcases in the Jacobean revival style.

QUARTERING
A decorative effect created by four sheets of veneer of similar grain, cut and laid so that the markings are symmetrically disposed.

QUARTETTO TABLE
This was a term used by SHERATON to describe a nest of four small stacking tables.

£££-£££££

QUATREFOIL
Gothic tracery in the shape of four arcs enclosed by a circle and separated by cusps. It originated in architectural stonework but is also used on furniture.

QUILT
This is a padded cover, usually made as a bedspread. A layer of wool or down is sewn between two materials with elaborately worked stitches following a geometrical or network pattern. The top surface is often decorated with an appliquéd design made from scraps of old material. Quilts were made throughout Europe from the 17th century, often as part of the marriage trousseau, and became especially popular in 19th-century America where the early settlers used up their old clothes to make elaborate PATCHWORK quilts. Many follow traditional patterns, while those of the Amish people have vibrant geometrical designs.

£££-££££

QUIMPER
A Breton FAIENCE factory which became important from the mid-18th century. The wares copy the Rouen potteries, with CHINOISERIE and ROCOCO motifs. In the 19th century the factory made good imitations of many of the 18th-century designs. Mark, from 1872 onwards, HB.

££-£££

▲ **Queen Anne** red and gilt japanned bureau-cabinet (£80,000–£100,000)

▼ **Cream and polychrome** toilet mirror (£9,000)

Simplicity was the hallmark of the time

QUEEN ANNE

The style that was in vogue during the reign of Queen Anne (1702-14) is one of much greater simplicity than the Baroque ornament of William and Mary. Queen Anne's favourite, Sarah, Duchess of Marlborough, summed up the mood by wishing to have things 'plain and clean from a piece of wainscot to a lady's face'.

In furniture ornament was at a minimum, the cabriole leg was introduced and forms became more curved and elegant. Walnut was the most popular wood, often inlaid with herringbone and cross-banding. Handles were brass, either pear-shaped or curved and attached to a solid brass back plate.

Queen Anne silver is of exceptionally high quality due to the influx of Huguenot smiths. Also under the influence of Huguenot refugees, the Spitalfields silk factories produced textiles of wonderful richness with brightly woven naturalistic flowers.

Delftware was produced in quantities in an attempt to undercut the large imports by the East India Company of Chinese and Japanese wares. It largely imitated Chinese BLUE AND WHITE decoration, although coloured examples are known. The decoration often arrived second hand, copied from Dutch DELFT, itself copying Chinese. The tulip craze had not completely died and vases to take them were made, along with tankards and POSSET POTS. In glass, the makers were building on the success of George RAVENSCROFT's lead glass and producing monumental baluster glasses that depend on simple form for their success, although some were engraved with arms or inscriptions.

Although unpretentiousness was the hallmark of the period, figured and burr veneers were used subtly and effectively, and JAPANNING in brilliant red and black with gold CHINOISERIE came into vogue. The CHEST-ON-CHEST, or tallboy, was developed at this time, and might be either DOUBLE-DOMED or have a straight cornice. Bun feet (flattened balls) were also popular. It should be noted that, with natural provincialism, American furniture historians fail to notice the demise of the Queen, and reckon the North American Queen Anne period to run from about 1725 to 1760.

▲ A huge painting of Queen Anne in her coronation robes, painted by Edmund Lilly. Size is against it — so only £4,000

▲ Blue-dash portrait charger, marking Queen Anne's coronation (£4,000-£5,500)

▶ Walnut chest of the Queen Anne period, heavily restored with later bun feet, hence low price (£3,200)

which leave parts exposed and rely on irregular shape, colour and texture for effect. The word *raku* means 'enjoyment of freedom' and the name comes from the Raku family of potters who began making the pieces in the Kyoto area early in the 16th century

▲ Ramsden punch bowl (£4,000). Ramsden & Carr tea caddy and spoon (£1,000-£1,500)

RACING TROPHIES

In 1666 Charles II began the popular custom of the monarch presenting a gold cup at Newmarket. By the 18th century horse racing was a well-established national pastime, with meetings held at organised courses. Among the most coveted trophies were the annual cups made for the races at Doncaster, Goodwood, Ascot and Richmond. Although occasionally gold cups were presented, these prestigious trophies were generally silver-gilt, decorated with a horse finial or racing scenes. They were a marvellous opportunity for silversmiths to promote themselves, none more so than RUNDELL, BRIDGE and RUNDELL, who were subsequently appointed the crown jewellers. Some of the most dramatic racing trophies, dating from the REGENCY period, are in the form of silver shields, sideboard dishes or small sculptures, the most famous being the Shield of Achilles designed by John Flaxman for the Goodwood Cup of 1833. Victorian trophies reached monstrous proportions, incorporating several figures, as firms such as GARRARD'S, Hancocks and Hunt and Roskell strove to outdo each other. They were frequently returned to the makers to be resold, or even hired out as centrepieces. The closing years of Victoria's reign

▲ Doncaster Cup, 1780s, by William Holmes, based on a design by Robert Adam (£25,000-£30,000, restorable)

saw a reaction, and a return to conventional cups based on 17th- and 18th-century designs.

RAKU

Bonfire—rather than kiln-fired—Japanese wares used extensively during the tea ceremony. They have thick black or dark-coloured glazes

RAMSDEN, OMAR (1873-1939)

An ART NOUVEAU designer of silverware, who was born and trained in Sheffield. There he met his partner Alwyn Carr, the two registering their marks jointly in 1898. They set up a workshop in London, employing a large staff of silversmiths, designers, chasers, engravers and enamellers. Carr appears to have designed, while Ramsden ran the business. Their work shows the influence of the ARTS AND CRAFTS MOVEMENT and the CELTIC REVIVAL, and is characterised by hammered surfaces, the marks not being removed by planishing (flattening on an anvil). They produced many ecclesiastical and presentation pieces. In 1919 the partnership was dissolved. Carr designed silver and ironwork on his own, while Ramsden carried on running the London workshop. After 1919, pieces are marked 'Omar me fecit'.

RATAFIA GLASS

An English 18th-century drinking glass with a long, narrow funnel bowl to hold a small quantity of a brandy-flavoured fruit cordial called ratafia.

 £££

Broadcasting all over the world

RADIOS

The practical development of wireless by Marconi and others had taken place by 1914, but it was not until 1922, when the first BBC stations started transmitting, that wireless really took off in Britain. From this point the output of wireless receivers, or radio sets as they came to be known, was prodigious, and over the next two decades more than 100 manufacturers entered the market.

The great names, Ekco, Ultra, HMV, Murphy, Philips and others, all contributed to the development of the classic British radio, achieving levels of technical excellence, sound quality and design that have ensured the lasting popularity of their products. Particularly appealing today is the way radios reflect the styles of their period, the result

of the radio being seen primarily as a piece of domestic furniture, and therefore closely linked to changing fashions in interior design.

Through the 1920s and 1930s radios expressed everything from revivalism and jazzy decor, with sunburst motifs galore, to the architectural modernism and cool elegance of ART DECO. Cases were often triumphs of applied design, with wood being the favoured material, followed by BAKELITE, whose use was pioneered by Ekco. It was the Ekco Bakelite factory in Southend-on-Sea that made the cases for most radios of the period.

The masterpieces of radio history, the circular Wells Coates designs for Ekco and the Gordon Russell range for Murphy, always fetch large sums. However, plenty of excellent valve radios of the 1930s–50s can be found for under £100 and, in good condition, will always sound far better than anything made more recently in Japan.

▲ Classic Bush Radio, 1948, valued at the Manchester Roadshow (£80)

▶ Radio speaker disguised as a figure of Confucius, made by Andia in papier mâché. German, 1930s. Seen at the Blenheim Palace Roadshow (£150–£200)

▲ The Lyric, early TV set with radio by Logie Baird and Jack Buchanan (£2,500–£5,000)

▶ Child's plate, c1920, by Heathcoate China, with the very rare subject of a crystal set (£40–£60)

Over the points, over the points

RAILWAYANA

Preserved steam lines flourish in Britain like nowhere else, a reflection of the nationwide nostalgia for the railways of the past. Some people collect actual locomotives and rolling stock but much more widespread is the popular fascination with the far more accessible relics of earlier ages of the train. An extensive literature and specialist auctions support this large market, and there are many collectors who do not wear anoraks.

The choice is very wide, ranging from the rare and expensive locomotive name plates and numbers to more widely available lamps and signalling apparatus, cast-iron and enamel signs, station seats, posters, tickets and other printed ephemera, uniforms, badges and buttons, crockery and domestic metalware, whistles and clocks, books and maps, even jigsaws and chamber pots — in fact anything that has an identifiable railway link.

Collectors prefer, and pay higher prices for, items that can be associated with the many railway companies that were operating before the formation of the big four, the SR, GWR, LMS and LNER, in 1923, but post-grouping relics are also desirable. There is less demand for more modern things from the time of British Railways, but their popularity will certainly increase in the post-privatisation era.

▶ One of a rare pair of telephones, used by railway platelayers, from c1890s until 1950 (£150-£250)

◀ Railway coach builder's tool chest, brought into the Derby Roadshow (£800-£1,000)

▼ Cab-side number plate from a North Eastern Railway locomotive (£2,500-£3,000)

◀ Name plate from a GWR locomotive, 1940s (£12,000-£13,000)

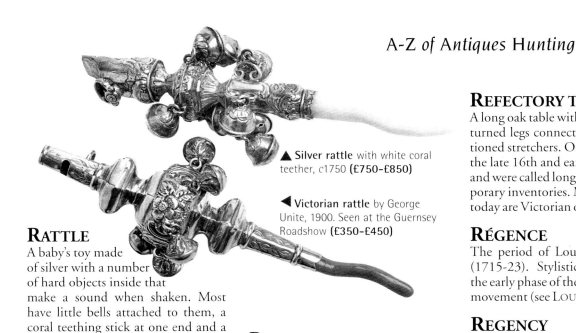

▲ **Silver rattle** with white coral teether, *c*1750 **(£750-£850)**

◀ **Victorian rattle** by George Unite, 1900. Seen at the Guernsey Roadshow **(£350-£450)**

RATTLE

A baby's toy made of silver with a number of hard objects inside that make a sound when shaken. Most have little bells attached to them, a coral teething stick at one end and a whistle at the other. Although known from Elizabethan paintings, marked examples only date from the late 17th century and have been much copied.

  £££

RAVENSCROFT, GEORGE (1618-81)

Probably the most famous English glassmaker, and the inventor of flint glass. He set up an experimental glasshouse in the Savoy, London, in 1673. Although it produced clear white glass, it was affected by crizzling (internal crazing). Encouraged by the Glass-Sellers' Company, he set up a second glasshouse at Henley-on-Thames and by 1675 had overcome crizzling by reducing the salts and adding lead oxide. His glass, marked with a raven's head, is more brilliant and heavier than Venetian, but follows Venetian and German patterns. His experiments, using only English raw ingredients, paved the way for British dominance of the 18th-century lead glass market.

R £££££

READING CHAIR

A chair with a curved yoke and wide arms, plus a lectern shelf and often candle stands attached to the back of the yoke rail. The reader could sit facing backwards and rest his elbows on the arms. They date from the 18th century and were erroneously called COCK-FIGHTING CHAIRS.

  ££££

READING STAND OR TABLE

A wooden, often mahogany, stand with a slanting top resembling a lectern. They were either designed to rest on a table or were free-standing with a tripod and an adjustable stem. In the 19th century they were also made in brass and followed a wide variety of designs.

  £££-££££

REEDING

A form of decoration which is the reverse of fluting. Derived from a classical column, it is a series of thin, parallel, convex ribs used to decorate stems, borders, furniture and legs from the late 18th century.

▲ **Mahogany reading table**, mid-Georgian, **(£4,500-£5,500)**

REFECTORY TABLE

A long oak table with four, six or eight turned legs connected by square-sectioned stretchers. Originals date from the late 16th and early 17th centuries and were called long tables in contemporary inventories. Most that are seen today are Victorian or later.

RÉGENCE

The period of Louis XV's minority (1715-23). Stylistically it describes the early phase of the French ROCOCO movement (see LOUIS).

REGENCY

The period from 1810 to 1820, when George III was largely insane and his son acted as Prince Regent. Stylistically, the term is gen-

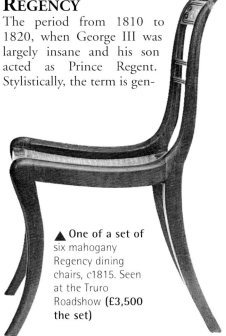

▲ **One of a set of** six mahogany Regency dining chairs, *c*1815. Seen at the Truro Roadshow **(£3,500 the set)**

erally applied to furniture which was inspired by NEO-CLASSICAL and Egyptian forms and was more flamboyant and robust than the delicate ADAM style which preceded it (see GEORGIAN).

REGULATOR

A particularly accurate clock dating from the 1720s onwards whose sole purpose is the accurate keeping of time, usually to set other timepieces by. They generally have a plain case to house the weights and pendulum.

RELIEF

A moulded or carved design which projects from the surface. Relief decoration was common in classical Greece

▶ The Sex Pistols' *God Save the Queen* in original sleeve (£800-£1,000)

GOD SAVE THE QUEEN
(Cook/Matlock/Rotten/Jones)

Original sound recording made by A & M Records Ltd.

Time: 3.10

AMS 7284
AMS 7284A*

℗1977 A & M Records Ltd.

SIDE 1
45 RPM

Copyright Control

SEX PISTOLS
Produced by Chris Thomas

Spinning into music history

RECORDS

Rock'n'roll began in 1954, with Bill Haley's single *Rock Around the Clock*, but is already a permanent fixture at the London auction houses. Copies of Elvis Presley's original Sun singles are now worth between £200 and £500, with each vinyl 7in worth two of the cumbersome old 78s.

The arrival of The Beatles in 1963 left its mark on record collecting: a mint-condition stereo copy of their 1963 debut LP, *Please, Please Me*, is now valued at £1,000 if it has a black label with gold lettering. The controversial sleeve of their 1965 American album, *Yesterday and Today* (called the 'butcher' sleeve because it depicts the group with pieces of meat and dismembered

dolls), was swiftly withdrawn, and today a mint copy can change hands for more than £1,000.

Despite never matching The Beatles' album sales, Bob Dylan had an equally swingeing impact on pop. His second album, *Freewheelin'*, is considered rock's most valuable record. A stereo version, containing four tracks deleted from later editions, was recently valued at more than £10,000. Today, even records from the late '70s Punk Rock explosion are proving collectable. Watch out for the second Sex Pistols single, *God Save the Queen*, on A&M, valued at £800 in mint condition with the original sleeve.

Many classic albums are now available on compact disc, with B sides and bonus tracks added, but collectors will accept no substitute

for the vinyl original. The exceptions to this rule are CD album samplers, which are increasingly valuable — as are authenticated, autographed record sleeves of such '60s rock icons as Brian Jones, Jimi Hendrix, Jim Morrison and John Lennon. But beware 'authentic' Beatles signatures — all four could imitate each other's hands, and so could their roadies!

◀ Two acetate discs by the High Numbers (later The Who), 1964. (£250-£300)

▲ Signed copy of the Beatles' French EP, 1964 (£1,000-£1,500)

◀ Elvis's second record. A 78rpm disc on the Sun label, 1954 (£250-£350)

▲ Beatles album *Yesterday and Today* with 'butcher' sleeve, later withdrawn (£700-£800)

▶ A selection of **78rpm** shellac discs, including (top) an early Berliner's 7-in record, dated 1901 (£10-£20)

and Rome, especially to decorate tombs and architecture. These designs provided the inspiration for NEO-CLASSICAL decoration and were much used by designers such as Robert ADAM and Josiah WEDGWOOD.

RELIQUARY
An elaborate container made to hold a fragment of the remains of a saint, generally a piece of bone or clothing, or even a splinter of wood from Christ's cross. They were usually made of silver or gold and often set with precious stones, sometimes with a rock crystal panel so the relic could be viewed. The most gruesome ones are shaped like the part of the body they contain, such as the heart, hand or even shoulder blade.

 ££££-£££££

RENT TABLE
A type of drum table, with either a polygonal or a circular top which revolves on a pedestal base. Drawers are set into the frieze marked with letters of the alphabet or days of the week, and were used for filing documents or collecting rents.

£££££

▲ Reproduction **George II** chair, 19th century. (£2,000-£3,000)

REPRODUCTION
A reproduction starts life as an honest copy of an antique design rather than as a deliberate forgery. Excellent-quality reproduction furniture and silver were made during Edward VII's

reign, which today provide a much cheaper alternative to period furniture. Problems arise when, over the years, reproductions become confused with the original object—for example, QING copies of MING dynasty porcelain can be extremely difficult to tell from the originals.

RESTORATION
The period from the restoration of Charles II to the abdication of James II. The style was much less severe than that of the Commonwealth as a result of the Dutch and French designs being brought to England by Royalists returning from exile. Walnut replaced oak, and C and S scrolls softened the rectangular forms of Commonwealth furniture. Caned seats and backs became popular and gilt gesso furniture was introduced, as well as lacquer cabinets and rich upholstered coverings such as velvet, brocade, and crewel embroidery.

RESTAURATION
The period from the restoration of the Bourbon monarchy in 1815 to the July Revolution of 1830. There was no abrupt departure from the EMPIRE style, although it became coarser and heavier (see also LOUIS).

REPOUSSÉ
Relief decoration on metalwork, especially silver, formed by hammering on the underside, so the decoration projects and the detail can be CHASED onto the surface. It is one of the most ancient metalworking techniques, and found on Greek silver, but especially popular in the 17th century and again in the 19th when earlier silver was often 'improved' with chased decoration.

REVERE, PAUL (1734-1818)
Famous for his ride, he was also one of the best American silversmiths. The son of Paul Revere the elder, a HUGUENOT émigré who settled in Boston, he made a range of silver in English domestic styles but was also an accomplished engraver. After the failure of his silversmithing business in the 1760s, he turned to engraving prints. He played an active part in

Through thick and thin

RIE, DAME LUCIE (1902-1995)

Britain's best-loved studio potter, Lucie Rie arrived in London as a refugee in 1938. In Vienna she had trained under Hoffmann at the Art School and won several prizes at the international exhibitions.

In England she came under the influence of Bernard LEACH, which had a disastrous effect on her work. His heavy-bodied, exuberant work with its thick glazes was quite alien to Rie's thin, elegant and understated output.

It was the arrival of another refugee, Hans Coper, 20 years her junior and arguably the greatest potter of the century, which gave Rie the confidence to return to her own style and philosophy. The two shared her studio in Albion Mews, London from 1946 to 1959, collaborating on a successful range of tableware in the 1950s. Much of her influence came from Japan and her bowls emulate the raku wares from the tea cermony. Vase forms could almost be metal and many of her glazes are copper or rusty iron coloured and patinated.

As she became better known, Rie was able to concentrate almost entirely on her studio pottery, the turning point in her career coming when she was given a one-woman show by the Arts Council in 1976, followed soon after by the award of an OBE. Subsequently she had exhibitions all over Europe and Japan.

Rie's output was large, but she remained true to the principle that a pot was first and foremost a vessel. She made massive, monumental dishes in stoneware with thick lava-like glazes, and at the same time bowls of extraordinary delicacy in porcelain. Decoration was minimal and usually restricted to incised lines, often resembling the gills on a mushroom. Colours were normally restrained, although a vibrant egg yellow is one of her most recognisable glazes. The surface texture was always an important part of the success of a piece and she was determinedly self-critical. In 1990 she suffered a severe stroke and sadly did not work again. Inevitably, with prices so high and such deceptively simple shapes and glazes, forgeries have appeared which can fool

▶ Rie/Coper stoneware bowl with tenmoku glaze, c1954 (£300-£400)

▼ Porcelain flared bowl with manganese glaze (£350-£450)

◀ Porcelain inlaid sgraffito bowl, turquoise with bronze glaze (£2,500-£3,000)

▲ **Porcelain bottle vase** with an amethyst glaze **(£1,500-£2,000)**

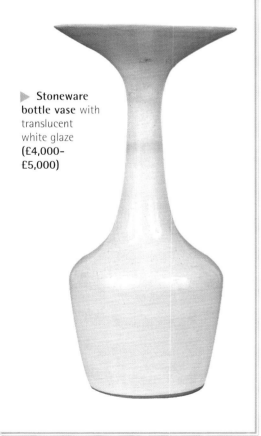

▶ **Stoneware bottle vase** with translucent white glaze **(£4,000-£5,000)**

politics, especially the American War of Independence, after which he turned to bell-founding and dealing in imported SHEFFIELD plate. His designs also changed from plain, early GEORGIAN shapes to more delicate, engraved NEO-CLASSICAL ones.

RHYTON

An ancient drinking vessel shaped like the head of an animal, a woman or, as below, a foot. Once full, it cannot be put down unless inverted so has to be drained in one go. Made in both silver and pottery it is the ancestor of 18th-century English mask jugs, TOBY jugs and fox-head STIRRUP CUPS.

£££-£££££

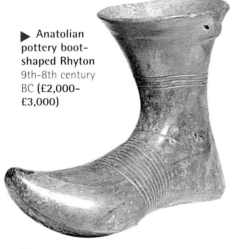

▶ **Anatolian pottery boot-shaped Rhyton** 9th-8th century BC **(£2,000-£3,000)**

RIBBON-BACK

A type of carved decoration introduced by CHIPPENDALE in his *Director*. The splats of the chair are naturalistically carved to look like interlaced ribbons tied in a bow.

RIDGWAY, JOB (1759-1813)

A Staffordshire potter who established a factory at Hanley before moving to Cauldon Place, Shelton, in 1802. He produced earthenware transfer-printed in blue, and also stoneware. The business was continued by his sons John and William, who made stone china known as

▶ **Teapot in robin's egg glaze** with silver open-work mounts, second half of 19th century **(£1,000-£1,500)**

Cauldon ware, which was exported in large quantities to the USA. Marks: J & W Ridgway, J & WR, J.W.R.

 S ★

RIESENER, JEAN HENRI (1734-1806)

A French ÉBÉNISTE who made furniture in the LOUIS XVI style, distinguished by outstanding craftsmanship, especially in the MARQUETRY and the way bronzes are applied. German by birth, he joined OEBEN's Paris workshop, becoming manager on Oeben's death. Several famous pieces, including the great *bureau du Roi*, were completed by him. He did not become a *maître* until 1768, so all his work up to that time has Oeben's stamp. In 1774 he was appointed *ébéniste* to Louis XVI and supplied spectacular furniture for Versailles. He also made MOTHER-OF-PEARL encrusted furniture for Marie-Antoinette, before abandoning ROCOCO curves and flourishes for straighter lines and more solid proportions.

RINGFLASCHE

A German bottle or jug with a ring-shaped body decorated with elaborate applied ornament. They were made of stoneware in the Rhenish potteries from the 16th century onwards.

££-£££££

ROBIN'S EGG GLAZE

A speckled, opaque, turquoise or purplish blue glaze, developed in the early 18th century at the imperial kilns of Jingdezhen. An all-over turquoise glaze is applied first and cobalt blue or iron red is then blown through gauze on to it.

One giant step for toys

ROBOTS

Japanese robots have made their mark on the toy market. The first were clockwork, tinplate models, such as the 7in- high 'Robot Lilliput', dating from the 1930s, but during the 1950s and '60s friction motors, batteries and radio controls took over from clockwork, and plastic from tinplate. The launch of the first Sputnik in 1958 was a giant imaginative step for toy-makers, and robots of all sorts proliferated. As well as the achievements of real scientists and spacemen, films such as the *Star Wars* series have left their mark.

Most robots were made in large numbers and exported widely. Generally they have survived in large numbers too and their value is limited, particularly if they suffered wear and tear in the hands of their original owners. International collectors seek the rare examples in mint condition and in their original boxes. Such robots can now command prices well in excess of £1,000.

▲ **Battery-powered** Japanese robot with original box. Seen at the Guernsey Roadshow (£120–£180)

◀ **Japanese clockwork robot,** based on Robbie from the film *The Forbidden Planet,* with box. Price depends on condition (£1,500–£2,500)

▲ One of a pair of Robinson &
Leadbeater figures, 1890s. Brought
into the Bexhill Roadshow
(£300-£400

ROBINSON & LEADBEATER

Makers of PARIAN who, unlike
MINTON, SPODE and others, often
coloured their figures and groups.
The factory was in production at
Stoke-on-Trent from 1864 to 1924.
The mark is R&L in a stamped oval.

ROCK CRYSTAL

A transparent, colourless quartz
which occurs naturally in many parts
of the world. It was especially popular in the Middle Ages and early
Renaissance, and from earliest times it
was carved into decorative objects,
incorporated into jewellery and caskets or mounted in silver gilt and
used for drinking vessels and salts. It
returned to popularity during the
19th-century GOTHIC REVIVAL.

ROCKING CHAIR

Although cradles on rockers, or
'bends', were used from the Middle
Ages, it did not occur to anyone
to make a rocking chair until the
mid-18th century. Legend credits
Benjamin Franklin with the invention
in about 1760, but the chairs may
already have existed in Lancashire.
The earliest were WINDSOR or LAD-
DER-BACKED types. In America the
Boston rocker, with a curved seat
dipped from back to front and a
high back with ornamental head
rest, developed from the Windsor
type. From the mid-19th century
BENTWOOD chairs with cane seats
became very popular in both Britain
and America.

▼ Wooden rocking horse,
carved and painted, with
remains of saddle and brass
harness studs. Mid-19th
century (£1,500-£2,000)

ROCKING HORSE

One of the oldest known rocking
horses is a solid-rocker example which
probably belonged to the future
Charles I in about 1610. However,
most antique survivors are 19th-
century or Edwardian. The best,
with finely carved and painted faces,
were made in Germany, which had
dominated the wooden toy market.
Swinging horses on frames were
less likely to throw riders than true
rockers. Leading makers include
W. Graeffer and Erste Schweizerische
Spielwarenfabrik. Their popularity
has never declined and they are still
made to traditional designs .

£££-££££

ROCKINGHAM

A pottery established in about 1745
on the estate of the Marquis of
Rockingham at Swinton, Yorkshire,
producing brown earthenware and
creamware. In 1785 it amalgamated
with the LEEDS pottery and began
making similar wares. From 1806
John and William Brameld acquired
the factory and developed the choco-
late-brown manganese 'Rockingham

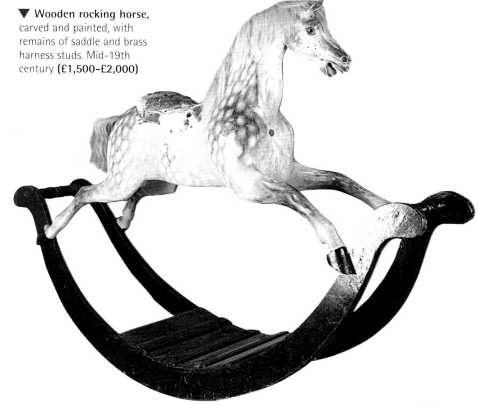

Time to lighten up a little

ROCOCO

A style that originated in France in the early 18th century and spread throughout Europe, reaching its English peak in 1735-55. The term is a combination of *rocaille* (rockwork) and *coquillage* (shellwork). Along with rocks and shells water movement dominates. It is a decorative, light, curvilinear style based on asymmetrical curves and 'S' and 'C' scrolls and leaf motifs, with later examples often incorporating CHINOISERIE and floral motifs.

It is the asymmetric development from the heavy, formal BAROQUE style of Louis XIV, ushering in a lighter, more intimate mood, which broke all the accepted rules of reason and restraint in decoration. Engraved ornament by designers such as Oppenordt, Meissonier, Pineau and Pillement was enormously influential.

It was particularly suited to interior decoration, wall panelling, plasterwork ceilings and chimney-pieces, some of the most extravagant schemes being executed in Austria and Germany.

Silver and porcelain are two of the greatest expressions of the Rococo, since they could fully assert it both as a three-dimensional, asymmetric shape and with details, whereas architecture and furniture had to retain a formal shape and relied mostly on Rococo decorative detail. Silver is its perfect medium, with the Huguenot craftsmen Paul DE LAMERIE, Nicholas Sprimont and Paul Crespin producing dramatic, curving, sculptural forms.

The newly discovered HARD-PASTE porcelain was also a good medium, with MEISSEN, FRANKENTHAL and NYMPHENBURG producing delicately painted services, and figures echoed in SOFT-PASTE at CHELSEA and SÈVRES.

Rococo furniture is characterised by deep carving, but on mirrors and girandoles it was possible to produce frames of great lightness and delicacy. Thomas CHIPPENDALE, Matthias LOCK, Thomas Johnson and John LINNELL all produced Rococo furniture designs.

▲ One of a pair of **Rococo** giltwood mirrors (£38,000 the pair)

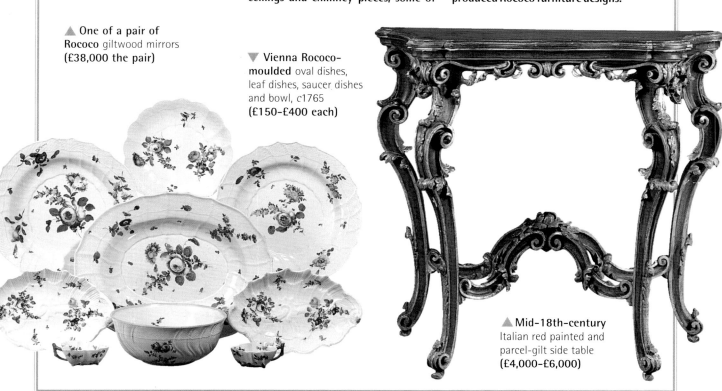

▼ **Vienna Rococo-moulded** oval dishes, leaf dishes, saucer dishes and bowl, c1765 (£150-£400 each)

▲ Mid-18th-century Italian red painted and parcel-gilt side table (£4,000-£6,000)

glaze'. A speciality was the Chinese-inspired Cadogan teapot, filled through the bottom. Porcelain was made from 1826 until 1842. Wares were decorated in a rich ROCOCO revival style with elaborate floral designs. Tea services would have only one saucer marked, otherwise there are various combinations of Rockingham, Brameld and a griffin. Pattern numbers reached only 2000. Forgeries by SAMSON of Paris are known.

 ££-££££

RODNEY OR SHIP'S DECANTER
A conical decanter with a shallow base for use at sea. It was named after Admiral Rodney and dates from after his 1780 victory at Cape St Vincent.

£££

ROENTGEN, DAVID (1743-1807)
The greatest 18th-century furniture-maker, Roentgen was the son of a Saxon cabinetmaker. His workshop was near Koblenz, but he had depots in Paris, Berlin and Vienna. French cabinetmakers, piqued by his success, forced him to join the Paris Guild. He supplied furniture to Louis XVI; sold Catherine the Great a quantity of items, and was appointed court furnisher to Frederick William II in Berlin. His furniture stands out from that of French contemporaries for its Germanic heaviness and architectural proportions, as well as *trompe l'oeil* MARQUETRY and elaborate clockwork mechanisms that make secret doors open at the touch of a button.

ROMAN POTTERY
Roman ceramics were made from the 1st century BC to the 4th century AD, but in no way rival the art of the Greek potters. The most common form is *terra sigillata*, also known as Samian ware, made throughout the Empire but especially in the Arentine potteries. Decorated with a red gloss slip, with trailed slip or incised ornament, it provided a cheap alternative to metal. It was imitated by WEDGWOOD and others in the 18th century. By the

▲ **Roman pot,** 2nd century AD. Seen at the Taunton Roadshow. No commercial value because of damage

middle of the 1st century AD, lead-glazing was introduced and vessels with a greenish-yellow glaze were produced. In the eastern provinces a glassy turquoise glaze was popular.

£££

ROMAYNE HEAD
A carved profile head in a medallion, often decorated with scrollwork and foliage. It originated in the Italian Renaissance and was introduced in the early 16th century to England, where it often appears on church furniture and panelling. On London buildings female romayne heads indicate ownership by the Mercers' Company.

ROSENTHAL
A flourishing porcelain factory founded in Bavaria in 1879 and still run by the Rosenthal family. It is well known for simplified ART NOUVEAU services and contemporary figures such as bathing belles, made in the early 20th century. It also made traditional products based on 18th-century patterns. Since the 1950s it has been one of the most innovative producers of ceramics.

££-£££

ROSEWOOD
A dark brown wood marked with very dark stripes and grown in Brazil, India

and the East Indies. When worked, it has a fragrant smell. It was almost as popular as mahogany during the early Victorian period. It fades in sunlight.

ROUNDABOUT CHAIRS
With a circular seat, a semi-circular back and six legs, these were made in the East Indies during the 17th and 18th centuries and are sometimes called 'burgomaster' chairs.

£££-££££

RUBY GLASS
A rich red glass made by the addition of gold chloride to the frit (the glass-forming mixture), invented by J. Kunckel and first produced in 1679.

RUDD TABLE
First illustrated in HEPPLEWHITE's *Guide* of 1788, it was described as 'the most complete dressing-table ever made, possessing every convenience which can be wanted'. It is named after a notorious courtesan and forger, Margaret Caroline Rudd. An elaborately fitted toilet table, it has mirrors at all sorts of angles and a plethora of drawers of all shapes and sizes.

R £££££

RUMMER
A large, short-stemmed drinking glass popular from about 1770 to 1850. The early ones have funnel-shaped, then ovoid, bowls, which gradually become much thicker and straight-sided in a

▲ **Lemon squeezer rummers,** left 1790 and right c1810 **(£120 each)**

bucket shape. The stem is thick, often with a knop, and the base either round, or square with the characteristic 'lemon squeezer' shape. The latter was copied in the 1920s, but examples tend to look flatter and whiter. 'Pub' rummers are heavier and more rounded.

RURAL OR RUSTIC FURNITURE
Furniture carved in a naturalistic way to look like the trunks and branches of a tree. It was first made in the mid-18th century as part of the 'cottage' style and was soon adopted as an accepted form for garden furniture. In the Victorian period it was made in cast iron, too, by firms such as COALBROOKDALE. The term also applies to simple, country-made furniture such as trestle tables, rush-seated chairs, stools, dressers and cupboards which were made from native woods often by local estate carpenters for use in cottages and the kitchens and servants' quarters of large houses. The many regional variations of WINDSOR and LADDER-BACK chairs are also described as rural furniture.

RUSSIAN PORCELAIN
The Imperial porcelain factory was founded in St Petersburg in 1744. After 1800 it concentrated on NEO-CLASSICAL works and employed artists from leading European factories such as SÈVRES and BERLIN. Elegant shapes, imitating Greek, Roman and Egyptian forms, were a speciality. Its outstanding achievement was the 1,000-piece service

Shy experimenter

RUSKIN POTTERY

Taking its name from the famous Victorian writer and critic, John Ruskin, the Ruskin Pottery was the creation of William Howson Taylor and his father Edward, an art teacher and painter who died in 1912. It was founded in West Smethwick, near Birmingham, in 1898 and its products reflected the Taylors' great interest in experimental and Orientally inspired glaze effects. By about 1910 the complex, high-temperature, reduction-fired FLAMBÉ process had been mastered and, from then on, helped by critical acclaim and awards at exhibitions, William Howson Taylor was widely regarded as one of the master potters of the modern world. By dedication and single-mindedness he built on his reputation during the 1920s, and he kept Ruskin and its small, skilled staff going until 1933, adapting the style to suit public taste.

When he closed the pottery, Taylor was already a sick man. He died a couple of years later, but not before he had destroyed all his notes and the records of more than 30 years of achievement. As a result, this man, who created some of the most spectacular and technically brilliant pottery to have been made this century, remains a shadowy figure. The surviving wares are the only witness to his genius.

▶ Ruskin stoneware vase with minor restoration (£350–£450)

◀ High-fired stoneware bowl and cover (£800–£1,200)

▶ Stoneware vase with cylindrical neck and flared rim (with hairline crack), 1908 (£1,200)

▲ **Russian plates,** possibly made for the Royal Yacht, with the monograms of Tsars Nicholas II and Alexander III (shown below) **(£3,000)**

created for Count Guryev. The factory flourished under Nicholas I, who commissioned several services and large presentation pieces. Products moved away from the EMPIRE style to neo-ROCOCO, influenced by Sèvres, MEISSEN and Oriental porcelain, as well as figurative groups in BISCUIT. Several private factories also flourished in the mid-18th century, notably that established by Francis Gardner at Verbilki, north of Moscow. After the Revolution the Imperial factory was taken over by the state and produced some important porcelain designed by the Russian Suprematist artists.

surface. It is used only with stoneware, and some potters—notably WEDGWOOD—abandoned it because it can be dangerous. It was first used in the Rhineland from the 12th century, and in England by DWIGHT in the late 17th. It was popular later with potters such as the MARTIN brothers.

SALTS

Being above or below the salt had great social significance from the medieval period through to the mid-17th century. There were three types of salt in use—primary salts, secondary salts and salt cellars. Primary salts could be massive, the largest surviving British example being the Rogers Salt, at 22in high. They were placed on the principal table between the host and the most important guest. People sitting at other tables were 'below the [primary] salt'. The social importance of the salt explains the elaborate forms to be found: ships, castles and monkeys survive, and we know others such as morris dancers and mermaids from inventories. With the development of more intimate family meals, the importance of the salt had declined by the late 17th century. The salt cellar remained independent from peppers and mustards until the second half of the 18th century when the condiment set developed. Up to the end of the 17th century salt was taken with a knife. Salt shovels then took over and were in turn replaced by salt spoons in the mid-18th century. Glass liners are comparatively recent, resulting from the popularity of pierced work in the mid-18th century. Today they are assumed by many to be an essential part of a salt, which they are not unless the salt is pierced. Always empty and wash your salts after use—never leave salt in them.

££-£££

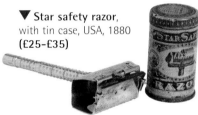

▼ **Star safety razor,**
with tin case, USA, 1880
(£25-£35)

SAFETY RAZOR

Until the late 19th century cut-throat razors were the norm. In Britain they were usually made by Kropp or Wilkinson. The first successful safety razor was the Star, patented by Kampfe Bros of New York in 1880. Competitors included Eastman & Krauss' Home Safety Razor (1891) and Hovendon's Midget (1893) and Wilkinson's Roller Safety Shaver (1904) in Britain. These had chunky wedge-shaped blades. Gillette's thin throw-away blade was perfected in 1903. In 1927 the Rolls Razor, with strops built into the case, was patented, and in 1931 the Schick Electric Razor was invented.

£-££

ST CLOUD

At least one FAIENCE factory was active at St Cloud from the 1660s, supplying the hospital and servants' quarters at Versailles. SOFT-PASTE porcelain was made from 1693, and from 1722 to 1742 there was a sub-sidiary factory in Paris. Products are well modelled and have a warmer, less shiny glaze than MENNECY. All sorts of pots were made, as well as jugs in the forms of men and birds, knife handles and snuff-boxes. Gilt was rarely used. After about 1730 the factory was influenced by MEISSEN, but from *c*1750 standards declined and the concern closed in 1766.

£££-££££

ST LOUIS

One of the the three major French paperweight factories along with BACCARAT and CLICHY. It was founded in 1767 in Lorraine and made flower, fruit and MILLEFIORE paperweights, some with dates between 1845 and 1849.

£££-££££

SALT GLAZE

A glaze which is produced by throwing common salt into a kiln at certain temperatures. This vaporises to a soda which blends with the clay giving a typical, pitted-orange

▶ **Pair of salts** by
Robert Hennell, 1778,
(£350-£550)

SAMPLER

Embroidered panels, dating from the 17th to the 19th centuries, originally worked in a variety of stitches to demonstrate the skill of the needle-woman or, more likely, needlegirl. This led to the creation of charming pictures incorporating pious mottoes, the alphabet, numbers, and animals, birds, buildings or anything else that appealed to the minds of 12-year-olds. One specific stitch became known as the sampler stitch. Samplers were done on a tough linen ground, and bear the maker's name, age, and the date (which was often unpicked later to keep the age secret).

£££

▼ Sampler map of Europe embroidered in 1795 by Jane Young, aged 10. Brought into the Huddersfield Roadshow (£150)

▲ Two sections of a sampler worked in 1663, seen at the Blenheim Palace Roadshow (£2,000)

SANG DE BOEUF

A deep plum-red glaze used in China from the Kangxi period, and imitated in Europe from the 19th century. It looks like coagulated ox blood, and is made from copper.

SARREGUEMINES POTTERY

A large factory in Lorraine, founded in about 1770 by Paul Utzschneider, which continued under his descendants until the late 19th century. By 1867 it was said to be the largest French factory of industrial ceramics, with 2,000 employees. It began by making cream-coloured earthenware and stoneware in the Wedgwood style and in 1794 acquired the models and materials of the Ottweiler pottery and porcelain factory. In the 19th century it produced tablewares with printed landscapes and was well known for its faience. Marks: Sarguemines or Sarguemine, U C or U & Cie.

££-£££

SATINWOOD

There are two varieties: East and West Indian. Both are rich golden-yellow with beautiful figuring. It was especially popular for furniture in the later 18th century. Many of SHERATON's designs were intended to be made in satinwood.

▲ Dancing shepherdess after 18th-century Meissen, but made in the second half of the 20th century, with detail of the mark, below (£200-£220)

From small fibs to blatant forgery

SAMSON OF PARIS

The biggest liers, it is said, begin with the smallest fibs. The most remarkable of all pottery and porcelain copyists — not to say forgers — began in the 1830s by innocently replacing broken items from services, garnitures and pairs. Edmé Samson set up his company in 1845, and it continued under Emile Samson and others until the late 1970s.

The range of Samson's activity was immense. Almost all the great 18th-century factories of France, Germany, and England were copied, and so too were MAIOLICA and FAIENCE, Bernard PALISSY plates, PERSIAN and HISPANO-MORESQUE dishes. Apart from MEISSEN figures (with a 'crossed cross' rather than exactly the crossed swords), SÈVRES wares and DERBY pieces — which often have CHELSEA marks — and

▲ Another identifying mark of Samson

Chelsea rabbit tureens, the most commonly met-with Samson copies are 18th century Chinese FAMILLE ROSE and VERTE export wares.

These are often painted, rather crudely, with phony coats of arms. With experience and the opportunity to compare true and false, a number of Samson characteristics become apparent. There is often a blueish, rather than the correct greyish, tinge to the glazes, which are applied to a shiny white LIMOGES-type body. The LAMBREQUIN or spearhead gilt borders, outlined in red, seldom vary, and are often crude compared to Chinese work. In the Oriental field Samson also produced large fish bowls and IMARI wares.

All Samson's English copies are in a hard, rather than the correct soft paste body. European groups and Chinese figures were sometimes taken from moulds, and are therefore smaller than the originals due to shrinkage. It is interesting to examine the pseudo-soft paste used for Samson CHANTILLY under an ultra-violet light. Instead of the expected pinky violet, it appears bright yellow. An irony is that not everything that is nowadays called Samson was actually made by them. Some 'Samson' is actually Herend, from Hungary. And Samson is now collectable, particularly in France.

▲ **Samson vase** inspired by 18th-century Chinese famille rose, c1890 (**£800–£1,200**)

A mass of minute details

SATSUMA

This class of decorative, high-fired earthenware is named after a region of south-western Japan. Quite how far back its origins can be traced is debatable. Some pots bear dates of the late 18th or early 19th century, but these may be spurious. Our knowledge of JAPANESE CERAMICS has a gap from the early 18th until the mid-19th century, but from the 1860s fine-grained, straw-coloured, crackle-glazed, high-fired earthenware (erroneously classed by some authorities as porcelain) began to flow to the West. By the early 20th century this had become a flood. Confusingly many were not made at Satsuma but at Kyoto.

Nobody denies that we have a mass of brilliantly enamelled and gilt vases, figures, bowls, koro (incense burners) and dishes, some of which are among the most minutely detailed ceramics ever produced. There is a huge number of decorators whose names survive only on their pots, but three of outstanding quality are Yabu Meizan, Kinkozan Sobei and Ryozan. Pots by this trio will make from the upper hundreds of pounds to several thousands.

Less well-decorated pieces can change hands for a few hundreds, and it is possible to buy a poor-quality vase for £10 or so. The best pieces have to be in good condition — collectors are fussy and there is still enough available for them to pick and choose.

Subjects depicted range from figures, including warriors and women and children, to birds, flowers and festivals, all giving a glimpse of Japanese life. One group, apparently dating from the third quarter of the 19th century is known as 'brocade Satsuma'. These dramatic vases, ewers and bowls can make several thousands of pounds. The Satsuma and Kyoto kilns also produced figures, although these are far less common than the wares.

◀Very high quality **Satsuma dish** made in Kyoto, c1900. Seen at the Blenheim Roadshow (**£2,000**)

▶ Two satsuma **pieces** shown to experts at the Bexhill Roadshow both c1900. The vase was valued at **£3,000-£4,000**: the dish (left) at **£4,000-£6,000**

SATYR

A mythological creature with goat-like hairy legs and tail, a man's torso and bearded face, and horns. Satyrs attended Bacchus, were spirits of fertility, and often represent untamed nature, licentiousness and lust. They appear on marriage chests and wine coolers and were popular as furniture mounts in the 18th century.

SAVONAROLA CHAIR

Also known as an X-CHAIR, this is a medieval style of chair with an X-shaped frame. It was used in various forms, particularly in 15th-century Italy (when perhaps the firebrand preacher Savonarola had one), was revived in England by Sheraton, and made in metal in the 19th century.

£££

SAVONNERIE CARPETS

The Savonnerie factory produced the finest carpets in Europe under the patronage of the French kings. Founded in Paris in 1627 in an old soap works, hence its name, it originally made carpets for royal use. Techniques derived from Oriental practice, with a close, Turkish-knotted pile of wool or silk on hemp warp and weft. The finest were woven with 90 knots to the square inch, and it took a skilled craftsman a year to make three square metres of plain carpet. The factory's finest work was during the reign of Louis XIV when, like the GOBELINS factory it was reorganised with LE BRUN as director. Nearly 100 magnificent carpets were woven for the Louvre. The richly patterned formal carpets of Louis XIV gave way to lighter ROCOCO patterns from the early 18th century. Under Napoleon many fine carpets were produced in the EMPIRE style. In 1825 the firm was amalgamated with the state-owned Gobelins.

£££££+

Using the pen as a sword

SATIRICAL CARICATURES

Colourful, witty and fun, political caricatures of the early 19th century provide a unique insight into the politics, religion and social attitudes of the time.

The caricaturists played upon every physical aspect of their subjects. Napoleon Bonaparte was a gift to them. They exploited his small stature and huge ambitions, portraying him as a dwarf, posing as a colossus. They glorified in the victories of Nelson and Wellington, yet when both men transgressed (Nelson with Lady Hamilton and Wellington with the emancipation of the Irish Catholics), they were quite brutal. Lady Hamilton is shown as fat and ugly, while Wellington is seen kissing the feet of the Pope.

Originally printed in black and white, many of these caricatures were coloured at the time, with many more done during the late Victorian era. Contemporary colourings attract the highest value. Rare examples by James Gillray for example, now fetch around £600. An average price from a specialist dealer, would be £60 to £70.

The caricaturist of the early 19th century was both an artist and a journalist, in much the same way as a newspaper cartoonist of today – although more influential. When most people could not read, they provided an insight into contemporary life.

An illustration of the caricaturist's power is provided by the instance of George IV as Prince Regent trying to bribe one of them with 100 guineas to stop portraying him as a drunkard and a lecher. The man took the money and thereafter portrayed the Prince as 'the former drunkard and lecher'.

▲ The caricature titled *Public Opinion* by Cruikshank, published in 1820, is a lampoon on the failed marriage of George IV and Caroline of Brunswick (£30-£50)

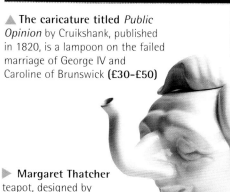

▶ Margaret Thatcher teapot, designed by *Spitting Image* artists, 1980s (£150-£200)

◀ Punch annual from 1867: odd volumes are worth upwards of £5

SAXTON, CHRISTOPHER (c1542-1606)

An English map-maker, he surveyed the country in the 1570s, and had county maps engraved and published. In 1579 they were issued together as an atlas. His maps were popular and much reprinted until they were superseded by those of John SPEED in the early 17th century.

£££

SCAGLIOLA

A material used since Roman times to imitate marble and PIETRA DURA. Marble dust, isinglass (animal gelatine) and colorants are applied to a GESSO ground, fixed under heat and highly polished. It was used mainly for architectural features and table tops.

SCENT BOTTLES

Made from Roman times in glass imitating agate and other stones. Clear glass bottles of the 15th and 16th centuries were simple forms decorated with beads or trails of glass. Milk glass was used in Germany, often decorated with figurative designs. Barrel-shaped bottles were produced in France, and opaque-white and blue glass bottles at Bristol. During the 18th century porcelain scent bottles in ingenious, often naturalistic forms were made throughout Europe—

▶ Scent bottles from a collection seen at the Taunton Roadshow

one notable maker in England was CHELSEA. Many enamel bottles were made by Battersea, Birmingham and the other Midland factories. They were decorated like snuffboxes, but designed for women rather than men. Two-ended bottles in coloured glass were popular 19th-century products.

££-££££

SCHOFIELD, JOHN (active 1776-94)

A fine English silversmith, never admitted to the Goldsmiths' Company. He registered a joint mark with Robert Jones in 1776 and his own mark separately two years later. He worked mainly in the NEO-CLASSICAL Adam style, specialising in candlesticks and candelabra.

◄ **Three pairs of steel scissors** brought into the Bexhill Roadshow, early 19th century **(£10-£20 each)**

SCISSORS

Invented by the ancient Egyptians, and more immediately descended from medieval weavers' shears. Silver-handled scissors with steel blades exist from the 17th century, although examples from before the late 18th are rare. The widest variety was made in the 19th century, often with decorative handles. Scissors were made of silver and silver gilt as well as steel, and tortoiseshell, ivory and mother-of-pearl might also be used in the handles. Some were made in the form of a stork, others could fold so the blades were concealed.

 £-££

SCONCE

A wall light with a candlestick attached to a reflecting back plate. Made from wood, brass, pewter, ORMOLU or silver, the back plate is often embossed with decoration or a coat of arms. From the late 17th century the back plate was sometimes a mirror. Elaborate ROCOCO examples were known as GIRANDOLES.

£££-£££££

▲ **One of a set of four** Edwardian silver wall sconces, 1901 **(£9,000 the set)**

Something to cash in on

SCOTTISH SILVER

Silver has been produced in Scotland for many centuries, but very little survives from before the late 17th century. Simplicity of form with little or no decoration is an important characteristic of most truly Scottish silver. This was a direct result of the economic situation: silver was treated very much as a 'cash' reserve, and as necessity dictated it could readily be turned into coin. It was therefore an advantage to have the bulk of the value tied up in the silver itself rather than in excessive decoration.

Some distinctly Scottish objects are to be found. The QUAICH, originally a shallow wooden drinking bowl, usually with two handles, was being made in silver from the 17th century onwards. THISTLE CUPS, which mostly date from the late 17th/early 18th century, owe their shape to the bold calix of strap work usually to be found applied to their lower body. Disc-end spoons from the 16th and 17th centuries are particularly important, their design being well ahead of anything that was being produced in England.

The 18th century saw the development of distinctly Scottish bullet teapots (a spherical shape), milk boats (looking rather like shallow sauce-boats) and extraordinary and rare oviform coffee pots (with serpentine handles, a spout with a tap, and standing on three legs). As the 19th century progressed and a tourist industry developed, much silver was made with Scottish decoration such as thistles, tartans and hunting pursuits. These pieces supplied a market but, although made in Scotland, can hardly be regarded as representative of true Scottish silver.

The first reference to a Scottish requirement for marking is in 1485. The earliest EDINBURGH marks known to have survived are from the mid-16th century. Edinburgh HALLMARKS up to

SCREENS AND SCRAPWORK

Movable screens to cut down on draughts have been used in Britain since the Middle Ages. 'A great folding skrene of seaven foulds, wth a skreene-cloth upon it, of green kersey' is recorded at Hengrave Hall, Suffolk, in 1603. However, it was really after the Restoration that screens became popular and elaborate, being covered with velvet, leather, needlework or Oriental lacquer. Either rigid or folding, traditional Chinese court screens can be vast. Lacquer screens imported during the 18th century and their British imitators may be well over 6ft high, and have six or seven panels. In the later 18th century, prints were often stuck to screens, with painted mounts and frames round them. During the 19th century, and the Victorian period in particular, this

▲ **Dressing screen** decorated with 18th-century mezzotints, 1840 **(£600-£800)**

the early 18th century can be confusing. The town mark — a castle — is straightforward. But the maker and the deacon (later on, the assay master) would each put their own marks on a piece, and sorting out what seem to be two makers' marks can be a problem.

Scottish provincial marks are particularly important for collectors. Outside the major centres such as Aberdeen, Glasgow and Inverness were the more unusual and rare places such as Arbroath, Cupar, Forres, Peterhead, Tain and Wick, whose marks were usually the most sought after. The vast majority of Scottish provincial pieces to be found are spoons (particularly teaspoons of the late 18th and early 19th centuries).

▼ **Inverness quaich,** late 18th century **(£1,500-£2,000)**

▼ **Scottish silver sugar bowl and cover,** (left) Glasgow, 1776 **(£700-£1,000).** George III Scottish silver milk boat with mythical fish handle, (right) Edinburgh, 1751 **(£500-£800)**

SCROLL

Based on a C curve, the scroll is fundamental to Graeco-Roman classicism. It appears throughout the history of European and Oriental decoration, in Celtic and Viking work, as a basic element in BAROQUE and ROCOCO styles and in a more restrained manner during the ADAM and CLASSICAL REVIVAL periods, and in eclectic Victorian ornament. Variations include scrolling foliage with rich, looping tendrils, S-shaped scrolls to adorn door pediments and bookcases, and scroll moulding— which resembles a loosely rolled piece of paper— used for edging furniture.

SEALS

Engraved seals for making impressions in wax have been a symbol of authority since ancient times. Not only did they ensure the authenticity of a document but a sealed letter or casket could not be opened without the receiver's knowledge. In the 17th century both literacy and correspondence increased greatly, and the introduction of Spanish sealing wax, a hard but easily melted material, made the owning of small private seals extremely popular. From the mid-17th century the seal developed into a fashionable piece of jewellery. Fob seals or signets were displayed on a CHATELAINE or fob chain. They were generally made of chased and embossed gold with the matrix of hardstone, steel or glass. Cheaper versions were made of PINCHBECK, tin or coloured glass in a metal mount. In the 19th century they were replaced by larger desk seals, the matrix being set in a heavy, ornamented handle, often in the shape of an animal or human head, shell or flower. Those put to professional use were plain and practical, but examples decorated with mother-of-pearl, ivory, lapis lazuli and obsidian were made for ladies. Two 19th-century inventions were the rotary seal with several different matrixes and the pipe-stopper desk seal which had the alternative function of tamping pipe tobacco.

fashion developed into more exuberant scrapwork, with printed images cut out and arranged in decorative patterns—on boxes and trays as well as screens—and then varnished. The proliferation of cheap printed images on packaging, cards and magazines made it a popular pastime in nurseries and drawing rooms.

🚢 🔧 🏰 **£££-££££££**

SCREWS

Hand-filed, tapered metal screws with slotted heads were used on furniture from the late 17th century, for example in the attachment of hinges. Lathe-made screws, which have a more regular appearance, were used from about 1760, again for hinges, and for securing table tops. Machine-made screws were in general use by the mid-19th century.

▲ **Large scrimshaw whale's tooth,** mid-19th century, 9½in long **(£2,000-£2,500)**

SCRIMSHAW

Designs scratched on bone, ivory—particularly walrus tusks—and whale teeth, shells or wood, by sailors to while away the time on long voyages. It was particularly popular on American vessels and is eagerly collected in the States, particularly after President Kennedy was photographed with pieces on his Oval Office desk. However, wildlife protection acts have restricted international trade.

🚢 **£££-££££**

🚢 🔧 ⚖️ 🏰 **£££-££££**

SECOND EMPIRE

The period covered by the reign of Napoleon III, who became French president in 1848 and emperor in 1852, abdicating in 1870. As a style it could not be more different from the EMPIRE of Napoleon. The Empress Eugénie, who was far more involved with patronage of the arts than her husband was, identified with Marie-Antoinette and therefore revived the Louis XVI style. The period is marked by its lack of originality and its vulgar and ostentatious adaptation of earlier styles. Reproduction furniture with over-elaborate mounts and marquetry in the Louis XIV, XV and XVI styles was made by BARBEDIENNE, Beurdeley and Grohé, while Christofle turned out similar reproductions in bronze and table silver, generally electroplated. Elaborate wallpapers were printed in imitation of Louis XVI *boiseries* and objects were also made in GOTHIC, Renaissance and BAROQUE revival styles. The deep-upholstered chairs and sofas with their curves, fringes and tassels are the period's most original innovation.

▲ Second Empire ormolu-mounted side table, mid-19th century (£14,000)

SECRETAIRE

Also known as an escritoire, this was originally a French term for various types of writing desk fitted with elaborate interiors, often containing drawers in which papers could be kept secret. Secretaires date from the 18th century and take a variety of forms, including fall front or *secrétaire en pente*, cylinder, roll top and *secrétaire à abattant*, which resembles an English secretaire. The English form stands against the wall, often incorporating a bookcase, and has a cabinet with a fall

'SERPENTINE'

Serpentine-fronted pieces of furniture are typical of the mid-18th century. The undulating line, with convex centre and concave sides is reminiscent of the 'line of beauty' which Hogarth advocates in painting. It is best suited to pieces like chests of drawers.

front, which pulls out to provide the writing surface, and closes vertically.

 £££££-£££££

SEDAN CHAIR

A portable seat enclosed in a box-like structure with poles at either end so two men could carry it. Sedan chairs were used to convey the nobility down narrow, crowded and dirty streets. They originated in Italy in the 16th century and remained in use until about 1800. They were generally made of painted and gilt wood with upholstered interiors and many examples are elaborately decorated with CHINOISERIE scenes, lacquer panels and brass mounts.

£££££-£££££

SEDDON, GEORGE (1727-1801)

An English cabinetmaker and the founder of the flourishing family business Seddon and Sons, which continued until the mid-19th century. Born in Lancashire, he was apprenticed in London in 1743 and by 1760 had set up his own cabinetmaking

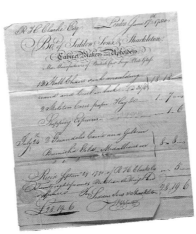

▲ A bill from Seddon, Sons and Shackleton, dated 1790

workshop. By the 1780s he was employing several hundred craftsmen and carrying a huge stock and range of furniture. He took his sons George and Thomas into the business, as well as his son-in-law Thomas Shackleton. Despite its huge output, very little furniture by the company is known. In the 19th century it provided furniture for Somerset House, London, and Windsor Castle, as well as making Gothic pieces to designs by William BURGES and John Pollard Seddon.

SET OF CHAIRS

Chairs for dining were made in sets from the 17th century onwards, and comprised at least six chairs with an arm chair for the host. In the 18th and 19th centuries, much larger or 'longer' sets were made, sometimes with more than 20 chairs, although these have usually been broken up into smaller sets since. The rarity of long sets means that they command much higher prices than would the same number of single chairs. Sets made up of chairs which are superficially similar, but did not start life together, are known as 'matched' or 'harlequin' sets.

SETO POTTERIES

Seto in Owari province was one of the most important ceramic-making centres of Japan, known as the 'six ancient kilns'. Ceramics have been made there since the 9th century. In the early Muromachi period (1368-1573) most prized products were the so-called 'flower' Seto wares, delicately incised with peonies, chrysanthemums, willow and prunus blossom. These were very extensively forged in the 19th century. In the 17th and 18th centuries it was best known for its tea-ceremony wares of brown or grey stoneware. It produced large quantities of kitchen ware in the 19th

A right royal result

SÈVRES

The Sèvres factory was originally established at VINCENNES, outside Paris, in the early 1740s. Early production seems to have been confined to porcelain flowers used for mounting on ormolu branches on table ornaments. Not until the end of the decade did serious porcelain production begin. The body was the most beautiful SOFT-PASTE or artificial porcelain ever produced. It is described as soft or *tendre* because the glaze was easily scratched.

The first pieces leaned heavily on MEISSEN and were decorated with stylised flowers and panels enclosing landscapes. By the early 1750s the chemist Hellot had established almost 150 enamel colours. The factory also developed two influential decorative elements. The first was a rich, thick, delicately tooled or *cisèle* gilding which enclosed the decorative panels and rioted across the rich ground colours that were the second landmark in the factory's achievement. These, a dark blue known as *bleu lapis*, a turquoise *bleu céleste*, a green, a yellow, and a pink rose Pompadour, produced an effect of depth not achieved elsewhere. The overall result was truly royal.

The hitherto struggling factory secured the patronage of Mme de Pompadour and LOUIS XV. This brought them monopoly powers over the gilding of porcelain in France. Simultaneously the King promoted the factory at court. The principal output was dinner services and sets of vases for chimneypieces. Each service was supplied with a table centre composed of figures in biscuit or unglazed porcelain, forming a wonderful foil to the rich colours and gilding.

Sèvres also produced plaques to enrich the grandest pieces of furniture. The detailed archives often make it possible to follow the production of a piece and establish its original cost and purchaser. In 1769 the factory discovered how to make HARD-PASTE, but most clients, in particular the King, preferred soft-paste, which remained in production until the end of the century. However, the Revolution, which removed the patron without paying his debts, caused great difficulties which were only resolved by the arrival of Napoleon, who restored the demand for splendid porcelain.

After Napoleon's fall, the factory's director Alexander Brogniart, who had assembled an outstanding team of painters, continued to supply the restored Bourbons until the abdication of Louis-Philippe in 1848. In the late 19th century the factory promoted studio porcelain, which is very collectable but has not yet achieved market recognition.

The factory mark was two Ls enclosing a letter for the date, A for 1753, B for 1754 and so on. The later years were marked with aa and bb, etc. Under Napoleon the words 'Manufacture impériale Sèvres' were printed in red with the date. A similar system was continued under the Bourbons, generally with the dates of firing, painting and gilding. Throughout its history Sèvres was the only factory to have a system of painters' marks. The patterns, porcelain and marks of Sèvres were much imitated. In addition, a lot of undecorated wares were sold off after the Revolution and decorated in England in the earlier style. These pieces are very difficult to identify.

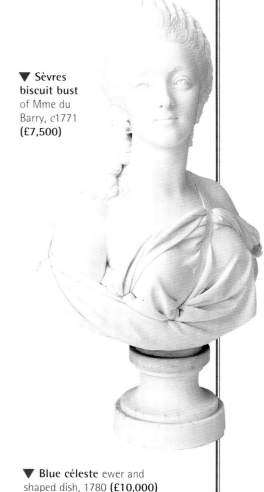

▼ Sèvres biscuit bust of Mme du Barry, c1771 (£7,500)

▼ Blue céleste ewer and shaped dish, 1780 (£10,000)

century, often decorated with freely painted birds and landscapes in iron black, brown or underglaze blue. The majority of the Seto wares seen in the West were made from the 1870s to the 1920s. The white body has a shiny glaze over a bright underglaze blue, painted in a quick, flicked style.

SETTLE

Dating from the Middle Ages, the settle is a long, sometimes curved bench with a high back and arms or sides at each end. The base is often built as a long chest with the seat hinged at the back to give access to storage space, or it is open, with up to eight legs. Although earlier examples are carved in the vigorous traditions of old oak, most settles have a panelled back and sometimes a panelled base. The bacon settle is usually very tall, with cupboards in which to hang bacon. The settle was an ideal piece of furniture for pubs and for 19th-century revivalists, who produced spectacular painted pieces. It was ideally suited to ART NOUVEAU treatment with copper and pewter panels and in the 1920s, with a somewhat lower back, the settle found a niche as a hall seat.

£££-££££

SEWING BOXES

Dexterity with a needle was one of the essential accomplishments for a 19th-century lady, and sewing boxes, filled with every accoutrement of the needlewoman's art, abounded. Such boxes were commonly of rosewood, mahogany or walnut, sometimes inlaid with mother-of-pearl, MARQUETRY, ivory or brass. Leather- or cloth-covered examples are also known. Inside, sewing boxes are beautifully appointed, often lined in velvet or satin, with decorative spools, and delicately wrought tools, each with its own fitting or compartment in an upper tray, over a well for further equipment or work-in-progress. The equipment typically included needlecases, scissors, thimbles, tape measure and pincushions. Sewing cases from the early part of the 20th century tend to be mass-

produced and much simpler, with only a few implements.

£££

SEWING MACHINES

It was not until 1830 and after many false starts that the French made a sewing machine that actually worked, and in America an inventor evolved a machine that would make a lock stitch—the first stitch not to imitate hand sewing. The production of successful sewing machines depended on the availability of interchangeable parts; each machine had to be identical with the next, and this was only possible with mass-production techniques and quality control, which the Americans had in abundance. In 1851 Isaac M. Singer patented the first truly practical sewing machine, which was widely advertised, and the sewing-machine industry pioneered instalment purchase. The potential was immediately seen, and a patent war broke out, resulting in an eccentric variety of machines shaped like Greek temples, dolphins or cupids, some elegant, some curious, but all having an overhanging arm carrying the needle mechanism, a continuous thread, and a handle to turn or a treadle to operate with the feet. Many were equipped with a wide range of accessories. Early sewing machines were open, with the works displayed, but they were soon covered in,

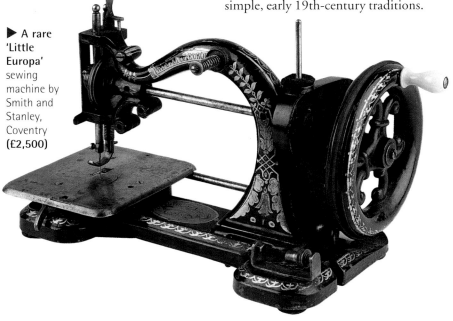

► A rare 'Little Europa' sewing machine by Smith and Stanley, Coventry (£2,500)

with hand-painted flower and similar motifs and inlay on the casing. The wooden domed covers were also very decorative. The ornate cast-iron stands of treadle machines have been topped with marble and sold as occasional tables for more than 20 years. Old sewing machines, long neglected, are often rusted up and virtually valueless.

££-££££

SGRAFFITO

A potted body is coated with slip and the design scratched through to expose the contrasting coloured base: one variety has the design engraved after the glaze has been applied In both cases the piece is then fired. The technique is common in both China and Europe, particularly 16th-century Italy.

SHAGREEN

Shark skin, polished so that the scales made a granulated pattern. It was usually dyed green or black and was used from the 17th century for covering boxes and tea caddies.

SHAKER FURNITURE

Efficient design and effective craftsmanship are the underlying principles of Shaker furniture. The sect, the United Society of Believers in Christ's Second Appearance, was founded in England in 1747 and soon spread to America where, by the 1840s, it had 6,000 members. The furniture follows simple, early 19th-century traditions.

Business on a plate

SHEFFIELD SILVER AND OLD SHEFFIELD PLATE

Without the development of old Sheffield plate, there would not have been a silver industry and assay office in Sheffield.

Old Sheffield, or fused, plate was devised by Thomas Boulsover in about 1743. A sheet of sterling standard silver was melted or fused onto an ingot of prepared and alloyed copper. This was rolled into sheets and objects were made out of this already plated metal (with all other forms of plating the object was made first and was then plated with silver). Boulsover concentrated on silver-plated buttons and it was not until about 1760 that a wider production developed on any scale with the establishment of firms such as Tudor and Leader.

Since it was impossible to cast old Sheffield plate, makers had to develop methods which avoided this. Candlesticks are a particularly interesting and important example. From the late 17th century until the 1760s (with only rare exceptions) candlesticks were cast. Old Sheffield platers stamped sections out of their prepared fused plate sheet, assembled these and then, to give strength and support, would put an iron rod inside and fill the interior with pitch. These are known as 'loaded' candlesticks. Retailers soon demanded the same in silver. As it was easier for the platers to produce silver, it was not long before large numbers of loaded silver sticks were being made. Sheffield has dominated this market ever since.

By 1773 the production of silver by the platers had increased to such an extent that an assay office was opened in Sheffield. The mark for Sheffield was a crown, which derives from the Crown and Anchor Tavern in Westminster, where the petitioners from Sheffield and Birmingham met when the Bill to establish the two assay offices was passed through Parliament. As a result of confusion with gold marking, in 1975 the crown was replaced by a rose. Sheffield is one of only three assay offices surviving in England today.

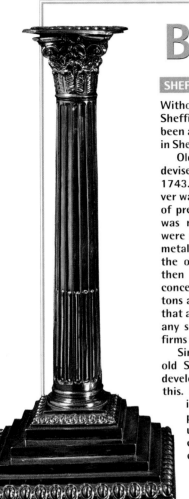

◀ **Pair of old Sheffield** plate candlesticks with Corinthian columns, c1770 **(£400-£600)**

Pictures by courtesy of Bonhams

Most was made for the celibate sect's dormitories and workshops, but in Mount Lebanon, New York, Shakers began making chairs and stools for public sale in the late 19th century. They have been produced commercially ever since. Although there are no longer any living Shakers, there are Shaker 'communities' centred around museums in America, producing furniture to authentic designs and techniques. There is now a Shaker shop in London selling products imported from the USA, sparking a revival. Shaker practicality encouraged low-backed chairs which could be stored under tables, wheels on beds and storage drawers built into walls. The best-known design is the Shaker Chair, a more elegant, elongated version of the Yorkshire LADDER-BACK.

Design is always strictly functional with no decoration. Native woods such as oak, maple, cherry, pear and walnut, either painted or stained to enhance the grain, are used.

SHANG

The earliest civilisation in China, the Shang dynasty ruled from c1500 to c1050BC. The era excelled in the making of bronze vessels cast by the *cire-perdue* technique. They reached a technical development never surpassed. At first they copied ceramic shapes but soon developed an identity of their own, influencing ceramic vessels in their turn. Forms are simple and robust, the richly decorated surfaces ornamented with stylised animal motifs. Shang pottery was still fairly primitive but saw some important innovations, the development of a high-fired stoneware and the use of a yellowish-green glaze. The pots were generally coil-constructed with geometric patterns impressed before the glaze was applied. High-quality, elegant, white-bodied wares were also produced, probably being intended for ceremonial use.

SHAVING STAND

A gentleman's toilet stand introduced in the mid-18th century. It had a wash basin, an adjustable shaving glass, receptacles for soap and perfume bottles and a cupboard and drawers below. Examples are illustrated in CHIPPENDALE's *Director* and SHERATON's *Cabinet Directory*.

£££-££££

An inspiration to them all

SHERATON, THOMAS (1751–1806)

Much of the furniture made in England between 1790 and 1800 is labelled 'Sheraton', particularly the elegant satinwood tables and chairs with tapering slender legs and spade feet, simply decorated with stringing and veneering. However, no single piece of furniture is known to have been made by Thomas Sheraton himself. His great influence on English furniture stems from the books of designs he published. Most significant of these was *The Cabinetmaker and Upholsterer's Drawing Book*, which appeared in four parts from 1791 to 1794. Many of its designs were executed by cabinetmakers all over the country.

Born in Stockton-on-Tees to a lowly family, Thomas Sheraton trained as a cabinetmaker, coming into his own as an author and designer only when he moved to London at the age of nearly 40. Although he had a palpable talent for furniture design and could perceive and create the fashionable taste, this was not his only interest. A Baptist minister, he also wrote philosophical and religious treatises. Sadly his brilliance at design and widespread influence did not make him rich, and he died in poverty. The late Victorian and Edwardian periods saw much furniture made in 'Sheraton Revival' style. But the term also covered pieces that owe more to HEPPLEWHITE and ADAM than to Sheraton.

▲ **Typical Sheraton** George III satinwood bonheur-du-jour (£10,000)

▶ **Burr-yew and marquetry** cutlery box with typical Sheraton motifs (£6,000–£8,000)

▼ George III satinwood tea caddy (£1,100)

▲ **One of a set of eight** George III mahogany dining chairs, after a design of Sheraton's, 1793 (£10,000)

SHELLWORK

Elaborate shellwork was carried out in Italian grottoes, from the 16th century. Later, and on a smaller scale, it became a domestic hobby. Most surviving examples date from the late 18th and 19th centuries when seashells were carefully collected and arranged in decorative patterns on caskets, mirrors and sometimes larger objects such as chair backs and sofas. Strange sculptures were also made and displayed under cloches.

▲ **Coffee pot** from a Shelley bone china 'Queen Anne' coffee set, nine pieces (**£350** the set)

SHELLEY

A large range of wares were made under this name by Wileman & Co from 1925 until after the Second World War. Previously they had operated as the Foley China Factory.

                    £-££

SHERRATT, OBADIAH (1775-c1846)

One of about 25 Staffordshire figure potters working in the Burslem area in the 1820s and 1830s. Only one piece, a mug, exists which is signed by him and there is no evidence to suggest that he actually made the dozens of figures attributed to him. He is traditionally associated with a type of figure group with bocage behind, raised on a stand with four or six legs.

                    ££££

▲ **Shibayama vase** inlaid with mother-of-pearl, stained ivory and tortoiseshell, c1900 (**£1,500-£2,000**)

SHIBAYAMA

Originally a 19th-century family of NETSUKE carvers, their technique of inlaying has seen the name attached to any such work. They used MOTHER-OF-PEARL, coral, turquoise, tortoiseshell and stains on wood or ivory INRO and netsuke. Later craftsmen applied their methods to a variety of products for export, in lacquer as well as ivory. Some Meiji (1868-1912) pieces are 'signed' Shibayama, but are unlikely to have been made by the family. Inlay can easily come off, and this makes a considerable difference to prices.

◀ **Sherratt-type** Staffordshire pottery group 'Tee Total', c1830. Restored and worth more if perfect (**£1,000**)

SHIP MODELS

The earliest ship models were made for the Admiralty in the mid-17th century, to accompany designs submitted to the Naval Board. These were beautifully made to scale by shipwrights in fine-grain box or holly wood. They generally have masts but no rigging and are extremely rare. More popular are the models made by French prisoners of the NAPOLEONIC Wars, some of whom were conscripted ivory and jet carvers. Organised production teams grew up within the prisons. The models were extensively forged in Brighton and Liverpool in the 1930s. From the early 19th-century plans were used

▲ **Ship model** of the *St. Anne*, 1926. Seen at The Guernsey Roadshow (**£350-**

for ships and the most common 19th century models are shipbuilders' full or half-block models which appear after about 1830. These were made once the ship had been built often as a gift to the owner, and the major building yards had special teams of modelmakers. Their models can be incredibly detailed, up to 8ft in length and with gold and silver-plated fittings.

££££

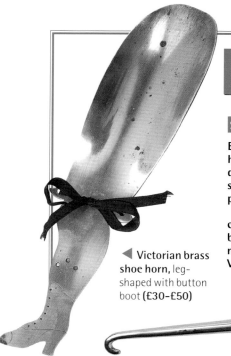

Let's get dressed

SHOE HORNS AND BUTTON HOOKS

Before horn was found to be ideal for shoe horns, calf hide with the hair on one side did the job. Ivory and brass have been used since the early 19th century and, later, plastics.

Button hooks date back to the 17th century, but few are known from the days before their potential as souvenirs and novelties was recognised by the Victorians. Again, all sorts of materials were used to decorate the handles, including gold, silver, tortoiseshell, semi-precious stones, shagreen and enamel. A popular late 19th-century novelty was a leg-shaped handle in TREEN or BOIS DURÇI and brass studs. The two implements were often combined, with the horn as the handle of the hook, and sometimes came in sets, along with glove stretchers and glove hooks, which are smaller versions of the hooks used for boots and gaiters.

◀ **Victorian brass shoe horn,** leg-shaped with button boot **(£30–£50)**

▲ **Chinese export** silver button hook, c1900 **(£75)**

SHOP MODELS

The models of butchers' shops, complete with painted joints of meat, made in the 19th century for display in butchers' windows, were not toys. They had glazed cases for static display. Dolls' shops, like dolls' houses, were also made, but these were toys, rather than static models.

                    £££

▲ **Carved and painted** butchers' shop model, 20th century **(£1,000–£1,500)**

SHUFFLEBOARD

A table up to 30ft by 3ft, on which to play shuffleboard. A description of 1686 refers to one made of pieces of wood about 18in long, 'being laid on longer boards for support underneath...so accurately glued that no shuffle-board whatever is freer from rubbs or casting.' Later used as dining tables.

SIDEBOARD

A mid-18th-century piece of furniture designed for gracious living. Robert ADAM envisaged it flanked by urns on pedestals, one for iced water, one for hot washing-up water. The pedestals contained a wine store and a plate warmer. The 18th-century sideboard was elegant, made in mahogany with or without inlay, and usually had six legs in two groups of three. There was a central drawer, with two side cupboards. The basic shape was retained in the early 19th century, with turned and fluted legs but in about 1830 the sides of the sideboard descended to the floor, and from the 1840s the centre section was built in, and the sideboard became a side cabinet. The solid sideboard made an ideal oak exhibition piece, and was useful for experimentation in GOTHIC, Aesthetic, ARTS AND CRAFTS, 'Quaint' and ART NOUVEAU styles.

▶ **Regency mahogany** breakfront sideboard **(£4,000–£5,000)**

Some were phantasmagoric with acres of inlay and massive decorative hinges. Between 1900 and 1914 some admirable reproduction 18th-century sideboards were made which, at first glance can be taken as original. Until about 1930 perhaps the most popular kind was 'Jacobethan' (old English without being too particular).

£££–££££

SIEGE COINS

To pay troops under siege, municipal plate would be cut up with shears into small pieces of roughly equal size. These were then struck with a crude punch, or perhaps the local HALL-

MARK, to validate them before being handed out as pay. Such coinage is typically square or oblong, rather than round, and often exhibits a remnant of engraved decoration from its previous incarnation. Siege coins were made at Newark, Colchester and Scarborough during the Civil War (1644-46 and 1648). Examples made under similar conditions are known from Ireland, and from the Low Countries and north-west Germany during the Thirty Years' War (1618-48). Civil War coinage made for Charles I from college plate in Oxford is not technically seige coinage, as it was plate melted down and properly struck with the King's head.

SILHOUETTE

Fashionable from about 1770 as a cheap substitute for a miniature or full portrait, the silhouette could be solid black or bronzed (John Miers, 1758-1821, was best for this), or adorned with details or clothing, and could be on paper, plaster, ivory, glass or another surface. Small silhouettes were done for miniatures and toys, such as snuffboxes, as well as for jewellery inserts. Larger ones of family groups were framed as pictures. During the 19th and 20th centuries, silhouettes were used on ceramics, commemorative and novelty ware.

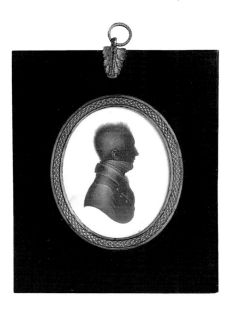

▲ **Silhouette by John Miers** with Field and Miers' trade label **(£200-£300)**

Status of the art

SILVER

Silver has been highly prized since before the time of Christ. Up to the early 17th century most pieces were gilded, giving the impression of gold. Here we look at three major English assay offices. (See also IRISH, SCOTTISH, BIRMINGHAM and SHEFFIELD silver).

Little Chester silver other than church plate and a few spoons is known from before the late 17th century. The 18th century saw increased production and growing numbers of goldsmiths. In particular, the Richardsons established a goldsmithing dynasty. They were followed at the end of the century by George Lowe who founded a business which continues to this day. Production declined in the 19th century, with only five Chester firms registering between 1863 and 1877.

In 1686 a system of HALLMARKS was started, which lasted only until 1697. In 1701 Chester was

◄ Exeter hallmark, 1701-1882

◄ One of the Newcastle hallmarks, used between 1702-1883

◄ A Chester hallmark, 1779-1962

► **Silver spoon** with maker's mark 'I.E.', Exeter, c1700 **(£300-£400)**

given an assay office which continued to mark silver until 1962.

Some fine things were made in the South-West during the 16th and 17th centuries, by silversmiths operating at such centres as Barnstaple, Exeter, Plymouth, Truro and Penzance, but it was only from 1701 to 1883 that Exeter Assay Office existed to regulate them. Even then many 'Exeter' products were made elsewhere, with Plymouth smiths predominating during the 18th century and Bristol spoonmakers during the 19th.

The most important period of Newcastle silver production was the 18th and early 19th centuries, although occasionally 17th-century pieces are found. Apart from flatware, the most common are tankards, mugs and two-handled cups — all, with practice, easily recognisable. An interesting, and distinctly Newcastle, feature is the amount of solder used in putting the foot on. It was usual practice virtually to flood the base with solder and remove the excess by turning on a lathe.

An ordinance of 1536 forbade any Scotsman to be apprenticed or to work in Newcastle. Despite this, a strong Scottish influence is often seen — notably in early 18th-century bullet teapots and later, single-struck flatware. Important Newcastle goldsmiths included Issac Cookson, who dominated the second quarter of the 18th century; the Langlands (sometimes with Robertson), in the second half; and the Reids during the 19th century. Of particular note is the engraved work carried out by Ralph BEILBY and his subsequent partner, Thomas Bewick. The three-castle turret mark of Newcastle was used officially for the life of the assay office, 1702-1884.

Money spinners

SLOT MACHINES

Some of the earliest slot machines were the HONESTY BOXES found in 18th-century inns, but the first patent was not applied for until 1857, when Simeon Denham invented a stamp-vending machine.

Today's wall-mounted models that dispense anything from chewing gum to condoms have much in common with that 19th-century forerunner, although their security devices are more sophisticated. With the Polyphon Music Slot Machines of the 19th century, cheap coin-operated entertainment became widespread. Penny arcades sprang up, particularly at seaside resorts, with machines offering fortune telling, shooting games, working engineering models, What the Butler Saw, haunted houses and church-yards, hangings and other executions and horse racing. There were also coin-operated strength, speed and sight testers, drink dispensers and electric shock machines.

The most popular items, then as now, were gambling machines. Developed in America under the lax US laws of the 19th century, many games, based on either roulette-type spinning arrows or dropping pennies, appeared in Britain by the end of the 19th century. British gaming regulations meant they had to be modified to include some element of skill.

A revolutionary development was made in America around the beginning of the 20th century, by a German émigré, Charles Fey, when he produced the first fully automatic three-reel gambling slot machine, called the Liberty Bell. This was the precursor of virtually every reel-based slot machine or 'one-armed bandit'. Very early slot machines are collectable, and therefore highly priced. Models from the 1960s often come up for sale in the Entertainment Auctions regularly held by the 'big four' London auctioneers.

◀ Green Ray slot machine, 1926 (£1,500-£2,000)

They were very popular again on children's ware of the 1920s and 1930s.

🧺 🪝 🏰🏮 **£££-££££**

SILK

The larva of the mulberry silk moth, native to China, is chiefly responsible for this natural fibre. It has been woven in China since at least the 2nd century BC. From Roman times, it was exported to Europe, and a silk-weaving industry grew up in Italy and Spain during the Middle Ages and the Renaissance, the lead later passing to LYONS in the late 17th century. In the 20th century, Spitalfields in London became well known for silk-weaving.

SKELETON CLOCKS

As the name suggests, these clocks display their

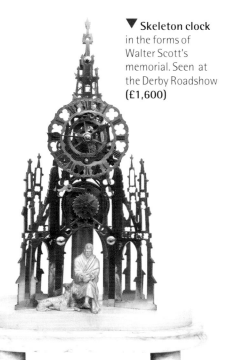

▼ Skeleton clock in the forms of Walter Scott's memorial. Seen at the Derby Roadshow (£1,600)

bare bones, which are protected under glass domes. They have pierced or fretted brass frames, and stand on wood or marble bases. Made in France from the mid-18th century onwards, they saw their greatest development in Britain (c1820 to 1870). They became increasingly complex, incorporating architectural motifs and elaborate striking mechanisms.

🧺 🪝 🏰 **££££**

SLAG GLASS

Press-moulded glass made from the last quarter of the 19th century in a streaked glass resembling marble. The colorants were the slag skimmed from metal furnaces. Green, blue, purple and black are the most common colours.

SLIPWARE AND SLIP

A method of decorating earthenware by trailing liquid clay in a contrasting colour on to the body, either from a tube as in TOFT ware, or by squeezing it from a bag, much like icing a cake. The finished ware is usually given a lead glaze before firing. Slip, liquid clay, is also used to join parts of a pot, the handle to a cup, for example. In slip-casting the liquid clay is poured into a plaster mould until a thickness has built up, the residue poured away and, once dried, the pot or figure released.

SMITH, GEORGE (active 1804-28)

Regency cabinetmaker, designer and upholsterer, who published several books of designs, favouring particularly Greek, Gothic, Egyptian and Chinese styles in the Regency manner. He was influenced by the Egyptologist and designer Thomas HOPE, but his designs tended to be more comfortable and robust.

SNUFF BOTTLES

Snuff became popular in China soon after the introduction of tobacco around the beginning of the 17th century, and it remained

◀ Unusual green glass overlay snuff bottle, depicting a twisted vine, 19th century (£700-£1,000)

Late Regency occasional table in the style of George Smith, c1825, (£6,000)

fashionable until discouraged by the 1912 Republic. Partly for climatic reasons the Chinese favoured small, stoppered bottles rather than boxes, with ivory spoons attached to the stoppers. Bottles were made in ivory, glass, porcelain, agate, crystal, amber, lacquer, horn and all the expected materials, plus a few which are more surprising such as dried fruit.

Stoppers usually contrast with bodies, and are generally plain where the bodies are carved, painted or inlaid. Inside-painted glass bottles are among the most commonly found, but most are of poor quality. The zenith of the fashion, as far as quality is concerned, was during the reign of Qianlong. Thereafter there was an element of mass production. Unusually among collecting fields, age plays a comparatively small part in making values. Collectors are most concerned with high quality.

££-££££

SNUFFER

The most comonly encountered candle snuffers are like scissors with boxes on top to take the 'snuff'—burnt wick—and three little legs below. They are generally silver plate and originally came with waisted oval trays. However, all sorts of ingenious alternatives were tried in the search to stop candles smoking or, like the blowpipe shown right, which was seen at the Guernsey *Antiques Roadshow*, to extinguish candles without spraying hot wax about.

££-£££

▶ Unusual silver blowpipe candle extinguisher, by Hamilton and Inches, Edinburgh (£100)

The snuff of life, taken a pinch at a time

SNUFFBOXES

The great period of snuffbox production was from the early 18th century to the mid-19th, when they were made in every conceivable material — gold and silver, tin and pewter, mammoth tooth and cowrie shell, porcelain and wood.

Snuff is a fine tobacco powder and to prevent escape and to preserve the aroma, boxes need tightly fitting lids, with snuff-proof hinges if any. These features often help to decide whether or not a box was originally for snuff. Size varies from about 1in wide up to table boxes, which may exceed 6in.

Among the most bizarre are Scottish 'MULLS' (simply the Scots for snuff box) made from an entire silver-mounted ram's head with the holder in the top of the skull and draped about with various equipment: serving spoon, rasp, rake, spike and so on. The whole was mounted on wheels to be pushed around the dining table.

Particularly in the mid-18th century and sometimes later, extravagant creations were produced as gifts for European royalty and aristocracy. These would be combinations of gold, precious stones and enamel, and today the best command enormous prices.

BIRMINGHAM became an important centre of box-making in England, with such makers as Matthew Linwood, Samuel Pemberton, John Shaw, Edward Smith and, most famously, Nathaniel MILLS producing a great variety.

Particularly sought after are 'castle tops' which have scenes on their lids and were made mostly in the mid-19th century. However, the best English boxes were made in London, notably those by Phipps and Robinson (late 18th/early 19th century), Rawlings and Sumner (mid-19th century) and John Linnit (early 19th century).

Fine snuff boxes were made in porcelain by CHELSEA, SÈVRES and MEISSEN, the exterior with either figure subjects or flowers, while the underside of the lid might be painted with the portarait of some dignitary or, not infrequently, something slightly pornographic.

► Treen snuff box carved as a shoe, 18th century. Seen at Luton Hoo Roadshow (£700 plus)

▼ Royal presentation snuffbox in Meissen porcelain, with portrait of Augustus the Strong by J.G. Herold, c1730 (£200,000)

► William IV table snuffbox, lid engraved with presentation inscription, Birmingham, 1838 (£300–£400)

A-Z of Antiques Hunting

▼ **Circular papier mâché box,** painted with a scene after Rosselli, 4in diameter, 19th century **(£150-£250)**

▲ **A pressed tortoiseshell box** with piqué point decoration, English, c1800 **(£180-£220)**

▲ **Oval varicoloured gold snuffbox,** inscribed inside 'Souvenir d'Amité', c1800 **(£2,000-£2,500)**

▲ **Chinese 19th-century soapstone** inkwell. Seen at the Wrekin Roadshow **(£20-£25)**

SOAPSTONE

The Chinese carved ornaments from this soft stone, which may be white, red or mottled greenish grey. Technically magnesium silicate, it was also used as an ingredient in SOFT-PASTE porcelain in 18th-century England. One problem with soapstone is that it may be masquerading as jade. It is softer than jade, more easily scratched —and it feels soapy.

SODA GLASS

Made by the Egyptians, Romans and Venetians, as well as by the English and others, this has soda as one of its most important ingredients. It has a slightly brownish or yellowish tinge, and is fragile and lightweight. It is also less resonant than lead glass, which replaced it in England from 1676. (See VENETIAN glass.)

SOFT-PASTE

This was produced in imitation of the true or HARD-PASTE Chinese porcelain. A wide variety of materials was used, including white clay and ground glass which fused when fired (at a lower heat than hard-paste) to make a glassy, white, porcelain-like material. Soft-paste was made to various recipes in Italy, France, and England until the end of the 18th century. It can be scratched by a knife, unlike true porcelain.

SOFT WOODS

According to the British Standards Institution, the term softwood

means, for practical purposes, the wood of conifers.

SOLITAIRE

In porcelain this means a CABARET tea or coffee set on a tray for the use of just one person. They were made by many late 18th- and early 19th-century factories. The game of the same name, played with beads or MARBLES which jump each other on a circular wooden board until only one should be left, is old, but was most popular in the 19th and present century. The name refers not only to the intended result, but also to the fact that it can be played by one person alone.

££-££££

▲ **Early 19th century solitaire** breakfast set, probably from Coalport or Davenport, c1810. Seen at the Truro Roadshow **(£600-£1,000)**

SONG

The Chinese dynasty which ruled from 960 to 1280. It was a period of great development in ceramics, particularly porcelain, the forms being amongst the most refined ever produced. Beautiful glazes were applied to stonewares, which, centuries later, became a source of inspiration to studio potters in the West. The Song dynasty was also a great period for classical paintings, sculpture and even furniture design.

Whichever way you look at them

SPECTACLES

The first spectacles were produced in England by Friar Roger Bacon (c1214–94), and in China and Italy at much the same time. Many of the earliest surviving examples were made in Nuremberg. The trade was established in London by the early 14th century, although the Spectacle-makers' Company was only incorporated in 1629. All the familiar types were present from early times: oval and round lenses — the Chinese favoured large round ones — Ds and half-moons, tinted lenses, bifocals from about 1716, pince-nezs, monocles and LORGNETTES.

Sometimes the spectacles would hinge on the bridge, enabling them to fold into a circle. Wig spectacles were hinged half-way along the arms to go outside a wig and be tied at the back. Early frames were leather; later iron, tortoise-shell, gold, silver, steel and plastics have been used. Prices can range from £5 for a common 19th or 20th century steel frame, to £2,000 or more for a 15th century leather-framed pair.

Often considerable craftmanship was lavished on spectacle cases, turning them from a functional necessity into a fashion accessory. Common materials are tortoiseshell, often with PIQUÉ work or SHAGREEN with gold or silver mounts. Occasionally the case would be a precious metal, engraved or even studded with precious stones. Interest lies also in equipment used by opticians to arrive at the correct prescription. In the 19th century, once lens-making in quantity became a realistic proposition, mahogany boxes of lenses in degrees of strength were made in numbers. Early this century, frames in a variety of styles became available and cards mounted with specimens are sought after.

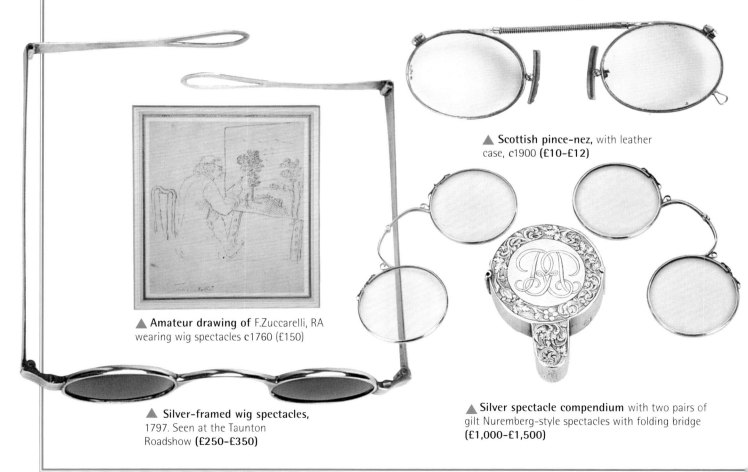

▲ Scottish pince-nez, with leather case, c1900 (£10–£12)

▲ Amateur drawing of F.Zuccarelli, RA wearing wig spectacles c1760 (£150)

▲ Silver-framed wig spectacles, 1797. Seen at the Taunton Roadshow (£250–£350)

▲ Silver spectacle compendium with two pairs of gilt Nuremberg-style spectacles with folding bridge (£1,000–£1,500)

◀ **Silver chatelaine spectacle case** with fretwork birds of paradise by George Unite, 1882 **(£200–£220)**

▶ **Velvet and cut steel** chatelaine spectacle case, c1870 **(£120–£150)**

SOUTHWARK POTTERIES

Much English DELFTWARE was made at Southwark, in London, at a factory set up in 1618 by the Dutchman, Christian Wilhelm. His designs in blue and white derived from Ming porcelain, and date mostly from 1628 to the 1640s. Biblical scenes in colour are also known from Southwark.

▲ **Map of Denbighshire,** London 1650, with original hand colouring. Price depends on edition and area **(£100–£1,000)**

SPEED, JOHN (1552-1629)

His is the major name in British antique maps. Speed's are among the best, finely engraved and bearing picturesque decorations. His maps of the counties of England and Wales (which drew heavily on the prior work of SAXTON and other cartographers) were published together as the *Theatre of the Empire of Great Britain*, forming the first printed atlas of the British Isles. This was issued repeatedly from 1611 until well into the 18th century. A description and history of each county is found on the reverse of Speed's maps, along with a list of important towns and villages.

£££-££££

SPELTER

An alloy of zinc, much used in the 19th century as a less expensive substitute for bronze, although it is lighter, softer and more prone to damage. It was cast in moulds to produce candlesticks and clock cases, and favoured by ART NOUVEAU artists for applied decorations. Figures were also made of spelter, usually in pairs, and at their best can be finished to resemble bronze, although the detail is always less fine.

SPHINX

A royal and religious symbol in ancient Egypt, the sphinx had the body of a lion and the head of the pharaoh. However, the Greeks and Romans preferred their mythological sphinxes with the head and breasts of a woman, the wings of a bird and the tail of a serpent. It was this subspecies of sphinx that was used in ornament from the Renaissance onwards, appearing in many forms, as a garden ornament, on gateposts, firedogs, candlesticks and furniture. The Egyptian sphinx became popular in France with Napoleon's Egyptian campaigns and appeared on English as well as French furniture in the early years of the 19th century.

▶ **Large spelter model of a dog,** 32in high, c1848. Seen at the Taunton Roadshow **(£300-£500)**

SPICE BOX AND SPICE CUPBOARD

Spices were a valuable commodity, and special containers were made for them, the best being air-tight. Wooden examples are known from Elizabethan times, in the form of small, turned barrels, but a better-known type is the shallow, circular box with radiating divisions, which became popular in the 17th century. Such a box might have a lid which could be screwed hard down, making it air-tight. Spice boxes were made of woods, including lignum vitae, walnut and, later, sycamore, but also metals (silver, tin and brass) and ceramics. Towers of interlocking boxes were made in the late 18th and 19th centuries, with from two to 10 labelled compartments stacking one above another. Pocket spice boxes were also made, complete with nutmeg grater. Small, square cupboards fitted with drawers and divisions were made to store spices and medicines from the late 17th and throughout the 18th century. Miniature chests-of-drawers served the same purposes.

££-££££

SPILL VASE

A cylindrical vase for holding spills (wooden sticks or paper tapers) for taking a light from the fire to light candles or pipes. Usually pottery or porcelain.

SPINDLE-BACK

A chair whose back consists of turned rods or spindles (a name taken from their similarity to spindles used in spinning yarn), which either run between the seat and the top rail, or vertically between two closer horizontal bars in the back.

£££

SPINET

A musical instrument with a small keyboard, with each note represented by one string and plucked by a quill or spine—hence the name. It is closely related to the harpsichord and the virginal (apparently so called because of its popularity in convents), but

became characterised by its wing-shaped case. It was popular in the 17th and 18th centuries until supplanted by the square piano.

R ££££

SPINNING WHEEL

Commonly associated with crones and fairy tales, the spinning wheel was designed to convert wool, flax or cotton into thread, so that they could be woven into cloth. By the late 17th century the foot-operated wheel had developed (using a treadle) so that the hands were free to manage the thread. The use of spinning wheels was not confined to cottage life, for spinning was also seen as a genteel accomplishment for 18th-century ladies. This is reflected in the woods of which the ornamental stands were made—mahogany as well as oak and beech.

▲ **19th-century spinning wheel** from the Museum of the Welsh Woollen Industry near Newcastle Emlyn

SPIRIT LEVEL

Finding a line parallel to the horizon—perfectly horizontal—is essential for surveying purposes, not least when cutting canals. Spirit levels do this by means of a bubble in a tube filled with spirit. The oldest form of the modern surveyor's level, complete with a telescope (about 20in long), bubble-tube and compass, dates from the late 18th century and is known as

a Y-level because the telescope is supported in Y-shaped bearings. This instrument was superseded in the 1840s by the 'dumpy-level', much used during the railway-building boom of 1848; this has a smaller telescope, about 12in long.

££-£££

▼ **Cast iron and brass spittoon** shaped like a tortoise, Chicago, c1880 **(£80-£120)**

SPITTOON

Spittoons, or salivariums into which to spit, were made of porcelain, creamware, and glazed earthenware by many factories. They might be incorporated in pieces of furniture, such as footstools. Less common are glass ones from Venice, Persia and China. Typically they are globular with a wide-flaring rim, or a high, funnel-shaped mouth. They may have a handle, and some have a spout.

££-£££

SPONGED WARES

Pottery decorated by applying colour, usually to earthenware, with a sponge. It produces an attractive mottled effect best seen on STAFFORDSHIRE tortoiseshell wares of the mid-18th century, when greens, browns and yellow were used. It also appears on the bases of Yorkshire TOBY JUGS and figures and occasionally on DELFT-WARE.

▼ **Mahogany spirit level,** inlaid with ivory, horn and brass. Brought into the Truro Roadshow **(£200-£300)**

200 years on

SPODE

One of the greatest and most successful of the Staffordshire porcelain and pottery factories, this was established in 1770 by Josiah Spode, and is still operating today.

In its early years the factory made CREAMWARE and fine stoneware, as well as introducing blue and white transfer-printed earthenware. It then became famous for bone china, the introduction of which is attrib-uted to a son of Spode, also named Josiah, in 1794. Josiah II also introduced New Stone China, a particularly fine stoneware, in about 1805.

Tea-sets, dinner and dessert sets were the main stock-in-trade in bone china, well designed in both form and decoration. From 1833 to 1848, Spode traded as Copeland and Garrett, thereafter as COPELAND, until in 1970 the name Spode was revived again.

▼ Pair of cranberry coloured Spode perfume bottles, c1830 **(£400)**

▼ **Dessert dish** with bat-printed decoration, c1820-25 **(£120-£150)**

◀ **Candlestick,** decorated with Imari pattern, c1830**(£400)**

SPUR MARKS
The unglazed marks left on the base of glazed pottery or porcelain by the spurs or stilts on which it was supported in the kiln.

SQUAB
A loose cushion used on a chair or stool, particularly those with wooden or cane seats. It may be tied to the chair-frame at the back.

STAFFORDSHIRE
The centre of the British pottery industry from the late 17th century to the present, with Stoke-on-Trent as the centre of the centre. The area is known as The Potteries, and the 'Five Towns' are Stoke, Burslem, Hanley, Longton and Tunstall, with Cobridge, Fenton, Longport, Shelton and Lane Delph nearby. The first notable products were the Elers brothers' stoneware and Thomas Toft's slipware. Thereafter almost everything has been made in the area, and almost every notable British potter and pottery has connections with the area, even if only by buying clay and materials there.

STAINLESS STEEL
An alloy of steel and chromium, first produced in Britain in the early 20th century. Its rust- and stain-proof nature made it ideal for tablewares. It was used from the 1920s, first for knife blades and then more widely.

STAMP CASES
Nineteenth-century silver novelties, often made in the form of a tiny, stamp-sized envelope, with a hinged opening, and often a ring fitting by

◀**Silver stamp case.** Birmingham, c1900. Seen at the Luton Hoo Roadshow **(£50)**

which they could be attached to a CHATELAINE.

££

STEAMER CHAIR
A folding, reclining chair of elegant curving shape, with adjustable back and separate leg rest, usually with cane seat and slatted back. It originated in the mid-19th century, but takes its current name from its use on the sundeck of luxury steamships in

▼ **Staffordshire rococo revival** porcelain inkstand, c1840 **(£500)**

Standing on ceremony

STANDISHES

An early name for inkstands, which were intended to hold writing equipment such as pens, ink, sand (or pounce), a taper (for sealing) and perhaps a bell.

Silver examples date back to the 17th century, but they became particularly fashionable in the second half of the 18th century, when Sheffield plate was also used for a less expensive alternative. Early examples were often made in the form of a casket, with internal subdivisions, while the tray type, bearing inkpot, pounce pot and so on, continued on into the 19th century, when there were also some very ornate, large inkstands.

Inkstands of other materials including wood, porcelain and ormolu were also made in the 18th and 19th centuries.

▼ **Silver inkstand** with cut glass bottles, by Henry Holland and Sons, 1866. Seen at the Bexhill Roadshow **(£800-£1,000)**

the early years of the 20th century. Passengers could comfortably lounge on such chairs, sipping cocktails, or recline with their feet up. Sometimes the name of the steamship company is on the back. Those marked 'White Star Line, Titanic' should of course be regarded with suspicion. Most surviving steamer chairs date from between the wars. Today, reproductions are fashionable for use in the garden.

£££

STEIFF
See TEDDY BEARS.

STEM CUP
A Chinese porcelain cup with a wide, shallow bowl raised on a stem which broadens out towards the base, rather like a wine glass without a foot. They were originally made during the early Ming dynasty, although the form is based on earlier vessels. They were also made in the early 18th century.

STERLING
The name given to the minimum standard of purity of English silver, which has been 925 parts of silver per thousand (92.5 per cent) since the early medieval period. There was a brief exception, in 1697-1720, when the BRITANNIA Standard (95.83 per cent) was used. After that both were allowed. The remaining proportion is copper or a base metal to lend strength and workability. Foreign silver may be of a higher or lower standard.

STETHOSCOPE
see MEDICAL INSTRUMENTS

STEVENGRAPH
Named after Thomas Stevens of Coventry who produced them from 1879, Stevengraphs are small silk pictures made on a Jacquard loom. They usually depict themes such as horse-racing and portraits of the famous. Their production continued until 1938.

££-£££

▶ **Rare Stevengraph** of the boxer Jake Kilrain. Brought into the Derby Roadshow **(£80–£100)**

▲ **Detail of a stiple engraved goblet,** by Frans Greenwood, c1742 **(£1,500–£2,000)**

STIPPLE ENGRAVING
Firstly, a method of engraving glass by pricking dots with a diamond to create an effect of light and shade. It was practised in the Netherlands in the 17th and 18th centuries, often on glass imported from Newcastle upon Tyne. Stippling has been revived in this country since 1935 by Laurence Whistler, to magical effect. Secondly it is a method of print-making in which wax covering a copper plate is pricked through to create a picture. the plate is etched and inked and run through a press on to paper. The resulting print is in tones of dark and light.

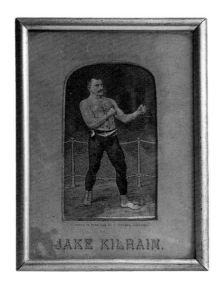

STIRRUP CUP
A cup made in the form of a fox's or other animal's head, traditionally used for pre-hunt tipples on horseback (hence the lack of stem or pedestal). Stirrup cups became popular from about 1760 to the mid-19th century and were made in porcelain, pottery, glass and silver. Not surprisingly a great many were made by a London dynasty of silversmiths named Fox, who were in business from 1801 to 1921.

£££-££££

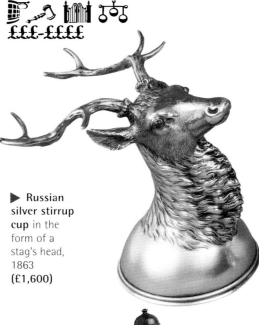
▶ **Russian silver stirrup cup** in the form of a stag's head, 1863 **(£1,600)**

▶ **German stoneware,** salt-glazed tankard with cobalt blue decoration, c1680, **(£700–£900)**

STONEWARE
A ceramic body, distinct from PORCELAIN or EARTHENWARE, made by firing clay containing a type of stone (usually feldspar) to a point where it is no longer porous. It is very hard and dense, resonant like porcelain, but usually grey or red rather than white, and non-translucent. It developed in Shang dynasty China,

and independently in the Rhineland in the 12th century. It was introduced to Britain in the late 17th century by John DWIGHT, who used a salt glaze to give shine to the brown body. Many refinements of stoneware followed, including Böttger's famous red stoneware (the forerunner to true porcelain at Meissen), Wedgwood's Jasper wares and black BASALTES, stone china (such as Mason's Ironstone and Spode's New Stone), Martinware and the work of some 19th- and most 20th-century studio potters.

STOOL

The oldest and, until the 19th century, the commonest kind of seat furniture, used in ancient Egypt and ever since. To qualify as a stool, a seat must have no back or arms. In Egyptian, Greek and Roman days stools were either four-legged or X-framed. These two basic designs have persisted, with three-legged variants appearing now and then (under milk-maids, etc). Many different types have been made over the centuries, to suit different fashions and purposes. From the 16th century, joint stools were made—robust rectangular stools of country wood, with turned legs and sometimes a decorative frieze. These are often fancifully called 'COFFIN STOOLS'. Upholstered stools became common late in the 17th century (see TABOURET), and thereafter more elegant, drawing-room examples on CABRIOLE legs. Special stools were made for music (round, adjustable height, or rectangular with a music well); to ease gout; to rest feet on; to use as a lavatory, and to conceal library steps.

▼ **Late Victorian** giltwood simulated bamboo stool **(£1,200–£1,500)**

▲ **William IV** four-light candelabrum, 26¼in high, 1833 **(£8,000–£12,000)**

▲ **Soup plates** engraved with coat of arms from an extensive service made for Alexander, 2nd Earl of Caledon, 1812 **(£29,000 for 18 pieces)**

▶ **George III** two-handled circular soup tureen and cover with lion's mask handles, 1803 **(£11,000)**

Silversmith who relied on designs supplied

STORR, PAUL (1771-1844)

Surprisingly for one of the country's foremost silversmiths, Storr was a member of the Vintners' Company, having been apprenticed to one of its members, William Rock. This was probably an 'apprenticeship of convenience' and the long-held belief that the London-born Storr was taught by Andrew Fogelberg makes sense.

He was freed in 1792 and his first mark was entered in partnership with William Frisbee, but less than a year later Storr registered a mark on his own.

At this time he moved into Fogelberg's Church Street, Soho, workshops (Fogelberg, it is believed, having retired to Sweden). His early work was good

but not particularly distinctive in design. By 1797, however, with the remarkable Portland gold font, made for the christening of the 3rd Duke of Portland, and which sold in 1985 for nearly £1million, Storr started to move into the top league.

His developing association with Rundell, Bridge and Rundell was of great importance. It supplied him with major commissions for banqueting plate, centrepieces and the like. Storr's early work was in the NEO-CLASSICAL style and later in the Neo-ROCOCO.

As so often with silversmiths, it is difficult to determine who was actually responsible for the designing — very rarely

were the marks those of the 'hands-on' maker. They were frequently those of the sponsors. Certainly Storr worked mainly to the designs of others, some of them artists of high standing such as John Flaxman, William Theed II and Thomas Stothard. He also borrowed the work of the Italian engraver Giovanni Piranesi. His reputation is largely based on the Regency classical pieces produced in conjunction with these designers — such as the Theocritus Cup, and the pair of 5ft-high candelabra by Flaxman in the Royal collection.

In 1807 the association with Rundell, Bridge and Rundell was formalised, Storr becoming a partner. This arrangement lasted until 1819 when Storr left

after lengthy arguments with Rundell. Many of his pieces thereafter illustrate how important the supply of designs had been to him. Although his standards of workmanship remained high, the artistic merits of much of his work became questionable.

Sadly, the fortune he accumulated was lost when he went into partnership with Mortimer, who ran their Bond Street shop ineptly. The firm survived, through Hunt becoming a partner in 1826, but Storr retired in 1838 and died in 1844. His firm continued as Mortimer and Hunt (1839-1843), Hunt and Roskell (1843-97) and Hunt and Roskell Ltd (1897 -c1965). Hunt and Roskell has recently re-opened, now owned by Aspreys.

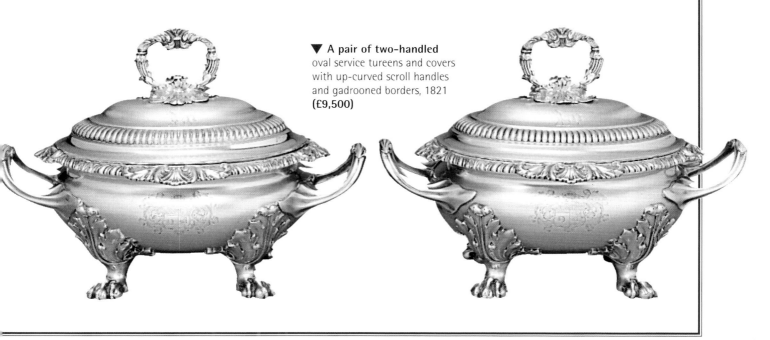

▼ A pair of two-handled oval service tureens and covers with up-curved scroll handles and gadrooned borders, 1821 (£9,500)

▲ Webb and Son cameo glass plaque made at Stourbridge, c1885 (**£14,000**)

STOURBRIDGE GLASS

Glass was made in the Worcestershire town of Stourbridge from the early 17th century. At first only flat glass for windows was produced, but by the 18th century output included fine table glass. In the 19th century Stourbridge became the most important English centre for fine decorative and table glass, both clear and coloured. Several factories were responsible for this, most notably Steven and Williams, Thomas Webb (famous for cameo glass) and Richardson (pressed glass).

£-£££££

STRADIVARI (STRADIVARIUS), ANTONIO (*c*1644 - 1737)

A native of Cremona, he made the most famous violins of all, the kind everyone dreams of finding in the attic and selling to become a millionaire. The trouble is that all too many people do find violins with exciting labels inside, declaring them to be the work of the master. Sadly, these are invariably facsimiles, most commonly made in what is now the Czech Republic. Around 600 true Stradivarius violins are known, and for the most part their whereabouts are well documented. Of course, there is a chance that another genuine 'Strad' may be found, but the odds are exceedingly long.

STRAPWORK

Ornament of flat, scrolling bands, curling and intertwining to resemble leather straps. It was a Renaissance fashion and widely adopted by engravers in the 16th century, affecting many of the decorative arts and

No stone unturned

STREETER, EDWIN (1834 - 1923)

Perhaps the greatest Bond Street jeweller of his day, Streeter was both self-made and self-destroyed. Scholarly as well as entrepreneurial, he published well-respected books on gems, and from about 1869 pioneered what was in effect a mail-order business through his splendidly illustrated catalogues. During the last quarter of the 19th century his business was one of England's most fashionable and important. He financed diamond miners in Africa, searches for rubies in Burma and pearl-fishing expeditions off Australia.

He was also a great campaigner for proper standards of HALLMARKING. Unfortunately, his enthusiasm for fine stones and his ever-open ear to the schemes of plausible adventurers led to the failure of a number of projects, notably a syndicate to mine emeralds in Egypt, and in 1905 the business went into liquidation.

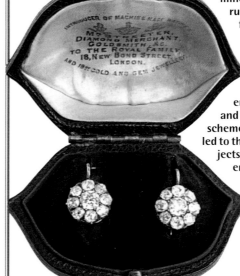

◀ Pair of diamond earrings by Streeter. Seen at the Wrekin Roadshow (**£2,500**)

finding particular favour in northern Europe in the late 16th and early 17th centuries. The 'Jacobethan' revival of 19th-century England brought a fresh outbreak of strapwork.

STRASBOURG POTTERY

It produced everything from extraordinary tureens in the forms of boars' heads, ducks or vegetables to enormous Continental stoves adorned with flowers and cherubs, not to mention table services, clock cases, bidets, BOURDALOUES and wall fountains, all in high Rococo style. Set up in 1721, it was responsible for some of the finest FAIENCE of the 18th century.

Strasbourg wares, made to simulate porcelain, enjoyed great success, particularly between the late 1740s and the 1770s. However, attempts to make porcelain itself undermined the success of the pottery, which closed in 1781.

£££-££££

STRAW WORK

This is a craft introduced to England from France in the late 18th century. It involved decorating boxes, mirror frames and other small items with flattened strips of straw, laid together in patterns like MARQUETRY or PARQUETRY The straw pieces might be tinted different colours to enhance the design, which could be pictorial or geometric. Straw work is well known in Britain through the work of NAPOLEONIC PRISONERS-OF-WAR.

STRETCHER

A piece of wood running horizontally between the legs of furniture, bracing the structure. In the late 17th century, stretchers became a decorative feature of chairs. They could be curved, serpentine, or X-shaped. By the end of the 18th-century they were no longer fashionable

STRINGING

A very narrow strip of wood or metal, inlaid into furniture to form a contrasting line, as a simple decorative feature. It is often used on table-tops.

STRIPPED

This is the fate that has befallen an enormous amount of pine furniture, which was originally intended to be finished with paint. The 1970s fashion for rustic charm set up a market for this humble wood, revealed in all its coarseness, but waxed to a dull sheen or varnished. The irony is that the distressed paint finishes removed by the strippers would have been highly fashionable in the 1990s, when trendy rustic charm wears an authentic hat. Most stripping was (and is) done by dunking the whole piece of furniture in a tank of caustic soda which loosens the joints. Hand-stripping is kinder, but more laborious.

STUDIO POTTERY

This is the name given to pottery made by artist-craftsmen working independently of factories, and therefore free to work on their own designs and to see each piece through every stage from conception to final firing. Each pot is therefore an individual work of art, rather than a mass-produced item, and many have departed from the rigours of useful shapes to explore the further limits of ceramic textures. The late 19th and 20th centuries saw a great flowering of such independent talent, and the term 'studio pottery' now implies the work of this period only. France, England, Germany and America have been the main sources of studio pottery.

Outside favourites

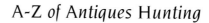

STREET FURNITURE

Until 10 or 15 years ago most street furniture was destroyed or left to rot when no longer needed. The unnecessary rape of iron railings from British cities in 1940 is well known, but the despoliation since by authorities and developers has passed almost unremarked. However, despite mockery, people began to put old gas lamps in their drives, and later to buy up the Gilbert Scott telephone boxes that were being ripped out by BT. Even earlier, there were serious collectors of metal insurance plaques. Tradesmen's signs, such as pestles and mortars, and pub signs that have been replaced are popular. The bollards or posts which were used to mark parish and ward boundaries have also sometimes been sold off as a result of street alterations. Some of the first were actually superannuated cannons with cannonballs on top – later the pattern was copied. All these, plus chunks and details of demolished buildings, are now sold by 'architectural antiques' dealers.

▲ **19th-century gas lantern** with new mechanical parts **(£400)**

▲ **House sign** for the Royal Insurance Company **(£95)**

▶ **Fire insurance sign,** 19th century **(£125)**

◀ **Sign from a** famous Chelsea pub, c1930s **(£400)**

▶ **Cast-iron** bollard, late 19th-century **(£70)**

▶ **Bollard** with St Pancras parish mark, late 19th-century **(£120)**

Pottery to take a shine to

SUNDERLAND LUSTRE

Pottery made by several factories in Sunderland in the 19th century, typically with mottled pink lustre around a black transfer print. Subjects are usually ships or the iron bridge over the Wear in Sunderland, applied to jugs and large bowls. Another popular line was pink-lustre wall plaques for the God-fearing, printed in black with inducements to piety: 'Prepare to meet thy God' and 'Thou, God, seest me'. Wares are marked by the various potteries in Sunderland.

◀ **Lustre jug commemorating** the Crimean War, c1854. Seen at the Bexhill Roadshow, damaged (**£150–£180**)

▼ **Sunderland plaque** by Dixon and Co, c1850 (**£80–£120**)

▲ **Transfer-printed mug** depicting Adam Clarke, a Wesleyan minister. Hand-coloured, c1840 (**£60–£90**)

▲ **Stump work or raised work,** mirror with panels closed, English, 17th century **(£20,000–£25,000)**

STUMPWORK

A type of needlework, popular in England in the 17th century, where the design—usually including figures, animals, butterflies, caterpillars, flowers and fruit trees—is built into high relief with stitching and padding. The figures may have carved wooden hands and seed-pearls, sequins and silver-wire decorations. It was used on small cabinets and mirror frames, or just worked as decorative panels.

SUNDERLAND TABLE

A rectangular or oval gateleg table with two flaps hanging almost to the ground from a very narrow spine. Most are in mahogany and date from the 19th or early 20th century.

 **£££–££££**

SWAG

An ornament that was particularly fashionable in NEO-CLASSICISM, and resembles a festoon of draped cloth, fruit, flowers or leaves. It was used as surface decoration in the decorative arts and in architecture.

SWAN-NECK

This is the name given to a type of hinged brass handle seen on CHESTS-OF-DRAWERS from the mid-18th century. It comes from the S-shape, reminiscent of a swan's neck, which

Time signals

SUJNDIALS

Despite splendid timepieces in the 17th and 18th centuries, sundials held their place because in the absence of telephone's 'at the third stroke', they were the only way to check and set clocks. On a good day, once the sundial is correctly orientated to the sun, it tells the time by a shadow cast by its gnomon (raised indicator) against a scale. The orientation is a problem with portable dials, so these are given a compass and adjustments to allow for changes of latitude. In the late 17th and 18th centuries church towers and country houses had fixed sundials (vertical and horizontal, respectively) against which clocks could be checked, and owners of pocket watches might also carry a pocket dial as a double-check. The coming of the electric telegraph and the railways in the 1830s led to a standardisation of time across the country, and sundials became decorative rather than useful. Many different kinds were made in the 17th and 18th centuries, ranging from simple, pocket examples to more precise, scientific pieces.

▲ **Dial by** Sevrin of Paris, c1760 **(£600–£800)**

◀ **Stone sundial** inscribed: 'For me dark days do not exist. I'm a brazen-faced old optimist.' **(£700–£900)**

---

forms the attachment at either end of the flattened oval handle. The scrolled pediments at the top of some 18th-century furniture may be called 'swan-neck pediments'.

SWANSEA

A range of earthenwares was made there from the mid-18th century onwards, but Swansea is better known today for the SOFT-PASTE porcelain it produced from about 1814 with the help of William BILLINGSLEY from NANTGARW. Several different types of porcelain were tried, some more translucent than others, but the decoration is invariably of high quality—usually birds, figures or flowers.

▶ **Swansea cup and saucer,** with gilt decoration, c1820 (£200-£250)

Much was sold unpainted, and subsequently decorated in London. After 1822, the factory reverted to earthenware, and it closed in 1870.

 £££-££££

SWASTIKA

Hijacked and reversed by Hitler so that it has become identified solely with Nazism, the swastika is an ancient symbol of prosperity and revival. It was used on early Greek jewellery and Etruscan burial urns, and even appears on early Christian gravestones as a form of cross. It is common as a border on Chinese porcelain, and is a Sanskrit and Hindu symbol.

SWEETMEAT GLASS

A small, shallow, glass vessel mounted on a tall stem, its bowl often moulded at the rim. It was used in England in the late 17th and 18th centuries for serving dry sweetmeats such as nuts and candied fruits.

£££

SYLLABUB GLASSES

Syllabub was a popular dessert in the 18th century, made from whipped cream flavoured with sherry, ratafia and spices. Special glasses were made for it from about 1725. Initially they were similar to POSSET pots but with one handle and no spout. Later, syllabub glasses were more like large, jelly glasses, some with a wider bulge at the top for the whipped cream.

££

The cutting edge

SWORDS

Before 1788 there was little standardisation of military swords as colonels of regiments were allowed to procure their own, to their own designs. British patterns can be collected from 1788, and the patterns for 1796, both infantry and cavalry, are well sought after as they were carried during the Napoleonic Wars (1793-1815). Officers were traditionally furnished with patterns to suit their mode of warfare — straight blades for heavy cavalry, slightly curved for light cavalry and slender, straight blades for infantry. Officer's swords often had beautiful blued and mercuric gilded designs on the blades, comprising crowned GR (for George III), flowering tendrils and sometimes a standing or mounted military figure. Infantry officers' swords often had 'For my Country and King' engraved on the blades. These lavishly decorated swords are very valuable today and, if in very good condition, realise in excess of £2,000 each. For the more modest pocket, swords with plain blades can be found between £250 and £500, depending on condition.

The later pattern dates for cavalry swords are 1821, 1853, 1864, 1885, 1899, 1908 (other ranks) and 1912 (officers). The last two patterns are still carried today on ceremonial occasions. Principal infantry patterns are 1803, 1822, 1845, 1892 and 1895. Regimental variations exist for both cavalry and infantry. Auction prices for 19th-century swords range from £200 to £400. PRESENTATION SWORDS can be bought from about £300. The highest prices (from £10,000 to £20,000) are achieved by swords given for valour by the Lloyds Patriotic Fund (mostly to naval officers during the Napoleonic Wars).

A preservation tip: due to the effects of finger acid, caused by the way some people examine swords, blobs of rust are often found on blades. To remove the rust use the edge of a copper coin — the copper, being softer than the steel, will not scratch the blade. Then treat the blade and hilt with beeswax to prevent damage by finger contact or air pollution.

▼ **Georgian 1796 pattern** light cavalry officer's sword (top) (£2,000)

▲ **11th Hussars** Levee pattern, (middle) (£2,000)

38th Middlesex presentation sword, (bottom) 1877 (£1,600)

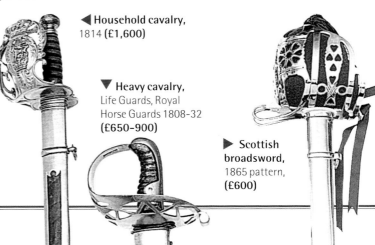

◀ **Household cavalry,** 1814 (£1,600)

▼ **Heavy cavalry,** Life Guards, Royal Horse Guards 1808-32 (£650-900)

▶ **Scottish broadsword,** 1865 pattern, (£600)

▲ George III mahogany tallboy with three small drawers in the top (£17,000)

▲ Table chair, mid-19th century made in 17th-century style (£800)

TABLE CHAIR
Otherwise known as a chair table, this serves both purposes—although not simultaneously. It is an arm chair, with a table-top hinged into the vertical position to form its back. For a table, the back is swung forward to rest on the arms. Such early examples of METAMORPHIC FURNITURE are also known by the terms 'monks' bench' or 'chair'. Some examples date from the 17th century but most are mid-19th century.

£££-££££

TABLE-LEAF CUPBOARD
To store the leaves of extending dining tables when not in use, a variety of cases was made from the REGENCY period onwards. Cases might be built into the backs of sideboards, or take the form of a large, lidded box with brass handles. Others held the individual sections in an open framework.

TABOURET
French word for a low, upholstered STOOL, introduced to England from France in the early 18th century. Tabourets were used at the court of Louis XIV according to strict rules of etiquette—it was a privilege to perch on one. Originally drum-shaped, hence the name, the tabouret later became rectangular with an upholstered seat.

TALLBOY
Also known as a CHEST-ON-CHEST, this piece of furniture is aptly named since only the tallest of boys could possibly hope to peep into the top drawers. It comprises two CHESTS-OF-DRAWERS, one above the other, and was a Dutch idea, introduced to England in the early 18th century, and made throughout the 18th and into the 19th. It usually has three or four drawers in the bottom part, and three plus a pair of small drawers in the top.

£££-£££££

TAMBOUR
A flexible shutter, made of thin strips of wood attached to canvas, which presents a reeded appearance from the outside. Used as a sliding door on night tables, or as a roll-top for desks.

TAMBOUR LACE
Not a true lace, this openwork fabric is made using a hook pulling thread through netting in interlinked chains to create the pattern. It takes its name from the way the fabric to be worked on is stretched over a circular frame, like a drumskin. It was popular in England and France during the late 18th and early 19th centuries.

Dishes at the heart of the meal

▼ **Mid–19th century** electroplated table centrepiece originally holding glass bowls for fruit and sweetmeats (£700)

TABLE CENTREPIECES

The earliest surviving English centre-pieces are the *surtouts* or ÉPERGNES that were first recorded in England around 1720, having developed in France in the very late 17th century. At first these incorporated a number of different objects. Standard would be a central tureen, supporting a dish surrounded by smaller dishes on branches. Some also had candle-holders, sets of three casters for sugar, salt and mustard (which was served dry in those days) and oil and vinegar bottles. By the second half of the 18th century the *épergne* had developed into a central basket supported on legs surrounded by smaller baskets on branches. Some examples were surmounted by canopies. Towards the end of the 18th century examples became taller and narrower, the small baskets often being in two tiers.

With the REGENCY, candle-holders are once more found, often as an alternative fitting to the baskets. An important development was the introduction of sculptural groups to the bases, and these gradually became more and more significant until, by the mid–19th century, centrepieces were produced which were purely sculptural, the baskets and other items having been dispensed with altogether.

An innovation in the latter years of the 19th century, and one which which remained popular well into the 20th century, was the assembling of a group of spill vases (holding flowers) to form an *épergne*.

▶ **Stourbridge glass** centrepiece with a pair of matching vases, c1870 (£400–£600)

TANG

The Chinese dynasty (AD618-906) which saw a great flowering of the arts in China, inspired by territorial expansion and new cultural and commercial contacts as the Chinese armies re-opened the silk route westwards to Persia. Excavations have shown that porcelain was made during this period, but it is earthenware for which the Tang dynasty is renowned. Little was known of this until, at the beginning of the 20th century, Swedish engineers building the railway system cut through Tang graveyards, exposing quantities of ceramic vessels and figures. Despite their purpose, the best of these tomb figures are among the most lively, vigorous and engaging of all pottery

◀ Large sancai figure of a guardian standing on a recumbent bullock, Tang Dynasty (£3,500–£4,500)

Putting a lid on it

TANKARDS

Effectively developing from the mid-16th century onwards, tankards are distinguished from mugs in that they have lids. Capacity ranges from a pint to half a gallon, with a quart being fairly standard in the 18th century. Tankards dating from before the early 17th century are usually tall and narrow with a domed lid, rather like a German beer *Stein* in form. During the second quarter of the 17th century English examples became lower and broader. Large numbers survive from the late 17th through to the late 18th century, when their popularity began to decline.

There are a number of interesting variations. Seventeenth-century PEG TANKARDS, with a vertical line of pegs on the inside, were passed around as a form of wager: participants had to drink down to the next peg in one go. If they did, they won. If not, there was a forfeit to pay.

In the eastern counties of Britain a Scandinavian influence was evident. In York examples were made in a more rounded form with pomegranate feet and thumb

▲ Charles II silver tankard, 1661. Seen at the Newcastle Emlyn Roadshow (£15,000-£20,000)

pieces. During the 1680s delightful CHINOISERIE examples were produced. In fine condition, these command very high prices.

An age-old myth is that the slot or hole cut in the base of a handle was to act as a whistle to summon a refill. It is, in fact, a simple piece of silversmithing to allow gases to expand more freely when the handle is soldered on.

sculpture, and caused a sensation when first shown to the European public early in the 20th century. So keenly were they collected that the enterprising Chinese started to augment the supply, and these latter-day forgeries are difficult to spot. Tang ceramics are not much collected by the Chinese themselves, because of their original purpose. The burying of figures and animals with the dead was common practice among princes, princesses, nobles and grandees, since it was essential to announce your high status to the spirits, and to be accompanied in death by the trappings you enjoyed in life. Thus were figures made of servants, guardian spirits, and all sorts of animals and pet birds.

Most seem to have been mass-produced, but a few may have been made to special order. Best-known are the Tang horses (with sloping backs and big bottoms) and the jaunty camels. Tang figures are decorated with coloured glazes (ochre, green, blue and brown), and usually have unglazed heads or faces, with the expression painted on. They are lightly fired, and easily absorb moisture, which the forgeries, being harder, do less readily. Tang pottery includes some beautiful vessels such as jars, ewers, vases, pots and boxes. These share the same colouring as the figures, but the glazes are often mottled or splashed together to create an overall pattern.

Stuffed and mounted for the study of nature

TAXIDERMY

The Egyptians preserved cats and occasionally other animals and birds, particularly the sacred ibis which was revered as a deity. But it was in VICTORIAN times that fascination with all things natural, and adherence to the Biblical idea that animals are to be used by man, led to amateur naturalists having animals stuffed to study them at close quarters.

Taxidermy (Greek 'taxis', arrangement, and 'derma', skin) is not for the squeamish. It involves removing the skin and all flesh and bone with the exception of the skull. All fats are scraped from the skin so that it does not putrefy, and it is then preserved with borax. A wire frame is covered with wadding, and the skin loosely arranged and padded with wood-wool (which was the stuffing for

▲ Roach in a bow-fronted case, caught by a Royal Duke, dated 1876 (£400)

▼ Unusual stuffed fox cub, early 20th century. Seen at the Newcastle Emlyn Roadshow (£200)

early teddy bears). Glass eyes are added, with tongues and mouths made of painted plaster, and some of these, particularly those of the big cats, can look surprisingly realistic. Finally, most animals were given settings of plants, grasses, and rocks made from PAPIER-MÂCHÉ, and sometimes a painted background scene.

Groups of animals set in bizarre, human-like scenes, are known as 'tableaux'. The most elaborate were the vast cases telling the tale of Reynard the Fox exhibited at the Crystal Palace in 1851. Scenes of weddings between kittens, boxing matches between rats and an appropriately populated 'Who Killed Cock Robin' were often often made by a taxidermist called Potter, and, although quite grotesque, can sometimes fetch high sums.

The Victorians were extremely keen on large displays of exotic birds, humming birds being a particular favourite. Many animals and birds are now protected under Wildlife

Acts and dealers must have licence to sell specimens. There was a vogue starting in the 17th century for bizarre assemblages of monkeys or fish resembling aquatic humanoids. These are now readily saleable.

Taxidermists also served hunters and fishermen who wanted a permanent record of their successes. Many tigers, lions, antelope and innumerable other game came under the taxidermist's knife, to end their days mounted on a study or library wall in one of Britain's country houses. H. N. Pashley of Cley, Norfolk, specialised in wildfowl, and was thrice winner of the Lord Lilford prize.

That there were seven taxidermists on as small an island as Guernsey in 1899 is

▲ **One of a pair** of little spotted kiwis with glass domes (£920)

an indication of the craft's popularity. Taxidermy gradually fell out of favour with collectors, but is now experiencing a revival. Fifteen or 20 years ago it was possible to buy a finely mounted, record-breaking pike for a few pounds, which today could fetch thousands.

J. Cooper & Sons made excellent stuffed fish, their value enhanced by bow-fronted glass cases with gilt lettering. Most top taxidermists recorded their work by a label or a name stamped on the mounting plaque. Look out for Cullingford, Rowland Ward, Spicer of Leamington and Hutchings. Fur, feather and skin can be damaged by moth and sunlight, and may be costly to restore. Also, good, moulded plastic fish are now being made to catch the unwary.

The comprehensive collection of British birds at the Booth Museum of Natural History, Brighton, East Sussex, is outstanding. It was bequeathed by Edward Booth, an ornithologist, who in the second half of the 19th century stuffed every piece himself.

► **Tantalus with three** cut-glass decanters and a drawer for cards and counters, c1880 (£250-£300)

TANTALUS
A decorative, lockable, wooden or electroplated stand or case for spirit decanters, in which they could be secured yet remain visible to tantalise, hence the name. A notable maker was BETJEMANN, and they were fashionable from the mid-19th century until the Edwardian period.

££££

TAPPIT HEN
The most prized type of Scottish pewter, a flagon with handle and hinged lid, vertical or slightly flared base, in-curving waist and flared neck. Most hold one Scottish pint (equivalent to three Imperial pints), and those encountered today date from 1750 to 1850.

£££-££££

TATTING CHAIR
A low-seated, high-backed chair with no arms and a caned seat and back, on turned legs, made in the mid-19th century in the High Wycombe area. Tatting is a form of lacemaking, and this chair is also known as a lady's sewing chair.

£££

► **One of a pair** of bronze and Sienna marble tazzas (£1,500-£2,000 the pair)

TAZZA
The Italian for cup, also used in the 16th and 17th centuries to describe a drinking vessel with a broad, shallow bowl mounted on a stem. It is now more generally used for any shallow dish on a central stem.

Changing fashions of a familiar ritual

TEA THINGS

Long before it became our national beverage, tea was thought to be a herbal remedy. It was imported from China in the mid-17th century and sold for as much as £10 a pound — equivalent to £800 today. Deemed beneficial to health, it was claimed to encourage longevity and to make the body 'active and lusty'. But so unfamiliar were we in those days, tea was spread on bread and butter or served as a vegetable.

Gradually it became an accepted alternative to chocolate and coffee, and was taken in coffee houses and pleasure gardens. Being so expensive, however, its enjoyment was limited to a very small proportion of the population, and vessels to contain it were made of precious metals such as silver.

It was not until the 18th century that the fashion for tea-drinking really developed. It became the vogue to drink tea after dinner (the mid-afternoon meal),

retiring to the drawing room where the lady of the house would brew up. The full-blown English tea ritual, with teapot, milk jug, sugar bowl, kettle and tea canister arranged on a tea table, gradually developed towards the mid-18th century. Early tea canisters were rectangular flasks with domed, pull-off tops. Before long they were made in pairs, sometimes with a larger box for sugar.

Lidded porcelain jars for holding tea were made as early as the 1730s at MEISSEN. In fact, probably the best name for ceramic tea containers is 'canisters'. The high value of tea encouraged the development of a lockable box or chest into which the canisters fitted. By the end of the century, the chests had taken over the decorative role from the canisters, and were made in a wide range of materials, predominantly wood, often beautifully inlaid with marquetry, but also tortoiseshell, ivory, enamel, mother-of-pearl,

and scrolled-paper work. Varying in shape, they could be rectangular, octagonal, round, oval, sarcophagus-shaped or even in the form of apples or pears. The larger chest-types might be fitted with metal receptacles (foil-lined to prevent tainting) for different teas, and a glass bowl for sugar. Smaller ones from the late 18th and early 19th centuries were themselves lined to hold the tea.

The term caddy, from *kati*, the Malay word for a measure of weight, was not applied to them until the late 18th century. Porcelain vases for holding tea were also made in the late 18th century — these oval jars with lids are sometimes erroneously known as TEAPOYS. Soon, tea services were being made by most of the major European factories which included a tea canister and trays for the teapot and spoons. Both blue and white and coloured sets were imported from China in huge numbers

▲ Elers Brothers red ware teapot, *c*1700, copying the Chinese (£400-£600)

including special orders with coats of arms. Enamelled glass and Battersea enamel canisters were also made. By the Victorian period, tea was cheaper, and plainer caddies reflected this.

Tea urns, often silver, were made in England from the 1760s. Later, copper examples were produced. Water is heated by a spirit burner, or by a red-hot iron core inside. This contrasts with the Russian samovar, in which water is heated by burning wood or charcoal inside a central funnel. Samovars have a fitting on top to hold a small pot of concentrated tea.

▼ Typical late George III tea set in silver, *c*1813-15, in rather worn condition (£700-£800)

▲ **Two from a set of eight Regency** parcel-gilt and painted tea canisters, as used in shops **(£3,000-£4,000)**

◀ **Composite set of silver** tea caddies, sugar box and teaspoons in case, 1705-46 **(£10,000-£12,000)**

▶ **Mahogany tea urn stand** with pierced fretwork gallery **(£4,500)**

◀ **Electro-plated kettle** and stand with spirit burner by Barnard, 1845. Seen at the Huddersfield Roadshow **(£500-£600)**

TEAK

One of the hardest and most durable woods, found in India and Burma. It has a golden brown colour, which darkens with age. It was used in the 18th and 19th centuries for campaign furniture, because of its tough qualities, and it has also occasionally been used for table tops, garden furniture, and ship furniture.

▶ **Mahogany** drum top 'teapoy', c1835 **(£2,500)**

TEAPOY

Often thought to be a term for a porcelain tea-vase, a teapoy is actually a small tripod table. The word derives from the Hindu word *tepai,* which means three-legged. A more common misuse from the 1820s is for a three- or four-footed pillar supporting a tea chest, as shown above.

£££-££££

TELEPHONES

A by-product of the increasing electronic wizardry of the modern telephone has been a widespread fascination with the classic instruments of the past, as collectors buy originals and replicas for use and as style statements. With their separate mouthpiece, the pedestal or candlestick telephones of the Edwardian era to the early '20s are decorative but impractical, so collectors tend to go for the elegant BAKELITE instruments of the 1930s. In Britain the most desirable model is the 162 series, first made in 1929, the earliest to have the hand set on the top. Its flared pyramid shape came in a number of colours,

If you go down to the woods today

TEDDY BEARS

It is not known whether Morris MICHTOM or Richard STEIFF made the first teddy bear. Whichever it was, the year was 1903. In that year, Mr Michtom's bear was apparently selling well in his Brooklyn, New York, store, and the Steiff bear was exhibited at the Leipzig Fair, attracting the attention of one of the biggest New York import houses, which is said to have placed an order for 3,000 specimens.

At home, the German bears appear to have been known as 'Freund Petz'. They borrowed their present name from the American President, Theodore (Teddy) Roosevelt.

Well-known makes now sell for huge sums but lesser bears and those in poor condition are not much sought after. Most popular are bears that have some form of identification, such as the Steiff metal button in the left ear (determining also the age) or a label. Otherwise they are hard to authenticate.

Early bears have some characteristics in common: they have long front limbs as they were meant to stand on all-fours in a bear-like position; they have a long snout and a hump on the back. They were stuffed with a wool which should be crisp and crunchy but is now normally little more than sawdust. Some were fitted with a growl, but these have almost invariably long ceased to function.

Do not be tempted to try and wash, repair or restuff teddies — this should always be left to a professional.

American and German teddy bears were manufactured from 1904. American firms include Columbia Teddy Bear Manufacturers, Commonwealth Toy and Novelty Co, Harman Manufacturing Co, IDEAL TOY CO and Knickerbocker. Among the Germans are BING, Bruin, Hermann, Schuco and Sussenguth. British manufacturers, who started large-scale production in the 1920s, included CHAD VALLEY, Chiltern, DEAN'S RAG BOOK CO, Ealon Toys, J. K. Farnell, MERRYTHOUGHT, Pedigree and Norah Wellings.

Beige and yellow are the most common colours, with black, silvery white, grey, rust and cinnamon being rarer and more valuable.

A 7in to 12in, beige Steiff teddy, c1920, in good condition, can be bought at auction for around £500 although earlier ones, as shown in the photographs, can fetch five times as much.

◀ Forged Steiff teddy bears as seen at the Huddersfield Roadshow. These duds are becoming quite common and are of no value. Beware

▶ 17-inch teddy by Steiff, 1904. Brought into the Manchester Roadshow (£1,000–£1,500)

▶ **Unusual English teddy** with expanding arms (£300–£500)

◀ **Ericsson No 16 'skeleton' telephone,** early 20th century (£150–£200)

with cream, green and red being much rarer than black. This instrument required a separate bell box. It was replaced from 1936 by the chunkier 332 series (with built-in bell), which is far more common. The 332s, too, were made in a range of colours. Both types are frequently adapted for contemporary use, along with other classic designs.

££-£££

TELESCOPES

These became widespread in Europe in the early 17th century, although their origins were probably much earlier. Refracting telescopes use lenses to focus light, while reflecting telescopes use mirrors. Refracting telescopes were the earliest to develop, and examples from the late 17th and early 18th centuries are covered in dyed vellum or fishskin. Mid-18th-century examples have long wooden tubes, while in the 19th century improved brass tubing made telescopes more compact. The brass could be covered with wood or leather, and some, particularly Italian examples, were elaborately decorated. Reflecting telescopes were more popular in the 18th century because they were free of the colour-disturbance effects of the refracting variety. The finest reflecting examples were made in London by makers such as James Short. DOLLOND invented his achromatic lens in about 1760.

£££-£££££

▶ **Large Steiff teddy,** c1908-09 Seen at the Taunton Roadshow (£2,000–£3,000)

A-Z *of Antiques* Hunting

TERRACOTTA

Italian for 'baked earth', used to describe red, unglazed earthenware, commonly used in bricks, but also decoratively. Terracotta wares emulating the ancient Greek style were made in the early 19th century by WEDGWOOD in the *rosso antico* body. It is also used for garden urns, flower pots and sculptural pieces.

TESTER

The canopy over a bed, which may be supported on a headboard and two posts, or four posts, or, if a 'half-tester', fly free from the head in apparent defiance of gravity. A chair of state and a pulpit may also have a tester; the latter for acoustic purposes.

◀ Rare brass thimble, c1730-50. Seen at the Guernsey Roadshow (£50-£60)

THIMBLES

Needlewomen's fingers have been protected by these short metal caps since Roman times, when thimbles were cast in bronze. Steel thimbles were common in the 18th and 19th centuries, and many were made of silver, although few are hallmarked. Georgian silver examples may be decorated with filigree work or applied gemstones, while many souvenir and commemorative examples were made in the 19th and 20th centuries. Thimbles were also produced from the 18th century in porcelain and enamel. Other materials include ivory, bone, hardwood, MOTHER-OF-PEARL, porcelain, glass and BAKELITE. Thimble cases were also made in a variety of materials, some with compartments for needles and pins.

      ££-£££

THISTLE CUP

A Scottish speciality, made of silver with a round base and flared rim (somewhat thistle-shaped), an S-shaped handle and lobed decoration rising from the base. Thistle cups were made in the late 17th and early 18th centuries. Thistle glasses, made in various sizes, were not necessarily for whisky. Around 1900 they were advertised as being for champagne.

££-££££

THONET, MICHAEL (1796-1871)

The pioneer of BENTWOOD. He developed a technique by which solid lengths of beech could be softened by boiling or steaming, and bent into frames for lightweight and functional chairs. Thonet patented his process in 1841, and established his business in Vienna in 1842. He streamlined his designs until they could be mass-produced—the best-known example, Chair No. 14, comprises only six parts. From 1859, when mass-production was established, Thonet exported much to the USA and the rest of Europe. By 1871 his company was the largest furniture-maker in the world. His designs are classics, pared down to the utmost simplicity and possessing considerable elegance. Perhaps the best example is his rocking chair, composed of flowing lines, functional yet decorative.

THUYA

Soft, close-grained, red-brown wood with mottled markings, used for inlays and veneers.

TIFFANY, CHARLES LOUIS (1812-1902) AND LOUIS COMFORT (1848-1933)

A great name in American decorative arts, Tiffany is synonymous both with American silverware through Charles Louis, and with original ART NOUVEAU designs through his son Louis Comfort. Charles Louis was a goldsmith and jeweller who set up in New York in 1837, initially as an importer and retailer of 'fancy goods' from Europe and the Far East. He soon developed a reputation for supplying fine jewellery specially commissioned from top European and American makers, using fine stones in designs inspired by many cultures—classical antiquity, Persian, Renaissance and Gothic as well as up-to-the-minute Art Nouveau. The silver side of the business also flourished. Tiffany won an award at the Paris Exhibition in 1867 for his display of silver. A further endorsement of his success as a manufacturer came from his spectacular array of royal patrons—23 by the 1890s, including Queen Victoria, the Shah of Persia and the Tsar of Russia. Tiffany silver

◀ Rare jack-in-the-pulpit favrile vase by Louis Comfort Tiffany, 20in high (£4,500)

followed the popular historic-revival and exotic-Oriental styles of the time, some of the most beautiful having delicate, Japanese-inspired designs encrusted with gold and copper details. Besides lavish presentation pieces, Tiffany was also known for high-quality household wares. Louis Comfort Tiffany studied as a painter in Paris, and was inspired by William MORRIS and the Aesthetic Movement, turning to the decorative arts in 1878 and establishing an interior design firm in New York a year later (his commissions included rooms in the White House). It is, however, his glass for which he is most famous, adding a new dimension to Art Nouveau with his studio glass and extraordinary lamps. He developed a type of iridescent glass which he called 'FAVRILE'. This was widely used in his lamps, typically as small fragments held in a network of metal, resembling stained glass, or as shades in the form of flowers. Lamps and other glassware such as goblets, vases, scent bottles and even stained glass windows and mosaics were made at the Tiffany Studios which he set up in 1900. His work was popular in Europe as well as America, and was widely imitated. After his father's death in 1902, he became art director of his father's company, and applied himself mostly to jewellery. Although the Tiffany Studios closed in the 1930s, the company continues today in New York and London.

££££-££££££

TIGER WARE

An old name puzzlingly given to stoneware which is not stripy, nor gold and black, but mottled brown on grey. Tiger ware, usually jugs, was imported into England in the 16th and 17th centuries from the Rhenish potteries, and was often mounted in silver. Similar ware was made by John DWIGHT of Fulham late in the 17th century.

TIGER'S EYE

An attractive form of chalcedony (quartz) which is brown, shot with lustrous yellow.

Wall to wall impressions

TILES

Although tiles were made extensively in the Middle Ages and, in DELFTWARE and CREAM-WARE, made a significant contribution to 18th-century interior decoration, most collectors tend to concentrate on those of the Victorian and later periods.

Thanks to technical developments, which radically changed both manufacturing and decorating processes, the 19th century was the great age of the tile. First to arrive were encaustic floor tiles with their multi-coloured patterns made from inlaid clays. First made by MINTON and other companies during the 1830s, they were subsequently used in huge quantities to decorate the floors of both grand and domestic buildings throughout Europe and many other parts of the world. Next, from the 1850s, came the moulded wall tiles with their colourful MAJOLICA glazes, adding rich pattern to many formal Victorian interiors.

The final, most influential achievement of the industry was the thin dust pressed tile, made for painted or printed decoration and produced by hundreds of potteries in thousands of patterns, reflecting the impact of contemporary styles from revivalism to ART NOUVEAU and ART DECO. Inspiration came from every conceivable source, with an emphasis on naturalism, the arts of Japan and the various styles of revivalism and the ARTS AND CRAFTS MOVEMENT. The patterns ranged from repeating motifs, to be used as ceramic wallpaper, to picture tiles made individually or in related sets, often for use in fire surrounds and furniture.

▲ 8in tiles from the 1860s. The upper one is stamped Minton (£5-£10) ▶

A-Z *of Antiques Hunting*

TIN AND TIN-GLAZE

Tin is a white metal which in its natural state does not corrode easily, and was therefore used to line vessels of other metals, such as copper, or for plating. It was also combined with other metals to make alloys such as PEWTER and BRONZE. Tin oxide, added to a lead glaze on earthenware makes a white, impermeable surface resembling porcelain. This is variously termed FAIENCE, MAIOLICA or DELFTWARE. The technique was imported from Persia around the 13th century. It was also occasionally used to whiten porcelain.

TINDER BOX

Being able to strike a light was of crucial importance before the development of electricity. Tinder boxes for this purpose were made of tinned iron in a number of forms. The most usual were round, with a candle nozzle in the lid and a handle on the side. Inside would be a flint and steel, and some combustible material (tinder) which the sparks could ignite. Small, pocket tinder boxes were also made, and other designs were based on flintlock or WHEEL-LOCK pistols.

£users£users£users£

TINWORTH, GEORGE (1843-1913)

A potter who worked at the DOULTON pottery from 1866, one of a group of artists who came there through the connection with the Lambeth Art School. Scrolling foliage with relief detailing was typical of Tinworth's work, but his subjects were wide-ranging, from children and animals to religious plaques.

TOASTING FORK AND TOASTER

Many different varieties of toasting fork developed from the two- or three-pronged fork used from early times for cooking meat. The most usual was three-pronged, while others had special brackets to hold cheese as well (the Georgians even designed a

◀ **Silver toasting fork** seen at the Truro Roadshow, c1740-50 **(£300)**

gadget to hold the cheese and bread together while toasting). Some toasting forks had extending handles to prevent the toasting of hands. Toasters combined a method of holding the bread with a trivet or hooks for hanging on the grate. The earliest were made to stand on the hearth on low feet, and might have slots for bread which could be rotated to cook both sides. The commonest type of toaster for use in front of a grate had spikes on a sliding frame of adjustable height. Others had an adjustable fork.

£users£users£users£

TOBY JUG

A pottery jug in the form of a figure with a tricorn hat, which forms the lip of the jug. Toby jugs were made by the Staffordshire potter Ralph Wood and his son from around 1760, and were widely copied by other potteries. Many versions were made, depicting different characters including a female one, Martha GUNN. The original Toby was probably Toby Philpot, about whom a song, *The Brown Jug*, was published in 1761. More recent characters, such as the First World

◀ **Staffordshire 'Thin Man'** Toby jug, 12in high, 1840 **(£250-£350)**

War leaders after models by Sir Francis Carruthers-Gould, the first newspaper cartoonist, have also been commemorated in jug form.

£users£users£users£

TODDY LADLE AND LIFTER

A toddy ladle is a smaller Scottish version of the punch ladle, usually silver with a whalebone handle. Toddy is made from whisky with hot water and sugar, and is served in a punch bowl. Another way of dispensing it is the toddy lifter, which looks like a small, slender glass decanter with a hole in the bottom. It is plunged into the toddy until full, then, with a finger placed over the neck aperture, lifted out and released over the glass. They became popular in the late 18th century and are thought to have been invented in Scotland, although also made in England and Ireland.

£users£users£users£

TOFT, THOMAS (d.1689)

Staffordshire potter renowned for his slipware. Thirty-one large dishes and three pots are known inscribed with his name and therefore attributed to him, but other names also appear on this style of 'Toft-ware', including Ralph and James Toft and George and William Taylor. Typical dishes are covered with white slip, then decorated in trailed dark brown slip with designs such as Adam and Eve, Charles II in the oak tree and the lion and the unicorn. Areas are filled in with orange, and details touched in with white dots.

TOMPION, THOMAS (1639-1713)

The most famous clockmaker of all, known as the 'father of English clockmaking'. He was admitted to the Clockmakers' Company in 1671 and produced many watches, bracket and LONGCASE

▶ **Toddy ladle** with whalebone handle, 1798 **(£150)**

300

clocks, as well as BAROMETERS and some LANTERN clocks. His workshop produced around 6,000 watches and about 550 clocks, and these were renowned for their accuracy. He was greatly esteemed, and on his death was described thus: 'the most famous and most skilful person at this art in the whole world, and first of all [to bring] watches to anything of perfection… he had a strange working head, and was well seen in mathematics'. In conjunction with the scientist Robert Hooke he is credited with innovations such as the balance spring and the cylinder escapement. His clocks had refinements such as perpetual calendar works, elaborate repeating mechanisms and astronomical detail. He was succeeded in the business by his nephew and partner George Graham.

TORCHÈRE

A small stand designed to carry candles, but also used for ornaments. Introduced in the early 18th century, it usually stood on three legs.

£££-££££

▲ Tortoiseshell and silver casket, Portuguese, c1750 (£4,500-£5,000)

TORTOISESHELL

A hard material of characteristic mottled dark brown and yellow appearance, widely used in decorative arts. Malleable when heated, it can be moulded. It can also be highly polished, and was often inlaid with silver PIQUÉ for use in small boxes. Large sheets were used to veneer BOULLE furniture. It came from the shell of the hawksbill turtle, and its use now, like that of ivory, is carefully monitored and restricted.

It must be wood

TREEN

This covers all manner of wooden domestic objects which cannot be described as furniture, and can include some remarkably decorative as well as useful pieces. Wood of all sorts has been carved or turned by country people for centuries, and early examples still exist, although most of the objects to be found today date from the 18th and 19th centuries.

Woods tend to be hard, since this is easier to work — fruitwoods, olive, walnut and yew are all encountered, while lignum vitae, the hardest of all (so dense that it sinks in water), produced some of the finest pieces. Ebony, mahogany and teak were also used.

The range of treen objects is very wide. Elegantly turned goblets were made, as well as more unusual pieces such as Scottish QUAICHS. Bowls in many sizes were produced, along with kitchen utensils such as spoons, butter pats, bread boards, rolling pins, ladles, skimmers and biscuit moulds. Many of these are plain and simple, with no

decoration or finish. More decorative are snuffboxes, needle cases, knitting sheaths, turned boxes and pots, pepper and salt holders, and apple and pear tea caddies. Welsh spoons are a distinct type of treen, highly carved as love tokens.

▶ Treen rosewood shoe with buttons. English apprentice piece, c1840 (£300-£400)

▶ Treen objects: (left to right) coffee mill, candlesticks and spice box (£600-£1,000 each)

TRANSFER PRINTING

A method of decorating ceramics and enamel, developed in the mid-18th century at the Battersea Enamel Works by John Brooks, and then taken up at the BOW and WORCESTER factories before becoming a widely used form of decoration on pottery and porcelain in the late 18th and 19th centuries. A design is engraved on a copper plate. The plate is inked and a print taken from it on paper which is applied to the ceramic body and removed, leaving the image to be fixed by firing. The image might be monochrome, or coloured in by hand. A technique for printing in several colours was developed in the 1840s by PRATT. Another technique is called 'bat printing', where a STIPPLE-ENGRAVED design is transferred using a 'bat' of glue instead of paper.

Blade runners

TSUBA

One of the most sought-after of the many collectable parts that go to make up the JAPANESE SWORD is the tsuba (the t is almost silent). This is the guard between the blade and the hilt, and serves to protect the sword-user's hands from being cut by the opponent's blade.

Tsuba are normally made from iron or bronze, and range from simple, plain and utilitarian examples to highly decorative pieces, incorporating precious metals, which are works of art in themselves. Look out for examples of the latter, particularly those that contain signatures, which can sometimes add to their value.

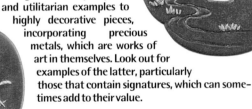

▲ Two sides of a Mito school tsuba, late 17th to early 18th century, unsigned (£60-£80)

TREMBLEUSE

A French term for an 18th-century cup and saucer adapted to be stable when held by a shaky hand. This was done by giving the saucer either a raised ring (of silver or ceramic), or a deep well into which the cup could fit. These were made at SÈVRES, also at the CHELSEA-Derby factory.

 ££-££££

TRI-ANG

Established as Lines Bros Ltd in about 1919, Tri-ang became a major toy-maker in the 1930s. Among their products were tin-plate toys, DOLLS' HOUSES and furniture, forts (for soldiers), garden wagons, carts, wheelbarrows, dolls' prams, and later bicycles and tricycles. In 1935 Tri-ang started to make 'MINIC' miniature clockwork vehicles, and from 1937 soft toys as well. 'Frog' model aeroplanes were also Tri-ang products. Today those toys in good condition have a value in the collector's market.

 ££-£££

TRIDDARN

A Welsh form of DRESSER or press cupboard with three tiers, the lower two with doors, the top open for the display of plate.

TROUBADOUR STYLE

The French version of the GOTHIC REVIVAL, *Style Troubadour* reflected a new interest in the medieval period, and flourished with the restoration of the French monarchy in 1814. Gothic architectural details found

▼ Tri-ang Regal Roadster lorry with original box, 1963 (£150)

their way onto furniture, tapestries, and small objects not always suited to such grandeur. The style was condemned in the mid-1830s, and soon went out of fashion.

TULA STEEL FURNITURE

Tula in central Russia was the seat of the armaments industry from its foundation by Peter the Great until modern times. In peaceful moments the workers made steel furniture and ornaments, decorated with cut facets. Catherine the Great made Tula furniture fashionable, especially after her visit to BOULTON's Birmingham works. FENDERS and FIRE IRONS were made, as well as elegant X-frame chairs and tables. The wares were sold at special annual fairs. After 1796 Imperial patronage ended abruptly, because Tsar Paul I loathed anything that his mother had liked.

R ££££-£££££

TULIPIÈRE

Tulips were all the rage during the RESTORATION, and appear as decoration on many works of art. To display fresh tulips, special vases were made of tin-glazed earthenware, not only at Delft, but also in England and elsewhere in Europe. There were two common forms, either with spouts spread out in a fan, or tall vases in the form of PAGODAS with corner spouts at every level. Porcelain tulipières were also made in Vienna and China.

£££-£££££

TUNBRIDGE WARE

A technique of mass-producing MARQUETRY designs was developed in the mid-17th century in Tunbridge Wells in Kent. It involved the gluing together of rods of different-coloured woods to form a picture or design when viewed in section (like a stick of seaside rock). A thin slice would be cut and glued onto the surface of the wooden object to be decorated, creating an instant marquetry design that could be readily repeated. Although earlier pieces exist, the technique came into its own in the early 19th century, and enormous numbers of

▲ **Tunbridge ware box,** possibly showing Stoneleigh Abbey, c1830 **(£400)**

wooden articles were decorated in this way. Subjects include geometric designs, but pictorial images were especially popular—views of Tunbridge Wells and landscapes, children, animals, birds and flowers. Countless small items were decorated in this way—mostly boxes, games boards, picture frames, napkin rings, watch stands, stamp boxes, pin trays and paper knives. Larger objects such as games tables and writing boxes were also made.

TUREEN

A large, deep, lidded vessel which may be silver, pottery or porcelain, for serving soup or stew. Smaller versions are for sauces. Shapes follow prevailing fashions, but tureens are usually oval or round. Examples in the form of animals' heads, swans or other creatures were made as novelties by factories such as STRASBOURG and CHELSEA. The latter's rabbit and bird tureens were copied by SAMSON.

TURKISH STYLE

Things Turkish had aroused much interest in the 18th century, but it was

▲ **Turkish-style** mother-of-pearl and composition inlaid wood table, late 19th century **(£1,300)**

▼ **Worcester partridge-**shaped tureen and cover, c1765 **(£7,000-£8,000)**

not until the mid-19th century that Turkish style became fashionable, initially for furnishing rooms intended for smoking. The association between Turkey and fine tobacco made this style appropriate, and characteristic elements included low-level seating, arcaded fretwork, small tables, brass incense burners and of course Turkish carpets, while some gentlemen topped it off with a fez while smoking. The Turkish OTTOMAN, a long, low, upholstered seat without a back, had been introduced to England earlier in the 19th century. Later, Turkish style was no longer confined to the smoking room, and it became fashionable to have a Turkish corner in the drawing room.

TURNING LATHES AND EQUIPMENT

The craft of 'ornamental turning', producing decorative woodwork by means of lathe and chisel, was popular among English gentlemen during the early 19th century. Treadle lathes and all sorts of specialist tools were made by many companies to supply the craze, but by far the best were made by Holtzapffel & Co, which was in business from the late 18th century to the 1920s, also making everyday tools. As this was a gentlemanly pastime, it was essential that HARDWOOD items had neither function nor commercial value, although they do have value today.

 ££££

TYG

A large drinking vessel with between two and 11 handles arranged around its body, and sometimes a number of spouts. Also known as loving cups, for communal drinking, they were made in both silver and earthenware, the latter being common in the 17th and 18th centuries. Many earthenware ones were decorated with trailing SLIP, sometimes with initials and dates. In more modern times, porcelain examples have been made for commemorative purposes by companies such as COPELAND.

 £££-££££

UNDERGLAZE DECORATION

A technique employed on ceramics where decoration is applied before the piece is glazed. Cobalt blue is the most common underglaze colour, but copper red, although more difficult to control, was used in China from the 15th century. Later, other colours such as manganese (purple) and green appeared. Imported Chinese blue and white wares were copied in Europe from the 16th century, at Bow and other English porcelain factories, and particularly in the 19th century in Staffordshire transfer-printed earthenware and in PEARLWARE.

UNICORN

The unicorn symbolised purity for the Egyptians and Persians and in Christian iconography it may represent the Virgin. It also symbolised the medieval courtly lover, and could be caught only by a true virgin. It is the emblem of Scotland, and thus a supporter of the Royal Arms. Its horn was believed to be the antidote to all poisons, and so the unicorn became a trade sign for apothecaries. The horns of various creatures were sold as those of unicorns—the most usual being those of Arabian gazelles, and the most spectacular: narwhal tusks.

UPHOLSTERY

This is what makes furniture bearable to sit on, cushioning the bottom and comforting the back with all sorts of padding and stuffing. The term also applies to all other furniture and furnishings supplied by upholsterers, the most spectacular examples in medieval times being beds. The idea

Red coat relics

UNIFORMS

The transition from suits of armour to scarlet cloth uniforms took less than 100 years. By the end of Elizabeth I's reign, the use of armour was already declining, and the English Civil War (1642-51) saw the last of the three-quarter-length armour. Soon, only steel helmets, breast and backplates were worn.

The basic clothing for 17th-century soldiers was a buff coat, made of cowhide, but, as many troops wore it, it became difficult to differentiate friend from foe. Various methods of discrimination were adopted, such as a coloured sash around the waist or a coloured plume in the helmet. Some regiments started to wear blue or scarlet coats, and by the end of the 17th century the buff coat had the addition of coloured cloth across the chest, with matching cuffs. This led to identifying regiments by colour.

By the 18th century most regiments had adopted scarlet with various colour facings, and British soldiers were known as the Red Coats. The French wore blue, the Austrians white. Short jackets or coatees were worn until the Crimean War when, during the bitter Russian winter, they gave British soldiers no protection around the waist — and many died from exposure. Khaki dress was adopted during the wars in Africa and India, and by the First World War the camouflage era had dawned.

Occasionally small batches of uniforms appear on the market and can be bought for around £50 a tunic. Officers' regimental tunics of the late 19th and early 20th centuries sell for around £200-£400, those of other ranks going for less. Early 19th-century coatees vary considerably in price, often realising £1,000-£2,000 at auction.

▲ Staff sergeant's uniform, Hampshire Regt., c1900 **(£350)**

◀ Victorian colonel's tunic, Royal Engineers, c1875 **(£600)**

of making upholstery integral with the frame of a chair, rather than just loose cushions, seems not to have taken a serious hold until the later 17th century, when chairs with upholstered backs and seats appear in numbers. Upholstery developed throughout the 18th century, building up ever thicker layers and becoming part of chair design. Eighteenth-century upholstery also involved drapes and curtains, with furniture to match. A great advance came in the early 19th century with the invention of coiled spring upholstery, patented in 1828, which paved the way for all those comfortable, deeply sprung Victorian chairs.

VALENCIENNES LACE

A type of linen pillow-lace made at Valenciennes in France, typically with scrolls and stylised flowers in the design. It was one of the finest and most expensive types of 18th-century lace. Production continued into the 19th century, and similar lace was made in neighbouring areas. Valenciennes lace was much imitated in the 19th century.

VALLAURIS

A centre of traditional craft pottery between Cannes and Nice on the French Riviera. Clément MASSIER (c1845-1917) was born there and had his Golfe-Juan studio nearby. Later, Picasso produced his ceramics at Vallauris.

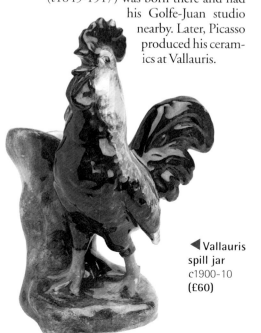

◀ Vallauris spill jar c1900-10 (£60)

VARGUENA

A 19th-century term for a 16th- or 17th-century Spanish type of desk, effectively a chest with a drop front which opens to reveal a fitted interior, often elaborately inlaid with complex designs. They generally stand on either a carved table-support or another chest. Both the interiors and the stands tend to contrast with the plainness of the exteriors.

£££££-£££££

VASE

Vases come in an enormous range of shapes, from the Campana (a classical, upturned bell-like urn with flaring sides above a shallow, two-handled bowl and a pedestal foot) to the SÈVRES *vaisseau-à-mât* in the form of a sailing ship, designed to conceal pot-pourri beneath the rigging. Vases were also made in sets, called GARNITURES, comprising one, two or three pairs of matching vases around a grand central one.

VAUXHALL PORCELAIN

Excavations at the recently discovered site of the the Vauxhall factory on the Albert Embankment in London have confirmed that wares previously attributed to William Ball's factory in LIVERPOOL were made at Vauxhall, which operated from 1755-64.

Evidence of a pottery and a glass works were found on the same site.

VEILLEUSE

A system for keeping food or drink warm by the bedside for invalids, it comprised a teapot, covered cup or bowl slotting into a hollow pedestal which houses a candle. These ceramic contraptions were made throughout Europe from the mid-18th century to the mid-19th. Clarke's NIGHT-LIGHT was a variant, and modern versions are still produced.

£££-££££

VENEER

Very thin sheets of fine wood applied to another surface, often a furniture carcass of some lesser timber. Full advantage can be taken of the decorative figuring of the wood by cutting veneers at particular angles and across areas of irregular growth such as roots and burrs—OYSTER VENEER is an example of this. Wood veneers were hand-sawn in the 18th century, and are thicker than those of the early 19th century, cut on a circular saw. Later in the 19th century machine tools cut veneers even more thinly. The term veneer also refers to tortoiseshell or ivory, applied in a thin layer to a different material.

A-Z of Antiques Hunting

VENETIAN GLASS

Glass was made in Venice from the 5th century AD, with the industry (by then flourishing) moving, for fear of fire, to the island of Murano in the lagoon at the end of the 13th century. Venetian glass owed its great success to the 15th-century development of *cristallo*, a thin, delicate soda glass ideal for elaborate trailing and threading, giving rise to fantastic wine glasses with winged stems formed of all sorts of curlicues and loops of glass. Venetian glass was widely copied elsewhere in the 16th century. This FAÇON DE VENISE is difficult to tell from true Venetian. Other characteristic types of Venetian glass were *filigrana*, with threads of white spiralling around the body, and MILLEFIORI. Extravagant chandeliers adorned with flowers and fruits were made in the 18th century, along with decorative mirrors. These are still produced to old designs.

VERNIS MARTIN

A general term for French 18th-century JAPANNING on wood, which takes its name from Guillaume MARTIN and his brothers. They had a monopoly to copy Oriental lacquer, but also developed a special coloured varnish which was particularly lustrous when applied in many coats. This became known as *vernis Martin*, and might be in any of a number of colours including yellow, grey, blue and green. It was applied to furniture, carriages and small items such as fans, boxes and bodkin cases. Now the term covers work by other craftsmen as well.

VERRE ÉGLOMISE

Glass decorated on the back with gilding, coloured designs and metal foils, sometimes seen as a frame to mirrors. It is an ancient technique dating from Roman times, but was revived in the late 18th century, by French frame-maker J. B. Glomy, after whom it is now named.

VESTA CASES

Named after the Roman goddess of the hearth, vestas were small wax matches with phosphorous tips. When first produced in the 1830s,

▲ Silver vesta cases, c1900, seen at the Luton Hoo Roadshow (**£30–£40 each**)

they were kept in small SNUFFBOXES, with rough striking plates. There were safety problems with this form, as a stray spark could ignite the lot. In the late 1860s, the distinct vesta case appeared, with the lid at the end. A small internal spring was added to ensure the lid could not accidentally flip open. By the end of the 19th century, vesta cases were being produced in large numbers (especially in BIRMINGHAM). Oblong forms were engraved, stamped, chased or enamelled. Others took the shape of pigs, owls, snakes, bottles, biscuits or bullets. The end came with the development of the petrol lighter around the time of the First World War.

££-£££

VICTORIA CROSS

Britain's highest award for military valour, this MEDAL was instituted during the Crimean War. The first were presented in June 1857. To date 1,351 have been awarded, including three bars. Until the First World War the metal came from a captured Russian canon, thereafter from a Chinese gun.

VIENNA PORCELAIN

Porcelain manufacture in Vienna was begun by C. Du Paquier in 1719. This factory produced most original and finely decorated wares in the late BAROQUE style. Black or iron-red monochrome, pale shades of green, pink and purple, CHINOISERIE scenes, mythological subjects and armorial wares predominated. Silver as well as gilding was a speciality. For inventiveness Du Paquier porcelains are without peer, but the factory was never a commercial success. It was taken over by the state in 1744. This second, State Period was the antithesis

▲ Victorian scrap-work screen, 1860-70 (**£200–£300**)

306

Lasting values from the days of Empire

VICTORIANA

The reign of Queen Victoria, which lasted from 1837 until 1901, was the longest in English history, and a period during which increasing prosperity extended to the middle classes, lending a new impetus to the arts and encouraging popular rather than exclusive styles. The term 'Victoriana' was an abusive label for a despised period which fell from fashion after the First World War. It is now getting the recognition it deserves.

In the early Victorian period, the NEO-CLASSICAL styles of the REGENCY continued, along with a new flourishing of ROCOCO, which fitted in with the dawning of romanticism. Porcelain, pottery and silver all expressed the neo-Rococo in frilly, feminine forms, and furniture developed curling legs and scrolling arms and backs. Victorian romanticism found expression in a fascination with the Middle Ages,

which inspired a more serious exploration of the GOTHIC style by PUGIN and others, with stained glass windows, panelled walls, suits of armour and dismal tiger skins. Already the eclecticism so typical of the High Victorian age was apparent, with curly Rococo rubbing shoulders with ponderous Gothic. Comfort was all-important, and furniture typically had ever more generous upholstery, with springs and deep buttoning contributing to a sense of ease and well-being at home.

By the time of the Great Exhibition in 1851, manufacturers were capable of the most extraordinary confections owing more to industrial expertise than to artistic sensitivity. The cleverer the technique and the more monstrous and remarkable the piece, the louder the public applauded it. EGYPTIAN, GREEK, ROMAN, Byzantine, LOUIS XIV, GOTHIC and Renaissance styles were all imitated — and sometimes

blended. Delight in gadgets and the machine age was apparent everywhere.

These excesses of historical and mixed-up styles pervaded the period. The typical mid-Victorian room was filled with furniture, cluttered with ornamental objects, and hung with heavy, dark drapes.

The ceramic factories in Stoke-on-Trent poured out a stream of utilitarian wares to a welcoming Empire that made full use of the newly developed machinery and techniques. The Victorian era was the last to see the general availability of cheap skilled labour combined with a wealthy middle class which could afford finely made objects in quantity.

Reaction came through the ARTS AND CRAFTS MOVEMENT, inspired by the critic John Ruskin and motivated by William MORRIS. Their idea was to improve decorative design, and encourage hand crafts rather than machine

▲ Victorian woollen flowers under a cloche, 12in high (£150-£200)

processes. Their designs were simple and promoted 'beauty with usefulness' rather than ornament for its own sake.

Another late Victorian development was the AESTHETIC MOVEMENT, which took its inspiration from the Japanese fashion, and promoted 'art for art's sake'. Aestheticism was a lifestyle, as well as a matter of art and design, and found a champion in Oscar Wilde. By the end of the Victorian period, modernists were looking to ART NOUVEAU on the Continent, while traditionalists were still reviving earlier styles.

▼ Royal Worcester jardinière, c1865 (£1,500)

▶ Typically sentimental painting by Victorian artist Arthur Elsley (£44,000)

▲ **Vienna cabaret** cup and saucer, c1860
(£300-£500 with stand)

of the Du Paquier era. Charming figures predominate, by L. Dannhauser and J. J. Niedermeyer. In pale pinks and yellows, they are easily spotted by the gilt decoration edging their bases. In the 1770s A. Grassi modelled brilliant caricature figures and an attempt was made to imitate SÈVRES CABARETS, painted with fine landscapes on coloured and gilt grounds. Von Sorgenthal took over the management in 1784 and had success with magnificent wares in the NEO-CLASSICAL taste. The entire surface disappeared under richly coloured and gilt decoration, including mythological subjects. 'Oriental' lacquered wares in red, black and gold were also outstanding. The death of Sorgenthal in 1804 was really the end of Vienna as a dynamic factory, but J. Nigg painted brilliant still-life plaques in the 1830s. Many pieces on the market are later imitations of Sorgenthal wares. Decoration is frequently printed. 'Painted' subjects are signed 'F. Boucher' and 'A. Kaufmann', although neither of them worked at Vienna. Du Paquier wares are unmarked; State Period wares impressed or painted in blue with the Imperial shield or beehive mark. Under Sorgenthal, this was accompanied by

the last three figures of the year (e.g. 804 for 1804). Subjects are often described in German on the back. Imitations have similar marks, thinly printed in underglaze blue or enamel.

VILLEROY AND BOCH

A German ceramic and glass factory, dating back to 1748 when a small FAIENCE concern was set up by François Boch. His sons developed the business, making cream-coloured earthenware as well, and in 1836 they united with the Villeroy family. Villeroy and Boch acquired several other factories during the 19th and 20th centuries, developing a range of decorative and utilitarian products .

£-£££

VINCENNES PORCELAIN

The forerunner to the factory at SÈVRES, Vincennes was established in 1738 to make SOFT-PASTE porcelain, and became the national porcelain factory of France. Early wares included naturalistic porcelain flowers, as well as small figures. Tableware followed in the late 1740s, decorated with Chinese-inspired designs or those borrowed from MEISSEN. Rich ground colours were developed in the 1750s, including several blues and pink. These were further enriched by elaborate gilding and enamel decoration in CARTOUCHES. BISCUIT figures were another speciality of Vincennes. In 1756 the factory moved to new premises at Sèvres, and was taken over by the king three years later.

£££-££££

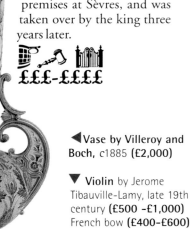

◀ **Vase by Villeroy and Boch**, c1885 (£2,000)

▼ **Violin** by Jerome Tibauville-Lamy, late 19th century (£500 -£1,000) French bow (£400-£600)

VIOLIN

Arguably the most important instrument in Western music since its development from the three-stringed type in the 16th century. It reached perfection between 1650 and 1730, particularly in the hands of such makers as the STRADIVARI and Guarneri families, although examples have been made all over Europe, most extensively in Italy, France and Germany. The front is pine, and the growth rings tell an expert whether it originated in southern or northern Europe, and possibly when—the rest of us can look at the label inside, and perhaps be misled. The back and sides are maple, the back acquiring its 'belly' by sculpting from a solid block. Earlier instruments are more dramatically modelled, with deep bellies. Many old instruments found today are 19th-century German or Czech, (with 'Stradivarius' labels) or French products, which have a certain flatness. German makers sometimes brushed on stain to imitate the patina of age around the rim. Certain fiddles made in countries with a strong folk tradition, such as Scotland or Norway, are of particular interest.

£££-£££££

VITRUVIAN SCROLL

Also known as wave-scroll or running dog, this is a pattern of repeated crested waves, much used in frieze decoration or on borders, particularly in classical or NEO-CLASSICAL design.

VoC

Monogram of the Dutch East India Company, a major force in trade in the 17th and 18th centuries. The company created a net of trade routes from Persia to Japan, with Batavia (now Djakarta) as its headquarters. VoC ships imported large quantities of merchandise from China, including silk, lacquer, tea and porcelain.

All sweetness and light

These are usually small boxes which open to reveal a hinged, pierced grille. Under the grille is kept a fine sponge soaked in an aromatic (sweet-smelling substance). Their function goes back to the days of the great unwashed when a lady or gentleman might find the stench of humanity or open sewers too much, and could simply open the vinaigrette and hope that the aromatic was powerful enough to overcome it.

The great period of vinaigrette production was from the end of the 18th century through to the middle years of the 19th when improved sanitation and personal hygiene rendered them obsolete. Most were produced by the toymen of BIRMINGHAM, but the best were usually made in London. In silver examples, the interiors, including the grille, were always gilded. Early grilles generally have simple geometric piercing (sometimes with similar engraving) or a filigree section inserted. Later grilles are often pierced and engraved with leaf or leaf and floral patterns. Unusual patterns such as musical instruments, birds and

▲ Silver vinaigrette by Samuel Hamilton, 1809, shown open below (£250) ▼

military trophies increase the value. The most common form of external decoration is engine-turned engraving as well as leaf scroll or leaf and floral engraving. Scenes add significantly to the value. These may be engraved, REPOUSSÉ or cast and were very much a speciality of the Birmingham makers. Some, such as Windsor Castle, are quite common, but the Bar Gate at Southampton, for instance, is rare and correspondingly valuable. Do beware of forgeries and be suspicious of any engraved railway or ballooning scenes: you may be lucky but most are modern engravings. For makers, see SNUFFBOXES.

▲ Gold vinaigrette with Roman micro-mosaic of a spaniel, c1820 (£1,700)

▶ Open vinaigrette showing grille with space beneath for sponge

WADE FIGURES

Wade is a Stoke-on-Trent firm that has specialised in making small pottery figures and ornamental giftwares, as well as a few larger items such as ornamental teapots. The figures often depict children, animals, and nursery rhyme and Disney characters such as Mickey Mouse, Donald Duck and Snow White and the Seven Dwarfs. These have become popular since the 1930s, and are collected, particularly by children. They have been inexpensive, but are now rising in price.

££-£££

Wade figure of a Russian girl, 1930s, ▲ rather flaked so value reduced (£100)

WAGER CUP

A cup, usually of silver, for wagers or drinking competitions on jolly occasions. Many are German in origin. The wager might be to empty a cup without spilling from its swivelled bowl, to empty a double bowl, or drink the contents of a windmill cup before the sails stop spinning.

££-££££

◀ Silver swivelling marriage, or wager cup (£1,000)

▲ **Cubist-style** Louis Wain ceramic cat, probably Czechoslovakian (**£300-£500**)

WAIN, LOUIS (1860-1939)

This is the man whose cats made him famous. Born in London, he studied art and then started drawing cats in 1883, depicting them humorously in human predicaments. Many of his pictures were published as postcards, which are now much collected, as are his original pen drawings, watercolours and oil paintings. He published annuals from 1901, and worked on strip cartoons in New York from 1907 to 1910. He developed schizophrenia and entered a mental home in 1918. Ceramic versions of his cats are collected today.

WAKE OR COFFIN TABLES

Irish mahogany tables with shallow drop-leaves either side of a long,

▼ **Wake table** made from a piece of Cuban mahogany, c1750 (**£20,000**)

narrow centre section, usually on square, chamfered legs. They date from around 1750-60, and take their name from the idea that a coffin might rest on the centre section (usually about 6ft by 15in) while the mourners sat around it. Despite their morbid associations, wake tables make ideal dining tables, and have been much faked and forged.

££££-£££££

WALDGLAS OR WEALD GLASS

An early type of glass, using potash from the ashes of burnt wood, and therefore made in wooded areas. Dark greenish or brownish Waldglas was made from the early Middle Ages in the forests (*Walde*) of Germany. From the 13th century, glass was made by the same process in the Weald of Kent, Surrey and Sussex. This Weald or Wealden glass was initially a lighter green than Waldglas, but later similar. A 1615 prohibition on the use of wood for industrial purposes put an end to this industry, which was deforesting areas of England as far afield as Newcastle-upon-Tyne and Stourbridge.

WALKING STICK

In past centuries, canes and walking sticks have been regarded as important dress accessories, rather than solely supports for the infirm. Latterly their role in male dress has been largely superseded by the more practical rolled umbrella. The most interesting part of a walking stick is the head, and all sorts of innovative and decorative ideas have been applied to it. Eighteenth-century

examples may open to reveal snuff, scent or perhaps a tiny mirror. In the late 18th and early 19th centuries, porcelain and enamel handles were popular, and might take various forms, human or animal. Walking sticks incorporating swords have been made from the late 18th century, and sticks have also been used to conceal all manner of other things, from a telescope to a fishing line, cigarettes to compasses. In the 19th century, ornamental examples were made in NAILSEA coloured glass.

£-£££

WALL, DR JOHN (1708-76)

One of the founders of the WORCESTER porcelain factory in 1751, who managed it until around 1774. Its wares during this period used to be referred to as 'Dr Wall Worcester'.

WALLPAPER

In use in the late 15th century as an alternative to tapestry or other wall-hangings, the earliest wallpapers were probably painted, although none survives to prove this. In the 16th

▼ **Three 19th-century walking sticks,** from left: with large ivory handle carved with coat of arms (**£300**); with ivory handle in form of a rose (**£150**); with silver handle (**£150**)

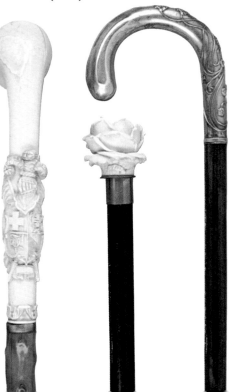

◀ **French wallpaper** panel by Zuber & Cie., 19th-century **(£6,000)**

century, woodblock printing was used, initially in black on white, but in 17th-century England colours might be added, and by the end of the century, flock wallpaper had appeared. Flower and CHINOISERIE patterns dominated in the early 18th century, and hand-painted Chinese wallpaper was imported. By the 1770s, France had taken the lead in wallpaper design. Repetitive floral patterns were enduringly popular, but there were brief fashions for scenic wallpaper and, in the 1760s, for print rooms with engravings stuck onto plain wallpapers. The 19th century saw a continuation of floral patterns, but also those imitating the tapestries of the past, and fashionable ART NOUVEAU designs. The great 19th-century French manufacturers of scenic panels, which have often been reprinted, were DUFOUR and Jean Zuber.

WALNUT

A hard wood varying in colour from light yellow-brown to greyish brown, with dark streaks. In England it was valued for furniture from the RESTORATION until mahogany became available in the early 18th century. It was also used for the best Italian, French and German furniture in the 16th and 17th centuries.

WARDIAN CASE

A glass case with a domed top, forming a mini-conservatory on a stand, under which plants could be grown. It was popular with Victorians as an interior decoration feature, and took its name from Nathaniel Bagshaw Ward who discovered that plants flourished in this way.

   £££

WARDROBE

Name given by Chaucer to a privy, but otherwise originally a dressing room—a 'guard-robe'—where clothes were kept. HEPPLEWHITE used the word in 1788 for a free-standing fitted cupboard for clothes, but such items were more usually known as clothes presses in the 18th century. From the 19th century, a wardrobe often included a long mirror.

WARMING PAN

The best way of taking the chill off a bed, in the days before hot-water bottles, was to slide one of these between the sheets. On the end of a long handle was a circular metal box (copper, brass or occasionally silver), sometimes with a pierced lid, into which hot coals were placed. These were in favour from the 16th century until they were ousted by the stone hot-water bottle in the 19th century. A warming pan was even the excuse for a revolution in 1688, when a fraudulent baby Prince of Wales was said to have been smuggled into the Queen's bed in one.

   **£££**

◀ **Walnut linen chest** c1730, seen at the Bexhill Roadshow **(£5,000–£8,000)**

◀ **Brass warming pan,** Dutch, 1614 **(£900–£1,000)**

WASH-HAND STAND

These are the descendants of the mahogany basin-stands of the 18th century, which were usually small square or corner pieces with a hole for the basin, and a shelf with a drawer beneath. Very complex pieces with many drawers and a mirror above were also made at the end of the century. The wash-hand stand, or wash stand, appeared in the early 19th century, and was a more substantial piece of furniture, often with a marble top with a circular hole for the basin, and frieze drawers beneath. A mid-Victorian example might have an unpierced marble top, splashback and sides, and be part of a bedroom suite. Victorian wash stands could be of mahogany, walnut or pine (originally painted, not stripped), and often had attractive tiles in the splashback. They might also have a cupboard beneath for a CHAMBER POT.

££££

WASSAIL AND BRAGGET BOWLS

The word wassail comes from a Danish toast. Traditionally a wassail bowl was a bowl of spiced ale offered from house to house on New Year's Eve, along with a song, in return for some gift—a pleasant form of 'trick or treat'. It is a turned, wooden bowl, sometimes with silver mounts, but the name is also given to two-handled loving cups, passed round on jolly occasions. Traditionally Bragget Day was the mid-point of Lent, when a specially powerful Bragget Ale would be mulled and served to all from a Bragget Bowl, before another 20 days' abstinence. The bowls are usually pottery versions of punch bowls.

   R ££££

Potter with his finger on the pulse of fashion

WEDGWOOD

Started by the great Josiah Wedgwood in 1759, this is the most important English pottery factory, which was highly successful and influential in the 18th century and continues in production today. Wedgwood was a shrewd businessman and a skilful innovator with his finger on the pulse of fashion, who understood and exploited the taste for NEO-CLASSICISM, creating wares renowned for their high quality.

The one-legged Josiah had boundless energy and was an entrepreneur as much as a potter, mixing and corresponding with the high society of the day. He was a partner of Matthew BOULTON, working with him on mounted JASPER and BASALTES wares. One of his earliest lines was a cream-coloured earthenware, printed or painted, which was so fine that it rivalled porcelain.

Known as Queen's ware due to Wedgwood achieving the royal patronage of Queen Charlotte in 1765, it also appealed to Catherine the Great of Russia, who ordered an enormous service painted with English landscapes in sepia. Each piece is painted with a frog as the service was destined for a palace known as La Grenouillière, hence its nickname the 'frog service'. This was completed in 1774 and is now in the Hermitage Museum in St Petersburg.

In keeping with neo-Classical taste, Wedgwood favoured simple, elegant shapes, with decoration emulating the antique. He developed fine stonewares, the most famous being BLACK BASALTES and JASPER WARE, the former being a plain matt black body, the latter having classical relief decorations in white on a blue, or sometimes green or lavender background. A wide range of products was made, including the famous PORTLAND VASES and tablewares, plaques for furniture and for mounting into snuffboxes, cameos for jewellery and all manner of small items. Such was Wedgwood's success that the factory's wares were widely imitated.

Josiah was against porcelain, and the factory flirted with porcelain production only briefly from 1812 to 1829, taking it up again in 1878. In the 19th century the firm also made PARIAN figures, while continuing production in the 18th-century styles. Important designers such as Dr C. DRESSER were occasionally employed in the late 19th century, and Eric Ravilious in the 1930s. Today the factory continues to produce versions of its 18th-century Jasper wares, as well as modern pottery.

Some of the most sought-after wares were those designed by Daisy Makeig-Jones in the 1920s: the Fairyland series. Brightly coloured pixies, elves and fairies are depicted in various dream scenes, the whole outlined by a gilt transfer.

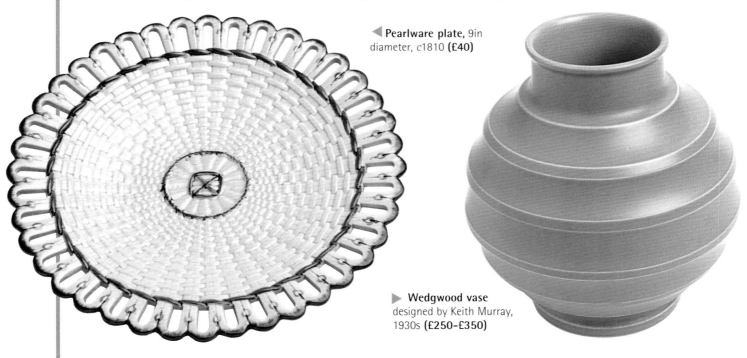

◀ Pearlware plate, 9in diameter, c1810 (£40)

▶ Wedgwood vase designed by Keith Murray, 1930s (£250-£350)

▲ **Large transfer-printed** earthenware dish, c1835 (**£300**)

▲ **Wedgwood fairyland lustre** malfrey pot and cover, 1920s (**£5,000**)

▼ **Small Rosso Antico vase,** impressed 'Wedgwood', 19th century (**£200-£250**)

WATCH STAND

So that owners could see a watch when not wearing it, stands were made on which it could be displayed like a clock. These might be of wood, ceramics, brass or other metal, and took many forms. STAFFORDSHIRE pottery examples are often pairs of figures framing a hole where the watch hangs.

££-£££

WATCHES see WRISTWATCHES.

WATERFORD GLASS

The most famous of Irish glass is typically deeply cut, this cutting being such a Waterford speciality that a few glass pieces were even imported from England for decoration at the factory. Glassmaking started in Waterford in the early 18th century, but was shortlived, and it was not until 1783 that the famous factory was established there, making lead glass rather than the earlier flint glass. Until it closed in 1851, the Waterford factory produced various tablewares, notably decanters, drinking glasses and bowls. As well as deep cutting, typical features include a design of arches and pillars around the body of a decanter, and swags, as well as good clarity. It is often said that Waterford glass can be distinguished by a bluish tinge, but this is now recognised to be a quality shared by glass from other sources. A mark, 'Penrose, Waterford', is found on a few of the Waterford wares. A new factory started production in Waterford in 1951, making glass in the traditional Waterford styles.

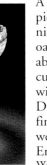

▲ **Waterford-type** Irish cut-glass bowl and detachable stand, c1825-30 (**£1,500-£2,000**)

££-££££

WELLINGTON CHAIR

A misleading name for chairs with a black-stained or ebony line on the top rail and uprights, supposedly in mourning for the death of the Duke of Wellington in 1852. In fact the fashion began in the REGENCY.

WELLINGTON CHEST

An early 19th-century English chest of many shallow, narrow drawers in a single tier, locked by means of a flap of wood which may be secured to prevent the drawers from being slid out.

£££-££££

WELSH DRESSER

A modern term for a piece of country furniture, commonly in oak, with shelves above and deeper cupboards beneath with frieze drawers. Dressers are not confined to Wales, and were made widely in England as well as Wales from the early 18th century until well into the 19th.

££-££££

WEMYSS WARE

This cheerful splashy pottery was made from 1880 to 1930 at the Fife Pottery in Scotland. It includes washbasins, jugs and other toilet wares, jam pots and tablewares, but most notably pigs, for use as door stoppers. These are decorated with loose, colourful cabbage roses, thistles, fruits, or a cock and hen design. The large pigs have painted eyes worthy of Barbara Cartland, and flowery livery to match, while the small pigs have

▼ **Rare large Wemyss pig,** early 20th century (**£5,000**); small pig with sponged decoration (**£500**); money box with shamrocks (**£400**)

◀ **Whitefriars glass,** from the M54 suite, c1930 (£15-20)

rather more piggy eyes. These decorative styles are the work of the Czech Karl NEKOLA. Production stopped at Fife in 1930, but the moulds were bought by another pottery and used until 1942. The pigs, in particular, have been imitated by other potteries.

 £££-££££

WHATNOT

An upright stand with three or more shelves, sometimes with a drawer beneath, and popular in the 19th century. It might be triangular rather than square, to fit into a corner. Many whatnots have been brutally cut down to form low tables, supposedly more appropriate to modern use.

£££-££££

WHEEL ENGRAVING

A technique with ancient origins, particularly popular in Europe from the 16th century. A design is ground onto a surface, such as glass, with an abrasive wheel, operated by a treadle mechanism. The decoration may be either superficial, or deep-cut in relief. Copper wheels were widely used. Many different sizes might appear on one vessel, pictorial effects being built up progressively.

◀ **A fine and rare** combined matchlock and wheel-lock gun with octagonal barrel, c1620 (£10,000-12,000)

▲ **Wheel-engraved** tumblers, dated 1845 (£1,000-£1,500 the set)

WHEEL-LOCK

A type of firing system for guns, invented in the early 16th century. A piece of pyrites was brought into contact with the roughened edge of a spring-driven metal wheel when the wheel was released by a trigger, producing sparks which ignited the gunpowder. The piece of pyrites was held in a 'jaw' which could be pulled clear of the pan containing the gunpowder, thus making the gun safe.

WHIELDON, THOMAS (1719-95)

A leading figure in the history of English pottery, who started a factory in Staffordshire around 1740, taking on such future great names as Josiah SPODE (as an apprentice) and Josiah WEDGWOOD (as partner from 1740 to 1759). He is best known for lead-glazed earthenwares decorated with coloured glazes (yellow, brown, green and blue in particular). His products included teapots and other pieces in the form of cauliflowers and fruit. He also made AGATE WARE, white salt-glaze, and black, glossy Jackfield ware. Firm attribution to Whieldon is rarely possible, since other factories made similar wares.

WHISTLE

The most commonly found whistles are silver whistle RATTLES

▶ **Zink-alloy** combined whistle and wick lamp, c1880-1900 (£10-£15)

and teethers, bosun's pipes, and police or railway whistles. Bosun's pipes are usually silver and consist of a downward-curving tube, with a 'keel' beneath and a ball at the end. They are played by raising a finger from a hole in the top.

 ££-£££

WHITEFRIARS GLASS

Founded in London in the 17th century, the Whitefriars glasshouse did not become significant until 1835 when, in the ownership of James Powell, traditional, hand-blown glass was revived following ancient Roman and VENETIAN forms, as well as 18th-century designs. From 1860, the factory made glass for William MORRIS, and coloured glass for windows to the designs of Pre-Raphaelite painters. It also made MILLEFIORI-style paperweights from the mid-19th century, and still does so, along with a range of hand-cut lead glass tableware. Its association with glass artists continues into the 20th century.

££-££££

▼ **Fragments of** 17th- and 18th-century wig curlers found on the Thames foreshore (£1-£5)

In vino veritas

WINE TASTERS, CISTERNS, ETC

Many silver items with wine connections are highly collectable. Most silver wine tasters are French, and most extant examples date from the late 18th century onwards. English tasters are quite rare, and with some two-handled, 17th-century items their true function is debatable. Massive wine cisterns survive, particularly from the late 17th and early 18th centuries. These were filled with ice and water, and flagons, bottles and pots were placed inside to cool the wine. Wine coolers, holding individual bottles, became popular at the end of the 18th century and were made in their largest numbers

◀ Dutch silver wine funnel, c1800 (£200)

during the REGENCY. The firm of Rundell, Bridge and Rundell must have been the largest supplier. Most wine coolers have been made in ELECTROPLATE since the mid-19th century.

With the increasing use of glass decanters, silver COASTERS made an appearance in the 1760s. Particularly sought after are double coasters of either wagon or 'jolly boat' form. With the compulsory labelling of wine bottles from the mid-19th century, many people began to serve directly from the bottle, so few silver coasters were made after this period.

For the same reason, production of BOTTLE LABELS or tickets declined rapidly. The variety of bottle labels is enormous, with shapes ranging from the common oblong forms through scrolls, crescents, escutcheons and eye shapes to shells, vine leaves, bats and four-leaf clovers: the more unusual the shape, the greater the value. The wording makes an enormous difference to price. Port and Sherry are common, but Bounce, Commandaria and Convent are rare.

Wine funnels became popular during the last quarter of the 18th century, although earlier examples are occasionally found. Up to the 1790s most have a detachable pierced bowl, with fixed and detachable rings to hold a piece of muslin to remove sediment. In addition there will be a 'thumb piece' by which the funnel can be attached to the side of a porcelain PUNCH BOWL.

▲ Victorian silver Burgundy jug with gilt interior and inscription, 1885 (£3,000–£5,000)

Except with rare, pre-1760s examples, the end of the funnel is curved to direct the flow of wine to the side of the decanter. A larger funnel, with the bowl fitting inside it, was to become popular at the end of the 18th century.

WIG CURLER

In the 17th and 18th centuries clay wig curlers were made in the same kilns as pipes. There were two usual patterns, one solid, like a waisted handle, the other drilled through and with flanged ends. They were heated and wound into wigs much like their metal and plastic successors.

WIG STAND

When not in use, a wig would suffer if just tossed aside, so special stands were made to keep its coiffure intact. These might be just a disc on a turned stem and base, or a head-shaped block on a stand. The former were wood, the latter wood or ceramic. The name has also been given to a tripod stand with drawers, holding a basin, but there is nothing to distinguish such pieces from WASH-HAND STANDS.

£££–££££

WILLAUME, DAVID (1658-1741)

An important and prolific HUGUENOT goldsmith who probably came to Britain around 1685, and registered his first known mark in London in 1697. He used advanced techniques and designs, and his work was good on a large or small scale, from wine cisterns to teapots and tablewares. He was so successful that he acquired a country manor by 1730. He also became involved in banking. His son and namesake took over in 1728.

WILLIAM AND MARY

The reign of William III and Mary II (1688-1702) saw the transition from the exuberance of the Restoration to the elegant sobriety of QUEEN ANNE. After 1685 the decorative arts were much influenced by French taste, introduced by the HUGUENOTs. The architect and designer D. MAROT was

▲ William and Mary walnut and marquetry chest-on-stand (£5,000–£5,500)

particularly important: he had innovative ideas for co-ordinating the decoration and drapery of rooms and furniture. New types of furniture during this reign included fall-front bureaux and box toilet mirrors.

A-Z of Antiques Hunting

WILLOW

A soft, yet resilient and flexible wood, pale in colour and flecked. In the 17th and 18th centuries, it was dyed black to imitate ebony. OSIERS, the young shoots, which are long and straight, have been used in wickerwork since ancient times.

◀ **Willow pattern** design transfer-printed on a plate by Dillwyn and Co, Swansea, 1820-30 (**£50**)

WILLOW PATTERN

A CHINOISERIE-style decoration found on ceramics, featuring a willow tree, a temple, a bridge with figures, a boat, an island and a pair of birds. Various stories have been dreamed up to weave these elements together. The pattern was introduced at the CAUGHLEY factory around 1780, and subsequently widely produced with variations. It was much used in English underglaze blue transfer-printed earthenware of the early 19th century by SPODE, WEDGWOOD, DAVENPORT and many others. Even the Chinese copied it.

WINDSOR CHAIRS

These originated in the beech woods of the Chilterns around High Wycombe, where 'bodgers' turned crude versions before passing them to craftsmen. The name can be traced to the 1720s and is now used for variations on the theme of solid moulded seat, turned legs and stick back with hoop or comb top rails. Sometimes there are nods to passing fashions, such as CABRIOLE legs or the OXFORD types, but the basic form persists into the mechanical age. ELM was commonly used for seats, and legs and spindles might be YEW. A popular type from the mid-19th century is the low-backed 'smoker's bow'.

£££-££££

WOOD, RALPH (1715-72)

The Woods were a famous family of potters whose factory in Staffordshire produced some of the most characteristic pottery of the 18th century. Ralph Wood specialised in rustic figures and groups, and TOBY jugs, coloured with lead glazes. His son, also Ralph, inherited the factory, and continued to make figures, but he used enamel colours.

WOOLWINDER

A woolwinder is an expanding wooden framework, working on the trellis or lazy-tong principle, which revolves on a metal shaft, usually with a wire-sided basket at the base. A skein of wool is placed on it, which winds as the frame is spun. When closed, a woolwinder resembles a hanging bat; when open, a distressed umbrella frame.

   ££-£££

WORK TABLE

A small table with drawers or a silk pouch beneath in which needlework and sewing equipment can be kept. Some are combined with games

▲ **Yew, elm and ash** Windsor chair, late 19th century. Seen at the Huddersfield Roadshow (**£1,500-£2,000 a pair**)

▲ **Regency combined** work and writing table, c1810-20 (**£1,500-£2,000**)

tables, with a CHESS board laid into the top. They were most used in the late 18th and early 19th centuries, and today are popular as occasional tables in drawing rooms.

££££

WRISTWATCHES

Long regarded as insignificant by comparison with the more dignified pocket watch, these have become highly collectable in the past 15 years, and the best can command substantial sums. The great majority were made after 1920, although occasional earlier examples may be found. By the end of the 1920s they had eclipsed pocket watches, becoming increasingly elaborate and diverse in the '30s, and taking on unusual forms and additional clever features. Particularly important makers whose names remain synonymous with the finest watches include Rolex, Patek Philippe, Cartier and Audemars Piguet—watches bearing

▶ **Swatch watch**, limited edition signed by Vivienne Westwood, 1990s (**£380**)

Lone survivor of a lost era

WORCESTER

Of the porcelain factories established in England in the mid–18th century, Worcester alone has survived in continuous production until today. The factory was founded in 1751 by John Wall, a doctor of medicine, and William Davis, an apothecary. They took over the small BRISTOL china factory in 1752 and produced a SOFT–PASTE porcelain. Unlike its rivals at DERBY, BOW and CHELSEA, Worcester porcelain could withstand hot liquids without cracking. As a result, the factory specialised in teasets, and on these the success of the factory rested.

Early productions in blue and white combine Chinese decoration with shapes copied from English silver. During the 1760s and 1770s the influence of MEISSEN and SÈVRES saw the introduction of coloured grounds, especially a deep blue and the celebrated 'scale blue'. Some Worcester porcelain was painted in London by James Giles. In 1783 the factory was bought by Thomas Flight for his sons. They were joined by Martin Barr and the company traded as Flight and Barr (1792-1804), BARR, FLIGHT AND BARR (1804-13) and Flight, Barr and Barr (1813-40). During the REGENCY period, superb painted decoration and lavish gilding resulted in some glorious productions. Two rival porcelain factories were established in Worcester by the CHAMBERLAIN family in about 1788 and by GRAINGER in around 1806. In 1862 the Worcester Royal Porcelain Co was established and the wares from this date are known as Royal

Worcester. The Grainger family continued until 1902. During the Victorian period Royal Worcester became famous for copies of ivory and for incredible pierced porcelain. James HADLEY modelled wonderful figures. During the 20th century hand painting became Royal Worcester's speciality, and signed pieces by the Stinton family and by Harry Davis are among the finest porcelains produced in England. From the 1930s figure-making was revived at Worcester, especially child subjects by Freda Doughty and animals by Doris Lindner. In recent times 'limited editions' have taken figure-making to new dimensions.

Worcester factory marks include the famous crescent, used from 1760 to the 1780s and incorporated into the Royal Worcester mark from 1852. Royal Worcester usually carries a date code which enables collectors to tell the year of a piece.

▲ Part of a tea service marked with a B for Flight and Barr, c1800. Seen at the Derby Roadshow (£1,000)

▲ Worcester urn-shaped vase painted in the manner of Thomas Baxter, c1810 (£7,500)

▼ Early Worcester teapot c1753-55 (£2,500) and three cups (£1,000 each if perfect)

Collector's items worth fighting for

WORLD WAR MEMORABILIA

Apart from the details such as cap badges, cloth divisional signs and regimental shoulder titles, the uniforms of the two World Wars might be considered a little drab. Nevertheless, an officer's tunic of the First World War with the rank on the cuff can fetch £150–£300.

The original Brody pattern First World War 'Tommy' helmet may reach up to £100, but Second World War helmets are still quite common. Also highly collectable are ephemera such as clothing coupons, identity cards, ration books, magazines and posters. Much can be bought for very little outlay, although a specialist auction house recently sold a collection of 31 Second World War posters for about £260.

Memorabilia of the German army are much sought after by collectors in Britain and America, with pickelhaubes (HELMETS) from the First World War being especially popular. A collection of imperial headdress was auctioned a little while ago for as much as £27,000.

The Third Reich has provided collectors of MILITARIA with a grand variety of badges and awards. Badge names include Infantry Assault, Tank Battle, Close Combat and Coastal Artillery, and there were also navy and Luftwaffe badges.

Combat awards are for numbers of engagements — 25, 50, 75 or 100. Many decorations come in three classes

— bronze, silver and gold. Quite a number of these awards and badges can be bought at auction for between £50 and £200 each.

The Third Reich dress daggers are pretty varied. The more common types — army, navy and air force — can be bought for £150–£300, depending on condition, but the rarer examples, including the SS Honour, Railway Protection Force, Diplomatic Corps and Technical Emergency Corps daggers, cost considerable sums — up to £2,000 each.

The fighting man spent more time hanging around in dank trenches or under a baking sun than actually fighting, and he often whiled

away the hours making useful or commemorative objects from the detritus of war. Collected today are Victory 'V' signs cut from copper or brass and mounted with spent .303 bullets. Empty shell cases were turned into gongs or waste bins or simply stand, polished in the hearth. A Second World War grenade will sell for around £15 but if in doubt about its safety — Check!

A word of warning to budding collectors — copies have been made of most Second World War German badges, awards and daggers, so if large sums of money are involved, buy only from reputable auction houses and dealers.

▲ First World War embroidered cards made in France and sent home from the trenches. Seen at the Manchester Roadshow (£40–£50 each)

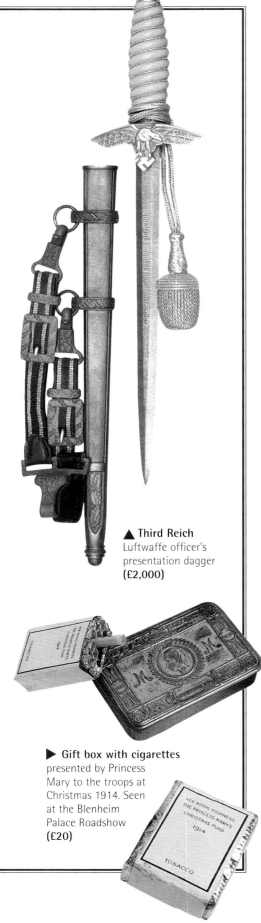

▲ **Third Reich**
Luftwaffe officer's
presentation dagger
(£2,000)

◀ **Gift box with cigarettes**
presented by Princess
Mary to the troops at
Christmas 1914. Seen
at the Blenheim
Palace Roadshow
(£20)

any of these names may command a premium. Inter-war watches are especially interesting and often unusual—perhaps rectangular or curved to the wrist. Novelties include the 'reverso', made to fold its face onto the wrist for protection; and early 'digital' types (not electronic), displaying hours and minutes separately. Small ladies' watches from the same period, excluding some ornate or bejewelled examples, are much less collected.

££-££££

WRITING BOX

Also known as a writing slope, this is a wooden, perhaps brass-bound, box which, when open, forms a gently inclined surface at which to write. At the top of the slope are inkwells, slots for pens and so on. Travelling boxes developed in the early 19th century and were particularly used by the army and navy in the Napoleonic Wars. The fashion continued until the later 19th century, and desk-top versions were made which are more upright. They are usually of mahogany or walnut, but more decorative exotic burr-woods were also used.

£££

X-CHAIR, STOOL AND STRETCHER

A chair with an X-shaped framework may be known as an X-chair or SAVONAROLA. Likewise a stool, supported on an X-shaped frame, is known as an X-stool—a type known from ancient Egypt. An X-stretcher

▲ **Savonarola chair** with an X-shaped frame, c1910 (**£400–£600**)

is one which runs diagonally from leg to leg, making the shape of a horizontal cross.

£££

XUANDE PORCELAIN

Chinese porcelain of the MING dynasty, made in the reign of the Emperor Xuande (1426-35). This is the best period of Ming blue and white porcelain, with lively decoration, subsequently much imitated. Underglaze red and polychrome decoration were also employed on some Xuande porcelain.

YEW

A wood long used in this country, dense and strong, golden brown in colour, and with a close grain and good figure. It was used for the framework of country furniture from the 16th century, and later for knobs, spindles and other furniture parts. Pieces such as gate-leg tables have been made throughout of yew. It was also used as veneer in the 17th and 18th centuries.

YONGLE PORCELAIN
Porcelain made during the reign of the emperor Yongle (1403-24), near the beginning of the MING dynasty. Its occasional appearances in specialist auction catalogues tend to be marked 'refer department', which means 'likely to be very expensive'. It includes very early blue and white decoration (see also YUAN), and also white wares with a secret decoration (incised before glazing and visible when the piece is held to the light).

YORKSHIRE DRESSER
A DRESSER with a clock fitted into the superstructure, common in Yorkshire and thought to have local origin, although not exclusive to that county.

££££-£££££

YU
Chinese Bronze Age wine vessel in the form of a bellied jar on a pedestal foot with swing handle and lid. They were made in the Shang and early Zhou dynasties. Later examples are ornate, with incised and relief decoration.

£££££+

YUAN
Mongol dynasty which ruled China from 1260 to 1368, during which time China was more accessible to Europeans than it would be again until the mid-19th century. Much was exported to Europe, including silk and porcelain. This dynasty saw the birth of BLUE AND WHITE decoration on porcelain, when cobalt was introduced from Persia. It is on strong Yuan roots that the MING reputation is built. Fine silver and lacquer work was also practised under Yuan rule.

▶ **Contemporary Zippo** brass lighter in the classic design (£10-£15)

ZEISS, CARL (1816-88)
One of the best makers of optical instruments in the world, he founded a company under his own name at Jena in Germany in 1846, which is still in existence. Zeiss's particular expertise was in optics (lenses), and the company applied this to a wide range of pieces, including microscopes and ophthalmic instruments. It also made optical instruments for the German war effort, such as naval binoculars and sniper sights. These wartime products are now highly collectable. The best Zeiss pieces included 'Jena' in the logo, rather than just the company name, and these are particularly sought after. Today the company is well known for binoculars and camera lenses.

ZIPPO LIGHTERS
These American cigarette lighters, guaranteed windproof and run on petrol, were very popular with American servicemen during the Second World War. It was they who introduced the lighters to Europe, often engraving them with military mottoes and giving them to their British sweethearts as mementos. A tall grille round the wick, with holes in it, acted as a shield against the wind. After the war, especially in the 1960s, their use became very fashionable in

Britain. Still produced, the steel lighters are distinguished by their rectangular, flat appearance and flip top.

£-£££

◀ **A metal-bodied zoetrope** with wood stand and paper strips (£400-£600)

ZOETROPE
Invented by W. G. Horner of Bristol in the mid-19th century, this is an optical toy based on the principle of the persistence of vision—a moving object is retained in the eye for a fraction of a second. A tin drum with slits cut in it has inside it a strip of paper painted with the successive stages of movement by a figure. Spin the drum and the figure appears to move.

£££

ZOGRASCOPE
This combination of a mirror and a magnifying glass on a stand reverses an image so that a printmaker can see how his finished work might look while preparing the plate. Invented in the second half of the 18th century, and most examples date from then.

£££

ZWISCHENGOLDGLAS
Translated as 'gold between glass', this applies to a glass vessel which has been decorated in gold on the exterior, then encased in another layer of glass. It was used in Roman times, then again by Bohemian glassmakers from the 18th century, particularly on beakers, where the decorated piece was enclosed in a closely fitting outer glass shell, the two parts being sealed together with resin.

INDEX

ACKNOWLEDGEMENTS

The Photographs

Principal photography by Clive Corless
Additional photography by Simon Farnhell

The Publishers and Headwater Communications are particularly grateful to Christie's Images, without whose co-operation this publication would not have been possible.

Acknowledgements are also due to: The Bridgeman Art Library, The Moviestore Collection, The National Trust Photo Library, Retrograph Archive, and Sotheby's.

The Experts

The Publishers and Headwater Communications are particularly grateful to the Producer of the 'Antiques Roadshow', Christopher Lewis, for making this book possible and providing consistent support.

Thanks are also due to the BBC team - the technicians and staff - who were always helpful despite the pressures of the television production schedule, and to the members of the public who, having queued for hours, waited longer while the photographers filmed their possessions.

The substantial role that David Battie has played in creating this book is recognised elsewhere. The Publishers and Headwater Communications would also like to thank Hugh Scully, Paul Atterbury, Hilary Kay, Christopher Payne and Ian Pickford for their expert assistance.